Media Tipping Points

Media Tipping Points

Analyzing and Predicting Global Events

Philip Gordon

Blue Matrix Publications

Blue Matrix Publications, October 2012
Philip Gordon : Media Tipping Points

First Published:

Blue Matrix Productions

USA:
2995 Woodside Rd. Suite 400
Woodside, CA 94062

France:
2 rue Despaty
Voisines, FR 89260

ISBN-13: 978-0984763832
ISBN-10: 098476383X

LCCN: 2011960810

Book Design: Steven Peterson

Printed in the United States of America

This Book is dedicated to my son, Jaike William-Pierre.
My sincere hope this provides his generation
a solution for our global survival.

"For God's sake, let's do something that changes the world."

—Nobel laureate Joseph Stiglitz

This Book is dedicated to my son, Jaike William-Pierre.
My sincere hope this provides his generation
a solution for our global survival.

"For God's sake, let's do something that changes the world."

—Nobel laureate Joseph Stiglitz

Current history offers a number of interesting case studies of tipping points and their relationships with global media. Each involves significant technological developments related to media and the impact on our world economically, culturally and politically. The three case studies examined here were selected on the basis of two main requirements—

1. Each is characterized by a defined "moment in time," where circumstances and events change as a result of the influences, or a phenomenon that could only be characterized as a tipping point, and

2. Each opened doors to new perspectives relative to the influence of media and the outcome and impact on global events and the creation of our new world reality.

ACKNOWLEDGEMENTS

My sincere gratitude and appreciation to the Centre d'Etudes Diplomatiques et Strategiques (C.E.D.S) in Paris, for assisting me to achieve my ambition and complete this book in my new home France.

Also thanks to the many individuals and colleagues who offered indispensable intellectual guidance and professional insights along the way. I thank as well the personnel at some of the 15 libraries and archives where I consulted texts and documents in United States, France and Great Britain, who were particularly helpful in facilitating my access to relevant information. In this regard, I would like to single out the library at Johns Hopkins University in Baltimore, Maryland, (MS-1979) and the Library at The Institute d'etudes Politiques de Paris.

Until recently, a book on this topic would have been impractical for a sole person to research efficiently, but the emergence of the Internet and the proliferation of material available through it allowed me to obtain texts and documents from governments, academic institutions, publications and libraries from around the world rapidly and at little cost. On occasion, search results yielded information that proved relevant and valuable from sources that one would not normally associate with the specific topics or locations being examined; this broadened my perceptions of the issues at hand, for which I would like to thank people I do not know but who brought the technology to the point where it could be used to such advantage.

Finally, I would like to thank my family and friends for the encouragement they lent in connection with my preparation of this book. Especially my wife, Anne-Lyse and my son Jaike, who were patient with me as it took time away from them and my business to do this research. Their impact on its completion was indirect but very real, and to the extent that it may have exceeded their interest in the topic itself, I am very grateful for their presence and understanding.

TABLE OF CONTENTS

LIST OF CHARTS, TABLES AND FIGURES

CHAPTER SEVEN

FOREWORD

This book addresses three comparative case studies in which the concept of the Tipping Point is evidenced during global events that are in many ways influenced by the media. The case studies were selected on the basis of (3) common key attributes: contagiousness, stickiness (during their development), and one dramatic moment in time that could be defined as a Tipping Point. These case studies were also chosen largely because their attributes included the (4) characteristics of people, organizations, media and events that could be categorically analyzed and compared within a conceptual framework, including recent events that were impacted by global media. The case studies are about the literature, trends, and information relative to media impact on global events in the context of the Tipping Point phenomenon, which are interpreted in the context of much broader event themes. These case studies represent only a few of the global events that meet the criteria for the Tipping Point Theory Analysis: Media Impact on Global Events.

The first case study, the presidential campaign of Barack Obama, was chosen in order to examine a narrower scope and timeframe for the analysis with a finite endpoint, and also because geographically, politically, economically, and culturally, only one nation is involved. In contrast, the second case study, the financial crisis of 2007 through 2010, involves more complex issues that impact other nation states and global economies. It requires an analysis on a much broader scale in time, 2007 to the present, with origins centered primarily in one country, yet in contrast to the first study, represented a larger field of data and information to analyze. The last case study, climate change, is included because, although the two first case studies provide a basis for understanding critical tipping point attributes and their characteristics, with its ongoing nature, it presents probable solutions and parameters for analyzing how tipping actually evolves and what its subsequent impact on a global scale could be. The climate change case study involves many nation states and many complex contemporary media development issues and technology changes integral to the research that is continuing to evolve. The correlations between these global events and media impact exhibited very strong cause and effect relationships between the tipping point attributes and the case study evolutions.

The case studies were also selected to be examined in this book on the basis of quantity and accessibility of information about the attributes and characteristics, their history in the context of media and impact, and emergence of a model theory framework to apply to future global events. These three case studies encompass relevant examples with regard to media impact and global events. They offer considerable variety in terms of their geographic locations as well as their scale, historical, social and political context, and consequently, they lend themselves to comparisons that exhibit these similarities and differences. In the course of comparing and analyzing them, consideration is given to the subdominant questions of why media has such an impact on global events, and why we have not already embraced the model for the purposes of addressing climate change. Throughout this book, many of the interpretations of the material are my own unless otherwise specified. References in the case studies are identified in alphabetical order so as to present a neutral and consistent way of referring to the sources in this context and therefore not implying any political or personal biases based on the order in which the references are named. Similarly, the text and information reproduced in the annexes are done alphabetically first, as they do not necessarily illustrate the timeline continuity of the events as they unfold during the case studies.

Other events in retrospect might have been chosen, such as the recent events involving Tunisia, Egypt, Libya, Bahrain, and other countries in the Arab region. But due to time constraints and limited knowledge of the culture and language, these and other more recent events were dismissed.

Part I

Tipping Point Theory and Global Media

INTRODUCTION

Tipping Point theory is a conceptual model framework application for analyzing *phenomena*, particularly in the context of media and global events, which helps to provide a strategy for international relations by collectively playing an important role in the interactions internally and between nation states. The Tipping Point theory model framework provides a means for analyzing and comparing global events that are impacted by various media types that arise and cross borders of nations and states that coexist and are codependent within the international system. The interpretation and adoption of the Tipping Point theory provides a potential opportunity to reduce the conflict among the world community in the future, since demand for resources that are only now becoming apparent, does not match future political, social and/or economic needs.

Part one of this version first reviews the concept of the Tipping Point theory that is fundamental to our analysis, defining and characterizing the *attributes* and *characteristics*. It then examines, presents and analyzes the academic literature on the subject of media and its global impact as relevant information from the sources that are directly involved with their creation and delivery. It attempts to explain the media impact from the perspective of its development and evolution in an international context and then discusses their relationships and interactions that exist within the medium and the world today and events that happened in the past and future.

While there are many published works about the broader concepts of media impact and global events, by the time one focuses on the narrow attributes and characteristics and concepts of our Tipping Point theory, the literature is fairly limited and almost none of it is relevant or recent. Additional research has recently been spawned by contemporary events (for example, the diplomatic cable discoveries from WikiLeaks and deployment via the Internet and their effect on nation state diplomacy); however, when the analysts discuss their impacts, they tend to summarize by providing a rather limited viewpoint based on previous published approaches and in doing so, they confirm how little has gone forth towards analyzing what impact the media really has on global events. Another example, which I cited earlier, is the recent Arab Spring region developments, which appear to be in epidemic form with many of the same attributes and characteristics of our model. Unfortunately, one has to put a finite limit on the scope and the timeframe for such an endeavor.

One development that emerges from this process is that nearly all of the underlying concepts that are critical to the analysis of media impact and global events have been subject to varying definitions, divergent theories and conflicting interpretations. It thus became essential to develop a workable definition of the *Tipping Point theory* and provide a perspective for the *attributes* and *characteristics* by which one can synthesize the information prevalent in the literature, and thereby constructing a solid framework from which to proceed with the subsequent examination of the *attributes* and *characteristics* in each of the case studies that form the core of this book.

Another highlight is that the media impact on global events, in terms of its analysis, when viewed in the context of contemporary media issues, appears to be more *ad hoc*, without a systematic process for problem-solving, forecasting and guidance for international management. This illustrates that the worlds' nations gravitate towards a more pragmatic behavior approach in their international event solutions, defying logic, and in doing so, often create additional problems, without focusing on the issues at hand.

The effort to understand media impact on global events presents challenges and highlights the very nature and essence of the Tipping Point theory and the concepts discussed here, particularly, anticipating when a tipping point will occur means you have to develop an approach to systematically identify it first, and then perhaps, deploy a "solutions methodology" to predict (or avoid) it on a extremely large global scale (when it is in fact detrimental to mankind). The analysis of the Tipping Point theory with regard to Media impacts on global events illustrates the huge gaps that exist in the application of this conceptual model. As such, while the application this theory and model, by my own admission, might be considered on the *periphery* of international relations, it does, in fact, find itself centered in the middle of the most, (if not all), of our most pressing global arguments.

For purposes of organization, Chapter One presents the definition of the Tipping Point theory and the *attributes* and *characteristics*, while Chapter Two overviews global media , development and key relationships.

CHAPTER 1
THE TIPPING POINT THEORY

Section 1.1 Tipping Point Theory: Defined

The Tipping Point Theory is defined in this context as the biography of an idea, where the idea can be very simple. It is an approach to understand the emergence of a trend, or the ebb and flow of a trend, for example: the election of the first bi-racial US president; or the meltdown during the international financial crisis; or the emergence of global climate awareness. The phenomenon of word of mouth, or any number of the other mysterious changes that influence everyday life and their relative impacts, is to think of them in this context as *epidemics.* Ideas, products, messages and behaviors as explored in this context spread just like viruses do.

Three attributes of The Tipping Point Theory are to be explored in the context of media impact and global events: first, the relationship to *contagiousness*, or spread of linkages in the characteristics; two, *stickiness*, the fact that little causes can have big effects; and three, that change happens not gradually but at one dramatic moment. In fact this third trait--supporting the notion that phenomena of epidemics can rise and fall in one dramatic moment--is the most important of the three attributes because it is this one that makes sense of the first two and perhaps permits the greatest insights into why global events happen the way they do with media influence.

This definition given to that one dramatic moment when during the epidemic, when everything can change all at once, and is termed in this context as, the "Tipping Point".[1] As global events evolve, the world is impacted in terms of the media delivery systems, population response, and the way countries are governed. Global events provide a context for the case study analysis of the media in context of these three (3) tipping point attributes. These collectively bring a sense of relevancy if viewed from the dual perspective of international relations and the world's future. Tipping Point Theory *attributes* are further analyzed with four (4) *characteristics*:

People, Organizations, Media and Events.

Each of these characteristics presents dynamic relationships on how they relate to the sequential attributes and the others in this context. The characteristics were captured in the research aiming at those most salient to the discussion and key questions regarding the existent of the phenomena of a tipping point. These characteristics are initially defined as:

- *People:* key individuals central to the studies and attribute progression
- *Organizations:* pivotal in their roles and responsibilities throughout the studies
- *Media:* types, audience, technology, participation and influence
- *Events:* global milestones, outcomes and moments reinforcing the underlying theory premises

Moreover, each of these characteristics evolved during different windows or duration of periods of time for each of the case studies that are cited in this book. Government, corporation, and private individual intervention with the media at any point in history are relevant in the discussion and become part of the argument as to how global events are in fact impacted and influenced. The Tipping Point Theory illustrates a conceptual approach for analyzing media impact and global events.

---

1 Malcolm GLADWELL, *The Tipping Point: How Little Things can Make a Big Difference*, New York: Back Bay Books, 2002.

What emerges from a review of the literature about this theory is that, while the concept is loosely defined, there exist significant variations on how it can be interpreted with regard to global event phenomena.[2] What follows is a more detailed definition of the Tipping Point Theory, its attributes and characteristics, and their relationships that are evident in our case studies regarding global events.

Section 1.2 Tipping Point Attributes

Section 1.2.1
Contagiousness Attribute:

I propose to explore for the contagiousness attribute in context with the Tipping Point Theory applied as it is characterized by the Broken Windows Theory. Broken Windows was the brainchild of James Q. Wilson and George Kelling. Wilson and Kelling argued that in effect impacts and events are the evitable result of disorder.[3] A simple application of this phenomenon suggests that if a window is broken and left unrepaired, i.e. the international financial system, whereby if it appears that the system is unregulated, unmanaged, or that no one cares about it, and no one is in charge, soon more windows will be broken, and the condition will spread sending a signal that anything goes. In countries or regions illustrating this example, financial oversights and lack of monitoring regulation are all the equivalent of broken windows and promote invitations to more serious financial meltdowns as is evident in events in Ireland and Greece that affected the entire European Union.[4] This is the epidemic of finance. Its effects are contagious -- just as a trend is contagious—in that it can start with just one broken window, or country bank failure, and spread instantaneously, particularly if the message is delivered via television or internet to an entire region's population in the world economies. The impetus to engage in a certain type of behavior is not coming from a particular kind of person or culture but from a feature of the environment, i.e. financial sector–banking. Contagiousness postulates that if a particular behavior in a community (or world) goes unaddressed, it signals that nobody cares about the community (or world) resulting in additional behavior of the same type. The contagiousness attribute proposes that there are people,

---

2 Ibid.

3 James WILSON and George KELLING, "Broken Windows. The Police and Neighbourhood Safety," *Atlantic Magazine*, 3, 1982.

4 Ibid.

organizations, and events moments within the global media environments that are capable of initiating these epidemics by starting with small, seemingly inconsequential causes that ultimately have large (global) impacts.

Broken Windows Theory in this context, viewed from the Malcolm Gladwell interpretation, states, "The success of any kind of social epidemic is heavily dependent on the involvement of (three types of) people with a particular and rare set of social gifts." According to Gladwell, economists call this the 80/20 Principle, which is the idea that in any situation roughly 80 percent of the "work" will be done by 20 percent of the participants.[5] These people are described in the following ways:

- *People* who "link us up with the world…people with a special gift for bringing the world together. They are "a handful of people with a truly extraordinary knack [… for] making friends and acquaintances." He characterizes these individuals as having comprised social networks of over one hundred people. To illustrate Gladwell cites a number of examples: the midnight ride of Paul Revere; Milgram's experiments in the small world problem; the "Six Degrees of Kevin Bacon" trivia game; Dallas businessman Roger Horchow; and Chicagoan Lois Weisberg, a person who understands the concept of the weak tie. Gladwell attributes the social success of connectors to "their ability to span many different worlds [...as] a function of something intrinsic to their personality, some combination of curiosity, self-confidence, sociability, and energy."[6]
- *Information specialists* or "people we rely upon to connect us with new information." They accumulate knowledge, especially about the marketplace, and know how to share it with others.[7] Gladwell cites Mark Alpert as a prototypical maven who is "almost pathologically helpful," further adding, "He can't help himself." In this vein, Alpert himself concedes, "A maven is someone who

5 Malcolm GLADWELL, The Tipping Point, op. cit.

6 Ibid.

7 Ibid.

wants to solve other people's problems, generally by solving his own.". According to Gladwell, mavens start "word-of-mouth epidemics" due to their knowledge, social skills, and ability to communicate. As Gladwell states, "Mavens are really information brokers, sharing and trading what they know."[8]

- Finally, *persuaders*, charismatic people with powerful negotiation skills. They tend to have an indefinable trait that goes beyond what they say, which makes others want to agree with them. Gladwell's examples include California businessman Tom Gau and news anchor Peter Jennings, and he cites several studies about the persuasive implications of non-verbal cues, including a headphone nod study (Wells and Petty)[9] and William Condon's cultural micro rhythms study.[10]

Section 1.2.2
Stickiness Attribute: Little Causes/Big Effects

The second attribute to be addressed is termed *stickiness.* In *The Tipping Point* Gladwell identified attributes and traits that make ideas sticky. I take this attribute beyond the scope of Gladwell's book. Gladwell was interested in what makes social epidemics *epidemic*. The focus here is how particular phenomena are constructed and what makes some stick and others disappear in the context of media impact on global events highlighted in the case studies. What I am looking for here are the same attributes, the same characteristics that are reflected in a wide range of case study applications. In general there seem to be six principles at work in order to make phenomenon sticky and these are:

- Simplicity, the golden rule -- it has to be simple and profound.

---

8 Ibid.

9 Gary WELLS and Richard PETTY, "The Effects of Head Movement on Persuasion: Compatibility and Incompatibility of Responses," *Basic and Applied Social Psychology*, 1, 1980, 219–230.

10 William CONDON, "Cultural Microrhythms," in *Interaction Rhythms*, 1974, New York, Human Sciences.

- Unexpectedness, it must generate interest and curiosity.
- Concreteness, the only way to reach everyone in the audience.
- Credibility, the credentials need to speak for themselves.
- Emotions, people must feel something.
- Stories, stimulating people to respond quickly.

I explore each these principles as further characteristic criteria for the four (4) tipping point theory characteristics of people, organizations, media and events.

On the other hand, the stickiness attribute is rather straightforward; there is a simple way to package information such as the Internet that under the right circumstances can make it irresistible. And all you have to do is find it. The presidential campaign of Barack Obama could be mostly characterized by this attribute, and the result correlated with available media technological tools he or his staff had at their disposal, and their methods and strategy for deployment.

Another example of little causes/big effects is where a specific content of a message renders its impact memorable: Popular children's television programs such as *Sesame Street* and *Blue's Clues* pioneered the properties of the stickiness factor, thus enhancing the effective retention of the educational content in parallel with its entertainment value.

Section 1.2.3
One Dramatic Moment Attribute: "Something Else" Tipping Point

The third and last attribute, that change happens not gradually but at one dramatic moment, supports the notion that epidemics can be created and influenced to end in one dramatic moment – this is the most important of the three attributes because this one makes sense of the first two and perhaps permits the greatest insights into why modern events happen the way they do. The attribute given to that one dramatic moment in the epidemic when everything can change all at once is called the tipping point or is termed *Something Else*.[11]

Based on these three attributes and the potential developments now exponentially gaining in world global media technology and also being readied for introduction in the not-too-distance future, one can correlate the analysis with a series of world impacting tipping points happening very soon. "*Something else* is when human behavior is sensitive to and strongly influenced by its environment", as Gladwell says, "Epidemics are sensitive to the conditions and circumstances of the times and places in which they occur." For example, "zero tolerance" efforts to combat minor crimes such as beating subway fares and vandalism on the New York subway that resulted in a decline in more violent crimes city-wide. Gladwell describes the *bystander effect*, and explains how Dunbar's number plays into the tipping point, using Rebecca Wells' novel *Divine Secrets of the Ya-Ya Sisterhood*, evangelist John Wesley, and the high-tech firm Gore Associates.[12]

Tipping points are "the levels at which the momentum for change becomes unstoppable." Gladwell defines a tipping point as, "the moment of critical mass, the threshold, the boiling point." Gladwell attempts to explain and describe the "mysterious sociological changes that mark everyday life." As Gladwell states, "Ideas and products and messages and behaviors spread like viruses do." Other examples of such "changes" in his book include the rise in popularity and sales of Hush Puppies shoes in the mid-1990s and the precipitous drop in the New York City crime rate after 1990.[13]

Section 1.3 Tipping Points and Global Events

The tipping point can be seen in a variety of global examples, for example, among them is population change. It is estimated that on August 26, 2011 the world's population reached 7 billion. And by August 10, 2045 the world's population is estimated to reach 9 billion (UN estimates). One could ask, in other words, when is the world population going to reach a tipping point? When will there be a scarcity of air, land, water, food, etc. in order to support the demands of societies and life-sustaining systems?

11 Malcolm GLADWELL, The Tipping Point, op. cit.

12 Ibid.

13 Ibid.

[14] The world's population, three centuries from now are projected to stabilize at 9 billion if fertility levels continue their decline, particularly in the developing world, but could also top more than 1.3 trillion if they remain unchanged from current rates according to statistics released by the United Nations. According to medium-level projections, women in every country will each have about two children in the decades to come, raising the world population from its current 6.4 billion to 9 billion in 2300 according to UN's Population Division.

The following is a list of milestones regarding population change and a graphic depicting the projections in a conservative sense.
3 Billion: 30 January 1960

4 Billion: 8 September 1974

5 Billion: 31 March 1987

6 Billion: 20 January 1999

7 Billion: 26 August 2011

8 Billion: 27 April 2025

9 Billion: 10 August 2045

---

14 Pentti LINKOLA, (1992). "The Doctrine of Survival and Doctor Ethics". Paints the prospective options by the worlds' population when the tipping point is reached in her book. "What to do when a ship carrying a hundred passengers suddenly capsizes and there is only one lifeboat? When the lifeboat is full, those who hate life will try to load it with more people and sink the lot. Those who love and respect life will take the ship's axe and sever the extra hands that cling to the sides".

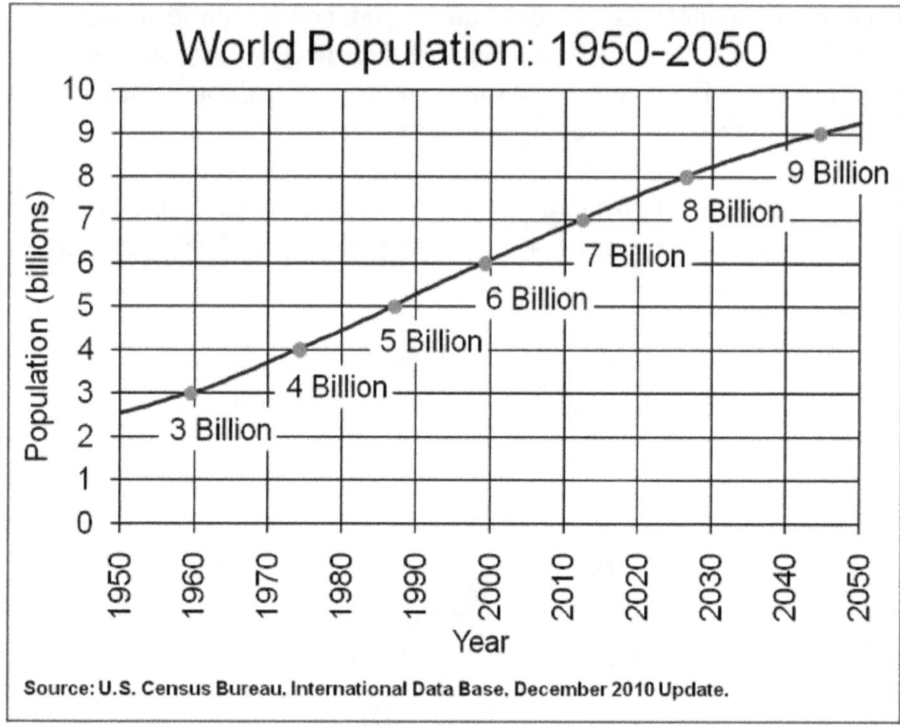

Figure 1: World Population 1950-2050 1[15]

Small variations in these forecasts will have enormous impacts in the long term, or a change such as one-quarter of a child under the two-child norm, or one-quarter of a child above the norm, would result in world populations ranging from 2.3 billion to 36.4 billion. If fertility levels remain unchanged at today's levels, however, world population would rise to 44 billion in 2100, 244 billion persons in 2150 and 1.34 trillion in 2300, according to the Division's new report, *World Population to 2300*. The UN said this clearly indicates that "current high fertility levels cannot continue over the long term."[16]

Given progress in extending life expectancy, people could expect, on average, to live more than 95 years by 2300. Japan, which is the global leader in life expectancy today, is projected to have a life expectancy of more than

15 U.S. Census Bureau, International Database, June 2011 Update, World Population 1950–2050, 2010.

16 United Nations Department of Economic and Social Affairs/Population Division (UNDES), "World Population in 2300 to be around Nine Billion Persons," December 9, 2003.

106 years by 2300.[17] In today's terms these figures alone present some startling statistics. Even at 7 billion, which is the population to be reached in August 2011, there is a growing awareness that the planet that we occupy is going through some significant changes that are either caused or aggravated by the existence and activities of mankind. With finite resources for land, water, food, and more importantly air, the additional influx and growth of population reaching anywhere between 9 billion to 44 billion and beyond presents some interesting analytical scenarios for a wide magnitude and range of potential tipping points that may occur as a result of the sheer need and scarcity of resources necessary for mankind for many of the basic requirements for life.

The example above is cited and described primarily to point out the magnitude and complexity of scaling and defining the parameters for any global event Tipping Point Theory case study analysis. One would hope that with the above example we can apply our methodology to define the attributes of contagiousness, stickiness, and a dramatic moment that would predict that tipping point for the world relative to population. We would need to make assumptions about the characteristics of each, particularly the people, organizations, the media systems, and the sequential events that would lead up to the tipping point. Our intent here is not to address population growth and to develop solutions for this challenge, albeit a worthy endeavor. Rather the intent is to point out the breadth and width and potential application of this theory.

Section 1.4 Tipping Points and Media Impacts

Media technologies have been integral to the representation of global events. In the current context, for example, the USA-led Iraqi Freedom War and the War on Terror were by most accounts of global international communication represented by news media, ignoring other genres, often neglected the crucial roles that audiences and newer technologies actually had within the real time global media culture.

The war in Iraq was one of the first major media events in which the technological infrastructure of the Internet Age facilitated the immediate and global dissemination of; images; video; text and multimedia from journal-

17 Ibid.

ists, civilians, and combatants via the Internet, Web, and mobile satellite networks that reached a worldwide audience, whereby both first and third world countries were exposed. For example, representations of Saddam Hussein's execution could not be 'controlled' by the Bush administration, as a video of his hanging was leaked and shown on television and over the Web.

It would be difficult to describe the degree to which the developments of the Internet has complicated the U.S. government's efforts to manage information surrounding war operations. The Bush administration no doubt tried to prevent all images of suffering and death occurring during the 2003 Iraq War (as was done during the 1991 Gulf War), with rare exceptions.

In response to a new global communications environment, the Pentagon has reportedly tried implementing electronic warfare (EW) strategies as outlined in the declassified *Information Operations Roadmap* commissioned by Donald Rumsfeld, US Secretary of Defense in 2003. Approaching the Internet as an enemy weapon and deployment system, the *Roadmap*'s objective is to "[p]rovide a future EW capability sufficient to provide maximum control of the entire electromagnetic spectrum, denying, degrading, disrupting, or destroying the full spectrum of globally emerging communication systems, sensors, and weapons systems dependant on the electromagnetic spectrum."[18] A major focus was the ability to disable cell phones, which, was presented by the Pentagon and journalists as a sign of "progress" in Iraq. Particularily, because they are commonly used as remote detonators for roadside bombs, or IEDs, activated by Internet messaging applications. The *Roadmap* called for "improvements in the capability "... to rapidly generate audience specific 'tipping points', commercial-quality products into denied areas" and "project . . . electronic attacks into denied areas by means of stealthy platforms."[19] Concluding that the actual goal of the information war on terror is to remove or control all non-U.S. communication and news from designated regions, suggesting a reductive model of media imperialism as we examine this technology. The expansion of telecommunications and technology in the world has meant that, in effect, the world has gotten more deeply connected and become "flat," as in Thomas

18 National Security Agency (NSA), *Information Operations Roadmap* (National Security Archive Electronic Briefing Book No. 177), October 30, 2003.

19 Ibid.

Friedman's famous formulation.[20]

In today's world (2012) cheap phone calls and broadband have made it possible for people to communicate instantly around the globe. Historically, with the arrival of the big ships in the 15th century, only goods could become mobile. With modern banking in the 17th century, capital then became mobile. Later in the 1900's labor became mobile with vast movements of populations searching for work opportunities. Similarly since the 1980's, three forces - politics, economics and technology - have pushed in the same direction to produce a more open, connected, exacting international media environment. These forces have given countries everywhere fresh opportunities to challenge positions on the world ladder, some for growth and prosperity goals, some not so admirable objectives. And now stretching into 2011, ideas are indeed more mobile with the technology.

Today people from all over the world have more access and are becoming more comfortable putting their own indigenous imprint on the world stage. "Local" and "modern" is now about how to communicate and coexist side-by-side with global and Western. The same is true of foreign policies, world conflict, and events. But there are some underlying realities. For example, basic issues of security influencing the global and immediate world neighborhood are critical components of any country's national security policy. And now with global technology reaching throughout the world so easily, no civilization can develop in a "hermetic box," which is apparent in the Arab region development of 2011-2. And importantly when it comes to religion and worldviews, countries are emerging from the backgrounds with rapid delivery and advanced security systems. These dynamics continue to present internal challenges overlaid with outside influences.

Section 1.5 Summary

As I have discussed, Gladwell describes the three rules of epidemics (attributes) in tipping points as:

- Contagiousness, the Law of the Few
- Stickiness, Little Causes/Big Effects

20 Thomas FRIEDMAN, *The World is Flat: A Brief History of the Twenty-first Century*, New York, Farrar, Straus and Giroux, 2005.

- One dramatic moment, Something Else,[21]

Whereas, these attributes have also been extended and applied in many fields, from the various sciences and economics to human ecology to epidemiology,

- In sociology, a tipping point (or angle of repose) is the event of a previously rare phenomenon becoming rapidly and dramatically more common. The phrase was coined in its sociological use by Morton Grodzins by analogy with the fact in physics that "adding a small amount of weight to a balanced object can cause it to suddenly and completely topple". Grodzins studied integrating American neighborhoods in the early 1960s. He discovered that most of the white families remained in the neighborhood as long as the comparative number of black families remained very small. But at a certain point when "one too many" black families arrived, the remaining white families would move out en masse in a process known as white flight. He called that moment the "tipping point."[22] The idea was expanded and built upon by Nobel Prize-winner Thomas Schelling in 1972.[23] A similar idea underlies Mark Granovetter's threshold model of collective behavior.[24]

- In climate science it has also describes the propagation and change of populations in an unbalanced ecosystem.

- In mathematics, as the angle of repose is seen as an inflection point.

- While in control theory, as the concept of positive feedback describes the same phenomenon, with the problem of balancing an inverted pendulum being the classic

21 Malcolm GLADWELL, The Tipping Point, op. cit.

22 Morton GRODZINS, *The Metropolitan Area as a Racial Problem*, Pittsburgh, University of Pittsburgh Press, 1958.

23 Thomas SCHELLING, "Dynamic Models of Segregation," *Journal of Mathematical Sociology*, 1, 1972, pp. 143–186.

24 Mark GRANOVETTER, "Threshold Model of Collective Behavior," *The American Journal of Sociology*, 83, 1978, pp. 1420–1443.

embodiment.[25]

- And finally, the tipping point in physics is the point at which an object is displaced from a state of stable equilibrium into a new equilibrium state qualitatively dissimilar from the first.

The discussion that follows, is premised on the development of a research and analysis methodology, utilizing, in fact, aspects of many of these interdisciplinary definitions, however, rooted predominantly of the Gladwell viewpoint and expanded here.

Before proceeding to the attributes and characteristics of each of the case studies, I propose to continue in chapter two with a review of global media.

Media Impacts and Global Events Website

For further information please visit the
Media impact and Global Events Website:

http://mdgparis.typepad.com/global_media_and_world_ev/

This website tracks, highlights, categorizes and provides a articles and commentary related to Tipping Point Attributes and Characteristics, as well as information and recent updates related specifically to the three case studies included in this version and other Media and Global Event issues.

25 Malcolm GLADWELL, The Tipping Point, op. cit.

CHAPTER TWO
GLOBAL MEDIA

From radio, film, television, to the Internet and mobile satellite networks, global media communication technologies have been integral to the Tipping Point phenomena and representation of world events. In this chapter I explore the way the media has always been eager to improve communication delivery technologies and how countries have developed new communication technologies and media since at least the 19th century.

Section 2.1 Media Impact and Global Relationships

The media has impacted the leading edge of global event reporting in the high-tech age. A few decades ago reporting was through newspapers, radio, and television. Things are different now as we are experiencing a social revolution of people-oriented reporting in real time. This element of intimate knowledge of the event or story being reported has dramatically changed the way we all view all of our global events. This revolution has intrinsically altered the way events are reported. The recent trends of people-oriented reporting is on the rise as reporting events becomes more personal and more accurate – however more subjective.

Most technologies described as the new media are digital, frequently having characteristics of being: interactive, networkable and manipulated.

Some examples are the Internet, websites, computer multimedia, computer games, CD-ROMS, and DVDs. New media is generally not described as television programs, films, magazines, books, or paper-based publications - unless they include technologies that facilitate digital interactivity.

There are several ways that new media might be described, The New Media Reader edited by Wardrip-Fruin and Montfort, defines it by using eight (8) concise propositions:

1. **The New Media Versus Cyber Culture** – Cyber culture is the social phenomena associated with the Internet and network communications (blogs, online multiplayer gaming), whereas, the new media is concerned more with cultural objects and paradigms (including digital to analog television, iPhones, etc).
2. **The New Media as Computer Technology Used as a Distribution Platform -** new media are the cultural objects that use digital computer technology for distribution. e.g. Internet, web sites, computer multimedia, blu-ray disks etc.
3. **The New Media as Digital Data Controlled by Software** - language of the new media is based on the assumption that, all cultural objects that rely on digital representation and computer-based delivery do share ocommon qualities. The new media is reduced to digital data that can be manipulated by software as any other data. Now media operations can create several versions of the same object.
4. **The New Media as the Mix Between Existing Cultural Conventions and the Conventions of Software** —new media is understood as the mix between older cultural conventions for data representation, access, and manipulation and newer conventions of data representation, access, and manipulation. The 'old' data are representations of visual reality and human experience, and the 'new' data are numerical data. The computer is kept out of the key 'creative' decisions, and is delegated to

the position of a technician."[26].

5. **The New Media as the Aesthetics that Accompanies the Early Stage of Every New Modern Media and Communication Technology** – "While ideological tropes indeed seem to be reappearing rather regularly, many aesthetic strategies may reappear two or three times...In order for this approach to be truly useful it would be insufficient to simply name the strategies and tropes and to record the moments of their appearance; instead, we would have to develop a much more comprehensive analysis which would correlate the history of technology with social, political, and economical histories or the modern period."[27]

6. **The New Media as Faster Execution of Algorithms Previously Executed Manually or through Other Technologies**—Computers are a huge speed-up of what were previously manual techniques. "Dramatically speeding up the execution makes possible previously non-existent representational technique." (This also makes possible many new forms of media art such as interactive multimedia and computer games. "On one level, a modern digital computer is just a faster calculator; we should not ignore its other identity, that of a cybernetic control device"[28]

7. **The New Media as the Encoding of Modernist Avant-Garde; The New Media as Metamedia**— Manovich declares that the 1920s are more relevant to the new media than any other time period. Meta-media coincides with postmodernism in that they both rework old work rather than create new work. The new media avant-garde is about new ways of accessing and manipulating information (e.g. hypermedia, databases, search engines, etc.). Meta-media is an example of how quantity can change into quality as in the new media technology

26 Noah WARDRIP-FRUIN and Nick MONTFORT (eds.), *The New Media Reader*. Cambridge, The MIT Press, 2003.

27 Ibid

28 Noah WARDRIP-FRUIN and Nick MONTFORT, *op. cit.*

and manipulation techniques can "recode modernist aesthetics into a very different postmodern aesthetics."[29]

8. **The new media as Parallel Articulation of Similar Ideas in Post-WWII Art and Modern Computing—** Post WWII Art or *combinatorics* involves creating images by systematically changing a single parameter. This leads to the creation or remarkably similar images and spatial structures. "This illustrates that algorithms, this essential part of the new media, do not depend on technology, but can be executed by humans." [30]

Section 2.1.1 Globalization and New Media

The rise of the new media has increased and accelerated the communication between people all over the world. It has allowed a wide distribution of views, information and ideas through blogs, websites, pictures, and other user-generated media. Flew stated that as a result of the evolution of the new media technologies, globalization occurs. Globalization is generally stated as "more than expansion of activities beyond the boundaries of particular nation states."[31] Globalization has shortened the distance between people all over the world by the electronic communication expressing this great development as the "death of distance." These forms of new media "radically break the connection between physical place and social place, making physical location much less significant for our social relationships"[32]

However, these changes in the new media environment also foster levels of tensions in the concept of what is public information. According to Ingrid Volkmer, "public sphere" is defined as a process through which public communication becomes restructured and partly un-embedded from national political and cultural institutions. This trend of the globalized public sphere is not only as a geographical expansion from a nation to worldwide,

---

29 Lev MANOVICH, "New Media from Borges to HTML," in *The New Media Reader*, 2003, Cambridge, The MIT Press, pp. 16–23.

30 Noah WARDRIP-FRUIN and Nick MONTFORT, *op. cit.*

31 Terry FLEW and Sal HUMPHREY, "Games: Technology, Industry, Culture," in *New Media: An Introduction* (second edition), 2005, South Melbourne, Australia, Oxford University Press, pp. 101–114.

32 David CROTEAU and William HOYNES, (2003). *Media Society: Industries, Images and Audiences* (3rd edition). Thousand Oaks, Pine Forge Press, 2003.

but also changes the relationship between the public, the media, and state.[33]

Virtual communities online transcend and extend geographical boundaries removing social restrictions. Howard Rheingold describes these globalized societies as self-defined networks that attempt to recreate what we do in real life. "People in virtual communities use words on screens to exchange pleasantries and argue, engage in intellectual discourse, conduct commerce, make plans, brainstorm, gossip, feud, fall in love, create a little high art and a lot of idle talk."[34] For Sherry Turkle, "...making the computer into a second self, finding a soul in the machine, can substitute for human relationships."[35]

While some of these perspectives suggest technology drives and therefore is a determining factor in the process of globalization, arguments involving technological determinism are generally looked down upon by mainstream media studies.[36] Often academics focus on the processes by which technology is funded, researched, and produced, creating a feedback loop in these the technologies, often influenced and transformed by the users who then feed into the process. Commentators such as Manuel Castells, refers to a soft determinism, contending that technology does not determine society. Nor does society set the course of technological change, since many factors, including individual inventiveness and entrepreneurialism, intervene in the process of technical innovation, social applications and scientific discovery, hence, the outcome depends on complex patterns of interactions. Indeed, technological determinism is probably not a problem, since technology is society and society cannot be understood without its technological tools.[37] This is distinctly different than stating that societal changes

---

33 Ingrid VOLKMER, *News in the Global Sphere. A Study of CNN* and its *Impact on Global Communication.* Luton, UK, University of Luton Press, 1999.

34 Howard RHEINGOLD, The Virtual Community: Homesteading on the Electronic Frontier, Cambridge, The MIT Press, 2000.

35 Sherry TURKLE, "Who am We?" *Wired*, 4.01, January 1996.

36 Raymond WILLIAMS, *Television: Technology and Cultural Form*, London, UK, Routledge, 1974; Meenakshi DURHAM, and Douglas KELLNER, *Media and Cultural Studies: Keyworks (KeyWorks in Cultural Studies)*, Malden, MA and Oxford, UK, Blackwell Publishing, 2001; Martin LISTER, Jon DOVEY, Seth GIDDINGS, Ian GRANT, and Kieran KELLY, *New Media: A Critical Introduction*, London, UK, Routledge, 2003.

37 Manuel CASTELLS, The Rise of the Network Society (The Information Age: Economy, Society and Culture, Volume 1), Hoboken, Wiley-Blackwell, 1996.

are driven by technological development, as highlighted in the theses of Marshall McLuhan.[38]

Manovich and Castells both argued that mass media, "corresponded to the logic of industrial mass society, which values conformity over individuality,"[39] and therefore, new media follows the logic systems of the postindustrial or globalized society whereby "every citizen can construct her own custom lifestyle and select her ideology from a large number of choices. Rather than pushing the same objects to a mass audience, marketing now tries to target each individual separately."[40]

Section 2.1.2 Social Change

The social media revolution has proven to be a powerful tool for a wide range of constituencies, from revolutionaries in the Middle East and North Africa to companies in the US and beyond. All types of political, economic, and cultural sectors are particularly interested in social media as a means of creating assemblies where people can learn to articulate, sell, and distribute their adverse views. However, by using the anonymity of the Internet and publicizing as many unfounded allegations as one can craft, the social media revolution can make it look as though there is a contagiousness in seeking this attribute of criticism against a particular country or individual, when in reality, all the claims emerge from a small group of self- interested parties. Despite such controversies, experts such as Andrew T. Stevens, an assistant professor of social media strategy at INSEAD, the international business school in France, have stated: "If I was a senior executive at a major corporation, I would have this on my radar screen as something to keep an eye on."[41]

Social movement media has a many-faceted and colorful history that has changed at a rapid rate since the new media became widely used. The Zapatista Army of National Liberation of Chiapas, Mexico was the first to make

38 Marshall MCLUHAN, *The Gutenberg Galaxy: The Making of Typographic Man*, London, UK, Routledge and Kegan Paul, 1962; Marshall MCLUHAN, *Understanding Media: The Extensions of Man*, Toronto, Canada, McGraw-Hill, 1964.

39 Lev MANOVICH, *op. cit.*; Manuel CASTELLS, *op. cit.*

40 Lev MANOVICH, *op. cit.*, p. 42.

41 Rhea WESSEL, "Activist Investors Turn to Social Media to Enlist Support," *The New York Times DealBook*, March 24, 2011.

widely recognized and effective use of the new media for communiqués and organizing in 1994.[42] Since then, the new media is used extensively by social movements to communicate, share, educate, organize, promote cultural movements, coalition build, etc. The WTO Ministerial Conference of 1999 protest activity was a landmark in the use of the new media as a tool for social change. The WTO protests used media to organize the original action, to communicate with and educate participants, and as an alternative media source.[43] The "Indy media" movement developed out of this action and has been a great tool in the democratization of information, which is another widely discussed aspect of the new media movement.[44] Some scholars respond that this democratization as an indication of the creation of a "radical, socio-technical paradigm to challenge the dominant, neoliberal and technologically determinist model of information and communication technologies."[45] A less radical view is that people are taking advantage of the Internet to produce a grassroots globalization, one that is (anti-neoliberal) and centered on people rather than the flow of capital.[46]

Many are skeptical of the role of the new media in social movements. Some scholars point out that unequal access exists to the new media creating a hindrance to broad-based movements, sometimes even oppressing some voices within a movement.[47] Others are skeptical about how democratic or useful it really is for social movements, even for those with access.[48] Activ-

---

42 Chris ATTON, "Reshaping Social Movement Media for a New Millennium," *Social Movement Studies*, 2, 2003, pp. 3–15.

43 Thomas Vernon REED, "Will the Revolution be Cybercast?: New Media, the Battle of Seattle, and Global Justice," in *The Art of Protest: Culture and Activism from the Civil Rights Movement to the Streets of Seattle*, 2005, Minneapolis, University of Minnesota Press, pp. 240–285.

44 Douglas KELLNER, "New Technologies, Technocities, and the Prospects for Democratization," in *Technocities*, 1999, London, UK, Sage, pp. 186–204.

45 Paschal PRESTON, Reshaping Communications: Technology, Information and Social Change, London, UK, Sage, 2001.

46 Douglas KELLNER, D. "Globalization and Technopolitics," in *The Future of Revolutions: Rethinking Radical Change in the Age of Globalization*, 2003, New York, Zed Books, pp. 180–194.

47 Herman WASSERMAN, "Is a New Worldwide Web Possible? An Explorative Comparison of the Use of ICTs by Two South African Social Movements," *African Studies Review*, 50, 2007, pp. 109–131.

48 Stephen MARMURA, "A Net Advantage? The Internet, Grassroots Activism and American Middle-Eastern policy," *New Media & Society*, 10, 2008, pp. 247–271.

ists cite that there are many new media components as tools for change that have not been widely discussed as such by academics.

The new media has employed less radical social movements using websites, blogs, and online videos to demonstrate the their effectiveness. This approach, the use of high volume blogs allowed numerous views and practices to be more widespread and gain more public attention. An example, the on-going Free Tibet Campaign, which has been seen on numerous websites as well. Another social change seen coming from the new media are trends in fashion and the emergence of subcultures such as: Cyberpunk, Text Speak, and others.

Section 2.1.3 National Security

The new media has also become of interest to the global espionage sectors. Accessible electronic database formats can be quickly retrieved and reverse engineered by national governments. A key interest to the espionage community are two sites, Facebook and Twitter, where individuals divulge personal information that can then be sorted, researched and archived for the creation of database files on a growing community of both people of interest and average citizens.

Section 2.1.4 Interactivity and New Media

Interactivity is now a familiar term for a number of the new media use options evolving the immediate dissemination of the digitalization of media, media convergence and Internet access points. In 1984, Rice defined *the new media* as communication technologies that enable or facilitate user-to-user interactivity and interactivity between user and information,[49] such as the Internet replaces the "one-to-many" approach of traditional mass communication with the possibility of a "many-to-many" form of communication. Individuals with the applicable technology can produce online media and include images, text, and sound about whatever they choose.[50] This new media technology shifts the approach of mass communication

49 Angela SCHORR, Michael SCHENK, and William CAMPBELL, *Communication Research and Media Science in Europe*, Berlin, Germany, Mouton de Gruyter, 2003.

50 Vin CROSBIE, "What is New Media?" 1998, *Sociology Central.* Retrieved from http://www.sociology.org.uk/as4mm3a.doc

and radically shapes the way the world is interacting and communicating. Vin Crosbie described new media in, "What is the new media?". He saw interpersonal media as "one to one," mass media as "one to many" and, finally; the new media as *individuation* media or "many to many."[51]

In the past, interactivity, assumed a definition related to the conversational dynamics of individuals who are face-to-face. This approach does not allow us to see its presence now in mediated communication forums. It's also viable in the applications of traditional media. In the mid-1990s filmmakers used inexpensive digital cameras to create films. Around the same time, moving image technology capable of being viewed on computer desktops in full motion had developed. Development of new media technology also provided new options for artists to share their work and interact. Other venues of interactivity also include, computer and technological programming, radio and television call –in guest speaker talk shows with listener participation in programs and letters to the editor forums. Interactivity in the new media has benefited everyone because people can express their views in more than one way with the technology.

Interactivity should be considered as a central theme in understanding the new media, as different media forms possess different degrees of it. On the other hand, various forms of digitized and converged media are not interactivel. Tony Feldman, for example, considers digital satellite television as a new media technology that employs digital compression to dramatically increase the number of television channels that can be delivered, in effect, altering the range of selections of what can be offered by the service providers, viewed from the user's point perspective, it still lacks a more fully interactive dimension. For this example interactivity is not an characteristic of all the new media technologies, compared to digitization and convergence.[52]

Terry Flew presents the position that "the global interactive games industry is large and growing, and is at the forefront of many of the most significant innovations in the new media."[53] Some examples of where interactivity in online computer games are, *World of Warcraft*, *The Sims Online* and *Sec-*

51 David CROTEAU and William HOYNES, *op. cit.*

52 Tony FLEDMAN, *An Introduction to Digital Media*, London, UK, Routledge, 1997.

53 Terry FLEW, *op. cit.*

ond Life. These games, which are product developments of the new media, establish relationships and experience a sense of belonging for users, despite temporal and spatial boundaries.. The new media have created virtual realities becoming extensions of the world we live in. These games can be used as an escape or to act out a desired life The new media changes continuously because it is constantly modified and redefined by the interaction between the creative use of the masses, emerging technology, cultural changes, etc.[54]

Section 2.1.5 Social Media and Data Revolution

The ***Social Data Revolution (SDR)*** is the shift in human communication patterns towards increased personal information sharing and its related implications, made possible by the rise of social networks in early 2000s. While social networks were used in the early days to privately share photos and private messages, the subsequent trend towards people passively and actively sharing personal information more broadly has resulted in unprecedented amounts of public data. Social data refers to that which individuals create, which is knowingly and voluntarily shared by them. Cost and overhead previously rendered this semi-public form of communication unfeasible, but advances in social networking technology from 2004-2012 have made broader concepts of sharing possible. The types of data users are sharing include geo-location, medical data, dating preferences, open thoughts, interesting news articles, etc. Technology continues to track user behavior with more and more precision, resulting in products and services that can be mass customized to a broad range of users.

Early examples of social data are Craigslist and the “wish lists” of Amazon.com. Both enable users to communicate information to anybody who is looking for it. They differ in their approach to identity. Craigslist leverages the power of anonymity, while Amazon.com leverages the power of persistent identity, based on the history of the customer with the firm. The job market is even being shaped by the information people share about themselves on sites like LinkedIn and Facebook.

54 Second Life, http://secondlife.com/whatis/#Be_Creative

Section 2.1.6 Social Authority

One of the key components in successful social media marketing implementation is building *social authority*. Social authority is developed when an individual or organization establishes itself as an expert in a given field or area, thereby becoming an "influencer" (per Galdwell) of a tipping point in that field or area. It is through this process of building social authority that social media is very effective. That is why one of the foundational concepts in social media has become that you cannot completely control your message through social media but rather you can simply begin to participate in the conversation in the hopes that you can become a relevant influence in it. These types of phenomena were integral and exhibited with the Facebook platform use during the recent 2011 *Arab Spring Uprisings*.

However, these types of conversation participation must be cleverly executed because people are, in general, resistant to direct or overt marketing through social media platforms. On the surface, this seems counter-intuitive, but it is the main reason building social authority with credibility is so important. A marketer (or *connector* to use the Gladwell term) generally can not expect people to be receptive to a marketing message in and of itself. In the Edleman Trust Barometer report in 2008, the majority (58%) of the respondents reported they most trusted company or product information coming from "people like me", inferred to be information from someone they trusted.[55] In the 2010 Trust Report, the majority switched to 64% preferring their information from industry experts and academics. According to Inc. Technology's Brent Leary, "This loss of trust, and the accompanying turn towards experts and authorities, seems to be coinciding with the rise of social media and networks." [56] Thus, using social media as a form of marketing has taken on whole new challenges. As the 2010 Trust Study indicates, it is most effective if marketing efforts through social media revolve around the *genuine* building of authority.[57] Someone performing a "marketing" role within a company must honestly convince

55 Edelman, *Edelman Trust Barometer 2008*, 2008. Retrieved from http://www.edelman.com/trust/2008/TrustBarometer08_FINAL.pdf

56 Brent LEARY, "Overemphasis on Brand Building Leads to Mistrust, *Inc.*, March 24, 2010. Retrieved from http://technology.inc.com/2010/03/22/overemphasis-on-brand-building-leads-to-mistrust/

57 Edelman, *Edelman Trust Barometer 2010*. 2010. Retrieved from http://www.edelman.com/trust/2010/

people of their *genuine* intentions, knowledge, and expertise in a specific area or industry through providing valuable and accurate information on an ongoing basis without a marketing angle overtly associated. If this can be done, trust with and of the recipient of that information – and that message itself – begins to develop naturally. This person or organization becomes a thought leader and value provider setting themselves up as a trusted advisor instead of marketer. *Top of mind awareness* develops and the consumer naturally begins to gravitate to the products and/or offerings of the authority/influencer.[58]

Of course, there are many ways authority can be created and influenced, for example, the participation in *Wikipedia*, which actually verifies user-generated content and information. Authority also provides valuable content through social networks on platforms such as Facebook and Twitter; article writing and distribution through sites such as Ezine and fact-based answers on "social question and answer sites" such as EHow. As a result of social media and the direct or indirect influence of social media marketers, consumers are as likely (or more likely) to make buying decisions based on what they read and see in platforms we call "social" but only if presented by someone they have come to trust. That is why a purposeful and carefully designed social media strategy has become an integral part of any complete and directed marketing plan (or as we will see in the case studies) but must also be designed using newer authority building techniques.

Social media takes many different forms, including Internet forums, weblogs, social blogs, micro blogging, wiki's, podcasts, photographs or pictures, video, rating and social bookmarking. By applying a set of theories in the field of media research (social presence, media richness) and social processes (self-presentation, self-disclosure) Kaplan and Haenlein created a classification scheme for different social media types in their Business Horizons article published in 2010. According to their findings, there are six different types of social media: collaborative projects, blogs and micro blogs, content communities, social networking sites, virtual game worlds,

58 Nathan LINNELL, "Social Media Influence on Consumer Behavior," *Search Engine Watch*, May 3, 2010. Retrieved from http://searchenginewatch.com/article/2049190/Social-Media-Influence-on-Consumer-Behavior

and virtual communities.[59] Social media technologies include blogs, picture-sharing, blogs, wall-postings, email, instant messaging, music-sharing, crowd-sourcing, and voice over IP, to name a few. Many of these social media services can be integrated via social network aggregation platforms such as:

Facebook, is a social network service launched in February 2004. As of July 2010,[update] Facebook had more than 500 million active users. Users typically create a personal profile, add other users as friends, and exchange messages, and it will include automatic notifications when they update their profile. Additionally, users may join common interest user groups organized by workplace, school or college, or other characteristics. The name of the service stems from the colloquial name for the book given to students at the start of the academic year by university administrations in the US with the intention of helping students get to know each other better. Facebook allows anyone who declares him or herself to be at least 13 years old to become a registered user of the website.

A January 2009 Compete.com study ranked Facebook as the most used social network service by worldwide monthly active users followed by MySpace.[60] *Entertainment Weekly* published its end-of-the-decade "best-of" list, saying, "How on earth did we stalk our exes, remember our co-workers' birthdays, bug our friends, and play a rousing game of Scrabulous before Facebook?"[61] Quantcast estimates Facebook has 135.1 million monthly unique U.S. visitors in October 2010. Social Media Today, as of April 2010, estimated that 41.6% of the U.S. population has a Facebook account.[62]

---

59 Andreas KAPLAN and Michael HAENLEIN, "Users of the World, Unite! The Challenges and Opportunities of Social Media," *Business Horizons*, 53, 2010, pp. 59–68.

60 Andy KAZENIAC, "Social Networks: Facebook Takes Over Top Spot, Twitter Climbs," *Compete Pulse blog,* February 9, 2009. Retrieved from http://blog.compete.com/2009/02/09/facebook-myspace-twitter-social-network/

61 Thom GRIER, *et al.*, "The 100 Greatest Movies, TV Shows, Albums, Books, Characters, Scenes, Episodes, Songs, Dresses, Music Videos, and Trends that Entertained Us Over the 10 Years," *Entertainment Weekly*, 1079/1080, December 11, 2009, 74–84.

62 Quantcast, "Facebook.com," October 31, 2011. Retrieved from http://www.quantcast.com/facebook.com

Facebook has been met with global event controversies. It has been blocked in several countries intermittently recently including, Egypt, Vietnam, Iran, Uzbekistan, Pakistan, Syria, People's Republic of China and Bangladesh. For example, on the basis of Anti-Islamic and religious discrimination content allowed by Facebook, it was also banned in many regions and countries of the world. The privacy of Facebook users is also an issue, and the safety of user accounts has been compromised several times. Facebook has recently settled a lawsuit regarding claims over source code and intellectual property. [63]

Facebook's role in the Obama Presidential Campaign and american political process was demonstrated in January 2008 when shortly before the New Hampshire primary Facebook teamed up with ABC and Saint Anselm College, allowed users to input live feedback during the January 5 Republican and Democratic debates. Over 1,000,000 users installed the Facebook application "US politics" in order to take part, and the application measured users' responses to specific comments made by the debating candidates.[64] This reaction and debate demonstrated that: Facebook was an extremely powerful and popular new way to interact and offer opinions. An article written by Michelle Sullivan of Uwire.com discussed how the "Facebook effect" was influencing youth voting rates, youth support of political candidates, and general involvement by the younger populations in the 2008 election. [65]

Illustrating the global reach of similar trends, in February 2008, a Facebook group called "One Million Voices Against FARC" organized an event whereby thousands of Colombians marched in protest against the Revolutionary Armed Forces of Colombia, FARC.[66] In August 2010, one of North

---

63 Roy WELLS, "41.6% of the U.S. Population has a Facebook account," *Social Media Today*, August 8, 2010. Retrieved from http://socialmediatoday.com/index.php?q=roywells1/158020/416-us-population-has-facebook-account

64 Russell GOLDMAN, "Facebook Gives Snapshot of Voter Sentiment," *ABC News*, January 5, 2007. Retrieved from http://abcnews.go.com/Politics/story?id=4091460&page=1#.Twrr-2Oonus

65 Michelle SULLIVAN, "'Facebook Effect' Mobilizes Youth Vote," *CBS News*, November 3, 2008. Retrieved from http://www.cbsnews.com/stories/2008/11/04/politics/uwire/main4568563.shtml

66 Sibylla BRODZINSKY, "Facebook Used to Target Colombia's FARC with Global Rally," *The Christian Science Monitor (Boston)*, February 4, 2008. Retrieved from http://www.csmonitor.com/World/Americas/2008/0204/p04s02-woam.html

Korea's official government websites, Uriminzokkiri, joined Facebook.[67]

Twitter is another social networking website owned and operated by Twitter Inc. that offers a service enabling its users to send and read messages called *tweets* via its social networking and micro-blogging platform. Tweets provides for text-based posts of up to 140 characters on the user's profile page. Users may subscribe to other users' tweets—this is known as *following* and subscribers are known as *followers*. Since its launch in July 2006, Twitter currently is estimated to have 300 million users as of 2011, generating over 300 million tweets and handling over 1.6 billion search queries per day.[68]

The social platform trend specific to Twitter's popularity was the 2007 South by Southwest (SXSW) festival (and actually a tipping point in itself), Twitter usage increased from 20,000 tweets per day to 60,000.[69] "The Twitter people cleverly placed two 60-inch plasma screens in the conference hallways, exclusively streaming Twitter messages," remarked *Newsweek's* Steven Levy. "Hundreds of conference-goers kept tabs on each other via constant twitters. Panelists and speakers mentioned the service, and the bloggers in attendance touted it." [70] Other Twitter milestones include, the first off-Earth Twitter message was posted from the International Space Station by NASA astronaut T. J. Creamer on January 22, 2010.[71] And in late November 2010, an average of a dozen updates per day was posted on

---

67 Laura ROBERTS, "North Korea Joins Facebook," *The Daily Telegraph (London)*, August 21, 2010. Retrieved from http://www.telegraph.co.uk/technology/facebook/7957222/North-Korea-joins-Facebook.html

68 "Your World, More Connected," Twitter Blog, August 1, 2011. Retrieved http://blog.twitter.com/2011/08/your-world-more-connected.html; Twitter Search Team, "The Engineering Behind Twitter's New Search Experience," *Twitter Engineering Blog (blog of Twitter Engineering Division)*, May 31, 2011. Retrieved from http://engineering.twitter.com/2011/05/engineering-behind-twitters-new-search.html

69 Nick DOUGLAS, "Twitter Blows Up at SXSW Conference," *Gawker*, March 12, 2007. Retrieved from http://gawker.com/243634/twitter-blows-up-at-sxsw-conference

70 Steven LEVY, "Twitter: Is Brevity the Next Big Thing?" *Newsweek*, April 30, 2007. Retrieved from http://www.msnbc.msn.com/id/17888481/site/newsweek/

71 Press release, "Media Advisory M10-012 – NASA Extends the World Wide Web Out into Space," NASA, January 22, 2010. Retrieved from http://www.nasa.gov/home/hqnews/2010/jan/HQ_M10-012_ISS_Web.html

the astronauts' communal account, @NASA_Astronauts.[72]

In other developments related to Twitter, *The Wall Street Journal* reported that Twitter elicited mixed feelings in the technology-savvy people (who have been their early adopters). However, some users are starting to feel too connected. *Nielsen Online* reported that Twitter has a user retention rate of 40%, many people stop using the service after a month, nevertheless, in 2009 Twitter won the "Breakout of the Year" Webby Award.[73] In February 2009, during a discussion on National Public Radio's *Weekend Edition*, Daniel Schorr stated that: "Twitter accounts of events lacked rigorous fact-checking and other editorial improvements". In response, Twitter responded to Schorr with two examples of breaking news stories that played out on Twitter and said users wanted first-hand accounts and sometimes debunked stories.[74]

In August 2010, South Korea intermittently blocked content on Twitter related to the North Korean government Twitter account. The account, setup with user name , @uriminzok, (loosely translated to mean *our people* in Korean), had 4,500 followers in less than one week. Very soon thereafter, on August 19, 2010, South Korea' banned the Twitter account for broadcasting "illegal information." BBC, US and Canada experts claimed that North Korea had invested in "information technology for more than 20 years" with knowledge of how to use social networking sites to their power.[75] With only 36 tweets, the Twitter account was able to accumulate almost 9,000 followers. To date, the South Korean has banned 65 sites, in-

72 Press release, "Media Advisory M10-012 – NASA Extends the World Wide Web Out into Space," NASA, January 22, 2010. Retrieved from http://www.nasa.gov/home/hqnews/2010/jan/HQ_M10-012_ISS_Web.html

73 Staff writer, "13th Annual Webby Special Achievement Award Winners," *The Webby Awards*, n.d. Retrieved from http://www.webbyawards.com/webbys/specialachievement13.php/; Ian PAUL, "Jimmy Fallon Wins Top Webby: And the Winners Are…," *PC World*, May 5, 2009. Retrieved from http://www.pcworld.com/article/164374/jimmy_fallon_wins_top_webby_and_the_winners_are_.html

74 Andy CARVIN, "Welcome to the Twitterverse," *National Public Radio*, February 28, 2009. Retrieved from http://www.npr.org/templates/story/story.php?storyId=101265831

75 Clark BOYD, "BBC News – North Korea creates Twitter and YouTube presence," BBC, August 18, 2010. Retrieved from http://www.bbc.co.uk/news/world-us-canada-11007825

cluding this Twitter account.[76] Twitter is also banned in China (but many Chinese people use it anyway). Chinese authorities respond to this use very seriously. In 2010, Cheng Jianping was sentenced to one year in a labor camp for a sarcastic post on Twitter.[77]

YouTube is a video-sharing website on which users can upload, share, and view videos created by three former PayPal employees in February 2005. Unregistered users may watch videos, and registered users may upload an unlimited number of videos. In November 2006, YouTube, LLC was bought by Google Inc. for $1.65 billion, and now operates as a subsidiary of Google. Before the launch of YouTube in 2005, there were very few easy methods available for ordinary computer users who wanted to post videos online. With its simple interface, YouTube made it possible for anyone with an Internet connection to post a video that a worldwide audience could watch within a few minutes. The wide range of topics covered by YouTube has turned video sharing into one of the most important parts of social networking culture.

Section 2.2 Media: Political, Cultural, Economic Relationships

Media has a enormous social networking and micro-blogging social and cultural impact upon society predicated upon the ability to reach a wide audience with a strong and influential message. Marshall McLuhan uses the phrase "the medium is the message" as a means of explaining how the distribution of a message can often be more important than content of the message itself.[78] Television broadcasting, for example, has control over the content society watches and the times in which it is viewed. This points out distinguishing feature of *Traditional Media* that *New Media* has challenged by reinventing the participation habits of the public. The internet creates an opportunity for a heightened level of participation, more diverse political opinions, social and cultural viewpoints. Perhaps suggesting that by allow-

76 Zachary SNIDERMAN, "North Korea's Newly Launched Twitter Account Banned by South Korea," *Mashable.com*, August 19, 2010. Retrieved from http://mashable.com/2010/08/19/north-korea-twitter-banned/

77 Andrew JACOBS, "Chinese Woman Imprisoned for Twitter Message," *New York Times*, November 18, 2010. Retrieved from http://www.nytimes.com/2010/11/19/world/asia/19beijing.html

78 Marshall MCLUHAN and Fiore QUENTIN, *The Medium is the Message*, Hardwired, San Francisco, 1967, pp. 8–9, 26–41.

ing consumers to produce information through the internet will result in an overload of information. In a democratic society, all forms of media can serve the electorate about issues regarding government and corporate entities. Some consider the concentration of media ownership to be the greatest threat to democracy. Media can be used for various purposes: For example, it can be used for advocacy, both for business and social concerns. This can include forms of advertising, marketing, propaganda, public relations, and political communication. Entertainment is another use, traditionally through performances of acting, music, and sports. Third, it can be used for public service announcements.

Another description of Media is *central media* which implies the ability to transmit tacit knowledge. The manipulation of large groups of people through media for the benefit of a particular political party and/or group of people is among its uses. Bias, political or otherwise, towards favoring certain individual outcomes or resolution of an event is inherent. "This view of central media can be contrasted with lateral media, such as email networks, where messages are all slightly different and spread by a process of lateral diffusion."[79]

Section 2.2.1 Relationships: Political

Certain groups tend to promote certain media strategies in an effort to further a political cause. Tipper Gore, the wife of previous US Vice-President Al Gore, was the founder of the Parents Music Resource Center and was the main figure in pushing for warning labels on music, even though she does not fit into the conservative demographic. Whereby, demands for the banning of certain songs or the labeling of obscene albums came specifically from conservative political groups in the United States. As such, she argued that such material had simple and identifiable effects on children and thus should be banned/labeled.

Political factions, as perhaps in this instance, sometimes use the media to influence new members into joining and following their groups.

Other political relationships media strategies include:

79 Marshall MCLUHAN and Fiore QUENTIN, *The Medium is the Message*, Hardwired, San Francisco, 1967, pp. 8–9, 26–41.

Control

Theorists such as Louis Wirth and Talcott Parsons emphasized the importance of mass media as instruments of social control. They pointed out, in the 21st century, with the rise of the internet, the two-way relationship between mass media and public opinion is beginning to change with the advent of new technologies such as blogging.[80]

Mander's theory is related to Jean Baudrillard's concept of *hyperreality*.[81] Using the 1994 O.J. Simpson trial as an example. The reality reported on in this case was merely the catalyst for the images that defined the trial as a global event, and made the trial more than it should have been. Essentially, hyperreality is where the media is not merely a window onto the world, but is part of the reality described, hence the media's obsession with media-created events.

Marshall McLuhan suggested mass media was increasingly creating a "global village." He pointed out, for example, there is evidence that Western media influence (in Asia) is the driving force behind rapid social change: "It is as if the 1960s and the 1990s were compressed together."[82] Highlighted by the recent introduction of television to Bhutan. Raising questions of "cultural imperialism" — and the de facto imposition through economic and political power and through the media of Western (and in particular US) culture.[83]

Other social scientists have made efforts to integrate the study of the mass media as an instrument of control. For example, in the study of political and economic developments in the Afro-Asian countries, David Lerner, emphasized the general pattern of increase in standard of urbanization, living, literacy and exposure to mass media during the transition from "traditional to modern society". Lerner states, "that while there is a heavy emphasis on the expansion of mass media in developing societies, the penetration of a central authority into the daily consciousness of the mass has to overcome profound resistance".[84] And, as a recently (2012), the govern-

80 Op cit
81 Op cit
82 Op cit
83 Op cit
84 David LERNER, The Passing of Traditional Society: Modernizing the Middle East, New York, The Free Press, 1958.

ment of Pakistan has even gone so far as to solicit bids ($10 million project) from technology companies to develop a system to cut off the internet service providers with a national-level URL filtering and blocking system. China and other governments, although with very little disclosure have implemented strategies for censorship and sanitizing the internet.

Content

The relation of the mass media to contemporary popular culture is commonly defined in terms of how dissemination occurs from the elite ruling class to the mass. The long-term consequences of significant control and concentration of ownership of the media, lead to accusations of media elite establishing a form of cultural dictatorship, continuing the recent debates about the influence of media barons such as Conrad Black and Rupert Murdoch. Murdoch has had his share of controversy in this regard, for example, the UK *Observer* (March 1, 1998) reported the Murdoch-owned HarperCollins' refusal to publish Chris Patten's *East and West* because of the former Hong Kong governor's description of the Chinese leadership as "faceless Stalinists" possibly being damaging to Murdoch's Chinese broadcasting interests.[85] In this case, the author was able to have the book accepted by another publisher, but this type of content censorship may be a beacon for the future. A related form is that of self-censorship by all level of members in the media in the interests of protecting their own careers.

Influence

It is indeed objectionable when a specific government tries to influence the printers and editors in addition to imposing many media laws. Every type of newspaper and other media forms are somehow under political influence and where there is political influence there will be false and fabricated news that will be published. In most countries, and more recently in developing controls, there are five sectors that are likely to be influenced by governments. These are:

1. Media: including newspapers, TV, radio, Internet, and books, etc.
2. Education: including schools, colleges and universities,

85 Nicholas CLEE, "The Bookseller," *Guardian Unlimited*, March 1, 2003, Retrieved from http://www.guardian.co.uk/books/2003/mar/01/featuresreviews.guardianreview30

students, and teachers.

3. Judicial: namely judges, lawyers, etc.
4. Medical: doctors, government or private.
5. Defense: members appointed for the protection of a country internally or externally, .i.e. police, army, navy, air force, etc.

Agendas

The agenda-setting process is perhaps an unavoidable part of large organizations that make up much of the mass media. Four main news agencies — AP, UPI, Reuters and Agence-France-Presse — claim together to provide 90% of the total news output of the world's press, radio and television.[86] Stuart Hall points out that because some of these media agencies produce material that often is good, impartial and serious, they are accorded a high degree of respect and authority. However, in practice the ethics of the press and television are closely related to that of the hegemonic establishment providing vital support to the existing order. Independence (e.g. of the BBC) is not "a mere cover, it is central to the way power and ideology are mediated in societies like ours."[87]

The public is in effect bribed by radio, television, and newspapers into an acceptance of biased, misleading, and status quo agendas. Greg Philo demonstrates this in his 1991 article, "Seeing is Believing," in which he illustrated the 1984 UK miners' strike were strongly correlated with the media presentation of the event, including the perception of the picketing as largely violent when violence was rare, and the use by the public of phrases that had appeared originally in the media.[88]

McCombs and Shaw further demonstrated agenda-setting in a study conducted in Chapel Hill, North Carolina, USA, during the 1968 presidential elections.[89] Here, a representative sample of undecided voters was asked to outline the key issues of the election as they perceived them. Concurrently,

86 Rajmohan JOSHI, Encyclopedia of Journalism and Mass Communication: Media and Mass Communication, New Delhi, India, Gyan Publishing House, 2006, p. 95.

87 *Ibid.*, p. 95.

88 *Ibid.*, p. 96.

89 Maxwell MCCOMBS and Donald SHAW, "The Agenda-Setting Function of Mass Media," *Public Opinion Quarterly*, 36, 1972, pp. 176–187.

the mass media serving these subjects were collected and their content was analyzed. They concluded, there was a definite correlation between the two accounts of predominant issues. "The evidence in this study that voters tend to share the media's composite definition of what is important strongly suggests an agenda-setting function of the mass media."[90]

Section 2.2.2 Relationships: Cultural

Fear in the face of huge power is the dictator's traditional tool for keeping people in check, but in fact by cutting off Internet and wireless service, most recently during Egypt's huge protests in January 2011, the president only confirmed that his fear of Facebook, Twitter, laptops, and smart phones empowered his opponents and exposed his weakness to the world, resulting in the toppling of his regime.

The new arsenal of social networks also helped to accelerate Tunisia's revolution, driving out the country's ruler of 23 years. It has also helped to ignite an epidemic that spread across the Arab world at breathtaking speed. The Egypt and Tunisia uprisings offer the latest encouragement for another way to look at the situation. While they are away for the world to keep up with friends and make blog posts, they also provide the same technologies that were hailed as a factor in the Iran Green Revolution. That led to stirring street protest that followed the disputed presidential election. But since the revolt collapsed, the government's role in monitoring the Internet has become a cautionary tale. As we know, the Iranian police eagerly followed the electronic trails left by activists, which led to their making thousands of arrests in the crackdown that followed. The government even posted photos of its hunt for its enemies inviting other Iranians to supply names and addresses. While the Iranian government has become much more adept at using the Internet to go after activists, it has, in fact, become a powerful political and economic force that protects the ayatollah's regime by creating an online surveillance center believed to be behind an army of hackers that it can unleash at any point against opponents. Repressive regimes around the world have fallen behind their opponents in recent years in exploiting the new technologies, and it is not unexpected when aging autocrats face younger, more technically savvy opponents. But in Moscow, to Iran, and to Beijing, governments have begun to climb the steep learning curve and

---

90 Ibid.

turn the Internet platforms around to their own political devices.

The countertrend debate that the conventional wisdom about the Internet and networking sites inherently tipped the balance of power in favor of democracy is mistaken. A new book, titled *The Net Delusion: The Dark Side of Internet Freedom*, by Eugenie Morozov has made a case in describing instance after instance of strong men finding their way to use the new media to their advantage.[91] After all, the very factors that brought Facebook and similar sites' products such future success also has incredible appeal for the secret police. A cyber surfing police officer can compile a dossier on a regime opponent without the trouble of street surveillance and telephone tapping required in the pre-net world. In Egypt in January 2011 the president resorted to traditional blunt instrument against the dissident and his crisis. He cut off the communications altogether, yet other countries have shown greater sophistication. While the fact that Facebook is a great database for government, now one has to believe that it is doing more good than harm, helping activists for virtual organizations that would never survive if they met face-to-face. But one has to be aware that they are speaking not only to their friends but to their oppressors as well.

Widney Brown, Senior Director of International Law Policy at Amnesty International, points out that these technologies are politically neutral. "There is nothing deterministic about these tools, Gutenberg's press, or fax machine, or Facebook. They can be used to promote human rights or to undermine human rights."[92] In China thousands of commentators are trained and paid to post pro-government comments on the web and steer online opinion away from the criticism of the Communist Party. The same is occurring in Venezuela where President Hugo Chavez first denounced the hostile Twitter comments as terrorism and then turned around and created his own Twitter feed. Scott Shane, a reporter at the *Times* Washington bureau, is the author of a book called *Dismantling Utopia: How Information Ended the Soviet Union.*[93] Yet Russia, much the same with the other governments mentioned, has managed to co-opt several prominent news

---

91 Eugenie MOROZOV, "The Net Delusion: The Dark Side of Internet Freedom," *PublicAffairs*, 2011.

92 Scott SHANE, "Spotlight Again Falls on Web Tools and Change," *New York Times*, January 29, 2011, para. 12.

93 Scott SHANE, Dismantling Utopia: How Information Ended the Soviet Union, Chicago, Ivan R. Dee, 1994.

media entrepreneurs with huge website followings that now strongly skew toward pro-Putin and the other anti-Georgia reports that went viral.

In Egypt Mr. Mubarak's government concluded that it was too late for simple monitoring and completely unplugged his country from the Internet altogether in addition to cutting off the country from television. This was a desperate move by an autocrat who had not learned to harness the tools his opponents have embraced.

Section 2.2.3 Relationships Economic

The media has a strong economic impact upon society. This is predicated upon the ability to influence a wide audience with a strong economically driven agenda. As previously pointed out, particularly with television broadcasting, and now the internet, each have a large amount of influence over the content society is exposed to and the frequency and times in which it is viewed. This is a distinguishing feature of New Media by altering the economic and purchasing habits of societies. The internet creates a (marketing) environment for presenting diverse entrepreneur, government and business viewpoints, and an increased level of consumer economic influence. These forms of media serve economic platforms, generally in favor of government and corporate entities, which typically have the most means to deploy them. Economic relationships and the concentration of media ownership by governments and large corporations are believed by some to be the greatest threat to democracy. Media can be used for various economic purposes: For example, it can be used for marketing, both for business and governmental concerns. This can include advertising, propaganda, public relations, and product/service communication. Political and governmental positioning and party economic strategy is another use, traditionally through use of disseminating and supporting economic driven agendas, not always without bias or (harmful) impacts. Third, it can be used for recent economic and development announcements.

In the same context as political and cultural relationships, economic relationships sometimes involve the manipulation of large societies and countries through these media outlets for the benefit of a particular political party and/or group of people. Bias, economic, political or otherwise, towards favoring certain individual outcomes or resolution of an events is inherent.

Section 2.3 Summary

What this chapter proposes to validate about Tipping Point theory and media applied in this context is, in fact, the leading edge equation for understanding current and future world events and ultimately, what will drive world societies closer together (or further apart). The questions about the great shift taking place in the world now will prove to be less about culture differences and more about global communication. Newspapers, TV, radio and all the other newer forms of media technology only reflect and document what is and has occurred. The next chapters will attempt to validate that when looking at specific case studies we can highlight when and why the tipping points arrive that result in world events, like rare moments in history, and possibly, we may have a unique opportunity to step out from the old protocols of how these events are perceived and influenced and into something new, a moment when one age ends and the future understanding begins.

Media Impacts and Global Events Website

For further information please visit the
Media impact and Global Events Website:

http://mdgparis.typepad.com/global_media_and_world_ev/

This website tracks, highlights, categorizes and provides a articles and commentary related to Tipping Point Attributes and Characteristics, as well as information and recent updates related specifically to the three case studies included in this version and other Media and Global Event issues.

Part II
Case Studies

INTRODUCTION

Current history offers a number of interesting examples of media impact on global events and their relevance to the Tipping Point Theory. Each of the following case studies analyzes and contrasts significant their attributes and characteristic relative to the media and the impact economically, culturally, and politically. The three case studies examined here were selected on the basis of two main criteria—1. Each exhibited the sequential progression of attributes and characteristics leading to a defined moment in time when circumstances and events changed as a result of the influences that lead to tipping points and 2. Each opens opportunities to understand media relationships to the world events around us, their impact and the creation of our new reality.

Most global events are connected with media in their reach and association, however, analysis constraints are not so easily addressed when researching the communication systems being employed and influencing the outcomes. Each of these case studies, however, is characterized by a media breakthrough and development (phenomena) and its application is salient to the study discussion. And, as in our last case study, Climate Change, the phenomena is simply not resolved.

Each of the case studies exhibit the attributes and characteristics central to the question of whether or not tipping points exist, can be analyzed, (and possibly controlled), and sometimes do (and do not) give answers to questions that are raised by them. These case studies provide the opportunity to address the questions by elaborating, analyzing and assessing specific examples.

Another element shared by each of the tipping point case studies examined here is that two are within recent memory. While this was not a selection criterion, per se, it shows that when compared, analyzed, and viewed in the context of other similar events in history, it allows their impacts to be observed and assessed in relation to possible future global events.

Overview of the Case Studies

Imagine you are born in 1961, and one day, 47 years later you run for the presidential office of the most powerful country on the planet. During your lifetime, major media technological tools become at your disposal to deploy (and guarantee) that you will win the US presidential race. This is why Barack Obama became the 44th president of the USA. The first case study examines the 2007-2008 *Obama Presidential Campaign*. The first case study will illustrate that prior to the start of the campaign, during the campaign, and on the election day itself, global media echoed the contagiousness and the stickiness attributes for his victorious campaign, which then lead to one dramatic moment, (tipping point), that dealt a devastating loss for the ill-conceived campaign of Senator John McClain and Governor Sarah Palin.

The second case study examines the *International Financial Crisis* from the period between Sept 1, 2008 and November 4, 2010 (and as this dissertation is being written – perhaps, still occurring), the world markets slipped into one of the worst financial tsunamis and complete loss of equity value and confidence in the banking system worldwide. The evitable impact (tipping point) was the one week financial casualty list (October 18, 2008) that included, Lehman Brothers, AIG Insurance, Morgan Stanley acquiring Citibank and Washington Mutual, the US federal bailout of Bear Sterns, and the 700 billion dollar US rescue package. The impact and effect on other world markets, IMF, Finland, other world funds was tremendous, not experienced since the Great Depression of 1930's. This crisis was carried, *blow-by-blow*, with ongoing updates on all the news media. As this event continued to unfold, it lead to a panic and selloff, a drop in the United

States stock market of over 700 points in just one day, and similar losses in markets worldwide, with a net value loss reaching 10 trillion and climbing (USD).

The final case study, *Climate Change*, examines similar types political, economic and cultural (and moral) issues related to this current global event. While not all the issues are common between each of the studies, there exists a certain amount of conceptual universality that reaches across and becomes generic to all. It also attempts to address the question: In context with the three tipping points attributes and characteristics research approach, does the application of the theory framework applied in the analysis and comparisons that follow, offer some potential long term solutions for climate change?

CHAPTER THREE
CASE STUDIES

One: Presidential Journey of Barack Obama

Introduction

This case study analyzes the presidential journey of Barack Obama that occurred during the presidential elections of 2008 in the United States. Barack Obama's revolutionary presidential campaign resulted in a culmination of never before experienced voter turnouts and added emphasis to the International Financial Crisis (2007 – 2010), which is analyzed in Case Study Two.

This study explores the Tipping Point attributes and characteristics of the presidential campaign of Barack Obama. The Tipping Point attributes include Contagiousness, Stickiness, and the One Dramatic Moment, as each unfolded during the presidential race between Barack Obama and John McCain. These attributes and characteristics were influenced by the various media developments and technological advancements that helped to shape the message of the campaigns, how they were delivered, how they were reported on, which events had significance, and the voter response.

The goal of this research is to understand the relationships between and among the attributes and characteristics individually and collectively. It is these relationships that shaped the campaign and its eventual outcome. The evidence of this case study suggests that the outcome didn't happen in a vacuum, it was the coalescence of the attributes and characteristics, as a media and social phenomenon led to the culmination of Barack Obama being elected as president of the United States.

Two research questions were paramount in this study. (1) How have analyzing the media delivery systems and technology used during the campaign, exhibited their influence on the reaction of the American voter? (2) What relationships between and among the various media delivery systems resulted in this outcome for this historic presidential campaign? Answering these questions within the case study takes the analysis to a higher-level.

Integral to this case study is a review of the actual campaign personalities and individuals, organizations, media agendas, technology structures and significant events that occurred and existed in 2008 to understand the conditions that proved dynamic for the evolution of the campaign. Also included are brief reviews of the historical state-of-the-art media in order to understand its contribution.

This research is formatted to develop a qualitative ratio framework to analysze the various attributes and characteristics of the Tipping Point theory. Part three's goal is to analyze and compare the complexity and the application of this theory. With these research questions in hand, this framework provides a methodology that can be applied to other global media events and similar tipping point phenomena in the other two case studies. The discussion that follows is based upon qualitative research from primary and secondary sources, and the bibliography and further references related to this case study appear at the end.

In this case study, I evaluate the Obama Campaign in the context of the US financial sector economic collapse, highlight many of the developments in the media, and analyze the campaign themselves. I examine how many skilled professionals orchestrated these campaigns and masterminded media strategies along the way for each of the two candidates.

Knowing when the tipping point occurred for the Obama Campaign is crucial in determining the media impact in effecting the 2008 election outcome. This research focuses on the contagiousness and stickiness of the communications that were disseminated by the campaigns and how the media treated it and, ultimately, how the voters responded. I also explore McCain's age and Obama's race. In addition, I evaluate how the outcome was tied to the unpopular incumbent George W. Bush (and how the McCain team tried to disassociate). The contagiousness and stickiness characteristics of the vice presidential candidates are also explored.

As part of this case study research, I examined the early developments and key issues in the summer of 2008, which candidate had the better energy policy, the competing agendas over the alternative tax policies, and finally, right up until the election itself, how the plans for saving the economy became so important. In the end, I propose an account of how the complexity of the attributes and characteristics, the strategies of the campaigns themselves, and the media technology were at work leading to the tipping point in the campaign and the ultimate result. I have divided the case study into three (3) attributes:

Contagiousness: The effects of the trends that resulted in an epidemic of forces in the messages that were used by the various sectors of media during the campaign. In doing so, I explore how the candidates' messages about themselves and their opponents played a large part in this attribute development.

Stickiness: Analyzing the shifts in momentum, some of which seemingly started small, ultimately leading to a larger impact during the campaign. These stickiness attributes, under the right circumstances, made the possibility of Obama's election a reality.

Dramatic Moment: When the epidemic resulted in a fundamental and irreversible/ irresistible change in direction for the campaign. The economic collapse led to the tipping point and the ultimate win for the Obama campaign. Understanding this final attribute makes sense of the first two and perhaps permits the greatest insight into why these events happen the way they do.

This approach is subdivided further into the four (4) specific sets of characteristics for each attribute: *people, organizations, media and events.*

Section 3.1 Contagiousness Attributes (C)

Most of the discussions in the media in the beginning of the campaigns were about the role of the candidates and their strategies relative to their message to try to get into the White House. There was a lot of rhetoric about the condition of the economy as well as the progress or lack thereof and the wars abroad in Iraq and Afghanistan. Almost daily there were media stories featuring issues on the economy, unemployment, housing starts, the Dow, gas prices and foreclosure rates. Everything early on in the campaigns was about trying to tie these complex issues to the candidates and also to the party the candidates represented.

I begin first by focusing on the Contagiousness of a combination of fundamental key individuals that assured that the Obama campaign was well aligned for a win for the Democrats.

Section 3.1.1 People

George W. Bush

The first Contagiousness attribute *person* begins with George W. Bush, whose inept handling of the economy, which showed from the onset of the campaign that the Republicans had a severe disadvantage. Regardless of party preference, the economic conditions and the disapproval of the presidency of George W. Bush alone might have been enough for Obama to win.

John McCain started his candidacy for president with the heavy dark cloud of President George W. Bush above him. Not since the 1968 presidential race of candidate Hubert Humphrey did a candidate need to decouple his fortunes from those of his party's incumbent. Bush's job approval was almost as poor as that of King George III among the colonists 240 years ago[94]. The failure of the Bush presidency is the dominant fact of American politics as it exists in recent history; it has been a key facet of the Democratic political strategy since early 2006. Even the success of the American troop surge in Iraq could not alter or change the feeling about the failed presidency of George W. Bush and consequently, the Democratic strategy for the remainder of 2008. A review of the Bush exit polls showed that just

---

94 Peter A. BROWN, "Bush not an Albatross," *Boston Herald*, January 15, 2012. Retrieved from http://www.bostonherald.com/news/opinion/op_ed/view.bg?articleid=1084447&srvc=next_article

11% said Bush would be remembered as an outstanding or above average president, which was by far the lowest positive end term rating for any of the past four presidents. Interesting enough, his surprising 25% approval rating on October 5, 2008 was only one percentage point higher than President Nixon's low of 24%, which was reached shortly before Nixon resigned, and only three points above President Truman's low of 22%. In other words, President Bush was very disappointing to most voters.[95] Both John McCain and his running mate Governor Sarah Palin of Alaska recognized that they were up against great odds and clearly did not want the contagious attribute link to the Bush administration to handicap their campaign.

John McCain

John McCain was a war pilot whose plane was shot down during a 1967 bombing run over Hanoi during the Vietnam War. He was imprisoned from 1967 to 1973 and tortured in what was known as the Hanoi Hilton. In other words, he was viewed as willing to put his country first, as when he was in prison, he refused to be released until those captured before him had been also released as well. Unfortunately, the economy displaced the concerns about the war from a long time ago, and the Wall Street issues and the bailout of September 2008 meant that McCain's veteran credentials lost much of their impact to create any contagiousness momentum for his candidacy.

The Obama media tactics clearly were to strengthen the tie between the incumbent Bush and McCain. This was demonstrated during the final presidential debate, when McCain made a decisive move to try to sever it, to proclaim that he was in fact a "maverick," as opposed to Senator Obama, who was also trying to characterize this image. During the final debate, Obama pointed out that McCain voted for 4 out of 5 of President Bush's budgets, so what was contagious and what people heard was that they were going to get the same economic package as the previous president. McCain's response was "I am not President Bush, if I wanted to, I would've run against Bush four years ago. I am going to get a new direction to the economy in this country." [96] What Obama strategists turned this rhetoric

95 Frank NEWPORT, "Bush Job Approval at 25%, His Lowest Yet," *Gallup Poll*, October 6, 2008, Retrieved from http://www.gallup.com/poll/110980/bush-job-approval-25-lowest-yet.aspx

96 John MCCAIN, "2008 third presidential debate against Barack Obama," Oct 15, 2008, Hofstra University, Hempstead, New York.

into was the fact that, McCain by his own admission, had voted *with* Bush over 90% of the time during his presidency.

This developing contagious characteristic (later contributing to stickiness and the dramatic moment) for the country was the state of the economy and, in a serious strategic lapse, McCain continued to be nonresponsive to the economic issues. He made problems for himself by stating that: "I am not George Bush," even calling to the effect that we were failing in Iraq and were going to lose. As he opposed his own party and his own president, he continued to sidestep the economic issues, which were paramount contagiousness issues in people's minds as they were considering who to select as the next president. The McCain campaign launched an attack on Obama's "celebrity status" in August, calling him Washington's biggest celebrity, however the media continued to present photos and videos of McCain embracing Bush in rally after rally. Also there was major coverage of McCain agreeing with Bush 90% of the time in congress and another video saying he couldn't think of a major issue on which he had disagreement with Bush. The Obama campaign made good use of these videos throughout the campaign. Spending more than 14 million USD to broadcast ads in order to familiarize the public with McCain's loyalty to the Bush agenda, Obama used it as the centerpiece of most of the ads prior to the party convention. The same message was underwritten by the Obama funds with just over 6 million USD in airtime between August 31 and the end of September. The paid for coverage featured pictures of Bush and McCain in frame after frame, as the words "the same" were overlaid on the screen. In other words, McCain and Bush had the same failure to understand the economy. Clearly this issue of being the "same" translated into a contagiousness attribute, as the voters, particularly Democrats, started to embrace the McCain-Bush link that further complicated McCain's chances in the general election.

The United States was unprepared for the financial meltdown; however, as a characteristic of contagiousness, the temperament of the next president was an important predictor of performance in the eyes of the voters. As such, this gave an important opportunity for the Republicans to cast Obama as a "prolific liberal who was not ready to lead," and they tried to put this out in the media with the implication that he was also an "unpatriotic radical who disdained American basic values."[97]

In retrospect, the faltering economy and the failed presidency of George W. Bush boosted the Democratic Party presidential prospects. And in a way, it was easier for Obama to establish that he was more ready to become the president than the counterpart McCain could assure that he was in fact in touch with the voters. The stereotypes that each tried to identify with became, in fact, a detriment to McCain when he tried to use his experience and his wisdom as a reason to vote for his party. Obama easily countered with "Out of Touch, Too Old" and mobilized the black votes to compensate for anything that was lost based on the reservations of whites and the under-energized constituency waiting to champion an "old age, standard-bearer."

What was interesting during this contagiousness period about stereotypes, the media offered reinforcement by which any mistake the 72-year-old McCain made could easily work to his disadvantage. At 72 and 47, respectively, both McCain and Obama were well above the minimum age the Constitution sets for election to the presidency. There have been only a handful of presidents younger than Obama. McCain had difficulty referring to Ronald Reagan's presidency from an age standpoint, as just after his inauguration, near his 70th birthday, Reagan was diagnosed with having Alzheimer's disease. Ronald Reagan was able to turn that around and basically said that he wasn't going to exploit, for political purposes, his opponent's youth and inexperience when in fact the 73-year-old incumbent was dealing with the 56-year-old challenger, former vice president Minnesota senator Walter Mondale.

Reagan had a distinct advantage in contrast to McCain. In so much as the economy had clearly improved during his tenure and during his reelection campaign, Reagan relied on simple themes in the media to bring about his contagiousness to the public consciousness instead of his age. McCain was slow to do any of these tactics, and his strategic campaign handlers missed some very real opportunities to refocus the American public away from the early contagiousness characteristic associated with his age.

97 Kate KENSKI, Bruce W. HARDY, Kathleen Hall JAMIESON, *The Obama Victory: How Media, Money, and Message Shaped the 2008 Election*, New York, Oxford University Press, 2010, p. 71.

The fact is that the American public knew that McCain was 72 years old, and this was being reinforced loudly and clearly in the media, while the Obama campaign team also reinforced this and pointed out that the energy and the vigor to meet the demands of the presidency was in fact a big difference (in the perceptions) of the two candidates. Interestingly enough, race was dealt with in the same manner as age in contrast, as much as it was left alone and continued to build in the American voters contagious consciousness as a basis for their decision to vote. It was in the back of their minds and surfaced only when faced with making a choice.

Whether the voters' feeling that McCain's senility was due to his date of birth and/or to the stereotypes that the media culture were putting in front and center, all led to the importance of this contagiousness. Was the American voter interested in electing the "elder of the tribe, the wise old man, or, the temperamental codger?"[98] Additional coverage about the perceptions of youth was rampant in the media, as was Obama's age at 47. Was he vigorous, energetic, and brimming with fresh ideas? Or was he wet behind the ears and not ready to lead? The focus by the media was understandable on the issue, as similarly 70 years or older was undesirable.

Age was a direct concern for the Republican nominee. McCain's awkward "gant" referenced memories of his war heroism, but also fueled the stereotype that a person his age became a media preoccupation and was contributing to a negative contagiousness. The American media covered the facts of his age and the potential prospect and the impact should he die in office, making the question about the credentials of his running mate important. As parallel the contagious perception that Sarah Palin (discussed in later section) was unqualified to be president continued to grow, the age issue became more and more problematic for the Republican ticket.

The Democratic campaign of Obama had contagiousness success in reinforcing the erratic nature and temperament of McCain in the media arena. There was a distinct political advantage gained by drawing attention to McCain's temperament. Erratic wasn't the only old-age-tied weapon in the Obama approach. McCain was characterized in the media as having a combustible temper. Some journals even reported it as "volcanic," and back in 1999, McCain's temperament was used against him by pro-Bush forces in

98 *Ibid.*, p. 59.

2000, even to the extent to allege that the Vietnam War veteran suffered a mental breakdown in Hanoi from which he never fully recovered. McCain tried to counter these allegations by releasing 1500 pages of medical records, including interviews with military psychiatrists showing that he had, in fact, a clean bill of health. Concerns about McCain's temperament also surfaced in the 2008 campaign when many thought that he often "acted on impulse," and even military commanders were slow to reinforce his levelheadedness. For example, Major General Paul Eaton, who was in charge of the training of the Iraqi military from 2003- 2004, said that "he thought it was a little scary. I think this guy's first reactions are not necessarily the best reactions… I believe he acts on impulse."[99] Many media analysts thought that the pick of Sarah Palin also was also impulsive.

Barack Obama

In contrast, in mid-September 2008 the media endorsements by McCain and paid infomercials tailored to individual states with tags such as "change is coming," had little effect, and even by mid-October the ads failed to produce results. For McCain it looked like more of the same as George W. Bush to the voters. McCain, in the voters' view offered this choice: higher taxes, and Obama meant: more money and fewer taxes for the working man. McCain tried to connect with another idea that Obama was *risky*, and McCain was *proven*, but the message never gained contagiousness momentum.

There was a significant derailment of the contagiousness of the presidential campaign of Obama in March of 2008 with the emergence of recorded statements by Obama's Chicago mentor and pastor Reverend Wright. In retrospect this could have led to some stickiness later for McCain's campaign if they had continued to be magnified by the McCain strategists. Obama's' vulnerability was magnified by the fact that Wright had officiated at Obama's marriage and baptized their children. Rewrites of Reverend Wright's ranting and words could not be re-contextualized by the Obama spin doctors. The pastor was recorded shouting to his enthralled congregation in 2003 "No, no, no, not God damn America, God damn America!" Within days the videos had been viewed by approximately half the country.

99 Mark BENJAMIN, "It's 3 a.m. Who do You Want Answering the Phone?" *Salon*, March 6, 2008. Retrieved from http://www.salon.com/2008/03/06/commander_in_chief_2/

Both the impact of the Wright revelations on Obama and the ineffectiveness of the Democratic response were reflected during the time between when the March 13 videos aired to a March 18 speech where Obama delivered a "more perfect union," which turned the whole issue around and stamped out the potential future impact to the campaign of this issue.

Republicans had tried to build on the contagiousness of this Wright issue and to point out that Obama had the same kind of anger in the manner and way the pastor had voiced them. The Wright issue was a central message of the Republican strategists, advocating that Obama seemed to have different values than most Americans. The point was the Republicans were trying to *stick* Reverend Wright and his sermons directly with the political journey of Barack Obama. To make it seem like both shared the same agenda, i.e. Barack Obama followed a preacher of hate, this whole controversy dominated media coverage and percolated through the Internet from March through early June. Republican ads that revisited this issue in the final weeks of the campaign created only a minimal stir as McCain tried to use Wright and his comments to illicit negative associations tied to race. The strategy was a potent one because negative characterizations about African-Americans affect opinions, and racial cues have been found to heighten race-based negative response and in this case might have led to a very delicate outcome.

The Republicans also tried to tie Obama to powerful underworld individuals, some of them African-American, where the ads stated that Obama allegedly engaged in misconduct or crime. Again there was an attempt to create a contagiousness about the stereotype of how could African-Americans be trusted with the presidency? There were other contagious attempts to create guilt by association. For example, in the last week before the election, a Republican ad sponsored by the National Rifle Association showed a terrified woman in her bathroom clutching a handgun pointing at her darkened living room, as the announcer intoned, "You don't want your child screaming in the middle of the night when a convicted felon breaks into your home." The point was that Republicans were trying to say that Obama voted four times to deny citizens the right of self-protection, even in their homes, and the reason that he did this, they alleged, was he was fighting a racial cue, that criminals are always of African origins.

Section 3.1.2 Organizations

The American voters were frustrated about the war, the faltering economy, and the way that a failing president had taken office as a result of the outcome of the previous election. This contagiousness *feeling of frustration* continued into the 2008 election. It translated into the way each party was being perceived by the other side and the way people reacted with voter registration. The numbers point out that an overwhelming 74% of those eligible to vote were registered by Election Day, an increase of 10.1 million. When compared to 2004, the Democratic registration had only increased 1.4% or 2.9 million it becomes an interesting contrast. The media was quick to point out that this did not always translate to the election of the advantaged party's presidential nominee, but one could see the *contagiousness* handwriting on the wall.[100]

Many voters were now identifying with whether a person was liberal or whether a candidate was conservative. Again, John McCain was more identified with the conservatives and less identified with the liberals. The other factor was the Democratic ticket was significantly more contagiously linked to the black, Hispanic, lower income, and those inclined to believe that their personal economic social situation had worsened in the past year. Race had become contagiousness characteristic for the political organizations and the media was well on its way to reinforcing the effect during the campaign.

The contradiction was that with an estimated $5.3 billion spent by the candidates, local parties and interest groups, the 2008 presidential campaign was the costliest in US history. A look at the distribution between the two major presidential campaigns and a historical comparison to previous campaigns reveals the simple fact that heavy media spending doesn't affect the outcome. The tsunami that hit the Republican campaign was built-in well before John McCain ever declared his candidacy and was only compounded to Obama's advantage of a very strategic media contagious and stickiness messages to the very end. Why, after Obama was spending significantly more than John McCain (because McCain had made a decision only to accept federal financing, and with Obama's tactical advantage with technology and his team of strategists), didn't the margin widen between the two

100 Malcolm GLADWELL, The Tipping Point: How Little Things can Make a Big Difference. New York, Back Bay Books, 2002.

candidates beyond what people were predicting early on? The amount of money Obama paid for media had little to do with his votes for getting into the office. The contagiousness was already in play, and the messages in the media, purchased with large sums of money that rolled into his campaign pockets, really didn't have an effect.[101]

Further adding to the organization contagiousness characteristic, halfway through Bush's second term, the 2000 elections swept the Democrats into control in the House and the Senate. At that juncture the economic woes of 2008 were the result of the Republican in the White House and Democrats on the other end of Pennsylvania Avenue. John McCain had no real strategy as he discussed the Iraq war, other than to say he would be a better commander-in-chief than Obama. The real question, however, was who is better at handling the economy? By downplaying the economy, McCain paid the price for under-nourishing this contagiousness characteristic and not moving undecided persons towards voting for him in the fall election. Also in retrospect, Senator John McCain ran an unusual campaign. As a Vietnam War hero, he was now trying to be portrayed in the media as surprisingly liberal, but this was primarily a reaction to reach a broader range of Americans and their opposition to George W. Bush. At one point again McCain tried to label himself as a "maverick" to draw contrast with Bush and therefore implying that he was not the same. With the economy becoming increasingly important contagiousness for the campaign, and McCain's' campaigning on Bush's side in 2004 and into 2008, and as a Republican who was supporting the tax reductions beyond the 2010 expiration date, these just didn't help. Also, his votes helped to nearly double the national debt. Obama seized on these issues in the media by indicating that McCain was embracing the current administration's economic policies and philosophy.

Further on, the "Chicago machine ties" attack by McCain failed to gain traction or become a contagiousness characteristic is a bit complicated. Obama was an Illinois senator, and the so-called Chicago machine had already backed his run for Congress, his successful bid for state Senate, and his party nomination for the Senate. But after mid-September, the economic collapse had all but wiped out the negative political impact and give-

101 Kate KENSKI, Bruce W. HARDY, Kathleen Hall JAMIESON, The Obama Victory: How Media, Money, and Message Shaped the 2008 Election, op. cit.

and-take or the attempt to make the Chicago Machine ties a detriment to the Obama campaign, since it was minor compared to the economy and garnered little media attention. Compared to the fears of a global economic meltdown that was dominating the media each candidate's political past seemed very minor in contrast.

Section 3.1.3 Media

While most of the developments in the media relating to the contagiousness occurred in nationally televised broadcast and ads, what was interesting was that, under the radar screen, the Obama campaign had opened a second-tier media assault on McCain's reputation on the radio, an understudied media venue that has been part of presidential campaigns for more than a century.

Radio

Both McCain and Obama tried to transmit their core messages in prepackaged radio biographies that became known as the Kansas values biographies. McCain's maverick credential was billed as defiance of the captors at Hanoi Hilton, and the Democrats used Obama's mother and maternal grandparents with roots in Kansas to establish his shared-voter values. Kansas values had been evoked long before in the history of presidential campaigns. Dwight Eisenhower launched his 1952 bid as the man from Abilene, who had come from the nation's heartland. Kansas was Middle America and Obama tried to develop contagiousness in the campaign that he was in touch with the values of the voters. He repeatedly tried to make arguments that linked his candidacy with a nation ready to change and end racial division.[102] Had the Republicans been more skillful in their attacks of their opponent, they would have had the potential to derail Obama's claim to basic Kansas values by suggesting that Obama authenticate and recount his life story since records of his citizenship were blurry. Meanwhile Obama was trying to sidestep his connections to the Chicago machine politics by reestablishing his values coming from Kansas. If McCain had deployed radio broadcasts properly, he might have been able to derail the contagiousness of these issues.

102 "Growing Doubts About McCain's Judgment, Age and Campaign Conduct," *Pew Research Center for the People and the Press*, October 21, 2008.

Internet and TV News

The Internet and TV news built a heavy presence for Obama. For example, the Cultural Communication Index (CCI) is used by the television news frequency index, TNF I, to show how strong the tie between McCain and the word *old* was throughout the election.[103] It was a visual and auditory advantage that Obama had over McCain with these two media sectors, such that, in the public's mind, McCain sounded too weak and looked too old next Obama. Ronald Reagan was about McCain's current age when he ran for reelection against Walter Mondale; Reagan looked 10 years younger than McCain at the same age.

Ad Campaigns

Reinforcing an existing contagiousness characteristic is easier to do than try to develop a new one. The Obama campaign clearly strengthened the contagiousness forces already in motion in the culture, such as the news reports, opinion columns, and comedy on TV as these mediums were making the same contagious *age* point. Throughout the post-primary, the Obama ad campaign built on this contagiousness reservoir to attach negative characteristics to the age of the Republican nominee. Visuals and the ad campaign messages reinforced this. For their part, the Republicans suggested that Obama was "not ready to lead, presumptuous, and a prolific liberal."[104] This was to counter what the Democrats portrayed about McCain who was "past his prime and out of touch with the concerns of middle America."[105] While age became a driving issue for the Democrats, the McCain campaign countered against Obama with three issues: one, that he was untrustworthy; two, the length of his elected service was short and he did not have the experience and wherewithal to create needed change; and three, he was a "self-important celebrity whose prime talent was speechmaking".[106]

---

103 (Note: the CCI, a tool developed by researchers at Stony Brook University, is not a standardized web searching tool with the output of many Internet spider searches). And what is being used in Internet and developed recently is called *Google stories*, whereby similar types of news stories feed and build on themes and strands of information to collectively show frequency and data trends about topics and phrases popular in media.

104 Kate KENSKI, Bruce W. HARDY, Kathleen Hall JAMIESON, The Obama Victory: How Media, Money, and Message Shaped the 2008 Election, op. cit., p. 71.

105 *Ibid.*, p. 71.

106 *Ibid.*, p. 71.

The Republican assaults heavily relied on the fact that Barack Obama was short on legislative and executive experience. Pointing out that if he won the presidency, he would had served less than four years in the U.S. Senate, and much of that time running for higher office. His state legislative pedigree consisted of three two-year terms as a senator.

In contrast to other presidential candidates, John Kennedy had served six years in the House and one full term in the Senate before becoming president, and Bill Clinton had 12 years' experience as governor prior to the Oval Office as well as being his state's attorney general, and Clinton had also chaired the National Governors' Association. Jimmy Carter had a double two-year term in the state Senate and one four-year term as governor prior to coming to Washington. And finally, George W. Bush came to the White House after six years as governor. Obama tried to counter this potential contagiousness issue about experience, referring to history and that Abraham Lincoln's national service consisted of one low-profile term in the House.

Internet: Viral Brew

There were two *viral* arguments that were part of the contagiousness that did not explicitly appear in the media but had bubbled throughout the campaign. The first was that Obama had violated the constitutional requirement that the president be a natural born citizen. The second suggested that Obama was of Muslim origins. Each of these contagiousness attempts were spread via viral e-mails and Web postings, but they were repeatedly debunked later by the fact-checkers in the media. People after the election still believed that Obama was a Muslim, although 25% voted for him.[107]

After researching the internet activity of the 2008 campaign, there were also two omissions in the streams of internet commentary: There was little discussion of the age stereotyping of McCain in contrast to the racial coding used to attack Obama. And if the internet media so often assumed that Obama was a Muslim, and should have disqualified him from the presidency.

By the time the American voters entered the voting booths, a contagious majority had concluded that McCain's age was more worrisome than Oba-

107 *Ibid.*, p. 98, 307.

ma's background, and that the economic change they were in the midst of would be better dealt with by the candidate who shared their values than by one who had considerable more experience.

Section 3.1.4 Events

Economy

Looking back at the economy in the fall of 2007, the Dow was setting record highs as early as October, 2007, at 14,164 points.[108] Yet, the country was anxious and the research polls showed that three quarters of the population believed that the nation was on the wrong track, i.e. by the second general presidential election to be held a year later, the Dow lost more than 4000 points to a close on October 7, 2008 at 9,477 points, and it still wasn't over--the bottom was not yet in sight. What became a contagious characteristic, and later stickiness and dramatic moment for the Democratic campaign for Obama, put simply, was the economic quarter that included the last five weeks during the campaign. It was so dismal that the closing months of 2008 were the US economy's worst performance in a quarter-century since quarterly records began in 1947.[109] At that point the contagiousness and stickiness were occurring, and a majority of the voters (53%) felt that the Democrats were better able to handle the economy, which then became the leading campaign and media issue in the presidential election. Most news accounts and media chatter between March and Election Day 2008 reinforced that Obama was on top of McCain on the economic issue. It wasn't just a perception, as most of the media was now echoing and reinforcing the message, this was the reality. How the American voters arrived at that conclusion is analyzed in the next section: Stickiness Attributes (S). The Wall Street meltdown really dominates the understanding of the September through mid-October timeframe in the campaign.. During this period, Obama's stickiness attributes began to transition and rise, and McCain's fell.

Section 3.2 Stickiness Attributes (S)

The stickiness attribute in this context as defined earlier proposes that there

108 *Ibid.*, p. 16.

109 Timothy R. HOMAN, "U.S. Economy: Consumers, Government Propel Growth (Update2)," *Bloomberg*, October 29, 2009. Retrieved from http://www.bloomberg.com/apps/news?pid=newsarchive&sid=aCi2EYr.5RhY

are exceptional characteristics of people, organizations, media and events in the global media environment that are capable of initiating epidemics – by starting with small, seemingly inconsequential events that can become and have alternately, large impacts. The stickiness characteristics of the Obama campaign are rather straightforward, as those that led to his tipping point could be characterized by the application of this study methodology and results that are correlated with available research. In retrospect it was a calculated method for deployment initiated by his campaign strategists that made it possible, in effect, to reinforce the stickiness attribute.

To begin this section, the focus of some of the stickiness characteristics during Obama campaign which started to gain strength during the period between June 7 and August 22, 2008 will be explored. During this time, there was a relentless wave of bad news, day after day, on the television, in newspapers and on the Internet about the economy. And the implications for the November election were becoming clearer, as costs of energy, oil, fuel, and generally just getting around and getting every product to market in the country was becoming too costly.

McCain tried to gain ground in the summer of 2008 and improve his potential stickiness, and in order to do so, he focused on the nation's energy crisis. That might yet have been possible if only energy and gas prices dominated and not the pressing media discussion of the fate of the economy. By the fall the Republican presidential nominee's argument failed to be here. However during this same timeframe, the Obama campaign shifted their emphasis and recognized how the growing stickiness potential connected the coming Wall Street crisis.

Section 3.2.1 People

Vice Presidential Selections

Joseph Biden

In the predawn hours of Saturday, August 23, 2008, with the Democratic convention scheduled to open in two days, the Obama campaign sidestepped the media by notifying its supporters electronically that Delaware Senator Joseph Biden had been given the nod for the Democratic vice presidential position. As soon as this information had landed in the inbox of the McCain campaign, it reminded the people that were still awake in the press about Joseph Biden's earlier doubts about Obama. Biden had denounced

Obama's poor foreign-policy judgment strongly and had argued, like many Americans, that Obama was not ready to be president. And now he was chosen as Obama's running mate.

Sarah Palin

Conversely, like most of the nation, the selection of Governor Palin of Alaska caught the Obama team by surprise. However from the onset, she was in trouble even before her first speech was delivered in St. Paul at the convention. Even before her acceptance address, the Republican campaign was dealing with false Internet rumors and charges related to her term as mayor. There was an onslaught of Internet attacks, and the Palin selection did not improve anything about people's perceptions of McCain's judgment and experience in making decisions, particularly for a partner to lead the Republican ticket. The McCain team was on the defensive facing challenges of lack of terrorist experience and sexist gender discrimination that was sourced by the liberal elite media bias. Her acceptance speech was continually being attacked, and her public record was also being challenged. An incident that was termed "Trooper Gate" by the bloggers raised serious credibility issues in as much as when she was the governor of Alaska, she had abused her office hours by firing a public safety commissioner who was reported as being pressured by the governor, linked to her ex brother-in-law, about his dismissal from his job as a state trooper. The state investigated this issue, and it dogged Palin for the rest of the campaign right up until the final determination when it was concluded that she had, in fact, not abused her power.

What is interesting and what was not leveraged as a stickiness characteristic for the Republican campaign is that Governor Palin actually had more experience managing a larger budget in Alaska than Obama had when he was a senator. Had the experience issue been raised during this time, it would have come out in a more favorable light and contributed to her stickiness. However, the media focused on personal issues, which were then reinforced by the Democratic strategic team. What happened was that the Palin selection undercut McCain's argument in an attempt to point out that Obama was not ready to lead. In fact, what became a stickiness characteristic was that Governor Palin was one heartbeat away from the presidency should McCain have to leave office. McCain's age was in reality, a stickiness stereotype that the American voter had fears of.

Statistics by Sam Harris and the *Los Angeles Times*, citing the actual tables of the Social Security Administration, suggested that there is at 10% chance that McCain would die during his first term in office. Should McCain survive his first term as president and get elected to a second term, there would have been a 27% chance that Palin would become the first female US president by 2015.[110] The real problem for Palin was establishing competence in a short 10 week period before the election. In contrast, at this time the increasing media exposure for Obama was interpreted and evolved as a stickiness characteristic of more confidence in his competence to lead by the American voter. Ultimately Palin and Biden squared off in vice presidential debates. By that time Senator Biden had already 10 debates to his experience, and introducing Palin as a new player guaranteed scrutiny from the media and immediately increased the influence of the media coverage on voter opinions that were otherwise undecided relative to the question of experience for the candidate.

Section 3.2.2 Organizations

Conventions

The 2008 presidential convention season was the most tightly compressed in recent memory as in just under 14 days Democrats and Republicans selected their vice presidential choices, nominated their presidential candidates, and moved on to serious campaigning. At this time there was a consistent focus and stickiness characteristic in the media that was being paid to politics, television for example: viewers tuned in for the convention speeches in numbers that handily surpassed the total for 2004. Statistically, John McCain attracted a larger audience than Obama, and Sarah Palin out drew Biden as well:

McCain: 38.9 million

Obama: 38.3 million

Palin: 37.2 million

Biden: 24 million[111]

110 Sam HARRIS, "When Average isn't Good Enough," *Los Angeles Times*, September 3, 2008. Retrieved from http://articles.latimes.com/2008/sep/03/news/OE-HARRIS3

111 Kate KENSKI, Bruce W. HARDY, Kathleen Hall JAMIESON, The Obama Victory: How Media, Money, and Message Shaped the 2008 Election, op. cit., p. 131.

In contrast, George W. Bush's acceptance address was seen by 27.6 million on TV as compared with John Kerry's 24.4 million in 2004 campaign.[112] There were other events occurring around the dates as each convention was competing with the Beijing Summer Olympics that were being held or with other global event competing for media space. It was interesting that on August 25-28 Senator Obama gave his acceptance speech before 84000 people in attendance at INVESCO Field in Chicago.[113] A review of the media at this time shows the reaction was obvious, that both conventions were a success, which is remarkable given the fact that a hurricane was bearing down on New Orleans as Republicans tried to gather for their opening.

Democrats

The Democrats used their convention as a way of filling in Obama's biography and to make people more comfortable with him, in other words, to get to know their candidate and increase his stickiness. The other Democratic objective with getting the message out about the economic objectives of the campaign was again, "change versus more of the same."[114] On the third convention night, the approach was to promote Obama's national security credentials. Speeches by Bill Clinton and the newly nominated Joe Biden reinforced the stickiness characteristics of important people throughout the campaign. Joseph Biden's acceptance speech was filled with many strange moments as he improvised beyond his written speech and said things that were not included in the original text, but the American voter overlooked the regular guy stumbles as a fellow American who seemed to understand how they felt. Although the Democratic vice presidential nominee speech was filled with oddities and mistakes, it had by now suggested that the stickiness effect was already on the viewer. Biden's speech indirectly affected voter preference by influencing Biden's favorable ratings, which in turn increased the number of voters for the Democratic ticket.

On Thursday 28th of August, Obama made a 52 minute acceptance speech at INVESCO Field that further attacked McCain and his alliance with George Bush. He argued that Bush was out of touch with the concerns of the middle-class and reinforced his agenda change. His acceptance speech at the convention was able to reframe John McClain's strategy to his own

112 *Ibid.*, p. 131.

113 "Obama Launches Historic Campaign," *BBC*, August 29, 2008. Retrieved from http://news.bbc.co.uk/2/hi/americas/7586375.stm

114 Barack OBAMA 2008 Presidential Campaign slogan.

benefit. Obama was no longer just a celebrity. Research collected six days after the conventions revealed that those who watched Senator Obama were more favorably impressed by him than those who did not view the speech. Hence television contributed to his stickiness. The bottom line regarding watching Obama's speech meant also an increased preference for the Democratic ticket.

Republicans

Not more than a half day after Obama's speech, Republicans tried to hijack the stickiness momentum and media coverage with the acceptance speech of vice president nominee Sarah Palin. Governor Palin's acceptance speech at the convention boosted positive perceptions of her with the bloggers, the press, and the public. In comparison, the Joseph Biden speech essentially lost on the night that included the address by Bill Clinton. The Palin speech elicited both media attention and congratulations. During her speech she used wit, sarcasm, charm, and radical and a full scale assault on the familiar cast of GOP targets: elitist adversaries, biased media, and high taxes. The speech improved the vice presidential nominee's public perceptions. Palin's acceptance speech was reflected in the media accounts in many sectors as her personal stickiness characteristic rose among those who had watched her convention speech. The goals for Republican convention were obvious. They wanted to distance themselves from a non-popular administration, to restore McCain's maverick appeal, and his reform appeal trying to make these other facets of his platform stick. The Republicans benefited from the stickiness attribute from their conventions, but the question still remained: What impact, if any, would the vice presidential nominees have on the general election and its outcome?

Section 3.2.3 Media

The research of the Obama campaign focused on the media characteristics that factored into the culmination of the tipping point for his presidential journey. Of note, the amount of information that was disseminated by each of the campaign teams was done so in such a way via the media, and the influence and impact could be correlated with the number of the dollars spent to reach the voters. Certainly there is an argument about how the contagious and stickiness attributes were put forth by each of the campaign teams in attempt to discredit the candidate on the other side. However, the economy's presence as a central issue of the campaign meant that the fundamentals of the media influence were indeed linked to the delivery systems and the way the messages were timed.

Not surprisingly, McCain consistently topped Obama on the question of who would be a better commander-in-chief, but when the question of who would handle the economy better became the nation's agenda, it became the central issue in the quest for the presidency. Had the war in Iraq been the central issue, in retrospect McCain would have done very well and would currently be, in my opinion, the United States president. But without question, the media "consumers", i.e. voters, were more likely during this time to see the economy as a central national issue. TV, journals and Internet sources were reporting the same conclusion.[115] Obama had a distinct advantage when it came to handling issues on the economy, as his campaign made a series of arguments that increased the stickiness attribute relative to the superiority the Democrats had on the issue. The belief that the Republicans were responsible for the Wall Street meltdown, a stickiness attribute that the Republicans could never reframe or reverse in the voters' minds, reinforced the notion that electing McCain was the same as re-electing Bush. The Obama campaign clearly had convinced a majority of voters who shared his perceived values that McCain was not able to fix the economy. By the end of the last debates, however, Obama was securely ahead of McCain as the election gap was over 10%. Approximately 50% of the voters believed that Obama could fix the problem, whereas only 40%, believed in McCain.[116]

Party strategies highlighted from the research during the campaigns are these:

- The impact of the tax increases and who would implement more favorable programs to aid the American voters. In this case, McCain was able to show some strength but not enough to reverse the stickiness already gathering momentum, and
- The selection of vice presidential candidates which had

115 Kate KENSKI, Bruce W. HARDY, Kathleen Hall JAMIESON, The Obama Victory: How Media, Money, and Message Shaped the 2008 Election, op. cit., p. 289.

116 "Growing Doubts About McCain's Judgment, Age and Campaign Conduct," *Pew Research Center for the People and the Press, op. cit.*

> some media influence in the public perception as well and created a minor stickiness attribute.

These were the repeated messages as communicated in the media during the entire campaign. The convention speeches were not surprising in shaping voter stickiness, as Joseph Biden's acceptance speech enhanced the public's favorable ratings of him, which improved the chances of the Democratic ticket. The convention acceptance speeches of both McCain and Obama increased their stickiness among viewers. However, the debates also provided significant feelings that, if elected, John McCain, would in fact, produce another Bush term. Specifically, the Obama campaigns' paid messages on broadcast, cable, and radio media delivery systems continued to drive home three stickiness perceptions that were all too important to the Obama candidacy:

- Obama shared voter values.
- Obama could handle the economy better than McCain.
- McCain equaled Bush.

In essence, these were the critical stickiness attributes of the Obama campaign. With their substantial bankroll, the Obama campaign had time to test and analyze the message delivery and how they would be deployed with the new technology mediums.

Obama early on had enlisted the support Eric Schmidt of *Google* whose team provided invaluable methods and procedures for maximizing the benefit of the Internet and creating stickiness through that medium. Schmidt, an informal adviser to Barack Obama for several months, later joined the Democratic nominee on the campaign trail. Clearly the Obama strategists were very pleased with this addition to their team:

> Schmidt will appear today with Obama in the tightly contested state of Florida to talk about the economy. Although Schmidt announced his backing of Obama in Monday's *Wall Street Journal*, he has been advising the campaign on technology and clean-energy issues for

most of the summer.[117]

For years, Schmidt was a major Democratic fundraiser and high-profile supporter of Democratic candidates, notably 2000 presidential candidate Al Gore, who now serves as a senior adviser to Google. But Schmidt had kept a low partisan profile during the 2008 campaign, offering up Mountain View's Google headquarters to all the presidential candidates for both parties during the primaries. Earlier in the year, he made supportive comments for energy independence plans proposed by both Obama and Hillary Clinton. Schmidt also showed up at the Democratic National Convention in Denver where he spoke to a group of bloggers whose convention-reporting headquarters were partly paid for by Google.

As Google grows, so does its interest in government. The Justice Department has yet to issue a ruling on Google's proposed ad-sharing deal with Yahoo, which some legislators believe would give Google too much control over online advertising rates. The company also has lobbied on issues such as Net neutrality; it opposes allowing telecommunications companies to set different rates for slower or faster levels of Internet service. A statement from Google said the company "of course remains neutral" in the presidential race. As for Schmidt, the statement continues, "...he believes that it is time for a change in America. In addition, his personal views on technology and energy are similar to Senator Obama's."

Online fundraising records indicate that among Google employees, Obama was much more popular than GOP rival John McCain. McCain enlisted former Hewlett-Packard CEO Carly Fiorina and retired eBay CEO Meg Whitman to join him on the campaign trail. Fiorina, however, was sidelined after suggesting none of the presidential or vice presidential nominees had enough experience to run a major corporation such as HP.

Section 3.2.4 Events

Energy

In early May 2008, when Obama was battling Senator Hilary Clinton for the Democratic nomination, Clinton stated that Obama was out of touch

---

117 Mary Anne OSTROM, "Google CEO Eric Schmidt to Stump for Obama," *Denver Post*, October 10, 2008. Retrieved from http://www.denverpost.com/entertainment/ci_10769458?source=rss

with the energy issue and the effect that high gas prices were having on the American voter.[118] McCain and Clinton both voted for a gas holiday tax program for the American public to demonstrate their willingness to listen to the economic problems that were facing the average American. This proposal, in effect, carried large liabilities, one being that the government would have to suspend taxes of up to 10 billion dollars in revenue, money that could have been spent for other transit improvements. Democrats countered with an expert consensus among economists who rejected the proposal by Clinton and McCain. At best, this tax holiday issue was a brief digression from the real stickiness issue that was unfolding in the media. The Obama campaign had successfully rallied conservatives and high-ranking economists of the day into supporting his agenda. Similarly, in the view of the American voters, for decades the country's elected leaders had been on the same page regarding well exploration and how to deal with OPEC. Obama's promotion of offshore oil well drilling brought up a consensus of memories recalling the 1969 Santa Barbara spill that hemorrhaged 200,000 barrels of crude oil across a square mile region, coating one of the nation's beaches into tar and left the ecosystem struggling.[119]

In a sign that the energy problem was worsening, on June 6 2008, the price of a barrel of oil reached near $34 a barrel, double that of the year before and up 42% since New Year's. At the same time, media headlines showed that the Dow had dropped 394.64 points to 12,209.81. At this same time, the average price at the pump had reached four dollars for the first time, and gas prices had jumped 29% in just his a year.

Obama had mustered enough delegates to win in the Democratic contest, a fact acknowledged by Hillary Clinton on June 7 when she threw her support to her former rival. McCain was already in general election mode by that time as he had wrapped up his party's nomination fight in early March. As the summer approached bringing along with it the year's peak driving times, whether or not prices would remain stabilized was an issue that was

118 "Growing Doubts About McCain's Judgment, Age and Campaign Conduct," *Pew Research Center for the People and the Press, op. cit.*

119 Flashing forward now to 2010 and the recent events in the Gulf of Mexico and the British Petroleum offshore drilling platform that collapsed and went on contaminating the Gulf for almost a month and a half is interesting. This regional and potentially global event was an economic and environmental disaster for Obama after he was in office, but his popularity seemed to ride the events.

missed by the media. By comparison in January of 2001, oil was trading at $32 a barrel.

The upwardly spiraling of oil prices dominated the news media, and a *Washington Post* ABC poll reported that high gas prices were causing the American voters' financial hardship. At this time McCain reversed his position on June 16 announcing his goal of eliminating our dependence on foreign oil. The oil issue created a clear stickiness attribute between the nominees and brought about a significant radio media attack on each other's position. During this time, incumbent president George W. Bush endorsed the lifting of the moratorium on offshore drilling in a move that placed the unpopular president and the prospective Republican nominee on the wrong side of the issue. Later in July, Bush followed up by rescinding the executive order for leasing for offshore drilling. Obama on the other hand, stuck to his agenda to keep the moratorium and prevent companies from drilling off the coast of Florida, saying, however, that he wanted to protect our coastline and still make investments that would reduce the US dependence on foreign oil and bring down gas prices for good. Obama also stated that McCain's position put the country's national security and economic interests at risk. The results were that media was trying to make this an important stickiness characteristic, i.e. oil energy security as the national purpose. During this time gas prices were at four dollars and five dollars a gallon, with no end in sight, because some politicians in Washington were saying no to drilling in America.

During this time, the Republicans continued to attack the Democratic position on the gas tax and went after Obama with a media blitz that cost over 3.6 million US dollars with a televised ad campaign that attempted to reinforce the message. From July 30 onward the election campaign theme became: "He's the biggest celebrity in the world, but is he ready to lead?" The Obama campaign launched a counterattack on July 8 with a TV media spot named "new energy" that aired just under 5000 times between July 8 and July 28 with a price tag of well over 2 million USD. Then another was produced called "new energy revised" that aired just over 8000 times from the end of July to the middle of October at a cost of over 3.5 million USD. The first television spot argued that gas prices and John McCain were part of the problem. The second spot reiterated the first claims about energy dependence, mileage standards, alternate fuels, and a tax cut for families, while pointing blame not to Bush but to Washington. During this time frame, Obama was on the wrong side of public media opinion, and 11 swing states were favoring the offshore drilling approach with only 30% opposed. When Obama saw this happening, he attempted to carefully modify his television strategy to avoid alienating environmentalists, particularly in the Florida region. It was something that didn't create any stickiness as many of the journals and news reports of the time felt that McCain and Obama were basically in a gridlock over energy. The Democrats in Congress, meanwhile, were scrambling to try to remove the drilling, which permitted some drilling under some circumstances in certain areas, an issue from the national debate for the fall elections. With the drilling issue a popular stickiness characteristic, media exposure focused on the energy prices and framed them as a cause for the United States' failing economy to benefit the McCain campaign. All this was short-lived as we know from the political perspective. The diminished importance of this stickiness characteristic is evident in the fact that the energy policy idea worked in the initial stages of McCain's campaign, and indeed later during the month of August, McCain actually was able to distance himself from Bush, even though, in fact, Bush and McCain were on the same voting page about the drilling issue. In retrospect, the Democrats acknowledged that McCain gained an advantage from the back and forth dialogue on energy. The Democrats admitted that they "mishandled the drilling issue" quoting a statement from Obama's chief strategist, David Axelrod.[120] What the Democrats were trying to do at that time was shift the discussion to the long term rather than the short-term. The stickiness of the energy issue led to a two-pronged media momentum shift for the Republicans at the time. Senator McCain was also gaining credibility in his area of strength, national security, and also in Obama's natural territory, economy. He also did this in a way to overcome his traditional conservative handicap. The subject of the drilling continued throughout the remainder of the campaign and clearly was not the main stickiness characteristic event.

Gustav Hurricane

The Republican National Convention took place at the Xcel Energy Center in Saint Paul, Minnesota, from September 1, through September 4, 2008. The first day of the Republican Party's convention fell on Labor Day, the last day of the popular Minnesota State Fair, yet because of Hurricane Gus-

120 Kate KENSKI, Bruce W. HARDY, Kathleen Hall JAMIESON, The Obama Victory: How Media, Money, and Message Shaped the 2008 Election, op. cit., p. 119.

tav, most of the politicking and partying did not start until Tuesday, the second scheduled day. This was the latest any major party convention has ever been convened, and the first one to take place entirely in September. Traditionally, the party who sits in the White House has the opportunity to select the date of its convention second, and normally the challenging party holds their convention in July while the incumbent party holds its convention in August. Later dates were chosen for both conventions because the parties wanted to schedule them after the Summer Olympics ended. It was also the second time in American history that an incumbent president did not attend his party's convention (although President George W. Bush did appear by satellite).

With the landfall of Hurricane Gustav on the U.S. Gulf Coast, the White House canceled the planned appearances of President Bush and Vice President Dick Cheney. Governors Bobby Jindal of Louisiana and Rick Perry of Texas also skipped the convention to remain in their states during the hurricane's landfall. The Monday, September 1, 2008, the convention schedule was compressed to two hours from seven. McCain called on the party to reduce partisan activities ahead of the hurricane's arrival. The Republican Party chartered a DC-9 to fly convention delegates representing the affected areas back home to their families. The last time a major hurricane struck in a presidential-election year was Andrew in 1992, which hit South Florida four days after the Republican Convention in Houston, Texas.

On March 26, 2008, the National Football League and NBC agreed in principle to move the kickoff time of a September 4 season-opening football game to 7:00 p.m. EDT instead of 8:30 p.m. EDT to accommodate the convention. The game ended relatively on time at 10:01 p.m. EDT, with NBC Sports handing off to NBC News within moments of the end of the game. According to Nielsen Media Research, 38.9 million Americans watched McCain deliver his acceptance speech—a half million more than had tuned in to see Obama the previous week.

Section 3.3 One Dramatic Moment Tipping Point (TP)

The third and last tipping point attribute, the one dramatic moment in the Obama campaign is supported by the notion that the epidemic can be created by one single event. The dramatic moment is the most important of the three attributes, because it makes sense of the first two and perhaps permits the greatest insight into why candidate Obama's campaign turned out the way it did. As we know, human behavior is very sensitive and strongly influenced by its environmental issues, and none was more pressing in the media, in terms of circumstances and their influence, than the economic decline that presented itself in mid-September of 2008.

Gladwell states: "Epidemics are sensitive to the conditions and circumstances of the times and places in which they occur."[121] In hindsight, Republican hopes were crushed by the unanticipated economic crash of historical proportions and McCain's response, which led to Obama's tipping point. The epidemic challenge that faced the McCain campaign was now a poor economy for which the Republican Party was being blamed as a result of George Bush's two terms in office. While Palin was adept at running a campaign, the McCain campaign needed to draw Democratic crossover votes and independent votes in order to win. After the results in the state of Tennessee, the addition of Governor Palin was detrimental to the Republican ticket. When the Republicans left their convention gathering in Minnesota, they were ahead in the public opinion polls. But just one week after McCain's acceptance speech, the country's new unemployment figures suggested the economy was becoming unhinged.

Section 3.3.1 People

The Candidates

The beginning of the dramatic moment in the campaign for president in the fall of 2008 began after the close of the Republican convention or on or around September 5 when the American voter woke to the news that the August jobless rate had risen to 6.1%, which meant nine and a half-million people were out of work.[122] For all practical purposes, the tipping point began on September 5 onward. The media could not contain themselves during the period between September 14 and October 12 of 2008. The economic collapse dominated the media, and it wasn't until October 13-19 that the topic moved to second place by reports about the October 15 presidential debate. This heightened level of attention in the media and now by

121 Malcolm GLADWELL, *The Tipping Point: How Little Things can Make a Big Difference*, *op. cit.*, p. 139.

122 Kate KENSKI, Bruce W. HARDY, Kathleen Hall JAMIESON, The Obama Victory: How Media, Money, and Message Shaped the 2008 Election, op. cit., p. 178.

the American public magnified the stickiness of all the media being consumed. In retrospect the average news consumer through TV and print did not see the economy as the most important problem. However the Internet was aware of the effects of the economy on the presidential campaigns, perhaps because the information was real-time, and not prepackaged and edited for presentation like TV and print news. The Internet had no advertising contracts and sponsors to appease and certainly didn't have an editorial agenda being dictated by corporate policy. The Obama team had all the one dramatic momentum they needed when John McCain stated: "The fundamentals of the economy are strong" on September 15, 2008.[123]

Section 3.3.2 Organizations

Republicans:
"Republicans are to blame for the economic free fall."[124]

By mid-September the Obama campaign continued their economic stickiness theme that they would use for the remainder of the election: McCain neither could, nor would, solve the economic financial crisis. The Obama campaign had what it needed, and McCain was out of touch with what was needed to deal with the crisis. For McCain's part, he believed in the underlying resilience of the US economy, perhaps being something that came from his Vietnam veteran days. McCain stated on September 15:

> You know that there's been tremendous turmoil in our financial markets and Wall Street, and it is, its, people are frightened by these events. Our economy, I think, still the **fundamentals of our economy are strong**, (emphasis mine) but these are very, very difficult times. And I promise you we will never put America in this position again. We will clean up Wall Street. We will reform government.[125]

---

123 *Ibid.*, p. 1.

124 "Growing Doubts About McCain's Judgment, Age and Campaign Conduct," *Pew Research Center for the People and the Press*, *op. cit.*

125 "McCain, Obama Blast Regulators, Managers for Wall Street Woes," *CNN Politics*, September 15, 2008. Retrieved from http://articles.cnn.com/2008-09-15/politics/wall.street.candidates_1_wall-street-financial-markets-financial-crisis?_s=PM:POLITICS

Democrats
What the Obama team did was immediately begin to bridge the stickiness to the tipping point from McCain's comment to the fact he didn't care about what was going on in the lives of most Americans. Obama countered:

Why else would he say that we've made great progress economically under George Bush? Why else would he say economy isn't something you understand as well as he should? Why else would he say today of all days just a few hours ago at the fundamentals of the economy are still strong?[126]

Obama responded and directed his response to voters to question both McCain's credibility and his capacity for empathy. "This morning Senator McCain said the fundamentals of the economy are strong. I ask you Senator McCain, what economy are you talking about?"[127] Within 24 hours another McCain statement referencing the turmoil about the difficult times was influenced and framed differently by the media, which cemented the Obama version in the public memory and added to the momentum. Within days the media was overwhelmed reporting on the Lehman Brothers collapse and the Dow "train wreck rush" towards 9000. They reported story after story about economic disaster occurring in the US market. Interesting, when doing the research with internet search keywords during this period, one finds that there are a tremendous number of hits and articles in newspapers and news transcripts about the way McCain botched the statement and failed to reframe it. But if you search for the entire statement that McCain uttered in his original statement, you find very few actual verbatim broadcast uses and newspaper accounts. The Obama campaign was capitalizing on this, and with their Internet media technological sophistication, the Democrats reinforced the truncated version and went screaming with capital letters *fundamentals* into the search engines.

Section 3.3.3 Media

The Final Campaigns
The campaigns during this time were quite interesting to review from a

---

126 John BENTLEY, "McCain Says "Fundamentals" Of U.S. Economy Are Strong," *CBS News Politics*, September 15, 2008. Retrieved from http://www.cbsnews.com/8301-502443_162-4450366-502443.html

127 Kate KENSKI, Bruce W. HARDY, Kathleen Hall JAMIESON, The Obama Victory: How Media, Money, and Message Shaped the 2008 Election, op. cit., p. 183.

media standpoint and Internet perspective, as the "fundamental" statement was screaming capital letters on the search engines and was now being linked to statements such as "job losses at 605,000 for the year," and "September foreclosures at 9800 a day."[128] One of the Obama ads at the time that was broadcast asked: "How can John McClain fix our economy, if he doesn't understand it's broken?"[129] There were several other slipups emphasized by the Democratic campaign within a week of the McCain remark that called his presidential powers into question, as on October 9 the Democrats cited other verbal lapses from the McCain during speeches. Central to the momentum of the tipping point moment was the Democrats media branding McCain as "erratic," as McCain moved from one position on the crisis to another and this feeling of herky-jerkiness, translated into a public perception of how he would handle the presidency if elected. All this translated into what the Democrats used as media logic of paired associations. If Wall Street failures precipitated an economic meltdown, then it was the Republican Party that deserved the blame.

Obama blamed the Republican philosophy of deregulation for the crisis on Wall Street and promoted this indictment of the Republican economic theory in the media coverage as well. What is important to note during this time is that the playing field between the two campaigns was anything but level. Clearly, the Obama side was out-spending the Republican side with their advertising, and the Democrats had very deep pockets and could really focus their funds and expand their media advertising, whereas McCain during this time had to split his ad space and costs with the Republican National Committee. By doing so, his message was diluted and had little impact to counter the Obama messages. The problem with the McCain ads, in retrospect, was that they were being written by lawyers who were trying to protect the party campaign position and John McCain, to protect everyone from liability, but they had no training in what ultimately would have been an influential message to reach the American voter. The September 15, 2008 Republican strategy team had planned and launched a series of television ads to attack the notion that the Democratic nominee Obama was not ready to lead. This might have been a good strategy and attracted substantial media stickiness interest and attention. However, by October

---

128 Kate KENSKI, Bruce W. HARDY, Kathleen Hall JAMIESON, The Obama Victory: How Media, Money, and Message Shaped the 2008 Election, op. cit., p. 184.

129 *Ibid.*, p. 184.

18th the preoccupation with the economic crisis precluded that any of these themes would get much play in the media.

The media attention on the economy was focused on the mishaps of McCain. For McCain's strategy team, the economy really took the campaign away from them. Trying to attack Obama's Chicago connections, the questions about his ancestry, his experience and leadership, and all the other typical campaign rhetoric was basically blown out of the water. The Democrats were now reinforcing their claim that McCain was just another candidate linked to the incumbent George W. Bush. And the Republicans were struggling to bring about any kind of campaign stickiness attacking Obama's readiness to be president. But at this point, the Republicans just couldn't make this stick. McCain worked aggressively to try to reverse the negative opinion of his comments on the economy, and he tried to show the country in two-minute ads for television that Obama was not ready to lead the country in this period of crisis. The Obama team successfully characterized McCain's response to the crisis as erratic, and the Republican team was trying to dissipate the impact of what had happened in mid-September.

McCain tried repeatedly with two-minute ads to try to reassure the American public and reframe his earlier comments. McCain's team spent on September 17 just under 4 million USD to restore the public confidence in their maligned candidate.[130] On the other hand, the Democrats reached into their fat bank account and started broadcasting the ad titled "real change," which offered a comforting and counseling approach that was aimed at shoring up the national polls and all the battleground state votes. The ad was successful in stickiness influencing of the public perception of Obama's trustworthiness, and the Republicans tried to counter with their own version of "foundation," which unfortunately was a quarter of the size of Obama's budget and certainly could not undercut the argument that had been laid out by Obama's two-minute barrage. Again, Republicans just couldn't make his position stick. Demonstrating the importance of the economy, the Dow Jones Industrial closing averages around the days of the presidential debates, the media coverage about the economy became increasingly focused and drew important stickiness attributes for the Obama campaign.

130 "Growing Doubts About McCain's Judgment, Age and Campaign Conduct," *Pew Research Center for the People and the Press, op. cit.*

Losing more than 2500 points between the first debate, September 26, and the last of the debates on October 15, what was key to the economic crisis was that the Dow had crashed through the 11,000 ceiling and continued to march downward, plunging through the 10,000 mark, and in the week between the second and third present presidential face-off went well by the 9000 barrier. Finally, the day of the final debate on October 15, 2008, it plunged another 733 points, which was its largest single day drop in history.[131] This impacted nearly half the US households who had a stake in the stock market, and a reported 55.3 million households owning mutual funds, the impact of this characteristic was sheer stickiness phenomena. And suddenly the American voter wanted one of the candidates to be in office who was up to the task of what appeared to be a Herculean effort of righting the devastated economy. As George Bush and his financial team were contemplating bailouts of the Wall Street giants and Congress was deadlocked in its decisions about what to do next, the Obama campaign reinforced the stickiness attribute in their favor by placing the crisis squarely on the incumbent Bush and the candidate McCain. At every opportunity in the media, the Democrats advanced their economic argument against the Republican nominee. And the televised debates were all about the public's perception that electing McCain would, in effect, produce another Bush term. Although the bailout bill was passed on October 3 and should have improved McCain's prospects, the $750 billion dollars had little effect, and the Dow continued to drop another 1800 points.

At the same time that the presidential debates had started on October 2, a rescue package had failed the first time it had been on the House floor. By October 2 it was not clear whether the bill would make it through on the second try. The media was more focused on the country's economic meltdown than anything going on in the debates, and the Democrats were pushing this point with the focus on the economy in their strategy. And by the October 7, by the second presidential debate, the wheels came off the Dow, and McCain was being paired in a negative light, and his poll numbers echoed the downward trajectory of the economy, as the Dow, a contributor to the tipping point, was approaching a total one-year decline of 5000 points. This translated to the voter belief that the country was on the wrong track economically, and the Republicans were being blamed for the crisis

131 Peter GOODMAN, "Market Suffers as Investors Weigh Relentless Trouble," *New York Times*, October 15, 2008.

and the effect on the campaign tipping point. In effect, electing McCain, was being translated into another Bush third term. TV, newspaper, Internet, and almost all forms of media reinforced this stickiness perception that the country was on the wrong track as it related to economy. The economic issues became *stuck* with the belief that the Republicans were responsible for the economic woes. Blaming the GOP for the economic woes was a favorable strategy for the Obama team, and the media reinforced the tipping point as it reinforced the public sentiment, and the American voter blamed the Republicans (McCain equals Bush), hence to vote for Obama, ensuring the stickiness attribute.

During the October 15 presidential debate, McCain attempted to push Obama on the defensive to try to assert control relative to the tax discussion. The media blasted front-page headlines, i.e. the *New York Times*: "McCain pressing Obama in the last and important debate."[132] McCain hammered his theme about *Joe the plumber* and *share the wealth* topics repeatedly during the third presidential debate, almost to the point that it was deemed annoying, as it was meant to make a stickiness impression on the viewer. The conclusion he had hoped to convey was that Obama was going to make the economy worse by raising taxes. McCain had everything to gain by this strategy during the third presidential debate. He knew he was fighting an uphill battle, and he also knew he had the audience opportunity to make a charge to resurrect his presidential hopes. But because McCain was almost redundant on his issues during the debate, the tone bordered on exasperation, trying to justify higher taxes without specifying as from whom they would be paid.

The issue of *spread the wealth* an attempted reframing by the McCain campaign by October 24, 2008, was translated in the media as a response to the perception that the government was taking tax payer money and redistributing it as the politician sees fit, was being portrayed as a form of socialism. Given the economic meltdown, the attacks by the Republican campaign that the Democratic plans constituted socialism were built on the presupposition that favor government intervention in the market. McCain, like Obama, supported the $700 billion rescue package or bail out, which

132 Jim RUTENBERG, "Candidates Clash over Character and Policy," *New York Times*, October 15, 2008. Retrieved from http://www.nytimes.com/2008/10/16/us/politics/16debate.html?pagewanted=all

gave taxpayers $250 billion share of major US banks. The Republicans tried to disassociate themselves with the term socialism and affix the label to the Democrats and the media so that the American voter would come to the stickiness conclusion that Obama was indeed a socialist. Obama's team had an interesting counterpoint, which was, "Why did Warren Buffett and Colin Powell endorse him if he was practicing socialism?". The media carried headlines that McCain attacked Obama's plans as a socialist strategy. Republicans in the final weeks of October tried to reinforce the socialism and spread the wealth message into their messages. The other thing that the share the wealth concept provided to the Republican campaign was to also frame Obama as a liberal while at the same time moving the potentially racial issue of welfare into the dialogue. Throughout this period both campaigns secured news time and space with ads and disseminated their positions on the web. These messages were an attempt to influence the news agenda, and depending on whose side you are on, it was all about either creating or stopping a dramatic moment from occurring. After the final presidential debate, the McCain tax message, as it was being presented in the media, seemed to change perception of his ability to handle the economy and also improved his favorability ratings and his stickiness at this moment. The problem was, when dealing with the national vote, considering the media only as national television, advertising spots, ads as the traditional campaign message delivery systems, was not enough to command enough of the vote to win. Obama had locked up many of the battleground states in early voting long before the McCain surge as an attempt to create his own tipping point.

Between October 29 and November 4 Obama media ads continued to attack McCain on both the economy and his links to George W. Bush. Meanwhile, Republicans countered with Obama as a tax-and-spend liberal whose agenda would only worsen their country's recession. At this juncture, with Election Day nearing, the Obama campaign tried to increase the reassurance with a detailed description of his proposals while McCain volleyed with their allegation that the democratic nominee was not prepared to deal with the financial crisis. It is on these issues during the closing weeks of the campaign that the media had its greatest impact on the outcome of the election. It is during this period that Obama's stickiness gathered momentum and widened the gap over his adversary. The media reinforced the position that Obama was better prepared to handle the failing economy and that electing McCain was just another continuation of the failed presidency of George W. Bush. Along with these aspects, the contribution of McCain's running partner, Palin, the prospect of her as a potential vice-president, particularly as it was being portrayed in the media, had the net effect of diminishing the Republican stickiness and any chances for success.

Between September 15, 2008 and October 15, 2008, the Republicans had attempted a comeback with their attacks on Obama's inability to deal with the wars in Afghanistan and Iraq. McCain clearly had one advantage and was portrayed by the media clearly as the candidate who could better deal with war. But the election stickiness was not about this issue, as the war was somewhat removed from the everyday consciousness of the American voter. Rather, the importance of the economy had enough stickiness attributes to ensure an Obama victory.

The Democrats used sustained national advertising as part of their strategy. They employed such themes as *common purpose* in telling the voters that they could choose "hope over fear and unity over division." This use of longer form media advertising characterized the Obama strategy in the final weeks and reinforced the stickiness attribute. At a cost of over 5 million USD, on each day of the last week of the election there were two minute TV ads titled: "defining moments," aired on national television. From October 28 to November 4 these messages were given additional exposure in Colorado, Florida, Iowa, Indiana, Montana, North Carolina, Ohio, and Virginia. The spots that aired from October 28 through November 3 were shown in Michigan, Missouri, New Mexico, Nevada, and Pennsylvania. The gist of this media campaign was similar to what Ronald Reagan had asked in 1980: "Are you better off than you were four years ago?" It was just phrased another way, "Will our country be better off four years from now?" The American voter was living in fear during this time as the economic system around them was collapsing, and most Americans felt if only George W. Bush had not been given another four years, perhaps this would never have happened. These two-minute advertisements were used before in prior campaigns, but at this juncture, with the flood of funds to Democrats, they were able to unleash a saturation of these ads, and at the same time Obama himself was exhibiting this low-key sense of confidence, comfort, and competence. In other words, he was already projecting his knowledge and feeling that he was moving towards his tipping point and he was going to win the election.

On October 29, at a cost of 3 million USD each, the Democrats unleashed eight half-hour advertising and TV campaign infomercials, highlighting their agenda promises with precision to cement their stickiness command of the issues in the eyes of the voters. At their core these pieces tried to link the solutions offered by the nominee, and they were carried on NBC, CBS, Univision, BCC, TV1, Fox, and MSNBC. These infomercials detailed precisely how Obama was going to restore the long-term health of the economy, help the middle class, and all the decisions he was going to make along the way to get the "American dream" back on track. Obama's media strategy during this time was to use a "nation in trouble," with home foreclosures, lost jobs, high gas prices, and record deficits. The national debt had never been higher, and the country in just the last month had begun historic economic meltdown. For each of the McCain charges and rhetoric that followed, Obama offered a rebuttal. These half-hour infomercials provided also convenient biographical vignettes for the closing argument in a campaign that was built on the persona of the Democratic nominee.

Thirty-three million viewers watched these Obama half-hour infomercials, topping the last game of the World Series, which, according to Nielsen ratings, only averaged 19 million viewers.[133] When you have an election that is changing the party in the White House, the new party has to prove he was capable as an opponent. From this perspective there was a statistical tie between Obama and McCain that existed as late as November 2, but the public perception had shifted as to which candidate could better handle this unexpected economic crisis. And from this viewpoint, Obama's lead improved by 12 points from 37 to 49% in the period from September 7 to November 2, while McCain dropped by eight points from 54 to 46%, again highlighting the attribute contributing to the tipping point in this case study, which occurred from approximately, September 15 to October 15, 2008.

Soon after becoming the presumptive nominee, the Obama team launched a biographical commercial campaign emphasizing his patriotism. Running advertisements in 18 states, including Alaska and North Carolina which were traditionally Republican. During this period, between June 6 and July 26, Obama spent $27 million as compared to McCain and Republican Na-

---

133 Kate KENSKI, Bruce W. HARDY, Kathleen Hall JAMIESON, The Obama Victory: How Media, Money, and Message Shaped the 2008 Election, op. cit., p. 246.

tional Committee's combined total of $24.6 million.[134]

On October 29 at 8:00 PM EST, Obama simulcast a 30-minute infomercial "American Stories, American Solutions" on NBC, CBS, Fox, Univision, MSNBC, BET and TV One, focused on issues including health care and taxation. An example of his influence on the media is the infomercial of an Obama speech live from Florida. The Fox network adjusted the second part of Game Five of the 2008 World Series, and delayed it by 15 minutes in order to show the commercial. The ad reached 30.1 million viewers across the other networks compared to ABC's *Pushing Daisies*, which garnered 6.3 million viewers.[135] Previously, the last presidential candidate to purchase a half-hour ad was H. Ross Perot who ran as an independent candidate in 1992.[136] The Obama campaign also bought a channel on Dish Network to screen Obama ads 24/7.[137] Wyatt Andrews reported on a "Reality Check" on the *CBS Evening News* the next day as to the doubts over the factual accuracy of some of the promises Obama made in the advertisement, given the government's enormous financial deficit. [138]

The Obama strategy team was particularly noted for their use of the Internet to rally supporters, an increase his momentum and make his policies known. "The integration of technology into the process of field organizing … is the success of the Obama campaign," says Sanford Dickert, who was

134 Jim RUTENBERG, "Taking to the Airwaves," *New York Times*, July 29, 2008. Retrieved from http://thecaucus.blogs.nytimes.com/2008/07/29/taking-to-the-airwaves/

135 Lisa DE MORAES, "Obama Enters the League of Must-See TV," *Washington Post*, October 31, 2008. Retrieved from http://www.washingtonpost.com/wp-dyn/content/article/2008/10/30/AR2008103002536.html

136 Elizabeth KOLBERT, "The 1992 Campaign: The Media; Perot's 30-Minute TV Ads Defy the Experts, Again," *New York Times (Late Edition)*, Oct 27, 1992, p. A.19

137 Dawn TEO, "Obama Campaign Buys Channel 73 on Dish Network," *Huffington Post*, October 2, 2008. Retrieved from http://www.huffingtonpost.com/dawn-teo/obama-campaign-buys-chann_b_131105.html

138 Wyatt ANDREWS, "Reality Check: The Cost Of Obama's Pledges," *CBS News*, October 29, 2008. Retrieved http://m.cbsnews.com/relatedfullstory.rbml?feed_id=0&catid=4557520&videofeed=36

John Kerry's chief technology officer for the 2004 campaign.[139] Further stating, "...but the use of technology was not the end-all and be-all in this cycle. Technology has been a partner, an enabler for the Obama campaign, bringing the efficiencies of the internet into the real-world problems of organizing people in a distributed, trusted fashion."[140]

Obama's use of the Internet also targeted 18 to 29 years old, the age group most reliant on new media for political information. Obama's campaign managers understood that the reason younger voters tended to ignore politicians was because politicians tended to ignore issues which most concerned them, which is why Obama received such a positive reaction from America's youth.[141]

Obama utilized forums and social websites such as MySpace and Facebook, and built relationships with his supporters and future supporters. The goal was establishing an upfront, personable and face-to-face quality to give supporters a sense of security and trust and inspiring them to rally others in their local communities. The Obama supporters themselves formed a nation-wide community and The Internet provided useful and effective tools, for example such as the "Neighbor-to-Neighbor" tool on (My.BarackObama.com) allowing them to reach a large number of people in a short time in their own community. These online communications led to Obama supporters orchestrating social activities such as sign making and door-to-door petitioning, as well as simply discussing their opinions about policies and issues they supported along with Obama.[142]

Obama's campaign was further bolstered by McCain's comparatively limited use of the Internet. Largely because McCain did not have the organi-

---

139 Sara Lai STIRLAND, "Obama's Secret Weapons: Internet, Databases and Psychology," *Wired*, October 29, 2008. Retrieved from http://www.wired.com/threatlevel/2008/10/obamas-secret-w/

140 Ibid.

141 "Growing Doubts About McCain's Judgment, Age and Campaign Conduct," *Pew Research Center for the People and the Press, op. cit.*

142 Michael XENOS and W. Lance BENNETT, "The Disconnection in Online Politics: The Youth Political Sphere and US Election Sites, 2002-2004," *Information, Communication, and Society*, 10, 2007, p. 443–64; Josh PASEK, Daniel ROMER, and Kathleen Hall JAMIESON, "America's Youth and Community Engagement: How Use of Mass Media Is Related to Civic Activity and Political Awareness in 14-to-22-Year-Olds," *Communication Research*, 33, 2006, p. 115–35.

zation of Obama's campaign, nor did he spend a comparable amount of money on this portion of the campaign. Obama's opportune timing and usage of online campaigning gave him significant advantage over McCain. [143]

Considering the impact of global media on the Obama campaign is the fact that in 2008 there was more readily available campaign-generated political information and, depending upon your perspective, misinformation, in more places than ever before. Access to the Internet made possible the experiences that could not happen in other forms of previous media delivery systems. The American voter spent countless hours watching the Obama campaign related videos on YouTube that garnered more than 50 million views for the 1800 videos. Interestingly most of the American voters were getting their political information from Internet sources such as YouTube. This translated into the people who received information on the Internet during the week or so before they voted would more likely have had a positive impression of Obama and were not as strongly affected as they would have been by hearing about the same as issue on talk radio.

Despite all the positive effects and stickiness of the web, it was a two-edged sword that undercut the Obama campaign on several key points during the election. For example, the vignettes featuring Reverend Jeremiah Wright's sermons supported the controversy that showed Obama in an unfavorable light; fortunately, this happened early in the spring and became a minor contagiousness issue to the raging tide of stickiness of the economy that would present itself later in the campaign.

The Internet provided real-time reporting, as the events and the voter count were being tabulated in the earlier swing states, as by the time voters had woken on the West Coast and prepared to go to the polls, the message on election day was well underway as the other voting decisions which happened earlier in the day, and in effect a tipping point during the campaign that had occurred was already being disseminated.

<u>*Micro-Targeting Cable and Radio:*</u> The Internet provided the ability to *micro target*, which completely changed the media playing field in 2008. Simply because he Obama campaign had such large differences in the

143 Sara Lai STIRLAND, "Obama's Secret Weapons: Internet, Databases and Psychology," *op. cit.*

amount of money that they could throw at very narrow focus of messages, some of them very deceptive, the campaigns became preoccupied throughout, with messages designed to sway the voter. Indeed prior to the advent of national radio, such micro-targeting was the norm not the exception. With the rise of extensive e-mail databases, housing profiles, information on individual purchasing patterns, lifestyle and voting preferences, group affiliations, etc., the targeting of information and messages became a *science* and was transformed by the technology that was available during the 2008 campaign.

Emails and Text Messages: Kenneth Plough, who is now Obama's technology secretary, as the campaign media guru, was able to deliver traditional messages in nontraditional ways, and by the end of the campaign, the Obama team had sent more than one billion e-mails. A million people registered as part of the Obama campaign's texting program. In contrast to campaigns in the past that would announce significant events to the press, and it would take sometimes days to disseminate, this way of reaching their supporters with an Obama campaign text message directly also to their supporters with the name of the president and vice president nominee on the signature line became very influential.

Section 3.3.4 Events

Economy

The economy was the central event to the agenda for the public and the media. And if you are on the Obama side of the equation, the Democratic version of why there were problems with the economy benefited them most. With the Obama campaign's success in bankrolling their platform, the news about the troubled economy and who is to blame was broadcast and heard in all the pivotal battleground states. In contrast, the counter claim was limited to fewer dollars to buy media time by the McCain campaign, and he had to split his messages with his colleagues in the Congress in order to afford to get his message across. From mid-January 2008 through Election Day, economy was the front, middle and foremost on the voters' minds. (The Iraq war and the fight on terrorism became a decidedly second distant cousin media-wise in comparison to the economy and its developments through January to October 2008). During the post-convention run-up, media activity about the economy, the foreclosure rates, the Dow dropping, and the slide of personal wealth became the momentum of enormous proportions for the American voter, and they were seriously scrutinizing and evaluating whether the candidates, either one of them, had the ability to fix it.

McCain: Attempt at a "Counter" Tipping Point: During the latter part of October 2008, it appeared that the McCain campaign had the offensive on the tax issue, and ultimately, may have created the possibility that its candidate would make a run for its own tipping point and swing the momentum in the race that otherwise had been lost.

After the October 15 presidential debate, prospects improved when Obama had a chance meeting with a typical, blue-collar worker who was labeled: "Joe the plumber," and in an apparent lapse on October 12, 2008, Obama made comments about "sharing the wealth" and was viewed as a patronizing tax and spend liberal. This misstep was telegraphed in the media by McCain to the extent that they claimed that Obama was out of touch with the American voter and tried to present this as enough of a response to McCain's earlier mistake about "the fundamentals of the economy are strong" statement. In the technological media stage of managed world politics, the under rehearsed statements of each opponent could be reframed in the media and by the adversaries' agenda in a different light. The McCain strategy team recognized the significance of Obama's stumble that happened before the third debate. This misstep was something that the Republicans considered an opportunity to define their position that they had been searching for. The notion that Obama said that he wanted to *share the wealth*, gave the Republicans back the advantage on the tax message, but unfortunately, without the deep pockets to really take advantage of it and broadcast this before the presidential debate, it was never exploited enough to offset, and for the 56 million viewers who watched the third presidential debate, the McCain campaign didn't have enough momentum from the issue.

McCain: End to His Counter Tipping Point Strategy: While the tax issue was hotly contested toward the middle and the end of October 2008, the McCain team failed to achieve a dramatic moment it was hoping for to move forward and on to victory, as the tax issue was clouded to by the healthcare reform issue that was also in the American voters' mind. On this issue Obama offered a seemingly better proposal, whereby McCain faced another serious hurdle that he was not going to overcome in the closing months of the general election. Because McCain's health care proposal was overly complicated, it invited attacks from the Democratic campaign relative to its emissions and its additional costs that the employer and employee would have to take on in order for benefits to be provided. Because it was a complicated proposal, Democrats had the opportunity to mislead voters in the media that, in fact, the Republican plan was inept and so confusing that even the media had trouble explaining it and reporting on it. A widely read AARP publication misstated the context of the McCain proposal as well. McCain on the other hand, wasn't helping his case, as his explanations came across as convoluted and difficult to understand, and when translated into the media muddied the details of the proposal, which let the allegations by the Democratic Party take hold. McCain's own website offered a complicated explanation of this proposal that also reinforced the Democrats' attack. The fact that Obama had quotations directly from the Republican nominee's website fortified the irrationality of the proposal. The Obama team launched a barrage of television ads that were aired 22,000 times, backed by extensive radio air time. Clearly the Democrats were attempting to put an end at any chance for the Republicans to create a tipping point. On this issue the Obama campaign benefited from its ability to outspend the McCain campaign, and on the healthcare issue picked up additional momentum from health labor unions and Planned Parenthood who in turn created their own media campaigns against McCain.

What seemed to finally squash the notion that McCain would have his own tipping point was that business organizations like the United States Chamber of Commerce, generally supportive of Republicans, said that his healthcare proposal would lead to an unraveling of the employer- based health care system. By October 27, 2008, the media began to focus on what businesses generally thought and now were promoting the Democratic alternative. In theory, the central Republican claims against Obama were beginning to take hold during this period, i.e. first, Obama would increase everyone's taxes, second, he would increase taxes on most small businesses, and he had voted to increase taxes on those making more than 42,000 USD.

McCain tried to make his case that small business would be the most affected by Obama's plans. The Obama strategists, on the other hand, tried to make a rebuttal argument that a very small percentage of small businesses would be affected with the ceiling of 250,000USD revenue per year as proposed as the limit of who would get the tax cut under the Obama plan.

The McCain strategy seemingly had impact, but the Republican strategists did not have enough funds for the audience to listen to their phrases and change their minds of the public.

The Tipping Point

As media technology has opened up new ways to inform, engage, and mobilize during the campaign, it also provided opportunities to insulate and send deceptive messages. Case in point, many voters who received text messages and e-mails during the final weeks reported that they thought the candidate Obama was a Muslim. For practical purposes, the Obama campaign's regular contagious e-mails to supporters blanketed them with reinforcing information that reframed all the events from the campaign's point of view and continued to offer strategy rebuttal arguments to be used to defend Obama's heritage and consequently go after the Republicans. The fact was that the targeting of the messages was working, and news media repeated the messages by dealing with them in broader terms. This was disheartening to the campaign for McCain, as news accounts that were paid for by the Republican campaign disappeared entirely or were regulated to just a brief mentioning by a nation that was obsessed and transfixed by the economic meltdown. The media and voters really weren't paying much attention to the misleading attacks about the tax issues or the race issue or Obama's origins. The basic fact was that the economic meltdown couldn't come at a better time for the Obama campaign.

On September 18, 2008, McCain stated: "The fundamentals of the economy are in good shape." With Obama's deep pockets and a media convulsion that was trying to keep up with the economic meltdown, the campaign strategy team in retrospect had little to do but to ride the epidemic of voter concern and momentum to the campaign's one dramatic moment or tipping point.

Section 3.4 Summary

The economy provided the necessary momentum and stickiness to propel Obama to his tipping point on or about the middle of September 2008, but the question that remains in this context of how will the Internet (or some other media innovation like it) play an increasing role in future campaigns, given the fact that the Obama campaign made extensive use of it to motivate voters to cast their ballots in 2008. Along these lines we can conclude also that campaigns that are able to raise enormous amounts of money will copy the Obama campaign model approach by offering forms of communication that can be proliferated on the Internet in "real time" almost immediately, capitalizing on the interactive potential of the new media. The downside with all this is that candidates promoting an agenda, who can spend and find investors to spend for them (and backers to spend for them), are able to raise more cash expanding the winning momentum against candidates who are left unwilling to please prospective patrons. For example, big oil and its influence on this past election may actually hurt the candidate in the future rather than help the candidate to sway voter opinion. Another drawback possibility is that the better financed candidate would have the ability to micro-target his audience and reach the voter without the benefit of rebuttal from the other candidate. In a truly democratic society, the opportunity to defend one's position and one's agenda would be canceled out. Rather than electing a better person with the better policies and better agenda, the American voter would be drowning in a media ocean of just one candidate's views and opinions that in effect distorts the reality and the potential for real solution and just adds to the chaos and confusion. The United States is a country that historically puts value in the clash of competing ideas, going back to the days of Washington, Jefferson, and Lincoln. However, recently not only in the media, but also in government agencies, and typically those engaging with the web, is a quest for solution to police the micro-targeting messages, including viral e-mails, and provide a venue for exposing both viewpoints equally before the election, not after.

During this case study, I researched the people, organizations, media, and events of the campaign, the tactics of Obama's campaign as they were employed. It presented McCain as an old-style liberal who could not possibly assume the mantle of change, denying John McCain as a self-professed "maverick" and ultimately, linking him to the unpopular incumbent George Bush. The Democratic messages amplified content to characterize John McCain as out of touch, asserting that he was erratic, and implying that he was too old to serve as the president and steer the journey in troubled economic times.

McCain's counter-strategy, which presented the argument that Obama was "not ready to lead" – a claim tied to fears, including some that were even race-based, that Obama was unpatriotic, angry, and a poser. This strategy failed during some distinct periods in the evolution of the campaign that followed the sequential tipping point attributes of contagiousness, stickiness, and ultimately the dramatic moment that led to the Obama victory. Once Obama took the lead in the polls in mid-September 2008, at the national level at least - he never lost it. Several key, fundamental economic issues changed within days surrounding the one dramatic moment. This case study exhibits how very difficult it is to calibrate tipping points precisely. Again, what I can offer is a somewhat bracketed approach, i.e., a relative timeframe as to when and why this particular tipping point occurred, as it does thereby serve as a functional model template for the remaining two case studies.

Another reason I considered these attributes and their characteristics important is that each exhibited an evolving interdependence and influence with respect to the media during this campaign. For example, when initial media reports cast energy policy in the early going as a central issue that was impacting the economy, McCain during this time gained a lot of momentum for his support of offshore oil drilling. By contrast, when the media refocused on the competence/incompetence issue and the knowledgeable or ignorant issue around Sarah Palin, the momentum or stickiness shifted. After the Republican convention, McCain was marginally ahead of Obama in the polls. However, during the timeframe between September 10 and October 14, 2008, which was close to the eve of the third and final debate, there was a such a shift and intense media focus on economy that it made it difficult, if not impossible, for McCain and his campaign to get enough media coverage of their own (and their counter strategies) on Obama's political associations and background.

From the beginning, McCain's response to the economic crisis was cast negatively by the Obama campaign and the press as a small issue that grew larger and later became a stickiness event. During the final weeks, the candidates' relative command of the economic crisis became the dramatic moment as to whether who would win as well as how he might govern.

Other issues such as tax policy became the yardsticks in the media by which voters assessed the candidates, amounting to a secondary back and forth banter leading up to these weeks. However, this really had little to do with the outcome, even after the last two debates on October 15, 2008 and October 28, 2000. Rather than resolving his stance on the economic crisis, McCain seemed to miscalculate its impact, and Obama countered that it was just the same rhetoric as the incumbent president, and therefore McCain was offering no real solution. In other words, these fundamental attributes outline a familiar pattern. Communications and global media reinforced to link the candidates to the conditions that political science analysts consider important in voting decisions. But even after the candidates' rhetoric, the analysis of tying voters to fundamental patterns could be estimated, there was, an unexplained variance critical to a tipping point occurring. Proceeding from contagiousness to the stickiness attribute, the unpredictable power of media communication factored in. And when deciding whom to vote for, it mattered little whether an individual thought he or she preferred Obama rather than McCain, but rather voters just wanted a solution to address the state of the economy.

Our case for the media impact on the campaign is premised on the notion that people do not make decisions on the basis of all available evidence, nor when they cast their ballots do they consider all the issues and influences potentially at play. Instead, some stickiness characteristics become more important and salient than others. The stickiness attribute applied in this matter assumes that individuals embrace media information for assessment on the basis of accessibility and how quickly and automatically they could search for solutions and how easily these answers (right or wrong) would come to mind. If the quantity of a particular issue was subject to a lot of media attention, it will be even more accessible in the media. For example, as discussions of the economy dominated the campaign, other issues received less attention. Then the economy became more salient to media consumers and other issues were featured less. By focusing on some issues and ignoring others, the media reinforced the stickiness, i.e. the criteria by which we evaluate a potential leader's policies and positions.

Issues can be made more salient by the stickiness attribute. Arguably, some issues would benefit one candidate more than the other if the content were disseminated, i.e. terrorism and/or the war in Iraq was more salient and for McClain stickier; however, when the stickiness focused on the economy or health care, Obama had the advantage. Stress old age and McCain is negatively influenced. Reinforce the notion of an angry black male with criminal ties, and Obama was disadvantaged, hence some characteristics of the unexplained variance.

The campaigns' contagiousness and stickiness attributes throughout the months were divided into several parts all discussed above. The first part, the preconvention months of the summer, McCain gained in part because the media reinforced contagiousness of the energy prices as a central problem in the injured economy, and offshore drilling for more oil had more support than the usual Democratic alternatives and therefore was carried in a favorable light in the media at that time. By contrast, the contagiousness of the Wall Street meltdown of major financial institutions vilified natural Republican allies, big business and Wall Street, thereby increasing the salience and stickiness of the economy issue, an issue which the Democrats enjoyed until Election Day as an advantage.

The stickiness attribute was primed throughout. Obama's media rhetoric of reassurance persuaded voters that the change he proposed was rooted in basic *shared value principles*. And during the period between June 7 to November 3, 2009 this same perception was shared by voters and increased each day leading up to the election. As scholars I trust that we will look at these contagiousness and stickiness attributes as being where the salient media messages of the campaign are organized and lead to a semantic structure of the campaign strategy resulting in activation of resources and a means for evaluation. Put simply, looking at these attributes in the context of the tipping point model is clearly a way to see the media impact on the campaign or any global event. Because both contagiousness and stickiness evolved and moved to the concept of tipping point to be more salient, in the end the campaign that had the financial wherewithal to purchase greater exposure for its media messages had a natural advantage. Since some of the topics in the media were more salient to some audiences than other topics, the use of targeted deployment media messages only magnified the contagiousness and stickiness of these effects.

Some of these media tactics moved voters by what psychologists call *selective exposure*. Specifically, if individuals and voters are drawn to speakers they admire and messages that they already agree with, they will go with them. Compounding the influence exponentially, the campaign strategists easily persuaded voters who were on the fence. As a result, I have to add to the relevant argument. This was an unexplainable phenomenon whereby individuals who were yet to be committed or influenced by the stickiness attribute. Or was it luck? Or, how much is too much?

There probably is, in any theory, a point or tipping point when there's too much. But we certainly have not discovered it. Countless events like these are actually shaping the tipping point attributes for our future. They start as small factors in the big game, and then later on they become so if they become contagious and sticky with significant attributes and characteristics, and then they try to develop a game and a strategy to gain media influence. "The world wants information quickly and instantly," said Kevin Merida, national editor for the *Washington Post*.

In our business, you have to shift to accommodate that. And if readers don't get what they want where they're looking, they go somewhere else and look. That's why we have to figure out how to get people what they want, and you keep up your own compass.[144]

As we turn to our next case study, the 2007-2010 global financial crisis, we will see similar patterns in the contagiousness and stickiness attributes and ultimately, the tipping point that to some degree is characterized by many of the same types of media communication delivery systems that delivered the messages in this first case study and contributed to the epidemic.

Media Impacts and Global Events Website

For further information please visit the
Media impact and Global Events Website:

http://mdgparis.typepad.com/global_media_and_world_ev/

This website tracks, highlights, categorizes and provides a articles and commentary related to Tipping Point Attributes and Characteristics, as well as information and recent updates related specifically to the three case studies included in this version and other Media and Global Event issues.

144 Jeremy W. PETERS, "Political Blogs Are Ready to Flood Campaign Trail," *New York Times*, January 29, 2011. Retrieved from http://www.nytimes.com/2011/01/30/business/media/30blogs.html?pagewanted=all

CHAPTER FOUR
CASE STUDY TWO

Two: International Financial Crisis 2007 – 2010

Introduction

As I conducted the research and formulated this Chapter about the second case study, the International Financial Crisis 2007- 2010 (it is now 2012), uncertainty continues to create nervousness over the future of the global and American economy. Now tsunamis, radioactive plumes, Middle East revolutions, the ongoing European debt crisis and a still weakened United States economy could undermine the recent gains. Some global issues, like the spike in oil and food prices, are quantifiable. But the long term, clearer picture depends on indicators yet to come, and recent history only highlight some of the attributes and characteristics of the complexity of global financial events and media influence. "The problem is not Japan alone — it's that Japan reinforces all the negative repercussions and our own weak recovery," said Stephen S. Roach, nonexecutive chairman of Morgan Stanley Asia and a professor at Yale. "It's difficult to know the tipping point for the global economy, but there are difficult headwinds now." The sequence of recent global events adds to a sense of global foreboding. Recently in Libya, American warplanes were flying and the oil producing wells stood silent. Troops from Saudi marched into Bahrain, moving across the Persian Gulf from Iran. In Europe, with the Greek crisis temporally adverted, finance ministers warn that hundreds of banks in other countries still carry billions of dollars in bad loans.

As surveys of global economists by *The International Economy Magazine* presented a majority view it as likely that some combination of Greece, Ireland and Portugal will still default on debt and force investors to take heavy losses. Oil prices continue to rise as of this writing. Japan, already the largest importer of liquefied natural gas, searches for energy to replace a damaged nuclear grid, as analysts expect these prices to rise too.

Finally, the United States, with an economic colossus burdened by the recent International Financial Crisis 2007-2010 that resulted in the worst long-term unemployment situation in nearly a century. If Japanese companies and investors retrench, selling some Treasuries and investing fewer yen overseas, the pain here could grow.[145]

In the years leading up to the start of the 2007-2010 International Financial Crisis, large amounts of foreign money flowed into the U.S. from rapidly-growing economies in Asia and oil-producing countries. These funds made it easy for the Federal Reserve to hold interest rates in the United States extremely low from 2002–2006 which contributed to easier credit conditions, which culminated in the United States housing bubble. Various types of loans (e.g., mortgage, credit card and auto) were extremely easy to obtain whereby consumers assumed an unprecedented debt load.[146] Additionally, as part of the housing and credit booms, financial agreements called mortgage-backed securities (MBS) and collateralized debt obligations (CDO) proliferated, these derived their value from mortgage payments and housing prices. These financial instruments enabled institutions and investors throughout the world to participate in the U.S. housing market. As housing prices fell, major global financial institutions which had borrowed and invested heavily in subprime (MBS and CDO markets) reported significant losses. Falling prices also lead to homes being worth less than the mortgage, and providing a owner incentives to option for foreclosure. The foreclosure *epidemic* that began in late 2006, drained substantial wealth

145 Michael POWELL, "Crises in Japan Ripple Across the Global Economy," *New York Times*, March 20, 2011. Retrieved from http://www.nytimes.com/2011/03/21/business/global/21econ.html?pagewanted=all

146 Paul KRUGMAN, "Revenge of the Glut," New York Times, March 1, 2009. Retrieved from http://www.nytimes.com/2009/03/02/opinion/02krugman.html?_r=1

from consumers and eroded the strength of banking institutions. Similarly, defaults and losses on other loan types also increased as the crisis spread from the housing market to other parts of the economy. Total losses estimated in the trillions of U.S. dollars globally.[147]

With the housing and credit bubbles, I researched how the tipping point attributes and media involvement influenced the financial sector to both expand and ultimately, to become increasingly fragile. Policymakers failed to recognize the increasingly important role played by financial institutions, particularly, investment banks and hedge funds, (also known as the shadow banking system). Some experts believed these institutions became as important as commercial (depository) banks in providing credit to the U.S. economy, however, not subject to the same regulations.[148] These institutions as well as certain regulated banks had assumed enormous debt burdens providing the loans (described above) and did not have a financial reserves sufficient to absorb large loan defaults or MBS losses.[4] Resulting in these losses impacting the ability of financial institutions to lend, diminishing economic activity. These concerns drove central banks to provide funds to stimulate lending and try to stabilize the commercial paper markets. Governments responded and provided bail outs to key financial institutions and assumed significant additional financial commitments.

147 "Executive Summary," *International Monetary Fund*, January 2009. Retrieved from http://www.imf.org/external/pubs/ft/weo/2009/01/pdf/exesum.pdf

148 Timothy GEITHNER, "Reducing Systemic Risk in a Dynamic Financial System," Speech, *Federal Reserve Bank of New York*, June 9, 2008. Retrieved from http://www.newyorkfed.org/newsevents/speeches/2008/tfg080609.html

Share in GDP of U.S. financial sector since 1860. [149]

From the period between Sept 1, 2007 and November 30, 2010 (and as this is being written – still occurring), the world markets slipped into one of the worst financial meltdowns since the 1930's, coupled with complete loss of equity value and confidence in the banking system worldwide. The inevitable impact (tipping point) worldwide was the one week casualty list (October 18, 2008), including Lehman Brothers, AIG Insurance, Morgan Stanley acquiring Citibank, and Washington Mutual, the federal bailout of Bear Sterns, and the immediate infusion of the 800 billion dollar rescue package by United States government and related global stimulus packages throughout the world. The financial crisis was carried, blow-by-blow, with updates on almost all media as a *living story.*

Recalling the Broken Windows theory, the brainchild of James Q. Wilson and George Kelling, which argued that, in effect, impacts and events are the evitable result of disorder.[150] A simple application of this phenomenon suggests the key research question for this study - if a "window" is broken

149 Thomas PHILIPPON, "The Future of the Financial Industry," *Finance Department of the New York University Stern School of Business at New York University, Stern on Finance blog*. Retrieved from http://sternfinance.blogspot.com/2008/10/future-of-financial-industry-thomas.html

150 James WILSON and George KELLING, "Broken Windows. The Police and Neighbourhood Safety," *Atlantic Magazine*, 3, 1982.

and left unrepaired, i.e. the international financial system, whereby, if it appears that the system is unregulated, unmanaged or, that no one cares about it and no one is in charge, soon more windows will be broken, and the condition will spread (contagiousness), sending a signal that anything goes. In countries or regions, illustrating this example, financial oversights and lack of monitoring regulation are all the equivalent of broken windows, and promote invitations to more serious events (as is evident in recent events in Ireland and Greece that have affected the entire European Union).[151] This is the epidemic of finance. It equates to that the effects are contagious - just as a trend is contagious - that it can start with just one broken window, or country financial failure, and spread instantaneously, particularly if the message is delivered via media networks to an entire region's population and the world economies. The impetus to engage in a certain type of behavior is not coming from a certain kind of person or culture, but from a feature of the environment, i.e. financial sector – banking. contagiousness postulates that if a particular behavior in a region or community (or world) goes unaddressed, it signals that nobody cares about the it resulting in additional behavior of the same type.[152]

Here I examine the Tipping Point theory attributes in the context of this global event and media impact, and the relationship to the panic and selloffs, the unprecedented drop in the United States stock market of over 700 points in one day, and similar losses in markets worldwide with a net value loss reaching 10 trillion in USD (and still climbing). Whereas sometime in October 2008, the world financial markets finally got the message. The world was riveted into a vicious credit crunch downward contagiousness, and it had reached the brink of frightening proportions. Stock markets worldwide plunged, currencies experienced violent ups and downs, and lending between banks stopped. Governments, in turn, poured trillions into bailout loans, equity infusions, and massive interventions. The United States Federal Reserve Bank, in a never experienced before move and unprecedented expansion of the powers, released 1.1 trillion USD of new lending in a period of about six weeks. This tsunami of money went to banks, to big insurers, to commercial paper users, and to money market funds. A 700 billion dollar bailout bill flew through American Congress on the promise that it would get at the root cause of the American crisis and

151 Ibid.
152 Ibid.

purchase the toxic assets from the banks' ledgers. European governments, led by Great Britain, attempted to outdo the American bailout and focus their infusion directly into the banks.

For the first time in history, finance ministers worldwide realized how lethal the new financial instruments created and brokered in the United States had saturated the global investment portfolios, and to what extremes the banks, especially in Europe, had gone in imitating the American corporate giants. A fashionable word in Europe was it could "decouple" its economy from the Americans, but this strategy quickly vanished as the European continent crept towards negative growth during the same time. The oil producing states-Russia, Venezuela, Iran, and the Arab states--that had linked their economies to the American consumer were faced with the same problems. Emerging economies-like Korea, Taiwan and Brazil--were staggering and caught up in the epidemic of the melt down. One country in particular, Iceland, which had taken a much riskier path, went bankrupt. The global crisis was indeed *Made in America*, despite imitators and those that followed its path. At its core it was a consumer binge on imported goods by the class of superrich who invented nothing and built nothing except for intricate chains of paper that people mistook for wealth.

Looking at the events from a tipping point perspective, the late spring of 2007 seems like a totally different era. The American financial markets were robust, consumer spending was continuing to grow, the market for investment grade credit was booming, and insurance premiums demanded for those who wanted to invest in riskier forms of debt were at an all-time low. Case in point, the S&P 500 jumped more than 9% just from March through May of 2007. One of the first contagiousness events came about in mid-June of 2007 occurred it was learned that two Bear Sterns mortgage hedge funds could not meet their margin calls. At that point, Moody's downgraded some of their subprime mortgage-based bonds. The fund sold some of its bonds to raise money, and the rest were just not salable at any price. This was the first time that subprime-related debt tumbled. While the experience was a wake-up call, financial analysts tried to remind the world that subprime mortgages were a small percentage of the overall financial market and that the problem had "been contained." This was the one of the first contagiousness *living stories* carried in the media, and it became the lead story and propagated (stickiness) throughout all of the media forms of distribution networks.

However, the contagiousness started to pop up all around the world related to subprime related funds, i.e. a 9 million dollar London hedge fund closed its door, there was a run on the big London mortgage lender, German and Swiss banks announced large write-offs, and in August of 2007, the Federal Reserve and the European Central Bank began to flood their economies with money. It was now a global problem and the media was all over it in huge proportions. What followed were additional revelations from big banks, especially Citigroup, announced they held hundreds of billions of long-term loans and mysterious off-balance-sheet entities called "SIV's" that they had financed in the short-term commercial paper market. The shock of these kinds of disclosures brought interbank lending to a screeching halt. In addition, other banks revealed they were holding billions in bridge loan commitments to finance highly leveraged private equity company buyouts.

The stickiness continued as the Federal Reserve came to the rescue and aggressively cut the base short-term lending rate in September and another in October 2007. At that juncture, the Stock market and the credit markets "shuttered" back to life. The problem was that the loss that was disclosed in October was shocking enough- 20 billion in asset write-downs, at Merrill Lynch and Citigroup, but the problem was they had grossly underestimated their losses to a point that and November, analysts were told they just did not know the value of these instruments that were at the center of their problem. The October 2007 fiasco was the first of many events which would follow in subsequent quarters as losses at major banks kept spreading along with the uncertainty about the real value of the bank assets.

Following a series of contagious and stickiness events, CEOs were fired, Federal Reserve interventions were more extreme, and in December 2007, the Fed tried to re-liquefy banks, exchanging treasuries for some of the riskier credit instruments. Through the spring of 2008, the epidemic expanded and continued as the Federal Reserve increased the instruments that they would accept as collateral for the loans to companies, but the attempts to turn back this rising tipping point virus, as it was now infecting the financial systems, became less and less successful. As the impact was felt worldwide, nervous markets teetered on the edge of the impending tipping point.

The first big bank to topple was Bear Stearns in March of 2008. Like most of the large investment banks, its trading ledgers were highly leveraged and depended on short-term financing. And because doubts spread about its overall portfolio, lenders finally refused to roll over its credit lines. Ultimately, bankruptcy was avoided only by a forced merger with J.P. Morgan. The events continued. Countrywide Financial, the largest American mortgage lender had to be rescued by the Bank of America in May. And in August, Fannie Mae and Freddie Mac, the two giant mortgage lenders with some 5 trillion dollars in home loans, were taken over by the US government. Lehman Brothers, which was bigger than Bear Stearns, was in worse shape, and with no merger prospects, Lehman filed for bankruptcy on September 15, 2008. This was the beginning of the tipping point, or one dramatic moment, in the international financial crisis. That very same weekend, the insurance giant AIG, petitioned the Fed for a large temporary loan and was rejected like Lehman, yet it was not even a bank. AIG was a guarantor of 300 billion of American mortgage-backed CDOs held by European banks. If AIG failed, the European banks would be forced to write off some hundred and 50 billion in assets. The Federal Reserve had to reposture with a $85 billion loan, which grew to $123 billion after some very difficult negotiations. Next Merrill saw the handwriting on the wall and merged with Bank of America. And that same week Morgan Stanley and Goldman Sachs petitioned the Fed to convert to full Federal Reserve status, basically surrendering their freedom from regulation for the assurance of federal aid should they need it. As the crisis spread throughout the world markets, the US announced its $700 billion bailout plan. And at that point, all European governments entered the markets in force. By November of 2008, one would have been hard pressed to find a major bank on the continent that did not receive a large infusion of government cash.

In 2012 at the time of this writing, while there was a soft rebound after 2009 into 2010, the stock market continues to be fragile, and the credit and lending markets remain semi-catatonic, particurily in Europe. This tipping point case study and the analysis of what happened, is not just a banking epidemic, as we will discover. The issues go much deeper than that.

The Attributes

From the narrative above as background, the goal is to identify some parameters and actions and reactions of the various media sectors during a defined timeframe between 2007 and 2010 for the financial crisis and identify the potential relationships to these attributes. The intent here is to further detail the characteristics and the attributes with the type of output needed to analyze and answer the fundamental research questions. These represent the key events and issues that play a role in this global event, and the tipping point qualitative ratio analysis framework constructed for this case study. An review of the notation for relationships and attributes is in order.

For the purposes of organization, I have divided the case study into three (3) parts: Section one is the analysis of the attribute of contagiousness, and/or, the effects of the trend, that results in an epidemic of forces. This approach is subdivided further into the four (4) characteristics that qualifies *people, organizations, media impact* and *events* that occurred during the attribute and affected the ultimate outcome. Section two examines the stickiness attribute, analyzing the shifts in momentum, some seemingly started small, and ultimately lead to larger impacts. And in section three, I explore the effects of the dramatic moment characteristics, when the epidemic resulted in a fundamental and irreversible change in direction. It is the understanding of this final attribute that makes sense of the first two and perhaps permits the greatest insight into why this event happened the way it did.

Said another way, one way to measure and pinpoint the tipping point of the International Financial Crisis is to quantify the relative impact of the various issues and their importance and characteristics. The objective is to provide a sense of qualitative influence and pneumatic control as to how these various attributes and characteristics led to the ultimate outcome.

Clearly, one can interpret these characteristics and attributes from many perspectives; however, the intent of our tipping point qualitative ratio analysis framework is to define where and when the one dramatic event occurred during the International Financial Crisis and then compare this to our other two case studies for similar analysis. This method for analyzing these attributes will be to simply look at the sequence of events in a chronological manner and observe the way the International Financial Crisis developed, how the various media sectors played their role and ultimately contributed to the worst global financial meltdown since the 1930s.

Section 4.1 Contagiousness Attributes (C)

There are those on Wall Street, PhDs, called *Quants*, who believe the stock market should behave in the same way as physical phenomena (like mortality statistics). They believe, for example, that death rates are the predictable function of a limited and stable set of factors and tend to follow what statisticians call a normal distribution, a bell curve. The economist Eugene Fama pointed out that stock prices rarely made big jumps or what he called a *movement five standard deviations from the mean*, as that probability, according to Fama, could occur once every seven thousand years.[153] But in fact they occur every three or four years. Investors react without any statistical orderliness. They change their minds. They do stupid things. They copy one another. And when the media is influencing what they know about the events around them, they panic.

Most of the discussions in the media in the early goings of the International Financial Crisis were about the toll that the big Wall Street banks were taking in the stock market. Along with the presidential campaign, the financial crisis seemed to be running a race for which issue was to be carried by the media as their lead story. Unfortunately (for all of us), the financial meltdown was a story so large and so complicated and had such impact, it affected the entire world.

While the initial discussions and media attention were about the vulnerabilities of the Wall Street banks and whether not the government should step in and try to resurrect these banks for the sake of the economy, it was only a matter of time, like dominoes, the big banking institutions, insurance giants, and the large corporations started to feel the pressure as they were all beginning to shoulder incredible debts with no real solutions. Almost daily, there were media stories featuring issues about the economy, the Wall Street banks, housing starts, the Dow and the way it was losing points, the gas prices, and foreclosure rates, and these only seemed to be increasing in frequency at the same time unemployment began to skyrocket. Everything in the early stages of the crisis, as it was presented, seemed to paint a picture that this was a limited and contained problem and would not spread to the entire US market, nor would it reach the entire global

153 Paul KRUGMAN, "How Did Economists Get it so Wrong?" *New York Times*, September 2, 2009. Retrieved from http://www.nytimes.com/2009/09/06/magazine/06Economic-t.html?pagewanted=all

economy. As we know in retrospect, this was not to be the case. But before I really look at how the media played its role during 2007-2010, my first focus relative to the contagiousness attribute is on a number of fundamental issues that assured that the US economy was on a path for a meltdown. The financial crisis had at least three (3) primary ingredients that were found throughout the attributes. These related to: – 1. loss of business vision, 2. demographic shifts, and, 3. gross economic mismanagement. We find these when we look at the each of the characteristics of people, organizations, media impact and the ultimate events of the crisis.

Section 4.1.1 People

Up until 1970, the United States possessed the most formidable array of industrial power ever seen. Then Americans backed off. As business administration migrated into graduate schools, executive ranks drifted farther and farther from the shop floor. The more important developments and analytical techniques for optimizing workflow and any new formulas could be completed without ever going near a factory. By 1980, American manufacturing and their control of the machine tool industry and the steel and textile industries were in catastrophic shape. There were attempts to react to the foreign competition onslaught, but it only revealed how incompetent the American companies had become. Another issue to consider is that people from the baby boom generation reached their 20s during the 1970s. What this amounted to was a huge influx of unskilled, untrained workers, which reduced productivity and placed a resultant downward pressure on wages. In contrast, 18 to 24-year-olds represented 4.3% of the population in 1960, and 5.6% of the population in 1970, but the total numbers of 18 to 24-year-olds jumped by 50%, from 7.6 million to 11.4 million in 1970. Sometime between then and the mid-1950s, the whole system began tipping towards an imbalance.

Baby boomers and Politicians

As the baby boomers had reached school age, the 60s brought a huge spike in college-age enrollments, and so began the culture wars that would mark the country's politics for years to come. The 60s ended sometime in 1971, about the time when Nixon took office in 1969, and the economy was already careening in the direction of its first economic crisis, and it was thought it was as bad as it could possibly get then.

By 1970, Nixon's second year in office, growth plunged to near zero while inflation was scraping by at 6%, and from the period 1971 to 1979, OPEC tripled their oil prices. The 1971 wage and price "90 day freeze" as it was originally called, lasted for three years. The decline of American tentativeness continued, and as an example, in 1977, the automaker Chrysler avoided bankruptcy only with the aid of last-minute government loans. Mix in social conservatism and the reaction of the traditional liberals, and it was clear that the rules of economics were not working quite the way they used to. Leaping forward to the last days of the Carter administration rarely had the American prestige and pride sunk so low. The American embassy in Iran was overtaken and 66 Americans were held hostage, with 14 released in the first few weeks, and the remaining 52 were held for 444 days. At that time the foreign policy was in shambles, and the economy was a mess as by 1980 inflation hit 13.5%. And by the end of Ronald Reagan's election in 1980, liberalism was dead, and the free market was getting to run wild. The review of the history of events at this stage is important context, as these times fostered the birth and rearing of the organizations that were developed and contributed to the contagiousness attribute of the financial crisis of 2007 through 2010. According to Gladwell, during this period America produced an oversupply of connectors, mavens, and salespersons who fed the hunger for continued economic growth and the environment that led to the stickiness attribute that follows.

Section 4.1.2 Organizations

From an economic point of view, a bank is a place where people put their cash so that it will be cared for, and at the same time, the banks are chartered with investing the money in assets that can't be liquidated without complicated maneuvers. So the banks needed to be highly regulated, and they were required to hold reserves and maintain substantial capital and pay into the deposit insurance system. In early 2008 the banks' deregulation actually promoted the contagiousness. At that time, the auction rate security system that contained 40 billion USD at its peak collapsed. This was parallel to the panic of 1907 in which banks experienced a similar collapse. Other bank-like institutions seemed to offer a better deal since they were able to operate outside the regulatory system when they got into trouble. What happened to the auction rate security phase was nothing more than a contagious series of bank runs. Investors and institutions, fearful of these unregulated instruments, started to pull out their funds, and it became the epicenter of the financial crisis. In June of 2008, Timothy Geithner, then president of the New York Federal Reserve Bank, tried to explain why the housing bubble had done as much financial damage as it did. Not realizing at the time was that the worst aspects of the crisis had yet to come. Geithner attributed the problem to *just* the housing bubble; however, it was, in fact, a whole range of badly designed financial arrangements. It was not just the auction rate securities that were developed by Lehman, for example, which he characterized as being non-banking financial system instruments and outside the regulatory arena. He later admitted that these financial arrangements were nonetheless banking functions that were affecting the security of the entire system. Auction rate securities had collapsed, asset-backed commercial paper had been reduced, and two of the five major investment banks had failed, with another merging with a conventional bank, and so the living story started to unfold.

Wall Street

Looking back, one of Reagan's first official acts upon assuming the presidency in 1981 was to eliminate the last remains of oil price controls. By the fall of that year, energy prices were in free fall. The American public reaction to the prices was astonishing, as consumers reduced optional driving and began the shift towards more fuel-efficient cars. Houses and household appliances, office buildings, and manufacturing plants were redesigned for greater energy efficiency. Oil production increased in fields that were once thought beyond viable. Reagan could be described as a man of simple and consistent principles. Case in point, take the clarity and determination of his anti-Soviet posturing that eventually led to the end of that regime. He also strongly believed in the core principles of the Chicago School–lower taxes, free markets, and minimal regulation. Two interesting developments were the major economic media stories of the 1980s: *leveraged buyouts* (LBOs) and the savings and loan crisis. The *LBO* lasted from 1982 to 1989. Simplified, it amounted to the underperforming, top-heavy conglomerates that were failing to measure up against foreign competition being bought up, scaled down, and refocused. Investors, on the other hand, took this as a signal in 1986, as the returns on these first waves of deals were so spectacular that more and more money began chasing these deals, and along with them the structures got more complicated, with bond piled on bond. Something called *PIKs* or *payment in kind* developed, whereas, if you missed a payment, the creditor was just given more bonds. (It's interesting that *PIK's* reappeared again in 2007 with the private equity takeovers).

This deal frenzy history of time lasted from 1986 to 1989 up until the spectacular bidding war for United Airlines in the summer of 1989, and then suddenly the banks started to refuse financing. Long-awaited deals in the *LBO* pipeline were brought to a screeching halt. Looking back, the bankers and the fund managers had already pocketed 80 million in fees and the people whom they represented, hundreds of millions more. The crisis in the savings and loan industry was a demonstration of the importance of regulatory oversight of lending institutions in modern financial markets. By the second half of the *LBO* boom, the end of the savings and loan fiasco had demonstrated the dangers of loose financial market regulation. In the markets, the contagiousness of the scent of money led the Wall Street bankers, the law firms, and the accounting firms into multimillion dollar settlements and penalties.

The entire economic profession was forecasting a major global recession when Clinton assumed the presidency, but Clinton inadvertently got his boom, a.k.a., the dotcom bubble. Before that time, in the mid-1990s, few people had even heard of the World Wide Web or the Internet before a startup company called *Netscape* issued its first stock in August of 1995. After that the tech stock boom was on. Looking back, the dotcom bubble was anchored in real technological developments The Internet revolution was as important as the railroad revolution parallel to the industrial age. However, the 1990's boom was rooted in the confluence of much broader contagious forces that laid the groundwork for the next attribute of stickiness. Baby boomers, the generation from the 1950s, who were now entering their 40s and 50s: their greatest period of work and output, and savings. Because 40 years of government investment was behind implementing the Internet, including most of its core technologies, and because it was built into a working worldwide system, it essentially shifted the strategy from an *organizational model from government* to a *private sector control model* in 1995. This had both characteristics of contagiousness and stickiness and became essential when one looks at the significant instruments and trading tools that were brought into high level of development in the 1980s and 1990s. These essential technologies created the bubble of the 2000's and later provided a broad platform of misuse and mismanagement by the beginning of the financial crisis in 2007.

Section 4.1.3 Media

The crucial media development of the financial crisis and thereby, a fundamental contagiousness attribute is best characterized by what can be termed a *living story*. In many ways and from many different perspectives, the 2007- 2010 International Financial Crisis could best be described in the media as a living story that was always evolving and contained a number of components to keep the audience focused on the media. The international financial crisis was a media living story, or stated another way, *a witch hunt for the villains*. The list is endless with regard to accusations as to why the problems developed and who created them. A popular notion that came from the right was that the Community Reinvestment Act, which forced banks to lend to minority homeowners, which was passed in 1977, was the culprit. The conservatives liked to blame Freddie Mac and Fannie Mae, citing that these government sponsored lenders had pioneered securitization of the housing bubble and created the fragility in the financial system. On the left, it was popular to blame deregulation for the crisis, specifically on the 1999 repeal of the Glass-Stegall Act, which allowed commercial banks to get in the investment banking business and inherently take on more risks. This contagiousness characteristic became a factor when things started to move in the wrong direction, as the risk-taking increased by institutions that were never regulated in the first place.

On July 19, 2007, the Dow Jones industrial average rose above 14,000 for the very first time. The Bush administration asserted that the economy's performance was continuing to be strong, flexible, and dynamic. And the housing market, which was not yet showed signs of being affected by the subprime market issues, as the impacts were being "largely contained", as stated by then Treasury Secretary Henry Paulson during his August 1, 2007 speech in Beijing.[154]

However, on August 9, 2007 the French bank BNP Paribas, suspended withdrawals from three of its funds, and the financial crisis was reaching across the ocean to Europe. This financial crisis was like nothing ever experienced in history, parallel forces with the bursting of the real estate bubble -comparable to what happened in Japan in the late 1980s, and the wave of bank runs -comparable to those of the early 1930s, meant the crisis was well on its way towards a tipping point. How did this incredible financial

154 US Treasury Secretary Henry Paulson, Beijing, China, August 1, 2007

crisis occur and how was this *living story* evolving in the media?

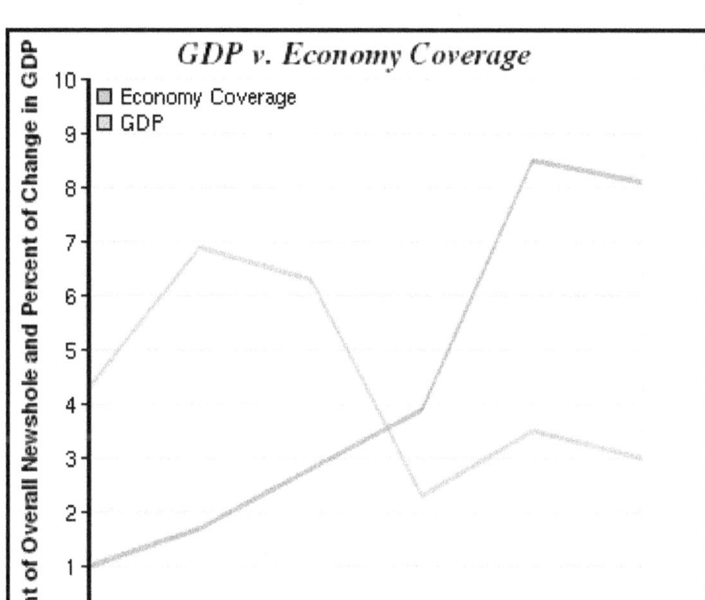

Living Story

The gravest economic crisis since the Great Depression was covered in the media largely from the top down, told primarily from the perspective of the Obama Administration and big business. It has reflected the voices and ideas of people in institutions more than those of everyday Americans.

Three top *living stories* dominated the media:

- efforts to help revive the banking sector
- battle over the stimulus package
- struggles of the U.S. auto industry

News about the banking industry and the government bailout was the most popular topic and accounted for 15% of the news. The Obama Administration's stimulus package was next (14%), and the U.S. automobile industry's financial troubles and plant closures was third, filling 9% of the media economic narrative. Together, these accounted for nearly 40% of the economic media coverage from February 1 through August 31, 2009. Other topics related to the crisis were covered much less. As an example, reporting of retail sales, food prices, the impact of the crisis on Social Security and Medicare, and its effect on education and the implications for health care combined only accounted for just over 2% of all the media economic coverage.[155]

In general, the topics that got heavier coverage were those that involved institutions. In February 2009, the coverage of the banking industry was driven by Treasury Secretary Timothy Geithner's program for distributing the remaining TARP funds (the program was started during the Bush Administration). And the announcement of the Public-Private Investment Program in March, with the results of bank stress tests covered in May and reactions by some TARP recipients to pay back the government loans.

Media attention on the stimulus package was focused on the heated debate in Congress over its passage. In February alone, stimulus coverage commanded 36% of all economic news, reflecting the effect and magnitude of the $787 billion program and also the congressional partisan battle in the U.S. Senate.

Media coverage of the auto industry often involved the issue of whether the government should be involved in taking over large segments of the troubled sector and whether it should let American automakers fail. Interestingly, the attention devoted to labor issues and worker layoffs in the car industry barely registered in the coverage. As the big three topics of banking, stimulus, and automobile dominated, there was less attention devoted to issues that might have had as much, and in some cases more, direct and immediate impact on citizens.

Perhaps no problem was more contributing to the media contagiousness than the housing market, which encompassed the sub-prime lending crisis, the home foreclosure epidemic, and the dramatic decrease in home values. U.S. home sales stood at a 12-year low in February 2009, the situation worsened as foreclosures in April rose 32% (compared with the same month a year before), and by June, home prices had declined 21% from

155 "Covering the Great Recession: How the Media Have Depicted the Economic Crisis," *Pew Research Center, Project for Excellence in Journalism*, October 5, 2009. Retrieved from http://pewresearch.org/pubs/1365/great-recession-media-coverage-driven-by-government-officials-and-business

one year earlier. Housing accounted for 8% of the total economic news, making it the no. 5 topic, in February.

Another media issue for many Americans was unemployment, as from February through August, the jobless rate climbed from 8.1% to 9.7%, the highest in more than a quarter century.

In February and March, when the fight over the stimulus package and the controversy over the TARP program were at their height, fully 56% of the economy-related news stories were triggered by a government entity such as the White House, Congress, a federal agency or a state government. That means more than half of the economy-focused stories during that time were reported as a *direct* result of some government action or statement.

This sheds some light on the questions of how aggressive and proactive the media itself was in promoting the economy story and contagiousness. Overall, about one-fifth of the economic stories during this same period were *triggered* (defined as origin) primarily by the initiative of journalists themselves. However, the degree of media *enterprise,* varied notably depending on the topic—and the bigger topics tended to have less press enterprise while the smaller ones had more. When it came to the big economic living stories, the media were more reactive. Coverage of the banking sector problems, for instance, press enterprise and investigations triggered only 14% of stories and on stimulus coverage 15%. The media were more proactive in monitoring the housing crisis (23%) and quite aggressive when it came to covering the unemployment picture, with press enterprise and investigation accounting for 35%. And in one significant story, the crisis's impact on ordinary citizens, press *enterprise* proved to be the (origin) for more than half (54%) of the stories. In short, when the coverage was heavily institutional and based on government action, the stories were coming *at* the press. And there was a delay factor. To cover the lives of ordinary people, journalists had to go out and find the stories for themselves and it resulted in more timely and immediate media accounts.

One example, a March 12 story in the *Kansas City Star* of a man who stole a bank's overnight deposit box in an economically hard-hit county in Southwest Missouri only to return the following night and give back that part of the loot that belonged to regular citizens. Illustrated some unorthodox ways in which the recession was affecting crime. The story told how the local sheriff was quoted saying the robber apparently could not bring himself to keep the "little people's money."[156]

This may reflect the fact that certain media groups and individuals who might otherwise play a role on media issues ranging from the Iraq war to the health care debate, could not organize and cover as aggressively on an issue as complex and multifaceted as the financial crisis.

Section 4.1.4 Events

The crisis of the *living story* contagiousness rapidly developed and spread into global economic shock, resulting in bank failures, rapid declines in stock indexes, and significant reductions in the market value of equities and commodities. Derivatives such as credit default swaps (CDS) also increased, strengthening the linkage between large financial institutions and their exposure. Moreover, necessitating the de-leveraging of financial institutions, whereby assets were sold a severe discounts to pay back obligations that could not be refinanced in tight credit markets, further accelerating the contagiousness of the liquidity crisis and resulting in a decrease in international trade.[157]

National ministers of finance, central bank directors and world political leaders, attempted to coordinate their efforts to calm global fears, but the contagiousness continued as media tried to report on the developing story. The currency crisis continued as investors sought safe havens transferring vast capital resources into stronger currencies such as the yen, the dollar, and the Swiss franc, ultimately leading many emerging nation economies to request aid from the International Monetary Fund. [158]

---

156 Ibid.

157 "Multinational Arrangements," World Academy Online, June 2009. Retrieved from http://worldacademyonline.com/article/33/460/multinational_arrangements.html

158 Mark LANDER, "West is in Talks on Credit to Aid Poorer Nations," *New York Times*, October 24, 2008. Retrieved from http://www.nytimes.com/2008/10/24/business/worldbusiness/24iht-24emerge.17215442.html?pagewanted=all; Martin FACKLER, "Trouble Without Borders," *New York Times*, October 23, 2008. Retrieved from http://query.nytimes.com/gst/fullpage.html?res=9B00E2DC103FF937A15753C1A96E9C8B63&ref=martinfackler

Banking

A number of media commentators contributed during this time that if the liquidity crisis continued, there could be an extended recession or perhaps worse, as the mounting development of the crisis created fears of a total global economic collapse. This financial crisis eventually yielded the biggest banking shakeout since the savings-and-loan meltdown.[159] Key bank leaders had trouble realizing the extent of the crisis and further fueled the media contagiousness by their own disclosures. For example, the investment bank UBS stated on October 6, 2008, "We would see a clear global recession with recovery unlikely for at least two years"[160]. Three days later UBS economists announced that the "beginning of the end" of the crisis, with the world starting to make the necessary actions to fix the crisis: with large scale systematic capital injections by governments and interest rate reductions to help borrowers in the United Kingdom. UBS emphasized the United States needed to implement similar systemic injections. UBS then later emphasized that in economic terms "the worst is still to come".[161] UBS quantified their expected recession durations on October 16, 2008: "The Euro zone's would last two quarters, the United States' would last three quarters, and the United Kingdom's would last four quarters."[162] At the end of October UBS revised its outlook downwards: "the forthcoming recession would be the worst since the Reagan recession of 1981 and 1982 with negative 2009 growth for the U.S., Euro zone, UK and Canada; very limited recovery in 2010; but not as bad as the Great Depression". [163]

Consumer banking trends and GDP worldwide was now being influenced by the media coverage. A Brookings Institution report in June 2009, stated that U.S. accounted for more than a third of the growth in global consumption between 2000 and 2007. "The US economy has been spending too much and borrowing too much for years and the rest of the world depended on the U.S. consumer as a source of global demand." With a recession in the U.S. and the increased savings rate of U.S. consumers, declines in growth elsewhere have been dramatic. For the first quarter of 2009, the annualized rate of decline in GDP was 14.4% in Germany, 15.2% in Ja-

159 Suresh GOEL, *Crisis Management: Master the Skills to Prevent Disasters*, Global India Publications, New Delhi, India, p. 183.

160 *Ibid*, p. 183

161 *Ibid.*, p. 183.

162 *Ibid.*, p. 183.

163 *Ibid.*, p. 183.

pan, 7.4% in the UK, 18% in Latvia, 9.8% in the Euro area and 21.5% for Mexico.[164]

By March 2009, the Arab world had lost $3 trillion due to the crisis.[165] In April 2009, unemployment in the Arab world was said to be a time bomb.[166] In May 2009, the United Nations reported a drop in foreign investment in Middle-Eastern economies due to a slower rise in demand for oil.[167] In June 2009, the World Bank predicted a tough year for Arab states.[168] In September 2009, Arab banks reported losses of nearly $4 billion since the global financial crisis onset.[169]

U.S.

Key US contagiousness financial indicators during this time - Real gross domestic product, the output of goods and services produced by labor and property located in the United States, decreased at an annual rate of approximately 6 percent in the fourth quarter of 2008 and first quarter of 2009, versus activity in the year-ago periods.[170] The U.S. unemployment rate increased to 10.2% by October 2009, the highest rate since 1983 and roughly twice the pre-crisis rate. The average hours per work week declined to 33, the lowest level since the government began collecting the data in 1964.[171]

---

164 Martin Neil BAILY and Douglas J. ELLIOT, "The U.S. Financial and Economic Crisis: Where Does It Stand and Where Do We Go From Here?," *Initiative on Business and Public Policy at Brookings*, June 2009. Retrieved from http://www.brookings.edu/papers/2009/0615_economic_crisis_baily_elliott.aspx

165 Marian NASTASE, Alina Stefania CRETU, and Roberta STANEF, "Effects of Global Financial Crisis," *Review of International Comparative Management*, 10, 2009, p. 695. Retrieved from www.rmci.ase.ro/no10vol4/Vol10_No4_Article9.pdf

166 *Ibid.*, p. 695.

167 Sahar BAHMANI, "Understanding the Current Recession and Its Global Impact," *Gulf Coast Economics Association, 2009 Conference Proceedings*, Savannah Georgia, November 5, 2009, p. 11. Retrieved from http://gulfcoastecon.org/63312/62060.html

168 *Ibid.*, p. 11.

169 Marian NASTASE, Alina Stefania CRETU, and Roberta STANEF, "Effects of Global Financial Crisis," *op. cit.*, p. 695.

170 "United States GDP Growth Rate," Trading Economics. Retrieved from http://www.tradingeconomics.com/united-states/gdp-growth

171 Mortimer ZUCKERMAN, "The Economy Is Even Worse Than You Think," *Wall Street Journal Opinion section*, July 14, 2009. Retrieved from http://online.wsj.com/article/SB124753066246235811.html

Europe

Following the crisis in Europe, on November 3, 2008, the EU-commission in Brussels announced a prediction for 2009 of an extremely weak growth of GDP, by 0.1 percent, for the countries of the Euro zone (France, Germany, Italy, etc.) and even negative number for the UK (-1.0 percent), Ireland and Spain.[172] On November 6, the IMF at Washington, D.C., launched numbers predicting a worldwide recession by -0.3 percent for 2009 averaged over the developed economies.[173] On the same day, the Bank of England and the Central Bank for the Euro zone, respectively, announced reducing their interest rates from 4.5 percent down to three percent, and from 3.75 percent down to 3.25 percent.[174] As a result, beginning in November 2008, several countries launched significant bailout packages for their economies.

US Reserve

The U.S. Federal Reserve Open Market Committee released a report in June 2009 stating:

"...the pace of economic contraction is slowing. Conditions in financial markets have generally improved in recent months. Household spending has shown further signs of stabilizing but remains constrained by ongoing job losses, lower housing wealth, and tight credit. Businesses are cutting back on fixed investment and staffing but appear to be making progress in bringing inventory stocks into better alignment with sales. Although economic activity is likely to remain weak for a time, the Committee continues to anticipate that policy actions to stabilize financial markets and institutions, fiscal and monetary stimulus, and market forces will contribute to a gradual resumption of sustainable economic growth in a context of price stability."[175]

Economic projections from the Federal Reserve and Reserve Bank Presidents included a return to typical growth levels (GDP) of 2-3% in 2010; an

172 Suresh GOEL, Crisis Management: Master the Skills to Prevent Disasters, op. cit., p. 185.

173 *Ibid.*, p. 185.

174 *Ibid.*, p. 185.

175 "Minutes of the Federal Open Market Committee," Board of Governors of the Federal Reserve System, June 23-24, 2009, Washington D.C. Retrieved from http://www.federalreserve.gov/monetarypolicy/fomcminutes20090624.htm

unemployment plateau in 2009 and 2010 around 10% with moderation in 2011; and inflation to remain at atypical levels around 1-2%.[176]

What is interesting is to look at these positions in context of the contagiousness attribute and how the media dealt with the issues and the impact on the economies.

Lower interest rates encourage borrowing. From 2000 to 2003, the Federal Reserve lowered the federal funds rate target from 6.5% to 1.0%.[177] This was done to soften the effects of the collapse of the dot-com bubble and of the September 2001 terrorist attacks, and to combat the perceived risk of deflation.[178]

Additional downward pressure on interest rates was created by the USA's high and rising current account (trade) deficit, which peaked along with the housing bubble in 2006. Ben Bernanke explained how trade deficits required the U.S. to borrow money from abroad, which bid up bond prices and lowered interest rates.[179]

Ben Bernanke, would explained in testimonies before congress, that between 1996 and 2004, the USA account deficit had increased by $650 billion, from 1.5% to 5.8% of GDP. Financing these deficits resulted in the US borrow huge sums from abroad, much of it from countries running trade surpluses, consisting of emerging economies in Asia and the major oil-exporting nations. The balance of payments required that if a country (such as the US) was running a account deficit it would also have a capital account surplus of the same amount, i.e. in the form of investments. Hence, the growing amounts of foreign funds (capital) that flowed into the US

---

176 Nick TIMRAOS and Chad BRAY, "SEC Brings Crisis-Era Suits," Wall Street Journal, December 17, 2011. Retrieved from http://online.wsj.com/article/SB1000142405297020373330457710231095578078 8.html

177 "Open Market Operations," Board of Governors of the Federal Reserve System, January 26, 2010. Retrieved from http://www.federalreserve.gov/monetarypolicy/openmarket.htm

178 Retrieved from http://online.wsj.com/public/page/news-opinion-commentary.html

179 Ben S. BERNANKE, "The Global Savings Glut and the U.S. Current Account Deficit," Remarks by Governor Ben S. Bernanke at the Homer Jones Lecture, St. Louis, Missouri, March 10, 2005. Retrieved from http://www.federalreserve.gov/boarddocs/speeches/2005/20050414/default.htm

financing its imports. This inflated the demand for various types of financial assets, augmenting the prices of these assets and conversely lowering interest rates. Foreign investors had funds to lend, primarily because they had very high personal savings rates (as high as 40% in China), or because of high oil prices. The Fed Chairman Bernanke referred to this as a "saving glut."[180]. Foreign governments also supplied funds by buying US Treasury bonds and attempted to avoid the direct impact of the crisis. US consumers used funds, essentially lent by foreigners, to finance consumption or to "bid up" the prices of housing and other financial assets. Financial institutions, in turn, used the consumer loans and packaged and invested in foreign funds with mortgage-backed securities (MBS).[181]

After which, the Federal Reserve funds rate rose significantly between July 2004 and July 2006[182] and contributed to an increase in the 1-year and 5-year adjustable-rate mortgages (ARM) , resulting in ARM interest rate increases more expensive for homeowners.[183] This also contributed to the deflating of the housing bubble, as asset prices move inversely to interest rates and it became more and more riskier to speculate in housing.[184] USA housing and financial assets dramatically declined in value after the housing bubble burst.[185]

The US Housing boom began to deflate in the fall of 2005 as prices rose to a point where purchasing a new home became out of reach for many Americans, even when the no down payment and *teaser* rate loans and sales of new homes began to trail off. Housing prices continued to rise for a while

180 Ibid.

181 Roger C. ALTMAN, "The Great Crash, 2008, A Geopolitical Setback for the West," *Foreign Affairs*, January/February 2009. Retrieved from http://www.foreignaffairs.com/articles/63714/roger-c-altman/the-great-crash-2008

182 Suresh GOEL, Crisis Management: Master the Skills to Prevent Disasters, op. cit., p. 71.

183 *Ibid.*, p. 71.

184 Sara MAX, "The Bubble Question, How Will Rising Interest Rates Affect Housing Prices?" *CNN Money*, July 27, 2004. Retrieved from http://money.cnn.com/2004/07/13/real_estate/buying_selling/risingrates/; Peter COY, Rich MILLER, Lauren YOUNG, and Christopher PALMERI, "Is a Housing Bubble About to Burst?" *Bloomberg Businessweek*, July 19, 2004. Retrieved from http://www.businessweek.com/magazine/content/04_29/b3892064_mz011.htm

185 Roger C. ALTMAN, "The Great Crash, 2008, A Geopolitical Setback for the West," *op. cit.*

as housing, like stocks, continued to lag behind in the lifecycle as relates to the prior year when it comes to trends as to whether prices were actually going to go up and sales are going to go down. By the late spring of 2006, the market weakness was starting to be evident. Prices began dropping then with increasing speed. By the second quarter 2007, according to the widely used *Case-Shiller Home Price Index*, prices were only down 3% from a peak a year earlier, and the course of the next year, they would fall another 15%, and in some regions, which had experienced the largest gains, like coastal Florida and California, the declines of course, were much larger up to 30 and 50%.[186] Lenders didn't really care if a borrower could make the mortgage payments. As long as the home prices kept rising, borrowers could always refinance or pay off their mortgage by selling the house. As soon as the home prices went the other direction, and houses became harder to market and sell, default rates began rising. Foreclosures impacted both the homeowner and the lender. As there was no way to go back to the bank to renegotiate these subprime loans because the loan originators had quickly sold the loans to financial institutions, which in turn, had divided them up into pools of mortgages into what is called collateral debt obligations, or *CDOs*, and then sold to investors. With this structure, there were too many legal obstacles, and there was no way to restructure the debts.

Another attribute of contagiousness in this living story came early in 2007, as the trouble with the subprime loans became apparent. The collateral debt obligations created some serious losses around February 2007 and the prices of shares had plunged. This began the contagiousness when it unraveled with the subprime lending. Without the financing, housing demand reacted and worsened the slump. As late as October 2007, many investors still believed that the senior shares of the *CDOs* were still well-protected, although eventually it became clear that nothing related to housing was a safe haven.

The size of the housing bubble was enormous, some estimated that housing had been overvalued more than 50% by the summer of 2006.[187] Simply stated, that meant that prices would have to fall by at least a third.

---

186 Vikas BAJAJ, "Home Prices fall for 10th Straight Month," *New York Times*, December 26, 2007. Retrieved from http://www.nytimes.com/2007/12/26/business/27home-web.html

187 Paul KRUGMAN, *The Return of Depression Economics and the Crisis of 2008*, New York, WW Norton, 2009, pp. 168–169.

In Miami, Florida, for example, home prices appeared twice as high as the fundamentals could justify, and in these areas they would fall by 50% or more.[188] What this meant was that anyone who bought a house during the peak bubble years was going to be in debt with the mortgage worth more than the house. In 2009, there were 12 million American homeowners with negative equity, and these homeowners were prime candidates for default.[189]

The contagiousness severity of a housing bust began to sink in, and it became clear that the lenders would lose a lot of money and so would the investors who bought these mortgage-backed securities. At the end of the housing bubble, it is estimated that the bust wiped out about US$8 trillion in wealth, and around US$7 trillion was in losses to homeowners and about 1 trillion in losses to investors.[190]

The key characteristic of the International Financial Crisis was the United States housing bubble, which peaked in approximately 2005–2006. This event became part of contagiousness (and later stickiness) that sent serious financial tremors into the markets in the first half of 2007 as late as early August, even though some people who felt that the housing slump and the subprime loans were contained, the stickiness had begun, as we will see in our next section.

Section 4.2 Stickiness Attributes (S):

The stickiness characteristics of the International Financial Crisis 2007-2010 that led to this tipping point are characterized by the application of this study methodology and results that are correlated with available media influence. In retrospect, this tipping point could never have been avoided. Miscalculated systems and methods developed for financial instruments, the institutions and the individuals that employed them, which, I would argue, largely influenced by the media continued the progression to the tipping point. We begin by analyzing stickiness attribute characteristic of people.

---

188 *Ibid.*, pp. 168–169.
189 *Ibid.*, pp. 168–169.
190 Ibid.

Section 4.2.1 People

"The function of the federal reserve is to take away the punch bowl just as a party is getting good," stated William Martin, who served as the chairman of the Federal Reserve for 18 years, spanning presidential administrations from Truman through Nixon.[191] Martin probably more than anyone established the standard definition of the Fed's role as "leaning against the wind, easing credit in hard times and tightening it before expansion gets frothy."[192]

From a historical perspective, examining the interest rate actions of the Alan Greenspan, chairman of the (FOMC) Federal Open Market Committee and real economic growth showed two things. The first was that before 9/11, the interest on Federal Reserve fund rate was already down to 3.5%, and after the attack, it went down quickly in steps to 1.75% and was held there through most of 2002. Economic growth was dismal in the first half of 2001 and recovered to a respectable, if somewhat anemic, rate of 2.4% during the first three quarters of 2002.[193] Second, in November 2002, amid distinct signs that the economy was sharply slowing, the Federal Reserve made a very aggressive half point cut in the funds rate, taking it down to 1.25%.[194] Growth again stayed sluggish in the last quarter of 2002 and in the first quarter of 2003, but rebounded strongly in the next quarter, in part due to the Bush tax cuts and the surge in Iraqi-related spending. At the FOMC meeting at the end of that quarter, the committee imposed yet another cut in the funds rate to only 1% the lowest since 1954. The committee stayed with a 1% fund rate for full year before starting a measured series of quarter-point fund rate increases and finally leveled out at 5.25% in early 2006. Looking back at Martin's strategy, it would appear that the FOMC chose to keep refilling the punch bowl until it was sure the party was really underway. But what really happened during this period was the

191 Gregory MANKIW, "How to Avoid Recession? Let the Fed Work," *New York Times*, December 23, 2007. Retrieved from http://www.nytimes.com/2007/12/23/business/23view.html?ex=1356066000&en=3337604c8708710a&ei=5090&partner=rssuserland&emc=rss

192 Richard LAMBERT, "Crashes, Bangs & Wallops," *Financial Times*, July 19, 2008. Retrieved from http://www.ft.com/cms/s/0/7173bb6a-552a-11dd-ae9c-000077b07658.html#axzz1jmaY8v3M

193 Charles R. MORRIS, The Two Trillion Dollar Meltdown: Easy Money, High Rollers, and the Great Crash, New York, PublicAffairs, 2008.

194 Ibid.

ignorance of the signs of rampant inflation in the price of assets, especially houses, and bonds of all kinds. Economists have come up with a multitude of reasons why central banks did not concern themselves specifically with asset prices in their sharp rise. Looking back, common sense demanded some intervention and regulation of the prices of a major asset class such as housing as it was soaring beyond all reason.[195]

In 2004, for example, *The Economist* magazine worried that the global financial system..."has become a giant money press and America's easy money policy had spilled beyond its borders..."[196] –this flood of global liquidity flowed into share prices and houses assets around the world, creating a series of asset price bubbles."[197] What is interesting is the European Central Bank in the spring of 2005 quietly criticized the asset price bubbles and monetary policy of the United States, but did little to stop the Federal Reserve strategy.

Alan Greenspan

A key contagiousness person during this time was Alan Greenspan. He created something called the Alan Greenspan "*Put*," defined as, no matter what goes wrong in the US economy, the Federal Reserve would come to the rescue by creating enough cheap money to buy everybody out of their troubles. From 2000 until mid-2005, the United States of America experienced a housing boom, part of a global real estate bubble that was pronounced the greatest in history. The market values of homes in many regions grew by more than 50%, and there was a frenzy of new construction. Merrill Lynch, one of Wall Street's leading banks at the time, estimated that about half of all American GDP growth in the first half of 2005 was housing related, either directly through homebuilding and housing-related purchases like new furniture, or indirectly by spending enabled by refinancing cash flows.

American Property Owners and Borrowers

Most Americans had considered their houses a reliable source of savings because their houses were usually their only highly leveraged asset. As a typical approach, people would buy 100,000 USD house, put down 20%,

---

195 Ibid.

196 "The Disappearing Dollar," *The Economist*, December 2, 2004. Retrieved from http://www.economist.com/node/3446249

197 Ibid.

and finance the rest with the conventional fixed-rate mortgage for 25 years. At 2% inflation, the house would be worth 168,000 by that time they would own it free and clear. This translated into a compound annual return on initial equity of almost 9%, and for most American families, this was the best investment choice they could ever make. But between 2000 and 2005, with values jumping 50%, changed many peoples perspectives. I.e. the stickiness trend became: buy a 200,000 USD house with 90% financing, which at the time was available to anyone, and turn around and sell it for 300,000 USD five years later, you would quintuple the initial investment equity, then turn around and put down another 10% down payment on a 500,000 USD home and wait for it to happen again.

Housing booms are generally triggered by demographics, as in the case of the 1950s, when family dynamics changed dramatically to compensate for the low birth rates of 1930s and 1940s. In contrast to the demographics of the 1990s, the housing market was calm in such a way that the real estate bubble of the 2000s was something that was conjured up in the world of the financiers. As long-term rates trended steadily downward in the second half of the 1990s, the big banks plunged headlong into the refinancing business. It took a couple of years for the consumers to catch on, as extracting money from houses was initially considered an exotic concept. The banks mounted large budget and lavish media advertising campaigns to stoke the enthusiasm for their loan programs. Refinancing jumped from $14 billion in 1995 to nearly a quarter trillion in 2005, and most of these resulting in higher loan amounts. By the 2000s, American property owners and borrowers had learned how to ride down the interest rate curve with abandon and were *stuck* to it in such a way that they kept going back to the well again and again.

Section 4.2.2 Organizations

The financial sector was led by several stickiness characteristics that started to come undone in October 2007 when the big banks and investment banks began reporting some 20 billion in losses, 11 billion of it at Citibank and Merrill Lynch, primarily in their prime subprime-based *CDO*s portfolios. Within weeks, these banks had to revise their estimates to more than $45 billion, including recalculations of third-quarter heavy losses. By the end of October the CEOs for Merrill Lynch and Citigroup had resigned or were fired. By November, the stickiness attribute was in full swing, and the financial markets were heading into an endless abyss. And the Federal Reserve could do nothing about it as the tsunami wall of money they kept floating into the market helped contribute to the dramatic moment to come in the following year.

Banks

The banks responded during this time, with a re-engineered application and approval process and tricks for automated credit scoring that sped up the application reviews that trimmed back the previous documentation requirements responding to the flood of borrowers racing to get loans. The media, news and advertising, was saturated with a period of proliferation of new affordable products and devices to make houses available to more marginal credit clients, and most of these products were strongly supported by community advocates for their own social and political reasons. These included a variety of adjustable rate mortgages, or ARMs, enabling borrowers to lock-in their expectations of continuously falling rates and rising property values. The borrowers were piggybacking their existing loans to finance the down payments and closing expenses. In the end, these subprime loans at higher interest rates and higher origination fees and riskier borrowers did not meet traditional lending tests but these were largely ignored.

By 2005 forty percent of all home mortgages were either for investment or as second homes purchases, and during this time, the banks were cheering on the American homeowner, in fact, proclaiming that they were losing tens of thousands of dollars by not grabbing one-year ARMs that were offering teaser rates of only 3.25% These rates would later balloon when borrowers were unable to make the payments. The problem was that Federal Reserve had no interest in looking into the growing signs of predatory behavior in the subprime banking industry that was epidemic in the banking sector.

Community advocates were pointing out there were some upsides to the financial boom in the housing market, as the national rate of homeownership in the United States increased from roughly 64% in 2002, all the way up to 69% in 2005. (Countrywide (acquired by Bank of America) later recounted their demise, and justified the proliferation of bad loans on the presumption that they were in fact assisting those who were previously unable (not qualified) to buy a home). They argued that statistics show that homeownership tends to stabilize communities by providing a solid base for family finances and help with planning families and futures. Unfortunately, like most booms and stickiness characteristics, the market epidemic inevitably veered into the direction of destructive access that led to the tipping point.

Subprime Lending

Subprime lending jumped from an annual volume of $145 billion in 2001 to $625 billion in 2005, an increase of more than 20% of total issuances. More than a third of these subprime loans were for 100% the value of the home, and quite a few included the fees added in. As a subprime crisis developed through the spring and summer of 2007 and contributed to the stickiness attribute, these risky mortgages counted for 15 to 20% of all outstanding mortgages, and in the context of a $12 trillion economy, any delinquencies within such a large group, would seem insignificant. What makes this subprime lending so important as a stickiness characteristic and so devastating is not the absolute size of the subprime and risky mortgages, but how during this time with the media promoted and reported on how they were being repackaged and resold and entered their way into the entire global financial system. The following paragraphs provide an, albeit brief, example of these complicated financial instruments that were now spreading in viral form throughout the world's economic systems.

Securities, Bonds and Equities

Back in June of 2007 equity markets in the United States were roaring ahead; however, there existed a persistent undercurrent of nervousness in the securities and bond markets. Suddenly, two Bear Stearns hedge funds that had invested primarily in mortgage-backed securities announced that they were having trouble meeting their margin calls. Merrill Lynch, which had the most exposure to these securities, asked for an additional $845 million USD in cash and securities to guarantee the Bear Stearns funds, funds which Bear Sterns didn't have. At that point Merrill Lynch discovered their initial exposure to $845 million worth of securities that now nobody would buy. Bear Stearns, which technically had no legal responsibility for the securities, came up $3.2 billion to close out its positions, and the world began to discover how deeply American subprime paper had infiltrated the global financial markets.

The media coverage of the casualty list of blue-chip financial companies began as big subprime linked bank losses included the Royal Bank of Scotland, Lehman Brothers, Credit Suisse, and Deutsche Bank. France's BNP Paribas had three big investment funds that could no longer value, and throughout the world, hedge funds were closing doors while governments were stepping in to bail out banks as asset management groups that went into liquidation. The Bank of England had to bail out Northern Rock the country's largest mortgage lender.

Section 4.2.3 Media

The relationship between the media living story and events was uneven, bringing up the questions: What was coverage and what was public opinion? Was the media reflecting public concern about the financial crisis and telling a living story they knew the public was interested in hearing? Or was the media manufacturing public concern, driving the crisis with consumer confidence, creating what former Senator Phil Gramm of Texas called "a mental recession"? Or was the financial crisis another example of how the media reflected, reinforced, and multiplied the public's concerns and, in effect, causing the tipping point? A number of factors in this case study suggest other issues than media coverage that may have influenced public opinion on a subject of the international financial crisis, ranging from personal experience to even perhaps the presidential candidates' views on the issue. However, the international financial crisis suggests the complex stickiness relationship between media and the public reaction. There were evident correlations between increased media and growing public anxiety.

Living Story

The media *living story* of the International Financial Crisis shifted repeatedly from a narrative about mortgages to one about recession, then a banking crisis, and then largely about gas prices—with a changing storyline and one that differed from media medium to medium.

Moreover, the connection between media living story and stickiness characteristic was uneven. Sometimes media coverage lagged months behind economic activity when the information was dependent on government data. Other times, the story tracked events erratically, as with housing and inflation. But when the events of the international financial crisis are easier to tell, as in the case of gas prices, media coverage was closely tied (in sync) to what is actually occurring in the marketplace.

The relationship between the media influencing the living story and public concerns about the international financial crisis is a complex issue. Going back to late 2007, Americans' attention to the crisis generally outstripped the level of media interest. While the public typically considered the economy its number one concern, the media had been far more interested in the presidential campaign—by a factor of nearly 5-to-1 between January 2007 and June 2008. The public attention to the living story and pessimism about the state of the economy both grew as the media began to pay more attention in 2008. Overall, the international financial crisis was the number two story in 2008 in the U.S. media, moving ahead of the Iraq war. But coverage did not come close to that of presidential campaign. For the first six months of 2008, the various media event characteristics that made up competing living stories during the financial crisis, including rising energy costs, (8% of the news),[198] with the next biggest event being inside Iraq (at 3%).[199] The race for president by contrast, was 37%.[200] Often the media coverage lagged behind these events, sometimes by months. In the first quarter of 2008, for example, media attention to a possible recession began to increase, though in reality the economy was strengthening some. Then as the economy began to weaken again in the second quarter, the media narrative shifted away from concerns about the economic slowdown. The only change in the economy that reliably predicts more media coverage during the year were rising gas prices.

While public attention to economic news did not always translate into media coverage, more coverage of the economy could be correlated to deepening public worries. Media coverage of the economy jumped in the first quarter of 2008, and the number of Americans who considered the economy to be ailing, doubled.[201] The economic picture improved slightly during that period. What Americans knew about the international financial crisis also varied based on what media they consumed. Parts of the economy were a bigger story in one medium than another, with some media generally less concerned overall. Gas prices, for instance, was a bigger TV story. Banking and housing were bigger stories in print. And unless there was a

---

198 "The Changing Narrative: How the News Media have Covered the Slowing Economy," *Analysis Report, Pew Research Center's Project for Excellence in Journalism*, August 8, 2001, p. 2. Retrieved from http://www.journalism.org/files/Economy%20report.pdf

199 *Ibid.*, p. 2.

200 *Ibid.*, p. 2.

201 *Ibid.*, p. 2.

clear political issue to argue about, the economy was not much of a story on cable news or on talk radio (at least, not during the key time slots when most people tune in). In January 2007, the international financial crisis was a third biggest story on cable news and talk radio compared to newspapers and network television.

Media Coverage

Coverage of the international financial crisis even when the events were continuing, however, did not keep growing. The *living story* subsided in September and October, falling to 2% and 3% of total news. In September economy coverage lagged behind wildfires raging in the West.[202] It began to pick up again in November and December as Americans were hit with double punch of rising gas prices and a 0.6% jump in the Consumer Price Index. But the media really began to focus on the crisis in a significant way in the first three months of 2008, particularly starting in late January. As the presidential primaries and caucuses hit full stride, the International Financial Crisis emerged as both a major living story and the leading public worry. From January through March 2008, the economic news in the media was well ahead of the war or any issue other than politics. And the topic remained at a roughly similar level of attention from then on.

As the *living story* evolved, the narrative in the media and what aspect of the International Financial Crisis was being talked about—changed fairly significantly. When it began, the focus was primarily a housing story. In the third and fourth quarter of 2007, almost half all the economic media coverage was about housing. With the beginning of 2008, the living story changed. Concerns about problems with the mortgage industry and its effect on housing broadened into *something* larger. The biggest focus of the coverage in the first quarter of 2008 was now whether the country was heading toward a recession. The stickiness characteristic in the media was led by a series of economic statements: 1. On January 9, 2008 the influential banking investment firm of Goldman Sachs released a report predicting a recession. 2. Federal Reserve Chairman Ben Bernanke publicly disagreed with that assessment a week later. 3. When the federal data on gross domestic product came out on January 30, it showed the economy in the fourth quarter of 2007 had slowed. And the media debate was on. For the first three months of 2008, almost half of media coverage was focused

202 *Ibid.*, p. 3.

on whether the recession was coming.

At the end of April 2008, a federal government reported the growth rate in GDP had picked up slightly in the first quarter, and with that news, discussion of whether the economy was in recession gave way to *something else*. Starting in April, the story of the international financial crisis became focused more on the price of gas and oil. From April through June, almost half of the crisis coverage was about rising energy prices. The second-biggest element of the living story remained housing, but it too had taken a turn. The story about defaulting mortgages had evolved into the living story more about a *crisis in banking* in general, than mortgages and foreclosures in particular.

The banking stickiness characteristic had begun earlier in the year. In January, Bank of America bought troubled Countrywide Financial (as referred to earlier), the nation's largest mortgage lender. In mid-March the investment banking firm Bear Stearns was on the brink of failure and was bailed out by an 11th hour purchase plan by J.P. Morgan Chase. The Bush Administration, in line with Federal Reserve, was also becoming more interventionist in an effort to calm investor fears. On March 12 the government authorized a $200 billion rescue plan for ailing banks. By the second quarter of 2008, other storylines that would loom even larger in the third quarter were beginning to emerge.

On May 27 the *Wall Street Journal* predicted that the Federal Reserve's intervention in the sale of Bear Stearns would lead to more regulation and oversight by the Central Bank. By July that prediction proved true, as the government moved to shore up troubled mortgage giants Freddie Mac and Fannie Mae.

The government information on the financial crisis data was often months behind. Congressional testimony and statements by government officials in press conferences and painted yet another picture and the reaction of the private sector, evidenced by the stock market, quarterly earnings reports, and the financial health of companies was another. Interestingly all of these stickiness characteristics were completely missed by the media narrative, lagging months behind what is going on in people's lives.

The most aspects the media was closely in sync with what is occurring.

However, the decisive factor on what was presented appears to relate to how easy the story was to tell. When the economy began to slow sharply in the fourth quarter of 2007, media reacted only modestly. The increase in media coverage of crisis woes came in January when economists began to anticipate the release of pessimistic GDP data for the quarter. (That report, issued on Jan. 30 2008, found that GDP growth for that period had slowed to 2.3%)[203] By that time, the coverage of a financial crisis picked up in the first three months of the year, the rate of GDP growth was actually increasing again. The pattern of the coverage media—which was largely dependent on official government reports—manifest again in the second quarter of 2008 when GDP growth slipped again (though the government report documenting this would not appear until late July). With the media thinking the economy was picking up again based on the previous GDP report, coverage of the crisis subsided as a living story. If the media relationship to GDP is generally one of being *behind events*, the pattern of coverage relating to several other key financial crisis indicators—such as the housing market and the Consumer Price Index—are yet, other important stickiness characteristics.

Starting in the second quarter of 2007, the sales of existing homes was on a steady downturn through the second quarter of that year.[204] Yet the media coverage of the problems plaguing the housing and mortgage markets vacillated wildly. There were major increases in coverage in August 2007 when President Bush unveiled plans to offer federal aid to those defaulting on mortgages, and in December 2007, when Treasury Secretary Henry Paulson introduced the idea of freezing mortgage interest rates to help homeowners. Yet each of those was followed by plunges in the amount of media coverage the following month—in September 2007 and January 2008. In September, the overall economy fell in news coverage as the war in Iraq generated greater media attention, and in January fears of a recession overtook all other economic concerns in the media. When the media would reduce its coverage of parts of the stickiness of this living story, trends in housing sales, for example, would actually improve. When the media would play up the negative aspects of the financial crisis, the housing market home sales would fall.

---

203 *Ibid.*, p. 6.

204 "Existing-Home Sales Fall in 41 States," *Associated Press*, August 15, 2007. Retrieved from http://www.msnbc.msn.com/id/20279235/

This is an important aspect of this characteristic of our case study. The stickiness of the pattern of up and down media coverage of housing was repeated in 2008. In March, media coverage of housing picked up again noticeably at the same time that media coverage surfaced of the Bear Stearns buyout after the bank was saddled with so many bad mortgages. It dipped again in May when a cyclone in Myanmar and an earthquake in China generated more coverage than the economy (not including energy prices). Coverage of housing then rose again in June.

The Consumer Price Index, which measures inflation in the economy, was during this period steadily rising, with one minor downturn, in August 2007. Here, too, coverage has ebbed and flowed—with only one obvious connection to the inflationary trajectory. In March 2008, there was a clear relationship between rising prices and a major spike in coverage. In that month, inflation grew at a rapid rate and rising food prices became a significant concern. Yet on other occasions, the relationship between coverage and rising prices is less clear. A significant jump in inflation during the second quarter of 2008, for example, was met with a general downturn in economic coverage.

The one aspect of the International Financial Crisis in which the media were most in sync with actual events was gas prices. From August 2007 through June 2008, coverage of energy prices almost exactly matched the arc of rising gas costs. And in the rare periods when prices fell, such as December 2007, that was matched with a corresponding drop in coverage of the issue. As the cost of gas soared throughout 2008, the amount of coverage grew at nearly the same rate.

Why was the stickiness attribute aspect of gas prices so closely tied to actual events? First, it was easy for the media to report—or anyone for that matter, even news executives—to be able to monitor gas prices in real time. One need only look at the signs at your local gas station on the way to work. And certain pricing milestones triggered an increase in coverage. (That was true in November 2007 when the average cost of unleaded regular hit $3 a gallon and again in June 2008 when the price reached the $4 mark).

Not only are gas prices an easy story to observe first hand, it also represented an easy story for the media to tell and perhaps also for the public to understand. (There are no confusing sets of conflicting data or complex economic jargon to parse, no indices made up of multiple elements to explain). Instead, *pain at the pump* is easy to illustrate visually and easy to connect to consumers. Media covered some aspects in *real time*—such as gas prices—because they are easy to see and reach consumers. Media covered other aspects more abstractly, because those elements were measured in data and statistics and released after the fact. The media, in a sense, was seeing just parts of the story, and describing the whole was elusive.

Media vs. Public Opinion

From August 2007 through the end of that year, for instance, about a quarter of Americans were paying very close attention to the financial crisis. This represented a fairly modest level of concern about that subject..[205]

The public's attention to prices at the pump seemed out of sync with coverage. In November, fully 44% of Americans surveyed said they were following news about energy prices "very closely." (At the time, such stories accounted for just 1% of the news). That gap between media and public concern continued into 2008, even as the media attention to the crisis and public interest in the subject grew. The lowest that public interest in the financial crisis ever dipped was to 36%. Media coverage of the economy, by contrast, filled 8% of the media coverage in 2008. There was a similar gap in media coverage vs. public interest in gas prices. In April, May, and June, more than 60% of Americans said they were following news about the subject "very closely." Yet this aspect of the living story accounted for only 3% of the coverage. Overall, Americans also tended to be more interested in the financial crisis in 2008 than the presidential race, though not by a substantial margin. The media agenda meanwhile, campaign coverage overwhelmed International Financial Crisis coverage (by nearly five to one).

It is hardly the case that the numbers for media and public curiosity about the news should be identical.[206] The media coverage about the financial crisis was a limited commodity, while anxiety is not. However, the gaps in media coverage reflect some of the largest discrepancies between press

---

205 "The Changing Narrative: How the News Media have Covered the Slowing Economy," *op. cit.*, p. 10.

206 *Ibid.*, p. 11.

coverage and public attention on any topic. So if it wasn't public opinion that was driving the living story of the financial crisis, then what was? The biggest catalyst for media attention appeared to be external events, the *something else* of the tipping point.

Coverage and Views about the Economy

Even if the media and the public were not entirely in sync about levels of coverage and interest in this living story, there does appear to be a correlation between how much coverage the media offered and how pessimistic people started to feel and react about their economic fortunes. In other words, even if the media did not, in fact, manufacture public concern, the more there was of media coverage may have reinforced those worries and confirmed for people that their fears were justified. As an example, in January of 2008, 26% of Americans considered the economy to be in excellent or good shape, while 28% considered it to be in poor shape. By March, after media coverage more than *doubled* from the previous quarter, those numbers had changed markedly for the worse. At that point 11% considered the economy to be in excellent or good shape, while the percentage of Americans who considered the economy to be ailing had *doubled* again to 56%.[207]

What's perhaps more dramatic is the relationship between public worry over rising oil and gas prices and the increases in media coverage. In January only 3% of Americans considered energy prices the most important problem facing the country. By July that number had jumped to 19%, compared with 17% who thought the war in Iraq was the top problem. Americans then considered the financial crisis the number one stickiness characteristic.[208] The increase in concern over gas prices coincided precisely with a increase in coverage of the issue. In short, in our next section, the one dramatic moment that led to this case study tipping point was reinforced in the living story being carried out in the media, and it impacted not only public opinion, but also their interpretation and their reactions to the financial institutions who were crumbling around them.

What Were the Top Media Stickiness Events?

Three major stickiness attributes events in the media accounted for nearly 40% of the overall economic coverage. 1. News about the banking industry

207 *Ibid.*, p. 12.
208 *Ibid.*, p. 12.

and the government bailouts was the most heavily covered item and accounted for 15%. 2. The stimulus package being presented by the Obama administration was nearly as large at 14%. And finally, 3. the US automobile industry financial troubles were third, accounting for 9% of the economic media. There were some interesting points about these characteristics. There was more coverage when they involved institutions. For example, a story about the banking industry was driven by Treasury Secretary Timothy Geithner's TARP fund proposal. And once it moved into Congress, the stimulus package commanded 36% of the news coverage reflecting the sheer magnitude of the $787 billion program involved in the battle that was occurring in Congress. Finally, the auto industry was being faced with American automakers who might fail and what the impact would be to worker layoffs and the other troubled aspects of the sector.

Who were the media originators of the stickiness characteristics?

Nearly half of the media stories were responses to a government action of some sort. And 32% were direct stories that came from the new Obama team or the White House or federal agency under Obama's control. Surprisingly, was the media themselves as nearly a quarter of all stories were generated by press initiative, primarily through investigative or enterprise journalism. Interestingly, about one fifth of the economic stories in the media were attributed primarily to the initiative of journalists. And when it came to the biggest economic stories, the media was more reactive in this regard. For example, the media was more proactive in responding to the housing crisis. And press enterprise proved to be a significant stickiness characteristic when it came to covering the crisis in fact on ordinary citizens. To summarize, the coverage was heavily institutional and based on government events (information given to the journalists) with the stories that were coming out of the press, whereas, to cover the lives of ordinary people, the journalists had to go out and find the stories for themselves.

Where were the major media stories that contributed to the stickiness characteristics coming from?

For obvious reasons New York, being the nation's biggest city, and Washington, DC, being the government capital, figured prominently in the international financial crisis media coverage. New York is the center of the financial banking industry. And Washington is the seat of the government, which scrambled to craft media responses to the crisis. Both of these cities are also home to a very large media network and major reporting bureaus.

The amount of stories that emanated from these two cities was overwhelming. Three quarters of all the economic stories came from these two cities, New York 44%, and metro Washington DC 32%.

Who was the lead person covered by the media stickiness?

Visibility of President Obama's administration far exceeded any other, with Obama as the lead person for 14% of all the economic stories from February 1 to July 3, 2009. This represented five times as much coverage as the number two person, convicted Ponzi scheme swindler Bernard Madoff, with just 3%. The number three and number five persons were also top Obama officials, Treasury Secretary Timothy Geithner and Press Secretary Robert Gibbs. The fourth leading person was Federal Reserve Chairman Ben Bernanke. Although he was dealt with in the media as an independent official, his response to the crisis was key to the media events.

The public's role towards some of the media events in this living story is more significant than in others. In the presidential campaign, it is the voter who decides elections. By contrast, the media coverage of a pileup on the interstate may be significant, but what consumers think about it will have a limited impact on the event. The economy is one of those living stories in which public attitude played a central role in the stickiness attribute.

As we started this case study we asked the question: Is the International Financial Crisis simply in our minds, as former Senator Phil Gramm suggested?[209] Perhaps not entirely. But to some degree, of course, all recessions, just as is true of all bull markets on Wall Street, are significantly influenced by consumer psychology. And the media information the public is operating with is a major determinant of that psychology.

During the international financial crisis, the public was focused on the living story in some ways *before* the media. Local media and national print seemed to sense a story first. And the tendency of television media to repeat the story of gas and energy prices ahead of other media outlets in influencing public perceptions of what was at the root of the economic slowdown.

That psychology was also influenced by an elusive timing epidemic – *something else,* embedded in the way the media would learn about eco-

209 *Ibid.*, p. 17.

nomic events. With its reliance on government data, much of the understanding of the economy was delayed. And a modest recovery might be occurring while the news, linked backwards to the previous quarter, was still highlighting a slowdown. Hence, as more information became available and released to additional media deployment channels, the public and the institutions and government leaders then became aware and continued to move well beyond the stickiness attribute. Looking back, the result is a partial, perhaps even blurry, image, like looking at parts of an elephant, photographed at different times, pieced together after it has already moved. The living story about the international financial crisis was perhaps too large and too complicated and presented such a psychological block to both the media and the general public, as well as our government officials, as it was too difficult to follow, interpret, and understand. In fact, there was no way of avoiding the tipping point.

Section 4.2.4 Events

Financial Instruments

As financial assets became more complex (and harder to establish market value), investors were reassured by the fact that both the international rating agencies and bank regulators, (who relied on them), accepted as valid some complex mathematical models which theoretically showed the risks were much smaller than actually proved to be in practice.[210] George Soros commented that: "The super-boom got out of hand when the new products became so complicated that the authorities could no longer calculate the risks and started relying on the risk management methods of the banks themselves."[211] Similarly, the rating agencies relied on the information provided by the originators of synthetic products. "It was a shocking abdication of responsibility."[212]

Sub-prime lending

The U.S. subprime mortgage value was estimated at $1.3 trillion as of March

210 Floyd NORRIS, "Another Crisis, Another Guarantee," *New York Times*, November 24, 2008. Retrieved from http://www.nytimes.com/2008/11/25/business/25assess.html?hp

211 George SOROS, "The Worst Market Crisis in 60 Years," *Financial Times*, January 22, 2008, Retrieved from http://www.ft.com/cms/s/0/24f73610-c91e-11dc-9807-000077b07658.html#axzz1jtkkWJ7H

212 Ibid.

2007, with over 7.5 million first-lien subprime mortgages outstanding.[213] With the easy credit conditions, evidence existed that both government and competitive pressures contributed to an increase the amount of subprime lending. Major U.S. investment banks and government sponsored agencies like Fannie Mae, played an pivotal role in the propagation of higher-risk lending. Subprime mortgages remained below 10% of all mortgage originations until 2004, spiking to nearly 20% and remaining there through the 2005-2006 peak.. The characteristic event linked to this increase was the April 2004 decision by the U.S. Securities and Exchange Commission (SEC) to relax the net capital rule, encouraging the largest (five) investment banks to dramatically increase their financial leverage and aggressively increase their issuance of mortgage-backed securities (MBS). Subprime mortgage delinquency rates stayed in the 10-15% range from 1998 to 2006, and then began to increase dramatically, rising to 25% by early 2008. This was stoked by additional competitive pressures on Fannie Mae and Freddie Mac to relax their underwriting policies, which further expanded the riskier lending.

Some analysts, like American Enterprise Institute fellow Peter J. Wallison, believe the roots of the financial crisis are born directly from the sub-prime lending practices by Fannie Mae and Freddie Mac, both government sponsored entities.[214]

On September 30, 1999, *The New York Times* reported:

> Fannie Mae, the nation's biggest underwriter of home mortgages, has been under increasing pressure from the Clinton Administration to expand mortgage loans among low and moderate income people...In moving, even tentatively, into this new area of lending, Fannie Mae is taking on significantly more risk, which may not pose any difficulties during flush economic times. But the govern-

---

213 "Will Subprime Mess Ripple through the Economy?" MSNBC, March 13, 2007. Retrieved from http://www.msnbc.msn.com/id/17584725#.Txf6qmOonus; Ben S. BERNANKE, "The Subprime Mortgage Market," Remarks by Governor Ben S. Bernanke at the Federal Reserve Bank of Chicago's 43rd Annual Conference on Bank Structure and Competition, Chicago, Illinois, May 17, 2007. Retrieved from http://www.federalreserve.gov/boarddocs/speeches/2005/20050414/default.htm

214 Peter J. WALLISON, "The True Origins of This Financial Crisis," American Spectator, February 6, 2009. Retrieved from http://spectator.org/archives/2009/02/06/the-true-origins-of-this-finan

ment-subsidized corporation may run into trouble in an economic downturn, prompting a government rescue similar to that of the savings and loan industry in the 1980s.[215]

The 1995 President Jimmy Carter's Community Reinvestment Act (CRA) of 1977 attempted regulating and strengthening with its anti-redlining procedures. The result a push by the administration for greater investment by financial institutions into riskier loans instruments. A 2000 United States Department of the Treasury study of lending trends for 305 cities from 1993 to 1998, showed that, $467 billion of mortgage credit was poured out of CRA-covered lenders into low and mid-level income borrowers and neighborhoods, and ,only 25% of all sub-prime lending occurred at CRA-covered institutions, and a full 50% of sub-prime loans originated at institutions exempt from CRA.[216]

Others have argued there were not enough of these loans made to cause a crisis of scope and magnitude. In an article in *Portfolio Magazine*, Michael Lewis, noted that "There weren't enough Americans with [bad] credit taking out [bad loans] to satisfy investors' appetite for the end product."[217] Essentially what contributed was that investment banks and hedge funds were taking advantage of financial innovation to make more loans. "They were creating [loans] out of whole cloth. One hundred times over! That's why the losses are so much greater than the loans."[218]

Predatory lending

Predatory lending refers to the practice of lenders to enter into unsafe or unsound secured loans for inappropriate purposes. For example a "bait-and-switch" method, used by mortgage company, Countrywide, who *advertised* low interest rates for home refinancing, then, when the loans were written, extensively detailed contracts were swapped with more expensive

---

215 Steven A. HOLMES, "Fannie Mae Eases Credit to Aid Mortgage Lending," New York Times, September 30, 1999. Retrieved from http://www.nytimes.com/1999/09/30/business/fannie-mae-eases-credit-to-aid-mortgage-lending.html

216 Robert GORDON, "Did Liberals Cause the Sub Prime Crisis?" *American Prospect*, April 7, 2008. Retrieved from http://prospect.org/article/did-liberals-cause-sub-prime-crisis

217 Michael LEWIS, "The End of Wall Street's Boom," *Portfolio.com*, November 11, 2008. Retrieved from http://www.portfolio.com/news-markets/national-news/portfolio/2008/11/11/The-End-of-Wall-Streets-Boom

218 Ibid.

loan products on the day of mortgage closing. Whereas, the advertisement stated that 1% or 1.5% interest would be charged, the consumer would actually be put into an adjustable rate mortgage (ARM), in which the interest charged, amounted to more than the amount of interest paid. This resulted in negative amortization. Credit consumers would not notice until long after the loan had been transacted.

Countrywide, sued by California Attorney General Jerry Brown for "Unfair Business Practices" and "False Advertising" " by placing loans to homeowners with weak credit, adjustable rate mortgages (ARMs), which resulted in homeowners making interest-only payments."[219] When the housing started to fall, homeowners in ARMs, had little incentive to pay their monthly payments, since much of their home equity had vanished. With a high rate of bad loans, Countrywide's financial condition deteriorated, resulting in the discounted sale of the lender to Bank of America. Countrywide later admitted to have involved itself in making low-cost loans to politicians for purposes of gaining political favors. Similarly, former employees from Ameriquest, at the time, a United States's leading wholesale lender, described a system in which they were pushed to falsify mortgage documents and sell the mortgages to Wall Street banks eager to make quick profits.[220] Practices such as these contributed to the stickiness events.

Increased Debt Burden

U.S. households and financial institutions were increasingly indebted or overleveraged during the years preceding the crisis. This added to their vulnerability during the collapse of the housing bubble and worsened the ensuing economic stickiness. Key statistics which support this include: the "free cash" used by consumers from home equity loans doubled from $627 billion in 2001 to $1,428 billion in 2005, a total of nearly $5 trillion dollars over the

219 Ibid

220 "Criminal Fraud: Mortgage Fraud Scandal Brewing," *Real News*, May 13, 2009. Retrieved from http://therealnews.com/t2/index.php?option=com_content&task=view&id=31&Itemid=74&jumival=3708

period, contributing to economic growth worldwide.[221] U.S. home mortgage debt relative to GDP increased from an average of 46% during the 1990s to 73% during 2008, reaching $10.5 trillion.[222] In addition, USA household debt as a percentage of annual disposable personal income was 127% at the end of 2007, versus 77% in 1990.[223] U.S. home mortgage debt relative to gross domestic product (GDP) increased from an average of 46% during the 1990s to 73% during 2008, reaching $10.5 trillion.[224] Finally, in 1981, U.S. private debt was 123% of GDP; by the third quarter of 2008, it was 290%.[225]

From 2004-07, the top (five) U.S. investment banks significantly increased their financial leverage, resulting in increased vulnerability. These institutions accounted for over $4.1 trillion in debt in fiscal year 2007, about 30% of US nominal GDP. Consequently, resulting in Lehman Brothers being liquidated, Bear Stearns and Merrill Lynch being sold at written-down prices, and Goldman Sachs and Morgan Stanley, in turn, effectively, becoming commercial banks, subject to stringent US regulation. With the exception of Lehman, all of required or received government support.[226]

In addition, Fannie Mae and Freddie Mac, owned or guaranteed nearly $5 trillion in mortgage obligations, were placed into conservatorship by the

221 Alan GREENSPAN and James KENNEDY, "Sources and Uses of Equity Extracted from Homes," Divisions of Research & Statistics and Monetary Affairs, Federal Reserve Board, Washington, D.C., March 2007. Retrieved from http://www.federalreserve.gov/pubs/feds/2007/200720/200720pap.pdf; "Home Equity Extraction: The Real Cost of 'Free Cash'," *Seeking Alpha*, April 25, 2007. Retrieved from http://seekingalpha.com/article/33336-home-equity-extraction-the-real-cost-of-free-cash; "Spending Boosted by Home Equity Loans: Greenspan," *Reuters*, April 23, 2007. Retrieved from http://www.reuters.com/article/2007/04/23/us-usa-greenspan-equity-idUSN2330071920070423

222 Colin BARR, "The $4 Trillion Housing Headache," *CNN Money*, May 27, 2009. Retrieved from http://money.cnn.com/2009/05/27/news/mortgage.overhang.fortune/index.htm

223 Ibid.

224 Ibid.

225 Martin WOLF, "Japan's Lessons for a World of Balance-Sheet Deflation," *Financial Times*, February 17, 2009. Retrieved from http://www.ft.com/intl/cms/s/0/774c0920-fd1d-11dd-a103-000077b07658.html#axzz1jtkkWJ7H

226 Stephen LABATON, "Agency's '04 Rule Let Banks Pile Up New Debt," *New York Times*, October 3, 2008. Retrieved from http://www.nytimes.com/2008/10/03/business/03sec.html

U.S. government in September 2008[227] These seven entities had a combined $9 trillion in debt or guaranteed obligations.

Financial Innovation and Complexity

The ongoing development of financial instruments of increased complexity were being designed, such as offsetting a particular risk exposure (such as the default of a borrower), or, to assist with obtaining financing contributed to the stickiness. Examples pertinent to the crisis included: 1. Adjustable-rate mortgages (ARM); 2. Bundling of subprime mortgages into mortgage-backed securities (MBS) or collateralized debt obligations (CDO) a form of securitization; and 3. Credit insurance called credit default swaps (CDS). The prevalence of these products increased the stickiness dramatically in the years leading up to the crisis. Certainly these financial innovations had an effect of circumventing regulations, such as, off-balance sheet financing, disguising the leverage (or capital cushion) reported by the major banks. Martin Wolf wrote in June 2009, "…an enormous part of what banks did in the early part of this decade – the off-balance-sheet vehicles, the derivatives and the 'shadow banking system' itself – was to find a way round regulation."[228]

Incorrect Pricing of Risk

Market participants did not accurately measure the risk inherent with financial innovation such as MBS and CDO's or understand their impact on the overall stability of the financial system for a variety of reasons. [229] The pricing models for CDOs clearly did not reflect the level of risk they were introducing into the system. Whereas, the average recovery rate for high quality CDOs has been approximately 32 cents on the dollar, compared to the recovery rate for "mezzanine" (placed in a more riskier position) CDO's, was approximately five cents for every dollar. The impact of massive losses on the balance sheets of banks across the globe left them during the crisis with diminished capital resources to continue.

227 Ibid

228 Martin WOLF, "Reform of Regulation has to Start by Altering Incentives," *Financial Times*, June 23, 2009. Retrieved from http://www.ft.com/intl/cms/s/0/095722f6-6028-11de-a09b-00144feabdc0.html#axzz1jtkkWJ7H

229 "Declaration of the Summit on Financial Markets and the World Economy," Office of the Press Secretary, The White House, November 15, 2008. Retrieved from http://georgewbush-whitehouse.archives.gov/news/releases/2008/11/20081115-1.html

Another example relates to insurance giant AIG. AIG activities involved insuring the obligations of these various financial institutions with the use of "credit default swaps" (CDS). The basic CDS transaction involved AIG receiving a premium, primarily in exchange for a promise to pay money to one party in the event another party defaulted. AIG lacked the financial strength to support its CDS commitments as the crisis stickiness progressed and eventually AIG was taken over by the US government in September 2008. The U.S. taxpayer provided over $180 billion in government support to this company between 2008 and early 2009.

This widely-used financial model formula assumed that the price of CDS could predict the correct price of these *mortgage backed securities*. It rapidly came to be used by a huge percentage of CDO and CDS investors, issuers, and rating agencies. According to one wired. com article:

> Then the model fell apart. Cracks started appearing early on, when financial markets began behaving in ways that users (of Li's formula – developed by the Wall Street *Quant*) hadn't expected. The cracks became full-fledged canyons in 2008—when ruptures in the financial system's foundation swallowed up trillions of dollars and put the survival of the global banking system in serious peril...Li's Gaussian "copula formula" will go down in history as instrumental in causing the unfathomable losses that brought the world financial system to its knees.[230]

The Gaussian copula soon became such a universally accepted part of the world's financial vocabulary that brokers started quoting prices for bond tranches based on their correlations. "Correlation trading has spread through the psyche of the financial markets like a highly infectious thought virus," wrote derivatives guru Janet Tavakoli in 2006.[231]

The stickiness characteristic continued, as two other events in the fall of 2007 started to be carried by the media. First, top banks which had committed to some $300 to 400 billion in bridge loans for private equity deals were still in the process of finalizing them when the subprime news started to hit the media. Because of the media influence and propagation of the stories,

230 Felix SALMON, "Recipe for Disaster: The Formula That Killed Wall Street," *Wired Magazine*, February 23, 2009. Retrieved from http://www.wired.com/techbiz/it/magazine/17-03/wp_quant?currentPage=all

231 Ibid.

many of these transactions were never completed, and others were watered down. The second event was much scarier. Commercial paper is the standard form of loans between interbank and intercompany for short-term borrowing. Typically, these loans from top drawer banks, trade with microscopic margins above the overnight fed funds rate, or its London equivalent, Libor. By early September 2007, the media was reporting that these margins had suddenly spiked up nearly 20%. Commercial paper and loans between interbank and intercompany for short term borrowing then came to a screeching halt and the media drove the living story well beyond the stickiness attribute.

Section 4.3 One Dramatic Moment Attributes (TP)

The third and last attribute, the one dramatic moment or tipping point in the 2007-2010 international financial crisis, is characterized by the notion that an epidemic can be created by one single event. As mentioned earlier, this is the most important of the three attributes because this one makes sense of the first two and perhaps provides the greatest insight into why the crisis (global event) happened the way it did.

Financial market behavior is very sensitive and strongly influenced by the environment in which it operates, and none is more pressing and immediate than the economic decline that culminated in mid-September 2008. The "power of context," as Gladwell states is that: "epidemics are sensitive to the conditions and circumstances of the times and the places in which they occur." The tipping point occurred in the international financial crisis when the "phenomena becomes rapidly and dramatically more common." The tipping point event is irreversible – comparable to wine spilling from a glass; just standing the glass upright will not put the wine back. As Gladwell states, "Ideas and products and messages and behaviors spread like viruses do.[232] The international financial crisis led to a tipping point with complex and integrated characteristics of the people, organizations, media and events.

Section 4.3.1 People

Timothy Geithner

In a June 2008 speech, then President and CEO of the NY Federal Reserve

232 Malcolm GLADWELL, *The Tipping Point: How Little Things can Make a Big Difference*, New York: Back Bay Books, 2002, p. 7.

Bank Timothy Geithner, (who later in 2009 became Secretary of the United States Treasury), reinforced the blame for the freezing of credit markets and liquidity panic on the entities in the shadow banking system (a parallel banking system discussed below). These entities were critical to the credit markets undermining the financial system and not subject to the same regulatory controls. Further, he reasoned, they were additionally vulnerable because they borrowed short-term (in liquid markets) to purchase long-term and risky assets. This meant that any disruptions in credit markets subjected them to rapid deleveraging, forcing them to sell their long-term assets at depressed prices.

In early 2007, auction-rate preferred securities, tender option bonds, variable rate demand notes, asset-backed commercial paper conduits, and other structured investment vehicles had a combined asset size of roughly $2.2 trillion. These assets financed increased with tri-party instruments to $2.5 trillion. Other assets held in hedge funds grew to roughly $1.8 trillion. The combined balance sheets of the then five major investment banks totaled $4 trillion. In comparison, the total assets of the top five bank holding companies in the United States at that point were just over $6 trillion, and total assets of the entire banking system were about $10 trillion leading him to conclude, in other words, the international financial system had reached its tipping point: "The combined effect of these factors was a financial system vulnerable to self-reinforcing asset price and credit cycles." [233]

Section 4.3.2 Organizations

Shadow Banking

Nobel laureate Paul Krugman described the panic in this shadow banking system, as "rivaling or even surpassing conventional banking in importance. Politicians and government officials should have realized that they were at the core of what happened to cause the crisis: they were re-creating the kind of financial vulnerability that made the Great Depression possible and, they should have responded by extending regulations and the financial safety net to cover these new institutions. Influential figures should have proclaimed a simple rule: "anything that does what a bank does and anything that has to be rescued in crises the way banks are should be regulated

---

233 Timothy GEITHNER, "Reducing Systemic Risk in a Dynamic Financial System," *op. cit.*

like a bank." He referred to this lack of controls as "malign neglect."[234]

Deregulation

The regulatory framework could not keep pace of the stickiness occurring with financial innovation, and the increasing complexity of the shadow banking system, such as derivatives and off-balance sheet financing. In some cases, laws changed or enforcement weakened in parts of the financial system. Key historical examples include the following: In October 1982, President Ronald Reagan signed into law the Garn-St. Germain Depository Institutions Act, which began the process of banking deregulation that helped contribute to the savings and loan crises of the late 80's/early 90's and the financial crises of 2007-2009. President Reagan stated at the signing, "all in all, I think we hit the jackpot".[235] Then in November 1999, President Bill Clinton signed into law the Gramm-Leach-Bliley Act, which repealed part of the Glass-Steagall Act of 1933. This repeal has been criticized for reducing the separation between commercial banks and investment banks. In 2004, the Securities and Exchange Commission relaxed the "net capital rule", which enabled investment banks to substantially increase their level of debt, fueling the increased use of mortgage-backed securities as a basis for subprime mortgages. The SEC conceded that self-regulation of these investment banks contributed to the stickiness of the crisis.[236]

Stated differently, financial institutions in the shadow banking system were not subject to the same regulation as commercial (depository) banks. Regulators allowed depository banks such as Citigroup to report significant amounts of assets and liabilities from off-balance sheets into complex legal entities called: *structured investment vehicles*, which in effect disguised the vulnerability of the capital base or risk taken. One news agency estimated that the top four U.S. banks would have to return between $500 billion and

234 Paul KRUGMAN, *The Return of Depression Economics and the Crisis of 2008*, *op. cit.*; Paul KRUGMAN, "Financial Reform 101," *New York Times*, April 1, 2010. Retrieved from http://www.nytimes.com/2010/04/02/opinion/02krugman.html?adxnnl=1&adxnnlx=1326978494-WOo7/m5tevHSi/qRiQCY5A

235 Paul KRUGMAN, "Reagan Did It," *New York Times*, May 31, 2009. Retrieved from http://www.nytimes.com/2009/06/01/opinion/01krugman.html

236 Stephen LABATON, "Agency's '04 Rule Let Banks Pile Up New Debt," *op. cit.*

$1 trillion to their balance sheets during 2009.[237] This increased stickiness media coverage about the uncertainty of the financial position of the major banks. Similarly, these off-balance sheet entities were also used by Enron, which in part, brought down that company in 2001.[238]

Fed Chairman Alan Greenspan, as early as 1997, lobbied hard to keep the derivatives market unregulated. The U.S. Congress and President allowed the self-regulation of the over-the-counter derivatives market, enacting the Commodity Futures Modernization Act of 2000. Derivatives such as credit default swaps (CDS) were used to hedge (or speculate) against particular credit risks. The volume of CDS outstanding increased 100-fold from 1998 to 2008, with estimates of the debt covered by CDS contracts, as of November 2008, ranging from US$33 to $47 trillion. Total over-the-counter (OTC) derivative national value rose to $683 trillion by June 2008.[239] Warren Buffett famously referred to derivatives as "financial weapons of mass destruction" in early 2003.[240] Each of these point out important stickiness characteristics of people and organizations were widely covered by the media.

Section 4.3.3 Media

Bad News versus Good News

A cover story in *BusinessWeek* magazine claimed that economists "failed to predict the worst international economic crisis since the Great Depression of 1930s".[241] An article in the *New York Times*, economist Nouriel Roubini,

237 David REILLY, "Banks' Hidden Junk Menaces $1 Trillion Purge," *Bloomberg*, March 25, 2009. Retrieved from http://www.bloomberg.com/apps/news?pid=newsarchive&sid=akv_p6LBNIdw&refer=home

238 Susan LEE, "The Dismal Science: Enron's Success Story," *Wall Street Journal*, December 26, 2011, p. A11; James K. GASSMAN, "What to Learn from the Fall of Enron, a Firm that Fooled So Many," *International Herald Tribune*, December 10, 2001, p. 10; Paul KEDROSKY, "How Enron Ran Out of Gas," *Wall Street Journal*, October 29, 2001, p. A22.

239 Stephen FIGLEWSKI, Roy C. SMITH, and Ingo WALTER, "Geithner's Plan for Derivatives," *Forbes*, May 18, 2009. Retrieved from http://www.forbes.com/2009/05/18/geithner-derivatives-plan-opinions-contributors-figlewski.html

240 "Buffett Warns on Investment 'Time Bomb'," *BBC News*, March 4, 2003. Retrieved from http://news.bbc.co.uk/2/hi/2817995.stm

241 Peter COY, "What Good are Economists Anyway"? *Businessweek*, April 16, 2009. Retrieved from http://www.businessweek.com/magazine/content/09_17/b4128026997269.htm

warned of such a financial crisis as early as September 2006, and the article goes on to state, "that the profession of economics is bad at predicting recessions." [242] According to *The Guardian*, Roubini was later ridiculed for predicting a collapse of the housing market and worldwide recession, while *The New York Times* labeled him "Dr. Doom."[243] The largest economic crisis since the Great Depression was covered in the media essentially from the top down. The perspective was slanted overwhelmingly from the direction of the political administration and corporate business interests.

Warnings Ignored?

The influence and impact of the media subsided when stories focused on the nervousness began to ease. For example, on the afternoon of April 3, 2009, the Dow Jones industrials closed over the 8000 mark the first time in two months. It was the fourth straight week that stocks had risen and marked a 20% increase over the market's low point back in March 2009. The media reacted with "real progress was being made in the road to economic recovery, but the worst may have ended."[244] When there were early signs of promise, the media coverage dropped off dramatically. Prior to April, the economy overwhelmed all other subjects in the media agenda. During February and March of 2009, almost half, 46%, of the media coverage in print and online and on radio and television was devoted to economy-related stories.[245] However, from April on, the media's attention about the economy issues continued to grow deeper into the summer, and by July and August economic focused media coverage outweighed other issues such as the health care reform, or terrorism, as it began to emerge as a *the* major news topic.

Stock Market

The decreased media coverage coincided with the signs that the recession

---

242 Stephen MIHM, "Dr. Doom," *New York Times*, August 15, 2008. Retrieved from http://www.nytimes.com/2008/08/17/magazine/17pessimist-t.html?pagewanted=all

243 Emma BROCKES, "He Told Us So," *Guardian*, January 24, 2009. Retrieved from http://www.guardian.co.uk/business/2009/jan/24/nouriel-roubini-credit-crunch

244 "Covering the Great Recession: Why Did Coverage of the Economy Decrease?" *Pew Research Center's Project for Excellence in Journalism*, October 5, 2009, p. 2. Retrieved from http://www.journalism.org/analysis_report/why_did_coverage_economy_decrease

245 Ibid.

that finally reached the bottom. It all began with the beginning of the bull market with stocks in March 2009 and the rising public opinion echoed the media about the economy. The stock markets offer one of the most carefully watched indicators for the media to monitor the economy in United States. With the capability of monitoring the economic pulse minute by minute on cable, Internet, and the news, the media could watch the market like a doctor watching the blood pressure of a patient.

In the early weeks of the year 2009 and in the new presidency for Barack Obama, the stock market readings were down, and coverage and pronouncements were accordingly down. For example, on March 6, financial mogul Donald Trump appeared on the *CBS Early Show* and said, "I think it probably will get worse and then eventually it will get better."[246] The question is when. Three days later the investor Warren Buffett declared on CNBC that the US economy had fallen off a cliff and a turnaround won't happen fast.[247] However, later that month the stock market began to reverse course. After the Dow had plunged below 7000 in the beginning of the month, it finished March of 2009 on a strong upswing. In early April it crossed the 7000 mark and exceeded 8500 in May in a long and steady march beyond the 9000 level.

Media coverage began to move in an inverse relationship with the markets during this time, as stocks began their steady climb. Press coverage of the economy generally began falling off. One dramatic moment of this reverse trend occurred in early April. As the Dow moved to over 8000, coverage of the economy from April 6 to April 12 plunged 17%, down almost 2/3 from the previous week.[248] The change in coverage was affecting the ordinary citizen as they were getting mixed signals through the press and the media, and there was less bad news about the economy as time went on. Signs of the good news began to coincide with the decrease in economic media coverage.

Another key reason the coverage of the economy in the media declined

---

246 Donald TRUMP, *CBS Early Show*, March 6, 2009.

247 Jennifer DAUBLE, "Billionaire Investor Warren Buffett Today on CNBC's 'Squawk Box'," *CNBC Squawk* Box, March 9, 2009. Retrieved from http://www.cnbc.com/id/29598302/CNBC_TRANSCRIPT_CNBC_S_BECKY_QUICK_SITS_DOWN_WITH_BILLIONAIRE_INVESTOR_WARREN_BUFFETT_TODAY_ON_CNBC_S_SQUAWK_BOX

248 "Covering the Great Recession: Why Did Coverage of the Economy Decrease?" *Pew Research Center's Project for Excellence in Journalism, op. cit.*

over time was that the Washington-based Congressional battles over the major issues of the stimulus package had subsided and along with them much of the media coverage. The stimulus battle took place in February and March and was eventually signed into law on February 17, 2009. The stimulus coverage in the media was a whopping 36% in February, but the rise of other events that were noneconomic stories in fact impeded it for the attention as the year continued to move forward.[249] Finally later in the summer the media coverage shifted gears entirely over the battle about the health care legislation and supplanted the financial crisis as a primary focus of the media attention and energy.

Media Influence

The International Financial Crisis was covered by the media in all sectors. Newspapers, network and cable television, radio news and news websites devoted much of their headlines to economy-related subjects.

But there are some major differences in the way that certain sectors of the media focused on the economic news. For example, newspaper front pages devoted the most attention to the economy from a more diverse range of sources and providing a higher level of enterprise reporting and the other media sectors. The network evening newscasts traditionally distinguished themselves by focusing on the impact of the lives of the average Americans. And cable television and talk radio focused more on the politics aspects of the economy, such as the stimulus package battle. The newspaper media sector consistently devoted the most attention to the economic financial crisis.

Online coverage of the economy was similar to the press overall. Thirty percent of the leading news coverage on websites was economy-related, which was very close to the 31% for the overall press.[250] However, the web differed in very small ways in that the media online followed the auto industry more closely, perhaps more than any other sector. But telling of the agenda of these websites is how they created the content. As an example, *Reuters.com* is a general interest news site, but the British-based news service the BBC derives most of its revenue from covering financial news for business clients.[251]

249 "Covering the Great Recession: How Economic Coverage Varied by Media Sector," *Pew Research Center, Project for Excellence in Journalism*, *op. cit.*

250 Ibid.

251 Ibid.

Coverage of the economy on the radio depended to a large part on the type of the program. The headline newscasts in the morning editions each devoted 30% of their time to the economic crisis.[252]

Each of these media sectors were had a partisan audience and agenda that mandated their coverage and their attempts to deliver and report on the widening living story that was ultimately leading to a tipping point.

Section 4.3.4 Events

Looking back at the international financial crisis, most of the US institutions simply denied there was a problem. Alan Greenspan in his 2007 book, *The Age of Turbulence*, recalled of the housing boom: "I would tell audiences that we were facing not a bubble, but a froth, with lots of small local bubbles that never grew to a scale that could threaten the health of the overall economy."[253] President Bush virtually never mentioned the housing boom in his public pronouncements while it was happening. He just referred to it only as a success. He boasted that mortgage rates were low and that over the past year the homeownership rate in America has reached record levels.[254] In addition, the Chairman of the President's Council of Economic Advisers said in 2005, "Housing prices have risen by nearly 25% over the past two years. Although speculative activity has increased in some areas, at a national level these price increases largely reflect strong economic fundamentals, including robust growth in jobs and incomes, low mortgage rates, steady rates of household formation, and factors that limit the expansion of housing supply in some areas."[255] Unfortunately, in hindsight, few could forseen the oncoming economic troubles due to the following events that were now unfolding.

252 Ibid.

253 Alan GREENSPAN, The Age of Turbulence: Adventures in a New World, Penguin Press HC, New York.

254 George W. BUSH, "President's Weekly Radio Address," August 6, 2005. In Robert J. Schiller, *The Subprime Solution: How Today's Global Financial Crisis Happened, and What to Do about It*, Princeton University Press, Princeton, NJ, p. 40.

255 Ben BERNANKE, "The Economic Outlook," Testimony before the Joint Economic Committee, October 20, 2005. Retrieved from http://www.house.gov/jec/hearings/testimony/109/10-20-05bernanke.pdf

Bubble Trouble

The tipping point was evident and with the crisis growing, and most media and politicians were unaware of it. Looking back at the stock market bubble of 1990s and the real estate bubble that followed it, similarly, media and leaders at the time, found it very difficult to see what was happening. While every tipping point is the outcome of a combination of attribute and characteristics, most importantly, the international financial crisis was the combination of factors which led to "denial thinking," as it was spread in a viral manner by the media and the institutions. In effect, the virus lent itself increasingly to validating the credibility (and false confidence) of this living story and self-justified the beliefs that the prosperity would continue. The existence of this *phenomenon* was hard to see as we cannot step back and observe the contagiousness and stickiness directly while it is occurring, and it was easy to underestimate and neglect the media influences.

Indeed, to conclude that the world is led by intelligent minds that act independently of the media events surrounding them is unrealistic; however, the magnitude of the contagiousness and stickiness attributes influencing the systems and thought patterns played a role in our collective financial reality. In a sense, intellectual arrogance exerted a growing influence over the meltdown of the world economy and the one dramatic moment. To successfully analyze and define when the one dramatic moment occurred, in effect, when it moved to the tipping point, the context of the characteristics of the previous two attributes must be factored into the end result. Understanding such a phenomenon is like understanding the growth and spread of a disease epidemic. Epidemics occur from time to time, and their origins confuse even the experts. The contagiousness and stickiness characteristics that lead to this tipping point occurred when the number of people and organizations catching the disease exceeded the removal rate of those unaffected. This *something else* or dramatic moment occurred when the epidemic rate exceeded the optimistic view of the market and became a widespread crisis. Followed by the escalation in the media of the arguments that would support the view, soon the epidemic spiraled, and that lead to a tipping point.

Important aspects of what happened that lead to this tipping point are the way the media influenced the media space, how many people were contacted, and the subsequent *rippling effect* in the media. The media constantly reported stories about housing price movements, and when the movements in the media tended to embellish and legitimize what people were feeling and thinking, it promoted the living story. With the housing bubble, under certain circumstances people were generally hoping and adapting to an excessively optimistic viewpoint based on the information that was being presented. The speculative bubble, in effect, caused an information cascade, to borrow a term used by economic theorists Sushil Gandhi, David Hirsch and Ivo Welch.[256]

The belief in investing in homes that became a collective belief fit the bubble after the late 1990s. The fact that this contagiousness and stickiness thinking caught on after 2000 wasn't something new, as the atmosphere of housing speculation dates back to the beginning of US history. Historian Aaron Sakolski, in his 1932 book *The Great American Land Bubble: The Amazing Story of Land Grabbing, Speculations, and Booms from Colonial Days to the Present Time* said, "America, from its inception, was a speculation."[257] Neither were the housing prices that contributed to the international financial crisis meltdown was not a localized phenomenon. This aspect of the living story was carried by the media to cover real estate everywhere. For example, in contrast to the housing boom in California in the 1880s, many people from other states rushed to Southern California to participate in it. During this meltdown, there was no suggestion of a national sense that it would affect every city outside of California.[258]

What has changed since that time and turned United States citizens into avid speculators in so many different places was the exaggerated attention brought on by media. Behind the housing crisis and the world energy crisis and the world food crisis, is the way all individuals throughout the globe are connected to the living stories in many different markets brought about

---

256 An *information cascade* occurs when those in a group disregard their own independent viewpoint and rely on collective information because they feel everyone else simply couldn't be wrong. And when they disregard their own independent information and act instead on general information, as they perceive it, they squelch the value of their own information. Over time, the group of the population melts into a further collective judgment, and the quality of the information declines." Robert J. SCHILLER, *The Subprime Solution: How Today's Global Financial Crisis Happened, and What to Do about It*, Princeton University Press, Princeton, NJ, p. 47.

257 *Ibid.*, p. 55.

258 Aaron M. SAKOLSKI, The Great American Land Bubble: The Amazing Story of Land Grabbing, Speculations, and Booms from Colonial Days to the Present Time, Johnson Reprint Corp.

by media technology. Before 2007, people stopped seeing the rise in prices as a bubble that would eventually end, and they got stuck in the momentum of a wild ride where they had no way of exiting. People began to believe what was carried in stickiness media that the boom times would never end...that a tipping point would never occur.

Real Estate "Myth"

Economist William Baumol stated in what has come to be termed "Baumol's Law" that the cost of those goods and services whose production is amenable to technological progress will tend to decline over time relative to the cost of goods and services that are by their nature not so amenable to technological progress.[259] This law suggests, therefore, that the price of homes, compared to the structural complements of the housing sector, such as of new tools, methodologies of construction and materials should fall over time. Yet actual building costs are really only affected by the availability of land and its value. In the U.S. Census for the year 2000, urban land area accounted for 2.6% of the total land area in the United States.[260] High-value homes in major cities were priced based on location relative to the rest of the built environment, not the unique value of the land. So there was a particular tendency during the housing boom to regard price increases as generally good news. The idea that public policy should actually validate the real estate values and prevent the collapse of home prices from ever happening is a fundamental error as a sudden drop in home prices indeed disrupts economy, producing undesirable systematic effects to the industry. But according to Robert Schiller, "...in the long run, home price drops are clearly a good thing."[261] In other words, the short-run/long-run paradox benefit calls to mind Keynesian economic theory: "...in the short run, we fear a sudden increase in the savings rate, which might trigger a recession, but in the long run, we want a higher savings rate, because we need the resources for investment for the future."[262]

In understanding when and why the one dramatic moment or tipping point occurred, it is important to look at the short run and the long run separately, particularly in terms of the international financial crisis, as the two are very

259 Robert J. Schiller, The Subprime Solution: How Today's Global Financial Crisis Happened, and What to Do about It, op. cit., p. 71.

260 *Ibid.*, p. 73.

261 *Ibid.*, p. 84.

262 *Ibid.*, p. 85.

different approaches. The short-term focus is on the subprime disaster, and the long-term focus is on the solutions that we are currently struggling with to reset the world economic balance. And perhaps we could also argue, the tipping point has yet to end.

Subprime Disaster

Between 1997 and 2006, the price of the typical American house increased by 124%.[263] And during the two decades ending in 2001, the national median home price ranged from 2.9 to 3.1 times median household income. This ratio rose to 4.0 in 2004 and 4.6 in 2006.[264] This housing bubble contributed to the stickiness characteristic by homeowners who refinanced their homes at lower interest rates by taking out second mortgages secured by the price appreciation. In a Peabody Award winning program, National Public Radio correspondents argued that, "a Giant Pool of Money ($70 trillion in worldwide fixed income investments) sought higher yields than those offered by U.S. Treasury bonds early in the decade. Further, this money had roughly doubled in size from 2000 to 2007, yet the supply of relatively safe, income- generating investments had not grown as fast."[265]

Wall Street responded to this demand with the MBS and CDO financial instruments discussed earlier, all designated as "safe" by the credit rating agencies. In effect, Wall Street was connected to this money by the mortgage market with enormous fees to those throughout the mortgage supply chain; from the mortgage broker selling the loans, to small banks that funded the brokers, to the giant investment banks. During 2003, the supply of mortgages which originated at traditional lending standards was exhausted. However, strong demand for MBS and CDO drove down lending standards, so mortgages still were able to be sold. This speculative financing bubble proved unsustainable, as the CDO in particular, enabled financial institutions to obtain investor funds to finance subprime and other

263 "CSI: credit crunch," *The Economist*, October 18, 2007. Retrieved from http://www.economist.com/specialreports/displaystory.cfm?story_id=9972489

264 Ben STEVERMAN and David BOGOSLAW, "The Financial Crisis Blame Game," *Bloomberg Businessweek*, October 18, 2008. Retrieved from http://www.businessweek.com/investor/content/oct2008/pi20081017_950382.htm?chan=top+news_top+news+index+-+temp_top+story

265 "Giant Pool of Money Wins Peabody," *National Public Radio, This American Life*, April 5, 2009. Retrieved from http://www.pri.org/stories/business/giant-pool-of-money.html

lending, which increased stickiness of the housing bubble (motivated by the generation of large fees).

By mid-September 2008, U.S. housing prices on average had declined by over 20% from their mid-2006 peak.[266] As prices declined, borrowers with adjustable-rate mortgages could not refinance to avoid the higher payments associated with rising interest rates and went into default. During 2007, foreclosure proceedings by lenders began on nearly 1.3 million properties, a 79% increase over 2006.[267] This increased to 2.3 million in 2008, an 81% increase compared to 2007. By August 2008, 9.2% of all U.S. mortgages outstanding were either delinquent (or in foreclosure).[268] By September 2009, it was up to 14.4%.[269] These instruments were integral to the unraveling and stickiness occurring during these periods.

Financial Institutions

The International Monetary Fund estimated that U.S. and European banks, "lost more than $1 trillion on toxic assets and from bad loans during the period between January 2007 to September 2009." [270] Total losses topping to $2.8 trillion from 2007-10 (U.S. bank losses hit $1 trillion and European bank losses reached $1.6 trillion). [271]

One of the first bank failures was a British bank, Northern Rock. This highly leveraged bank requested security from the Bank of England. Which in turn, led to a contributing stickiness characteristic *investor panic* and a bank run in mid-September 2007. Liberal Democrats calling to nationalize the in-

---

266 "A Helping Hand to Homeowners," *The Economist*, October 23, 2008. Retrieved from http://www.economist.com/node/12470547?story_id=12470547

267 RealtyTrac Staff, "U.S. Foreclosure Activity Increases 75 Percent in 2007," *RealtyTrac*, January 30, 2008. Retrieved from http://www.realtytrac.com/content/press-releases/us-foreclosure-activity-increases-75-percent-in-2007-3604?accnt=64847

268 "Delinquencies and Foreclosures Increase in Latest MBA National Delinquency Survey," Mortgage Bankers Association, September 5, 2008. Retrieved from http://www.mbaa.org/NewsandMedia/PressCenter/64769.htm

269 "Delinquencies Continue to Climb in Latest MBA National Delinquency Survey," Mortgage Bankers Association, November 19, 2009. Retrieved from http://www.mbaa.org/NewsandMedia/PressCenter/71112.htm

270 "U.S., European Bank Writedowns, Credit Losses," *Reuters.com*, November 5, 2009. Retrieved from http://www.reuters.com/article/2009/11/05/banks-write-downs-losses-idCNL5541556200911O5?rpc=44

271 Ibid.

stitution were initially ignored; but February 2008, the British government relented, and the bank was taken into public hands (having failed to find a private sector buyer). Northern Rock's problems point to the stickiness characteristic that would soon impact other banks and financial institutions.

Initially, as this aspect of stickiness spread, bolstered by the media coverage, companies affected were those directly involved in home construction and mortgage lending. But as the virus spread, over 100 mortgage lenders went bankrupt during 2007 and 2008. Leading to investment bank Bear Stearns' collapse in March 2008 resultant fire-sale to JP Morgan Chase. This stickiness characteristic of the crisis hit its peak in September and October 2008. Several major institutions either failed, were acquired after diminished value, or, subject to government takeover. These included Lehman Brothers, Merrill Lynch, Fannie Mae, Freddie Mac, and AIG.[272]

Global Markets

During September 2008, the International Financial crisis hit its most critical moment. The equivalent of a bank run on money market mutual funds was occurring. These are funds which frequently invest in commercial paper which is issued by corporations to fund their operations and payrolls. Withdrawals from money markets were $144.5 billion during one week, versus $7.1 billion the week prior.[273] This froze the ability of corporations to replace (rollover) their short-term debt. The U.S. government then extended insurance for money market accounts similar to bank deposit insurance with Federal Reserve programs to purchase commercial paper via temporary guarantees (TEDs).

The TEDs increased, an indicator of perceived credit risk in the general economy, with a high reached in July 2007, and continued to remain volatile, then rose even higher in September 2008, to a never before reached record of 4.65% on October 10, 2008.[274]

---

272 Roger C. ALTMAN, "The Great Crash, 2008, A Geopolitical Setback for the West," *op. cit.*

273 Diya GULLAPALLI and Shefalli ANAND, "Bailout of Money Funds Seems to Stanch Outflow," *Wall Street Journal*, September 20, 2008. Retrieved from http://online.wsj.com/article/SB122186683086958875.html?mod=article-outset-box

274 "Ted Spread," *Bloomberg*. Retrieved from http://www.bloomberg.com/quote/!TEDSP:IND

As these stickiness events were occurring, during a pivotal meeting on September 18, 2008, Treasury Secretary Henry Paulson and, Federal Reserve Chairman Ben Bernanke testified before key legislators and proposed a $700 billion emergency bailout. Bernanke was reported to have said: "If we don't do this, we may not have an economy on Monday."[275]

The Emergency Economic Stabilization Act (also called the Troubled Asset Relief Program: TARP) was signed into law on October 3, 2008.[276] Economist Paul Krugman and U.S. Treasury Secretary Timothy Geithner tried to explain the crisis as the implosion of the shadow banking system, which had increased in size to nearly equal the importance of the traditional commercial banking sector. In the absence of the ability to obtain investor funds, investment banks and other entities, could not provide funds to mortgage firms (and other corporations). This meant that nearly one-third of the U.S. lending system was frozen and continued to be frozen into June 2009. The Tipping Point was now evident and impacting at an alarming rate. Media was overwhelmed with stories echoing the events.

According to the Brookings Institution, the traditional banking system did not have the capital to close this gap as of June 2009: "It would take a number of years of strong profits to generate sufficient capital to support that additional lending volume."[277] They went further to indicate that some forms of securitization are "likely to vanish forever, having been an artifact of excessively loose credit conditions."[278]

The Tipping Point

During the period between June 2007 and November 2008, Americans had lost an estimated average of more one quarter of their collective net worth. By early November 2008, the S&P 500, was down 45 percent from its 2007 high. Housing prices had dropped 20% from their 2006 peak. Total home equity in the United States, which was valued at $13 trillion at its

---

275 Joe NOCERA, "As Credit Crisis Spiraled, Alarm Led to Action," *New York Times*, October 1, 2008. Retrieved from http://www.nytimes.com/2008/10/02/business/02crisis.html

276 "Bailout is Law," *CNN Money*, October 4, 2008. Retrieved from http://money.cnn.com/2008/10/03/news/economy/house_friday_bailout/index.htm

277 Martin Neil BAILY and Douglas J. ELLIOT, "The U.S. Financial and Economic Crisis: Where Does It Stand and Where Do We Go From Here?," *op. cit.*

278 Ibid.

peak in 2006, had dropped to $8.8 trillion by mid-2008 and falling more in late 2008. Total retirement assets, Americans' second-largest household asset, dropped by 22 percent, from $10.3 trillion in 2006 to $8 trillion in mid-2008. During the same period, savings and investment assets (apart from retirement savings) lost $1.2 trillion and pension assets lost $1.3 trillion.

Taken together, these losses totaled a staggering $8.3 trillion. Since peaking in the second quarter of 2007, US household wealth was down $14 trillion. [279] Cash used by consumers from home equity extraction, (which had doubled from $627 billion in 2001 to $1,428 billion in 2005 as the housing bubble built), ballooned to a total of nearly $5 trillion over the period.[280] U.S. home mortgage debt relative to GDP increased from an average of 46% during the 1990s and to a staggering 73% during 2008 reaching $10.5 trillion.[281] U.S. homeowners had borrowed significant equity in their homes to fund their lifestyles and they could no longer do once housing prices collapsed.

To offset this decline in consumption (lending capacity), the U.S. government (and U.S. Federal Reserve) committed $13.9 trillion, $6.8 trillion which was invested or spent as of June 2009.[282] In effect, the Federal Reserve has gone from being the lender of *last resort* to the lender of *only resort* for a significant portion of the economy. The Tipping Point had occurred in the US and was now spreading epidemically throughout the globe, fueled in part, by the media platforms that attempted to report the story.

The International Financial Crisis may have been a result of a deeper crisis, which is systemic of capitalism itself. According to *Samir Amin*, an Egyptian economist, the constant decrease in GDP growth rates in Western

279 Roger C. ALTMAN, "The Great Crash, 2008, A Geopolitical Setback for the West," *op. cit.*

280 Alan GREENSPAN and James KENNEDY, "Sources and Uses of Equity Extracted from Homes," *op. cit.*; "Home Equity Extraction: The Real Cost of 'Free Cash'," *op. cit.*; "Spending Boosted by Home Equity Loans: Greenspan," *op. cit.*

281 Colin BARR, "The $4 Trillion Housing Headache," *op. cit.*

282 "Government Support for Financial Assets and Liabilities Announced in 2008 and Soon Thereafter ($ in billions)," *FDIC Supervisory Insights Summer 2009*, Federal Deposit Insurance Corporation, Retrieved from http://www.fdic.gov/regulations/examinations/supervisory/insights/sisum09/si_sum09.pdf

countries since the early 1970s created a growing surplus of capital that did not have sufficient profitable investment outlets in the real economy. The alternative was to place this surplus into the financial market, which then became more profitable than productive capital investment, especially with subsequent deregulation. According to Amin, this tipping point phenomenon (has) led to recurrent financial bubbles (such as the internet bubble) and is the deeper cause of the financial crisis.[283]

John C. Bogle wrote in 2005, "a series of unresolved challenges that have contributed to past financial crises and have not been sufficiently addressed to face capitalism. Corporate America went astray largely because the power of managers (financial) went virtually unchecked. They failed to keep an eye on (these geniuses to) whom they had entrusted the responsibility of the management of America's great corporations."[284].

Section 4.4 Summary

What is interesting is that when the Financial Crisis Inquiry Commission released their report in January 2011, it hardly made for compelling reading because so little had changed as a result of the international financial crisis in both banking and regulation. The report shows chapter and verse about the bumbling management of the largest banks in the United States (and by the federal government) and, the fact that these institutions are even bigger than they were before the crisis. With these too-big-to-fail institutions now larger than ever, we are almost certainly poised to go through another tipping point like the one just analyzed in the not too distant future.

In the Commission Report, reviewing the period between 2000 and 2006, confirms the Federal Reserve did not exert any authority on predatory lending, and only a total of three institutions were referred to prosecutors for possible fair-lending violations on mortgages. The regulators were coddling bank managers, and executives were busy telling their investors that everything was in great shape. The report specifically highlights Countrywide Financial, the subprime lender. On August 2, 2007, Countrywide's

283 Samir AMIN, "Financial Collapse, Systemic Crisis?" World Forum for Alternatives, Caracas, October 2008. Retrieved from http://www.globalresearch.ca/index.php?context=va&aid=11099

284 John C. BOGLE, *The Battle for the Soul of Capitalism*, Yale University Press, New Haven, CT.

access to crucial mortgage financing had dried up, and commercial paper investors would not buy its obligations. Confirmed in a report quoting Angelo R. Mozilo the company's chief executive.[285] Yet the company's chief financial officer said in a statement that very same day that Countrywide had plenty of liquidity and had experienced: "...no disruption in financing its ongoing daily operations, including placement of commercial paper."[286] The credit rating agency Moody's reaffirmed the company's triple A rating at the same time. Two weeks later, Countrywide drew down its 11.5 billion credit lines, signaling extreme distress to the markets. The stock plunged a few months later, and the lender was taken over in distress by Bank of America.[287] This commission report also pointed out how Citigroup silenced the *ticking time bombs* that were shoved around on its balance sheet and soon were evidenced by enormous losses. In retrospect, the US government poured mountains of cash to help these banks through the crisis. This report adds to understanding of the events describing how the Treasury Department actually changed the tax code to assist and benefit banks in acquiring weaker institutions. Case in point, the Constitution of the United States provides for the fact that only Congress can write tax rules, however the Internal Revenue Service issued its new position on this with its notice 2008 – 83, released on September 30, 2008.[288] Hence, the reason that Wells Fargo stepped in to top Citigroup's proposal to buy the beleaguered bank Wachovia. The fact remains that the IRS was changing the code on the fly for the banks who wanted to get something for nothing out of the crisis.

Referring again to Mr. Mozilo, the report highlights the made comments to the commission describing his company: "as having prevented social unrest by providing loans to 25 million borrowers, many of them members of minority groups".[289] What he failed to understand and comprehend was that the throngs of loans that were made resulted in foreclosures and evictions and contributed to the tipping point epidemic. Mr. Mozilo was

285 Gretchen MORGENSON, "A Bank Crisis Whodunit, With Laughs and Tears," New York Times, January 29, 2011. Retrieved from http://www.nytimes.com/2011/01/30/business/30gret.html

286 Ibid.

287 Ibid.

288 Gretchen MORGENSON, "A Bank Crisis Whodunit, With Laughs and Tears," *op. cit.*

289 Ibid.

unaware of the consequences of his failure, and he even went on to say: "...and probably made more difference to society, to the integrity of our society, and any company in the history of America."

Does another financial crisis lie in with this kind of thinking? Commission investigators reviewing the United States Troubled Asset Relief Program (TARP) also seem to think so. By stepping in to save these big banks in 2008, the bailout did little more to reassure troubled markets and encourage high risk behavior by protecting the risk takers from the consequences of failure. What is occurring right now in Europe (2012 - Greek Crisis) probably will occur again in United States, as additional bailouts and debt reinforcement only potentially fuel more bad behavior (reinforcing the *Broken Windows* application) with potentially disastrous tipping point results. Upon reviewing the report, one finds that it falls short on several key points regarding the 2007- 2010 International Financial Crisis and the essential question of "What did the Wall Street bankers know and when did they know it?" How was the impact of the media integral to the developments and information at the time?

The bottom line was that the banks were clearly engaged in a system of self-dealing, pushing instruments of finance that they were having trouble selling. Banks such as Merrill Lynch knew going into 2007 that they were in trouble, and there was an agreement on the street, in so many words of: *you buy my bad products and I'll buy yours*. The point was that they were trying to sell each other otherwise unsellable pieces in order to complete deals and generate fees. Such arrangements were only made to prop up the value of assets that were otherwise collapsing. Citigroup provided the commission documents that suggested how overleveraged the Citi structured CEO's securities in fact were during this time, but that information was not released in the report. And certainly only later reached the media. The other fundamental question was concerning the credit rating agencies and how this was reported. How were the banks able to create tens of billions of CDOs in the spring of 2007 after the market was already falling apart? Moody's, for example, reported in March of 2007 that they knew the activities by banks like Merrill Lynch, Citibank and UBS. These banks were still furiously doing transactions to clear out their balance sheets. Moody's knew the banks were making new CDOs to create the illusion that and lure buyers for bad assets to avoid taking losses on. Moody's credit did not downgrade the CDOs for months afterwards. The report is seriously deficient about these facts. In context, the report was prepared under a timetable that was too short, its budget too small, and its commissioners too partisan. And, all these bankers knew that their lawyers could fight any subpoena for documents for more than a year rather than handing over any documents that would tell the real living story. There are those who believe that the transcripts of the interviews with the bankers would tell the real story, and some academics may believe they have a better take on what actually happened during the financial crisis on Wall Street. Yet, when these events are juxtaposed with the media coverage, public, financial and market reactions, one concludes the tipping point theory attributes and characteristics were in place.

As I turn to the final case study: *Climate Change*, I proceed with a similar approach the highlighting the contagiousness and stickiness characteristics and ultimately what could be this study's global tipping point, indeed, potentially influenced by many of the same types of media communication systems that delivered the messages and influenced and impacted the first two studies.

Media Impacts and Global Events Website

For further information please visit the
Media impact and Global Events Website:

http://mdgparis.typepad.com/global_media_and_world_ev/

This website tracks, highlights, categorizes and provides a articles and commentary related to Tipping Point Attributes and Characteristics, as well as information and recent updates related specifically to the three case studies included in this version and other Media and Global Event issues.

CHAPTER FIVE
CASE STUDY THREE

Three: Climate Change

Introduction

Much has been said recently about the increasing need to fuel our cities and economies and the toll it is taking and effect on our planet's energy resources. This last case study explores some of the political, economic, cultural, and moral issues relevant to climate change as global event. From the onset of this case study I would like to begin by framing the discussion:

> Science is about probability, not certainty. And the persisting uncertainties in climate science leave room for argument. What is a realistic estimate of how much temperatures will rise? How severe will the effects be? Are there tipping points beyond which the changes are uncontrollable?[290]

In approaching this study, my expectation was to find a blistering controversy about climate change with no clear position. However, my research points out an overwhelming consensus, and even though mainstream me-

290 Andrew C. REVKIN and John M. BRODER, "Facing Skeptics, Climate Experts Sure of Peril," *New York Times*, December 7, 2009, p. A1, A8.

dia was pretty much on the same page, doubt had worked into in all the reports about climate change, as for every scientist warning of global warming, there was another scientist saying that the claims were inaccurate. Countless scholarly reports are cited herein where essentially all of the world's leading scientists and academics appear all to be speaking with the same voice. They all say the same thing…that the world's climate is changing dangerously, and humans are to blame. My initial research question became "Why had climate change become a media debate?" Media and technology had influenced the other two case studies and their outcomes to a large degree. Was perhaps the murkiness or confusion on the climate change issue brought about by an organized media campaign as well? Or was it financed by the biased agendas, such as those of the coal and oil industries, to make us think that climate change science is somehow still controversial, that climate change is still unproven?

This case study first presents two parts, the first concerning the contagiousness attribute--identifying research, trends, and facts that exist-to-date. The second explores the stickiness attribute—and presenting how the system of sharing of the truth has clouded the issue and pointing out some of the media impact on this *living story*. My objective is a redirect towards a *global consciousness*. I also explore whether or not it is possible that this new global consciousness, fostered and promoted by media platforms, could be focused to address our future global reality with new technologies (and those which are still evolving) in order to avoid a global event. Finally, the study discusses the potential tipping point, or one dramatic moment for climate change.

My intention is more than just to present a research collection of articles, conclusions, and opinions. Rather, I attempt to detail a complete narrative put in context of the tipping point attributes and characteristics similar to that of the Obama Presidential Campaign and the International Financial Crisis studies. This third case study will illustrate that climate change as a global event is directly related to media impact and is really a conversation that needs to be had as we have arrived at a critical juncture in human history. By mastering our new (and innovative) media technologies and utilizing the media influence for our global consciousness, I explore whether or not we are capable of outperforming the inevitable and changing the course of history, in effect to remake the global environmental landscape and rewrite the future.

Before I begin I would like to make two important points. The debate about climate change is mostly conducted by people who live in cities where everything is artificial. Where they don't actually experience the changes that are taking place in the real world, and, the scientists, who have been telling us the truth when they say the world is at risk, and if we listen to those who are manipulating the media, we are in trouble.

Climate Change Defined

Climate change is the increase in the average temperature of the Earth's near-surface air and oceans since the mid-20th century and its projected continuation. Global surface temperatures have increased 0.74 ± 0.18 °C (1.33 ± 0.32 °F) between the start and the end of the 20th century.[291] The Intergovernmental Panel on Climate Change (IPCC) concludes that most of the observed temperature increases since the middle of the 20th century were caused by increasing concentrations of greenhouse gases resulting from human activity such as fossil fuel burning and deforestation.[292] Climate model projections summarized in the latest IPCC report indicate that the global surface temperature will probably rise a further 1.1 to 6.4 °C (2.0 to 11.5 °F) during the twenty-first century.[293] Global temperatures are predicted to cause sea levels to rise and will change the amount and pattern of precipitation, probably including expansion of subtropical deserts. In addition, the continuing retreat of glaciers, permafrost and sea ice is expected with warming will be strongest in the Arctic. Other likely effects include: increases in the intensity of extreme weather events, species extinctions, and changes in agricultural yields.

The Attributes

To begin, some parameters in this case study are outlined for the various climate change tipping point attributes. The goal is to identify the actions and reactions of the various media sectors involved in the climate change living story and identify the potential inter-relationships of these attributes and characteristics. From the research, these attribute relationships are identified and are analyzed

291 *Climate Change 2001: The Scientific Basis*, Contribution of Working Group I to the Third Assessment Report of the Intergovernmental Panel on Climate Change (IPCC), H.T. Houghton, Y. Ding, D.J. Griggs, M. Noguer, P.J. van der Linden, X. Dai, K. Maskell, and C.A. Johnson (eds.), Cambridge and New York, Cambridge University Press, 2001.

292 Ibid.

293 Ibid.

and compared in the following chapters in construction of our tipping point qualitative ratio analysis framework. The characteristics represent the key people, organizations, media, and events that impact this global event.

The influence of the media and the messages (delivered by and with the media technology) is a complicated issue to identify with for a future tipping point. One can easily interpret these attributes and characteristics from many perspectives. However, the intent of my research is to define why and when the one dramatic event might occur and compare this to the other two case studies via a similar analysis. This method for analyzing these attributes is, simply stated, to look at the sequence of events in chronological manner and observe the way they develop and how the various media sectors play their role.

Section 5.1 Contagiousness Attributes (C)

An analogy about climate change is that we are standing on a cliff, and behind us is a *considerable crowd* – (7 billion people and counting), and below is a beautiful shimmering pool. Some people say you can jump into that pool without any risk, as people have been doing this for ages without any problems, while others issue a warning and say the weather has been eating away at the foot of the cliff causing big rocks to fall into the water, and the risk of jumping grows more frightening by the day. In terms of the *considerable crowd* (world's population), below are the milestones that have already been reached and current forecasts for the future:

3 Billion: 30 January 1960

4 Billion: 8 September 1974

5 Billion: 31 March 1987

6 Billion: 20 January 1999

7 Billion: 26 August 2011

8 Billion: 27 April 2025

9 Billion: 10 August 2045[1]

World Population: 1950-2050

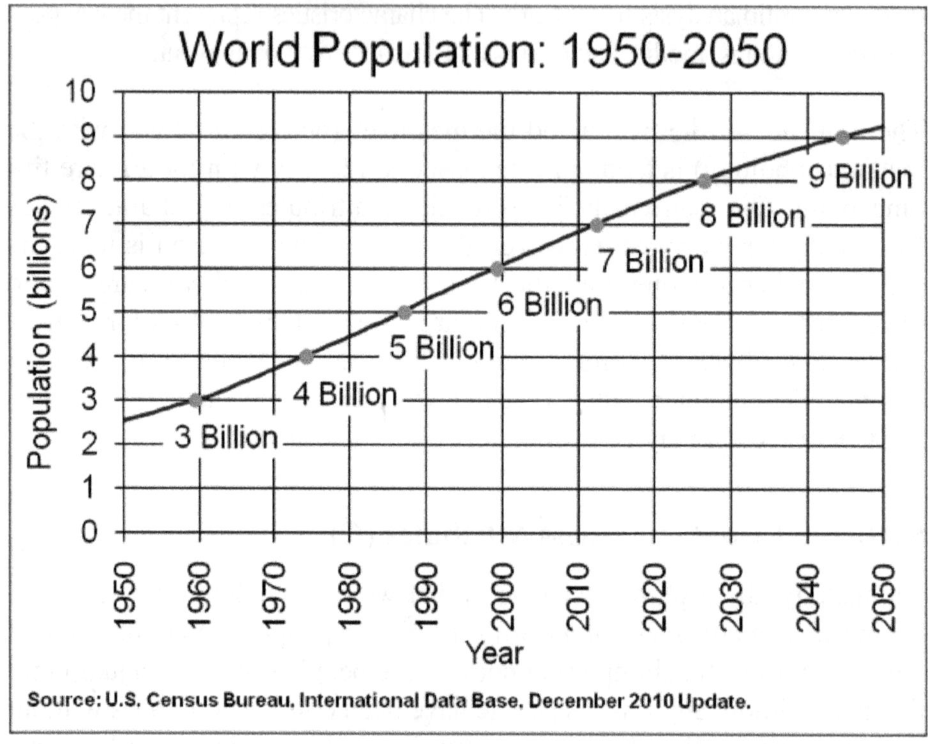

Source: U.S. Census Bureau, International Data Base, December 2010 Update.

The world's population three centuries from now will stabilize at 9 billion if fertility levels continue their decline, particularly in the developing world, but they could also top more than 1.3 trillion if they remain unchanged from current rates according to statistics released by the United Nations. According to medium-level projections, women in every country will each have about two children in the decades to come raising the world population from its current 6.4 billion to 9 billion in 2300.[294] But even small variations in these forecasts will have enormous impacts on the (world) ecosystems in the long term. As little as one-quarter of a child under the two-child norm, or one-quarter of a child above the norm, would result in world populations ranging from 2.3 billion to 36.4 billion. If fertility levels remain unchanged at today's levels, however, world population would rise to 44 billion in 2100, 244 billion persons in 2150 and 1.34 trillion in 2300 according to the UN Population Division Report, World

294 United Nations Department of Economic and Social Affairs/Population Division (UNDES), "World Population in 2300 to be around Nine Billion Persons," *op. cit.*, p. 1.

Population to 2300. The UN said this clearly indicates that "current high fertility levels cannot continue over the long term."[295] Given progress in extending life expectancy, the UN said, people could expect, on average, to live more than 95 years by 2300. Japan, which is the global leader in life expectancy today, is projected to have a life expectancy of more than 106 years by 2300.[296]

With regard to climate change, the people who we are listening to in the media sometimes are just not qualified to make pronouncements, and many have forgotten entirely whose interests they are supposed to be protecting, and some are quite willing to sacrifice a substantial number of people if they think there's a profit to be made in the process. And, the tipping point attributes and characteristics in the media that are influencing this phenomenon may be affecting the evolution. That's what this case study strives to answer about this global event: If we listen to media and people who have obvious conflicts of interest, do we risk falling off the cliff? In the past two decades in particular, given that complex ecosystems are being affected by human (mankind) activities, has there also been an organized agenda on the world's trust and a corresponding collapse in the integrity of the global consciousness? Great institutions of science and government seem to have lost their credibility, and the watchdogs, who many thought were the media, may have lost their focus. Entities such as the Intergovernmental Panel on Climate Change (IPCC) are questioned, and enterprises such as WikiLeaks only become more powerful. This provides the backdrop of my research as I explore each of the attributes and their characteristics.

Section 5.1.1 People

Scientists, as of the writing, are 90% sure that climate change is happening and that we, humans, are responsible. But with science, skepticism is part of the territory. As in the past, scientists doubting the certainties of the world have advanced the human body of knowledge. No scientist would deny the facts of a widely accepted conclusion without making a verifiable argument to the contrary. Genuine scientists, adhering to a very strict

---

295 "World Population in 2300 could Stabilize at 9 Billion, UN Estimates," United Nations News Centre, November 4, 2004. Retrieved from http://www.un.org/apps/news/story.asp?NewsID=12439

296 Ibid.

discipline, set out their theories and their experiments carefully and then subject them to review by other scientists. All scientists who approach the understanding of climate change have a certain degree of research that has underpinned their work for many years. For example the *greenhouse effect*, by which gases such as carbon dioxide absorb heat and set up a warming blanket around the world, was first proposed by the French mathematician and physicist Joseph Fourier in 1824. In the 1850s, the Irish physicist John Tyndall came up with a way to measure the capacities of various gases, and by the end of the 1850s effectively proved Fourier's theory. By the end of the 19th century, scientists had advanced the theory even further and predicted that humans might actually increase the temperature of the earth by burning fossil fuels, and in the process, increase the amount of carbon dioxide in the atmosphere.

Every living thing on the earth is composed of carbon in one form or another. Plants absorb the carbon dioxide and then convert the carbon into carbohydrates and then release the oxygen back into the atmosphere. Soil absorbs dead plants over the hundreds of millions of years into the swamps or into oceans and then they become covered with layers and layers of carboniferous matter. Under perfect conditions, heat and pressure convert these massive carbon files to coal, oil, or natural gas. Over the last two centuries humans have been digging up the stockpiles of fossil fuels and setting fire to them as energy sources to support their activities, releasing the resulting carbon dioxide back into the atmosphere. Scientist estimate a doubling of the atmospheric carbon dioxide, will increase the temperature as much as 3.8°F.[297] And most recently, a report of the IPCC estimated that this doubling of carbon dioxide will increase the global average temperature by between 3.6 and 8.1°, as the concentration of carbon dioxide in the atmosphere has already risen since 1850 by more than one third, from 280 ppm to 385 ppm, with indications that the planet will reach a doubling of this number near the middle of this century.[298]

The American oceanographer Roger Revelle was one of the first people to explain the *greenhouse effect* to the former US Vice-president and Noble Laureate Al Gore when they were both students at Harvard in the 60s. In

297 *Climate Change 2001: The Scientific Basis*, Contribution of Working Group I to the Third Assessment Report of the Intergovernmental Panel on Climate Change (IPCC), *op. cit.*

298 Ibid.

1957, Revelle published a paper in which he predicted global warming. He said at the time that humans were in fact conducting "a great geophysical experiment" and had no conception of the impacts.[299] In February of 1965, then-President Lyndon Johnson said in a message to Congress, "This generation has altered the composition of the atmosphere on a global scale through...a steady increase in carbon dioxide from the burning of fossil fuels,"[300] and in 1979, the National Academy of Sciences report authored by scientist J. Charney said, "There appears to be a consensus that climate change will result from man's combustion of fossil fuels and changes in land use."[301] Scientists understand that even a small increase in the average temperature of the globe could throw off the equilibrium that existed on the earth since a long time before the beginning of mankind, and scientists then began warning about global melting of the glaciers in the collapsing ice caps. They also warned about the floods, droughts, and rising tides. Scientists studied changes in the world's living conditions that would be more dramatic than anything in human history and more sudden than anything that had happened in hundreds of thousands of years.

The politicians during the 80s used the climate change question as a means to becoming the president of the United States. Presidential candidate George H. W. Bush, running against democrat contender Michael Dukakis, said that he would talk about the global warming and he would act.[302] In 1988 the world community gathered to create the Intergovernmental Panel on Climate Change, and Bush signed into law the National Energy Policy Act to:

> ...establish a national energy policy that would quickly reduce the generation of carbon dioxide and trace gases as quickly as feasible

---

299 Roger REVELLE and Hans SEUSS, "Carbon Dioxide Exchange between Atmosphere and Ocean and the Question of an Increase of Atmospheric CO2 during the Past Decades," *Tellus*, 9, 1957, p. 18-27.

300 United States. "Restoring the Quality of Our Environment," Environmental Pollution Panel, President's Science Advisory Committee, Washington, D.C., White House,1965.

301 Jule G. CHARNEY, "Carbon Dioxide and Climate: A Scientific Assessment," National Academy of Sciences Summer Studies Center, Washington, D.C., National Academy of Sciences, 1979. Retrieved from www.atmos.ucla.edu/~brianpm/download/charney_report.pdf

302 James HOGGAN and Richard D. LITTLEMORE, *Climate Cover-up: The Crusade to Deny Global Warming*, Vancouver, Canada, Greystone Books, 2009, p. 19.

> in order to slow the pace and the degree of atmospheric warming... to protect the global environment.[303]

This is all a matter of history, scientific history, the point being that in 1988 when the IPCC was created, no one seemed to be confused about climate change. With every new report and with every new experiment that was published in legitimate peer-reviewed scientific journals, the science community all appeared to agree. Even among the scientists who studied the scientists and those who researched the exhausted web of knowledge between the period 1993 and 2003, for example, as was done in a study by Naomi Oreskes, a professor at the University of California, not a single scientist was found to have taken exception to the consensus position.[304]

Section 5.1.2 Organizations

Intergovernmental Panel on Climate Change (IPCC)
The Intergovernmental Panel on Climate Change published the following on its website:

> ...Weather station records and ship-based observations indicate that global mean surface air temperature warmed between about 0.4 and 0.8°C (0.7 and 1.5°F) during the 20th century. Although the magnitude of warming varies locally, the warming trend is spatially widespread and is consistent with an array of other evidence detailed in this report. The ocean, which represents the largest reservoir of heat in the climate system, has warmed by about 0.05°C (0.09°F) averaged over the layer extending from the surface down to 10,000 feet, since the 1950s...
>
> ...Virtually all the 20th century warming in global surface air temperature occurred between the early 1900s and the 1940s and during the past few decades. The troposphere warmed much more during the 1970s than during the two subsequent decades, whereas Earth's surface warmed more during the past two decades than during the 1970s. The causes of these irregularities and the disparities in the timing are not completely understood. One striking change

303 *Ibid.*, p. 19.
304 *Ibid.*, p. 20.

> of the past 35 years is the cooling of the stratosphere at altitudes of ~13 miles, which has tended to be concentrated in the wintertime polar cap region.[305]

The IPCC's conclusion accurately reflects the current thinking of the scientific community on this issue. The confidence in the IPCC assessment is even higher today than it was 10 or 5 years ago, but uncertainty remains because: 1. of the level of natural variability inherent in the climate system on time scales of decades to centuries; 2. the questionable ability of models to accurately simulate natural variability on those long time scales; and 3. the degree of confidence that can be placed on reconstructions of global mean temperature over the past millennium based on proxy evidence. Despite the uncertainties, there is general agreement that the observed warming is real and particularly strong within the past 20 years. Climate change simulations for the period of 1990 to 2100 based on the IPCC emissions scenarios yield a globally-averaged surface temperature increase by the end of the century of 1.4 to 5.8°C (2.5 to 10.4°F) relative to 1990.[306]

Maintaining a vigorous, ongoing program of basic research, funded and managed independently, will be crucial for narrowing these uncertainties. The media role in addressing and presenting these questions is a priority, with agendas, corporate interests, and global value judgments becoming particularly important when assessing the potential impacts on natural ecosystems. The complexity is difficult at best, and, whether or not there is a tipping point in the concentration of greenhouse gases that, if exceeded, would cause dramatic changes to the Earth system or, whether or not the tipping point consequences, as a function of the concentration of greenhouse gases, are sufficiently known that the scientific community can define an acceptable level based on an analysis of potential risks and damages.

The future of Climate Change in fact, depends on the nature (e.g., rate and magnitude of concentrations of greenhouse gases) and the sensitivity of the climate system. Whereas, determining acceptable concentrations of green-

---

305 David G. VICTOR, *Climate Change: Debating America's Policy Options*, New York, Council on Foreign Relations Press, 2004, p. 143-144.

306 *Climate Change 2001: The Scientific Basis*, Contribution of Working Group I to the Third Assessment Report of the Intergovernmental Panel on Climate Change (IPCC), *op. cit.*

house gases depend on: 1 the ability to determine the sensitivity of the climate system, 2. knowledge of the full range of the other influential factors, and, 3. an assessment of the risks and vulnerabilities. Both the IPCC and the U.S. National Assessment of Climate Change Impacts assess potential climate impacts using approaches that are "scenario-driven."

In other words, the current models utilize a range of climate sensitivities to assess the potential impacts on water, health, forestry, agriculture, human, and the coastal zones, nationally and by region. Differences among climate model projections are sufficiently large to limit the ability to define an "acceptable concentration" of atmospheric greenhouse gases.[307]

In addition, technological breakthroughs that could improve the ecosystem capabilities to adapt are not known. The potential impact of Climate Change increases as a function of the sensitivity of the respective climate model. If globally, average temperature increases approach 3°C (5.4°F) - in response to doubling of carbon dioxide, this is likely to have substantial impacts on human activities and natural ecosystems. Another fact is middle and high latitude regions are more sensitive to Climate Change than other regions, and significant impacts in these regions are likely to occur at lower temperature levels of global warming. There could be significant regional impacts and particularly those aspects of the ecosystem which are less able to adapt to change than are human systems.

In summary, the IPCC is made up of scientists from all over the world and clearly has no vested interest in misleading the public with their peer-reviewed documents, yet:

- How does (did) the media present the findings from such reports?
- What is the amount of media coverage relative to other global events?
- How is it being consumed by the populations of the world? Do they understand it?

---

307 Committee on the Science of Climate Change, National Research Council, *Climate Change Science: An Analysis of Some Key Questions*, Washington, D.C., National Academies Press, 2001.

- Is it buried in the media space with little mention or emphasis in the media agenda because of its competition with so many other events for the front page lead story line?
- Does it fit a *profile* of attributes and characteristics similar to the first two case studies?

Energy Industries

One of the largest opponents of action on Climate Change has historically been the fossil fuels energy industry, particularly, the oil industry such as *ExxonMobil*, which consistently publicizes papers attempting to minimize the threat of global warming. In 1998, Exxon began providing financial support to individuals and organizations who offered opposing views to the scientific consensus that human activities were the leading contributing factor to Climate Change such as the *Competitive Enterprise Institute*. ExxonMobil also helped create the *Global Climate Science Team* who were active climate contrarians.

According to a study by the *Union of Concerned Scientists*, between 1998 and 2005, ExxonMobil dispersed roughly $16 million to organizations that were challenging the scientific consensus view.[308] After heavy criticism from the media and environmental groups during late 2006 and early 2007, ExxonMobil sought to distance itself from these activities and organizations. In 2005, the ExxonMobil went as far as to oppose a shareholders' resolution to explain the science behind its denial of Climate Change.

In recent years, other companies have increasingly come to accept the existence the projections, sources and consequences; for example, the Chairman of *British Petroleum*, John Browne, declared a *need for action* in 2002.[309] And, Lord Oxburgh, past-executive chairman of *Shell*, said in a speech at the 2005 *Hay-on-Wye Festival*: "We have 45 years, and if we start now, not in 10 or 15 years' time, we have a chance of hitting those targets. (Referring to reducing carbon emissions) But we've got to start now.

---

308 "Smoke, Mirrors & Hot Air: How ExxonMobil uses Big Tobacco's Tactics to Manufacture Uncertainty on Climate Science," Cambridge, MA, Union of Concerned Scientists, 2007. Retrieved from http://www.ucsusa.org/assets/documents/global_warming/exxon_report.pdf

309 Ibid.

We have no time to lose."[310]

Interestedly, one sector of the energy industry that has provided little opposition to the greenhouse gas arguments is the nuclear industry. *Margret Thatcher* became one of the first major political figures to suggest that nuclear power was actually a green solution. Nuclear power produces fewer CO2 emissions than fossil fuel plants; although the exact level remains somewhat controversial. However, Greenpeace maintains that nuclear power produces about one third of the CO2 emissions (as equivalent fossil fuels energy) over the lifetime of an installation.[311]

Politics

Politics have impacted the political debate, decisions and legislation over the science discussion and response to climate change. The political struggle involved various scientific organizations, governmental bodies, and special-interest groups. Support for action to mitigate increasing global warming, with ratification and implementation of the *Kyoto Protocol*, is a high agenda item on the political left. However, one the first politicians placing global warming on the political agenda was *Richard Nixon* in 1969. Nixon thought environmental topics (such as greenhouse effect and acid rain) should be legislated by a division of NATO. The reaction to his proposals by the NATO allies was moderate, yet his initiatives gained impact in the civil field. Also, *Margaret Thatcher* was involved in bringing an anti-carbon discussion in the public agenda. In Germany *Angela Merkel*, then Secretary of the Environment (during the conservative *Helmut Kohl* government), lead the *German Kyoto Delegation* and took a substantial role in advancing the Kyoto agreement possible.[312]

In some countries, the political right is fighting on a platform of strong action against global warming, while in others, the political right either opposes action to mitigate global warming or disputes the scientific consensus on global warming, instead leaning in a direction of adaptation policies. All European countries have ratified the Kyoto Protocol and support strong reductions in greenhouse gas emissions.

---

310 Ibid.

311 Ibid.

312 Andrew PURVIS, "Heroes of the Environment: Angela Merkel," *Time*, October 17, 2007. Retrieved from http://www.time.com/time/specials/2007/article/0,28804,1663317_1663319_1669897,00.html

United States

The Bush administration launched a disinformation campaign designed to intentionally mislead the American public on the issues and any limits on "climate polluters," according to a report in *Rolling Stone* magazine that reviewed hundreds of internal government documents and interviewed former government officials. "They've got a political clientele that does not want to be regulated," says *Rick Piltz*, a former Bush climate official, a whistleblower on the White House censorship of global-warming documents in 2005. "Any honest discussion of the science would stimulate public pressure for a stronger policy. They're not stupid."[313] Bush's disinformation campaign on global warming began almost as soon as he took office. With his carefully orchestrated delay policies, the White House blocked even modest reforms and replaced them with token investments in futuristic solutions like hydrogen cars. "It's a charade," says *Jeremy Symons*, a representative on Vice-President Dick Cheney's' EPA energy task force, the industry group that met in secrecy to implement the administration's energy policy. "They have a single-minded determination to do nothing—while making it look like they are doing something."[314]

The Bush White House went as far as to move key portions of a key report from the *Center for Disease Control and Prevention* (CDC) presented to the *U.S. Senate Environment and Public Works Committee* highlighting the impacts to human health by global warming. One CDC official, familiar with both versions, the CDC version and the version given to the Senate, the version given to the Senate was "eviscerated."[315] The White House then prevented the Senate (and thus the public) from receiving key CDC projections in the report about, 1. diseases likely to flourish in a warmer climate, 2. increased injuries and deaths from severe weather such as hurricanes, 3. more respiratory problems from drought-driven air pollution, 4. an increase in waterborne diseases including cholera, 5. increases in

---

313 Tim DICKINSON, "The Secret Campaign of President Bush's Administration To Deny Global Warming," *Rolling Stone*, June 20, 2007. Retrieved from http://www.desmogblog.com/sites/beta.desmogblog.com/files/The%20Secret%20Campaign%20of%20President%20Bush%20rolling%20stone.pdf

314 Tamás FARKAS, *The Investor's Guide to the Energy Revolution*, Raleigh, NC., Lulu.com, 2008, p. 234.

315 "White House 'Eviscerated' CDC Testimony Regarding Climate Change and Health," *Associated Press*, October 24, 2007. Retrieved from http://www.commondreams.org/archive/2007/10/24/4772

vector-borne diseases including malaria and hantavirus, 6. mental health problems such as depression and post-traumatic stress, and, 7. how many people might be adversely affected because of increased warming.[316] The Bush White House pressured American scientists to suppress discussion of global warming according to testimony taken by the U.S. House of Representatives,.[317]

"High-quality science" during this time was "struggling to get out," as the Bush Whilte House pressured scientists to edit their research on global warming to follow the Bush administration's skepticism. "Nearly half of all respondents perceived or personally experienced pressure to eliminate the words "climate change," "global warming" and other similar terms from a variety of communications."[318]

Similarly, senior officers of the *Government Accountability Project*, testified to the U.S. House of Representatives, that the White House attempted to bury the report *National Assessment of the Potential Consequences of Climate Variability and Change* produced by U.S. scientists pursuant to U.S. law. Some U.S. scientists resigned their jobs rather than give in to White House pressure to underreport global warming.[319]

The United States, a signatory to the *Kyoto Protocol*, has neither ratified nor withdrawn from it— and their representative, *Condoleezza Rice*, remarked that the Protocol was "unacceptable" at the time it was presented to her.[320] The protocol is non-binding over the United States unless ratified. Former US President, *George W. Bush*, would submit the treaty for ratification, believing it would strain the economy. Instead, he choose to empha-

---

316 Ibid.

317 Deborah ZABARENKO, "US Climate Scientists Allege White House Pressure," Reuters, January 30, 2007. Retrieved from http://www.commondreams.org/headlines07/0130-10; written testimony of Dr. Grifo before the Committee on Oversight and Government Reform of the U.S. House of Representatives on January 30, 2007.

318 Rick PILTZ, Written testimony of Rick Piltz before the Committee on Oversight and Government Reform of the U.S. House of Representatives on January 30, 2007.

319 Deborah ZABARENKO, "US Climate Scientists Allege White House Pressure," *op. cit.*

320 Jeffrey KLUGER, "A Climate of Despair," Time, April 1, 2001. Retrieved from http://www.time.com/time/magazine/article/0,9171,104596,00.html

size the uncertainties in the Climate Change issue.[321] Pentagon published a report in October 2003, titled "*An Abrupt Climate Change Scenario and Its Implications*" for United States National Security by *Peter Schwartz and Doug Randall*. The authors conclude by stating:

> "This report suggests that, because of the potentially dire consequences, the risk of abrupt climate change, although uncertain and quite possibly small, should be elevated beyond a scientific debate to a U.S. national security concern."[322]

Even with this as the government position, a total of 195 US cities, representing more than 50 million Americans have committed to reducing carbon emissions to 7% below 1990 levels. In 2005, California (the world's sixth largest economy) committed to reducing emissions to 2000 levels by 2010, 1990 levels by 2020, and 80% below 1990 levels by 2050. Approaches to meet these targets include requirements for renewable energy as a proportion of electricity production and tighter automotive emissions standards. *The Union of Concerned Scientists* has calculated that by 2020, drivers would save $26 billion per year if California's automotive standards were implemented nationally.[323]

The Bush Administration continued to work to undermine the state efforts to mitigate global warming. Then Transportation Secretary, *Mary Peters* directed US efforts to urge governors and dozens of members of the House of Representatives to block California's first-in-the-nation limits on greenhouse gases from cars and trucks, according to e-mails obtained by the US Congress.[324]

---

321 "President Bush Discusses Global Climate Change," Office of the Press Secretary, The White House, June 11, 2001. Retrieved from http://georgewbush-whitehouse.archives.gov/news/releases/2001/06/20010611-2.html

322 Natalie GOLDSTEIN and Kerry Harrison COOK, *Global Warming*, New York, Checkmark Books, 2010, p. 164.

323 "Fuel Economy Basics," Cambridge, MA, Union of Concerned Scientists, 2007. Retrieved from http://www.ucsusa.org/clean_vehicles/solutions/cleaner_cars_pickups_and_suvs/fuel-economy-basics.html

324 Zachary COILE, "How the White House worked to scuttle California's climate law", San Francisco Chronicle, September 25, 2007. Retrieved from http://articles.sfgate.com/2007-09-25/news/17261302_1_auto-emissions-greenhouse-gases-e-mails

Meanwhile in Europe, at the Vatican, Pope Benedict XVI told up to half a million people over a hillside near the Adriatic city of Loreto on the day the Catholic Church marks its annual Save Creation Day, that world leaders must make courageous decisions to save the planet "before it is too late."[325] And Canada, with its liberal government during the 1990s, agreed to Kyoto but did not subscribe to the increase of greenhouse gas emissions and did little to meet its targets. Canada's current conservative government has claimed that, due to increased emissions since 1990, it is impossible to meet the Kyoto targets, and to do so would be disastrous for the Canadian economy and subsequently, have withdrawn their ratification.

Australia has now officially signed the Kyoto ratification. Only doing so after the new Labor government came into power on December 3, 2007. The previous coalition government objected to ratifying the treaty, with their argument it would unduly impact Australian jobs, especially, "when countries such as China, India and the U.S. were not party to it".[326] Japan is preparing to force industry to make big cuts in greenhouse gases, taking the lead in a country struggling to meet its Kyoto Protocol obligations.[327] However, the recent 2011 nuclear plant shutdowns brought about by the earthquake and Tsunami may have altered their position as they search for immediate and long term energy solutions. Russia ratified the Kyoto Protocol in November 2004 after a deal with the European Union to gain WTO membership. With Russia's ratification, it completed the requirements of the treaty to come into force, based on nations totaling 55% of the world greenhouse gas emissions.[328] The UK government commissioned a *Stern Review* on the economic effects of climate change and it was published in October 2006. *Tony Blair's* reference to the assessment was that it showed that scientific evidence of global warming was "overwhelming" and its consequences "disastrous."[329]

---

325 Philip PULLELLA, "Pope Urges, Save the Planet Before it's too Late," *Reuters*, September 2, 2007. Retrieved from http://www.enn.com/top_stories/commentary/22598/print

326 "Rudd Ratifies Kyoto," *The Age*, December 3, 2007. Retrieved from http://www.theage.com.au/news/national/rudd-ratifies-kyoto/2007/12/03/1196530553722.html

327 Ibid.

328 Ibid.

329 "Climate Change Fight 'Can't Wait'," *BBC*, October 31, 2006. Retrieved from http://news.bbc.co.uk/2/hi/business/6096084.stm

Section 5.1.3 Media

But what was occurring in media during the time between 1993 in 2003? Two brothers, *Jules and Max Boycott*, published an article in the peer-reviewed *Journal of Environmental Change* in 2003, titled: "*Balance as Bias: Global Warming and the US Prestige Press.*" They researched the libraries for all the prestige dailies in the United States, the *New York Times*, the *Wall Street Journal*, the *Washington Post*, and the *Los Angeles Times*, and analyzed their coverage of climate change between 1998 and 2002. Their results found that the scientific press was almost 100% in favor of acceptance of the consensus on climate change.[330] In contrast 53% of the stories in these four newspapers quoted a scientist on an opposing side of the issue, an opposition spokesperson, or according to Gladwell, a "salesman." These self-appointed salespersons were from think tanks and even had scientific credentials related to the topic at hand. The experts were geologists and economists commenting outside their field of expertise, but not climate scientists. The issue is that a journalist in the current information age finds it almost impossible to stay current on every issue, especially when it has to do with science, and to protect their agendas, they frequently fall back on the *notion of balance*.[331] They interview one person on one side of the issue and one person on the other. The doctrine in most North American newsrooms is that both sides will wind up angry about the coverage; however, the reporter in question probably got the story "about right." But when it comes to science, which is a discipline in which there are legitimate subject experts, there is a process by which people who offer theories are weighed and measured by scientific peers. There is a process that these people use to decide and to recommend if the information in the research is relevant to the issue in question. While scientists have been growing more convinced about the proof and impact of climate change for most of the past two decades, the media conversation about climate change, on the other hand, with their influence on the general public, has been drifting towards confusion, producing conflicting stories that attempt to minimize the problem and exaggerating the solutions thereby making it more difficult for the public to understand the *living story.*

---

330 Maxwell T. BOYCOFF and Jules M. BOYCOFF, "Balance as Bias: Global Warming and the US Prestige Press," *Global Environmental Change*, 14, 2004, p. 125-136.

331 Ibid.

Age of (Mis) Information

The scientific academies in every major nation in the world have all stepped forward issuing statements affirming that climate change is a potential global crisis, and that all humans are both the principal cause and our only hope for a solution. The IPCC, acknowledging that in science there must always be room for error, has said, "There is a greater than 90% chance that the world as we know it, is going in this direction if we don't change the course."[332] In other words, the consensus is, we have a problem with climate change, and the diagnosis is that humans are generating the greenhouse gases. If you take a survey of Americans and ask them whether the climate is changing, just over 70% of them will say yes.[333] If you asked how many feel that humans are responsible, the number drops below 50%.[334] If you view this from a political perspective, these kinds of numbers are not going to change anything. Half the people don't even acknowledge a problem, and the media, has yet to create contagiousness for addressing the solution. Solving climate change is not going to be easy. If we are to avoid the tipping point, it will demand major changes in the way we consume energy, shape our cities, and source our food.

From a political perspective, US president *Barack Obama*, included on his agenda climate change. Americans would like to believe that there is no real difference between Democrats and Republicans on the issue; however, nothing could be further from the truth. Eighty-four percent of the Democrats say the earth is warming, compared to 49% for the Republicans. In 2008 Republican numbers were going down, dropping from a total of 62% only a year earlier. And when they were asked if humans are responsible for global warming, 58% of Democrats said yes, but just 27% of Republicans agreed. Another interesting fact about the numbers that came out of the Pew poll is that among Democrats with college education, 75% believed humans were responsible for global warming with Republicans at only 19%.[335] The only way to explain these differences is by the way that these

332 "World Energy Outlook 2011 Executive Summary," International Energy Agency, Paris, France, 2011. Retrieved from http://www.worldenergyoutlook.org/docs/weo2011/executive_summary.pdf

333 "An Increase in GOP Doubt About Global Warming Deepens Partisan Divide," *Pew Research Center for the People and the Press*, May 8, 2008. Retrieved from http://pewresearch.org/pubs/828/global-warming

334 Ibid.

335 Tbd

groups are influenced by media and the types of the media that they consume as characteristics that support the contagiousness and stickiness aspects of this event. In general, Democrats seem to be better informed about science, while Republicans are better informed about the controversy. The complexity is a reflection of the Internet age and how global media distorts the facts. Whether through agendas, understaffing, or entities with an actual intent to misinform, most global media throughout North America and even in Europe have failed to inform the readers and audiences about the important issues related to global climate change. The world is returning to an oral culture. People have grown accustomed instead of reading to getting their news from television and radio, and these two media sources struggle with complexity and resist careful criticism. The complexity of this contagiousness as an influence is a real problem for climate change, as when it comes to judging and criticizing sources of information: TV and radio present problems for the listeners. When you look at expert reports side-by-side, it's easy to point out the inconsistencies in the text, and it is easy to keep track of differing levels of authority behind different pieces of information. However, to try to compare two video reports, on the other hand, is almost impossible to do. However, some technologies have recently been introduced that are able to track the viral facts and impacts of phrases as they propagate throughout the different media environments, and as of this writing, it appears to be new science applied to the analysis of media impact that is just developing with the tools available. Examples of these technologies are: recordedfuture.com and memetracker.org. Another could be the relationships identified in the qualitative ratio analysis framework developed here.

There are an infinite number of media choices now available on the Internet and cable TV that contribute further to our abilities to become extremely well-versed in arguments that reinforce our political, economic, social and scientific assumptions If you are someone who is well-read, you work through a daily barrage with the *Wall Street Journal*, the *National Review* etc., constantly trying keep up with television reports that additionally barrage their audiences with stories that suggest there is a scientific controversy about climate change. Every new article that muddies the water, no matter how obscure, finds its way into the pages of these publications or onto the airwaves. Every new winter snowstorm in Florida is presented as counter evidence that the globe is not warming quickly enough. There is a steady diet of *contagious doubt*, which can't help but influence people who are trying to stay informed.

The contagiousness of media is not merely a matter of partisan outlets picking out a selection of events that tend to reaffirm established audience bias. Whatever would have been maintained as a reasonable standard of accuracy cannot be weeded out because of the obvious manipulation. In worst-case scenarios, networks like *Fox* and newspapers like Canada's *National Post* throw caution to the wind, publishing and broadcasting the works of *Stephen Malloy* and *Fred Singer*, so-called climate change experts, without mentioning to readers or viewers that these persons are taking money from industries that they are trying to defend. *Milloy* is an individual who has spent his entire career in public relations and lobbying, getting his funding from companies that include *Exxon, Phillip Morris, Edison Electric Institute*, counsel to *Monsanto Corporation* in return for declaring that environmental concerns to be "junk science"[336] Effectively justifying his position as executive director of *Philip Morris* and part of the *American Petroleum Institute* whose plan is to sow doubt and confusion about climate change, Malloy continues to lobby against environmental regulation of all kinds. His website *junkscience.com* is an attack on environmental issues and the people who promote them. *Fox News* brings *Malloy* into the studio and forgets to mention that he's actually an industry lobbyist. They don't let the audience know that he is not a journalist committed to a balanced or even accurate account. Rather he is a registered corporate lobbyist who has been paid to spin the issue to the advantage of his clients. The *National Post* is inclined to follow the same approach. The paper publishes pieces by *Malloy* and *Singer*, again with no mention of their corporate funding and affiliations. The *Calgary Herald* continues to load up its paper with opinion pieces with outrageous accusations saying that scientists are faking claims of climate change so that they can obtain government funding for additional research. This is one of the favorite clever tactics of the contagiousness *salespersons*.

Early in 2008 *Lawrence Solomon* published the book version of a collection of people who were against the consensus scientist opinion. The title of the book: *The Deniers: The World-renowned Scientists Who Stood up Against the Global Warming Hysteria, Political Persecution, and Fraud*

336 James HOGGAN and Richard D. LITTLEMORE, Climate Cover-up: The Crusade to Deny Global Warming, op. cit., p. 156.

(and Those Who are too Fearful to Do So). *Solomon* acknowledged that he couldn't find a single serious scientist to actually deny the global consensus.

Few reporters and journalists do have the kind of time and freedom to contact people all over the world. Neither do they have the necessary resources and attention span to do so. The media business has an agenda whereby they need to fill up the daily *void*, and most journalists wind up running ragged just to meet the responsibilities of a given day. The situation has gotten even worse as major media has consolidated. Although there are more individual outlets in North America today for immediate distribution, the total number of reporters has been declining for more than 20 years. Media professionals are working harder, specialists are stretched thinner, and media empires like *CanWest Global* are always looking for more ways to repackage the same content information for more distribution in more markets. It's not a surprise that media falls back on the journalistic precedent of quoting one source on one side of the issue and another on the other. It's no surprise that they tend to stand back as long as they can, in effect not committing themselves on a controversial story until there is absolute agreement from all sides. With a complicated issue such as climate change it is especially risky for media who have a closer relationship with creating contagiousness than they do with the scientists at the local think tank.

The scientists, on the other hand, are also part of the problem for continuing public confusion. Scientists are a media-shy group to start with and for good reason. It is part of their professional character not to promote media attention, especially by leaking controversial results to the mainstream media before the research has undergone a formal peer-review process at a respectable scientific journal. The problem is that scientists are inclined to practice supply-side science relying on the trickle-down effect and the diffusion model to get the word out.[337] The basis for their research and the way they disseminate the results is qualified with its own built-in control measures that, in a way, ensure this approach produces the very best conclusions and evaluations. The problem with advanced technological me-

337 Lawrence SOLOMON, The Deniers: The World Renowned Scientists Who Stood Up Against Global Warming Hysteria, Political Persecution, and Fraud**And those who are too fearful to do so, Minneapolis, MN, Richard Vigilante Books, 2008.

dia environments that are available today is that confusing and contrary arguments can originate and be promoted by contagiousness to ensure the public that there is no immediate crisis. There is not a peer-review system set up for the media and the journalists and the reporters, as they pick up information as it is available on the Internet, cable, and newspapers around them and regurgitate the storylines back into their own reporting. The same *phenomena* occurred in the international financial crisis during which it was difficult to report the complexities of the crisis as it was occurring. When the message was simple, as when the gas prices were going up at the pump, media had no choice but to report events accurately and up-to-date.

Perhaps the good news about global media generally is that we seem to be moving in a better direction. Most media outlets have abandoned the balance model, i.e. telling both sides of the story on a particular issue when covering climate change. They no longer regularly solicit or allow a quote from the other side every time they run a story about global warming. The problem is that it's past the time for those responsible in global media to check their facts and start to share them ethically and responsibly, as the public deserves the truth.

Political Pressure on Scientists

US officials have edited scientific reports from US government scientists, many of whom, such as *Thomas Knutson*, have been ordered to refrain from discussing climate change and related topics.[338] Furthermore, climate scientist *James Hansen, Director of NASA's Goddard Institute for Space Studies*, stated in a *New York Times* article in 2006 about his superiors at the agency who were trying to "censor" information "going out to the public." NASA denied , saying that it was just requiring that scientists make a distinction "between personal and official government views in interviews conducted as part of work done at the agency".[339] Similarly, scientists working at the *National Oceanic and Atmospheric Administration* have made complaints; government officials said they were enforcing long-standing policies requiring government scientists to clearly identify

338 Duncan CAMPBELL, "White House Cuts Global Warming from Report," *Guardian*, June 20, 2003. Retrieved from http://www.guardian.co.uk/environment/2003/jun/20/climatechange.climatechangeenvironment

339 Juliet EILPERIN, "Climate Researchers Feeling Heat From White House," *Washington Post*, April 6, 2006. Retrieved from http://www.washingtonpost.com/wp-dyn/content/article/2006/04/05/AR2006040502150_pf.html

personal opinions as such when participating in public interviews and forums.[340] The BBC's current affairs series *Panorama* investigated the issue and was told that, "...scientific reports about global warming have been systematically changed and suppressed."[341] According to an *Associated Press* release on January 30, 2007:

> Climate scientists at seven government agencies say they have been subjected to political pressure aimed at downplaying the threat of global warming. The groups presented a survey that shows two in five of the 279 climate scientists who responded to a questionnaire complained that some of their scientific papers had been edited in a way that changed their meaning. Nearly half of the 279 said in response to another question that at some point they had been told to delete reference to "global warming" or "climate change" from a report.[342]

Critics from the *Wall Street Journal* claim that the survey was itself unscientific. Lastly, attempts to suppress scientific information on climate change and other issues have been described by *Chris Mooney* as a "war on science."[343]

The book *Hell and High Water* asserts that there has been a concerted, disingenuous, and effective campaign to convince Americans that climate change science is not proven, and that global warming is just the result of natural cycles and more research is needed. Further, the book claims government *salespersons* suggest falsely that "technology breakthroughs" with hydrogen cars and other fixes will eventually solve the issue. It recommends voters demand immediate government action to curb emissions. *Tyler Hamilton*, in his review of the book for *The Toronto Star*, wrote:

> ...it offers alarming detail on how the U.S. public was being misled by [the Bush administration] (backed by conservative political

---

340 Ibid.

341 "Climate Chaos: Bush's Climate of Fear," *BBC*, June 1, 2006. Retrieved from http://news.bbc.co.uk/2/hi/programmes/panorama/5005994.stm

342 "Groups Say Scientists Pressured On Warming," *CBS News*, February 11, 2009. Retrieved from http://www.cbsnews.com/stories/2007/01/30/politics/main2413400.shtml

343 Chris MOONEY, *The Republican War on Science*, New York, Basic Books, 2005.

> forces) that is intent on inaction, and that it's also on a mission to derail international efforts to curb emissions.[344]

Also, research papers presented at an *International Scientific Congress* on Climate Change in 2009 (under the sponsorship of the *University of Copenhagen* in cooperation with nine other universities in the International *Alliance of Research Universities* (IARU), maintained that climate-change skepticism, prevalent in the USA, "...was largely generated and kept alive by a small number of conservative think tanks, often with direct funding from industries having special interests in delaying or avoiding the regulation of greenhouse gas emissions."[345]

Media Cover-up

Is there a media cover-up? Do you remember hearing any good news from the mainstream media about Climate Change? Instead, the headlines proclaim: "Record Low 2009 and 2010 Cyclonic Activity Reported: Global Warming Theorists Perplexed"? Or "NASA Studies Report Oceans Entering New Cooling Phase: Alarmists Fear Climate Science Budgets in Peril"? Opportunities by the media to capitalize on disasters are certainly not lost on some U.N. IPCC officials and they are influenced by the coverage. During a special press conference called by IPCC spokesman *Kevin Trenbert,* stated, "Experts warn global warming likely to continue spurring more outbreaks of intense activity."[346] But there is *something else* evident: *Christopher Landsea*, a U.S. expert on the subject, responded to the IPCC that no research had been conducted to support these claims. After receiving no replies, he proceeded to publicly resigned from all IPCC activities and the press conference received extensive global media coverage during the issue of cover-up into the public arena.

Many of the Climate Change alarms from media center upon concerns

---

344 Tyler HAMILTON, "Fresh Alarm over Global Warming," *Toronto Star*, January 1, 2007. Retrieved from http://www.thestar.com/article/166819

345 William FREUDENBURG, "The Effects of Journalistic Imbalance on Scientific Imbalance: Special Interests, Scientific Consensus and Global Climate Disruption," *Climate Change: Global Risks, Challenges and Decisions, IOP Conf. Series: Earth and Environmental Science* 6, 2009 532011.

346 Larry BELL, "Hot Sensations vs. Cold Facts," Forbes, January 28, 2011. Retrieved from http://www.forbes.com/sites/larrybell/2011/01/28/hot-sensations-vs-cold-facts-3/

that melting glaciers will lead to a disastrous sea level rise. A December 2005 BBC program reported that two massive glaciers in eastern Greenland were melting and resulting in massive amounts of water "racing to the sea." The commentators warned that the continued recession would be catastrophic.[347] The glaciers' "erratic" behavior as reported, was later recounted and spread in a Nov. 13 *New York Times* article titled: "As Glaciers Melt, Science Seeks Data on Rising Seas.".[348]

Fueling the confusion, a recent study conducted by U.S. and Dutch scientists which appeared in *Nature Geoscience* concluded, "that previous estimates of Greenland and West Antarctica ice melt rate losses may have been exaggerated by double. Earlier projections apparently failed to account for rebounding changes in the Earth's crust following the last Ice Age referred to as glacial isostatic adjustment."[349]

Nils-Axel Morner, department head of the *Paleogeophysics and Geodynamics Department at Stockholm University* in Sweden, argued that any concerns regarding rising sea levels are unfounded,

> "So all this talk that sea level is rising, this comes from the computer modeling, not from observations…The new level, which has been stable, has not changed in the last 35 years…But they [IPCC] need a rise, because if there is no rise, there is no death threat…if you want a grant for a research project in climatology, it is written into the document that there "must" be a focus on global warming…That is really bad, because you start asking for the answer you want to get."[350]

Other world climate alarms were sounded when reported in the media in September 2007 that satellite images revealed that the Northwest Passage– a sea route between the U.K. and Asia across the top of the Arctic Circle– had opened up for the first time in recorded history. However, the "recorded history" dates back *only* to 1979 when satellite monitoring first began, and it failed to note that the sea route froze again just a few months later

347 Ibid.

348 Ibid.

349 Larry BELL, Climate of Corruption: Politics and Power Behind the Global Warming Hoax, Austin, TX, Greenleaf Book Group, 2011, p. 84.

350 Larry BELL, "Hot Sensations vs. Cold Facts," *op. cit.*

the winter of 2007-2008.[351] The Northwest Passage has certainly opened up before. In February 2009 scientist discovered that they had previously been underestimating the re-growth of Arctic sea ice. This estimate of size was a large as the state of California (twice as large as New Zealand). They reported that the errors were attributed to faulty sensors on the ice.[352]

Unfortunately, these observations and positions aren't what most people generally receive from the media. Instead, media delivers sensational statements and dramatic images that leave catastrophic impressions of drowning polar bears and caving glaciers.. Many intentionally target impressionable young minds and sensitive big hearts to spread the panic with messages of fear and guilt.

For example, *The North Pole Was Here,* a children's book authored by *New York Times* reporter *Andrew Revkin*, warns kids that someday it may be "easier to sail than stand on the North Pole in summer."[353] Larry Bell, author of *Climate of Corruption: Politics and Power Behind the Global Warming Hoax* and a professor at the University of Houston, had this to say about the book:

> "Imagine such images through their visualization: How warm it must be to melt that pole way up north. Poor Santa! And Rudolph! Of course it's mostly their parents' fault because of the nasty CO2 they produce driving them to school in SUVs. Lots of grown-ups are sensitive people with big hearts too. Don't we all deserve more from the seemingly infinite media echo chamber of alarmism than those windy speculations, snow jobs and projections established on theoretical thin ice?"[354]

The problem with Larry Bell is that his background is space exploration and not climate science. In other words, he is not qualified to come to these conclusions.

---

351 Ibid.

352 Ibid.

353 Ibid.

354 Larry BELL, Climate of Corruption: Politics and Power Behind the Global Warming Hoax, Austin, TX, Greenleaf Book Group, 2011, p. 84.

Section 5.1.4 Events

The *U.S. National Assessment of Climate Change Impacts* provides a basis for summarizing the potential consequences of climate change. *The National Assessment* directly addresses the importance of climate change by considering climate scenarios from two recent models:

- The Hadley Model of the United Kingdom
- The Canadian Climate Model

These two models forecast very different globally-averaged temperature increases [2.7 and 4.4°C (4.9 and 7.9°F), respectively] by the year 2100. A key conclusion from the *National Assessment* is, "that U.S. society is likely to be able to adapt to most of the climate change impacts on human systems, but these adaptations may come with substantial cost."[355]

The main conclusions from these reports focus on agriculture and forestry, water, human health, and coastal regions: In the near term, agriculture and forestry are likely to benefit from CO2 fertilization effects and the increased water efficiency of many plants at higher atmospheric CO2 concentrations. Crop distributions will change, thus requiring significant regional adaptations. However, the combination of geography and different climatic regions of the United States, by factoring in advances in genetics, increases the US's ability to adapt to climate change. However, the actual conclusions depend on which of the climate scenario model above are considered, with hotter and drier conditions increasing the potential for declines in both agriculture and forestry. On the regional scale and in the longer term, the future seems uncertain.[356]

In addition, the tendency of droughts, as projected by the models, is an important concern in every region of the United States, even though it is unlikely to be realized the same everywhere in the nation. Any significant climate change impact is likely to result in increased costs because the US's investment with specific local development in water supply infra-

355 Committee on the Science of Climate Change, National Research Council, *Climate Change Science: An Analysis of Some Key Questions*, *op. cit.*

356 Committee on the Science of Climate Change, National Research Council, *Climate Change Science: An Analysis of Some Key Questions*, *op. cit.*, p. 19.

structure, is largely designed to the current climate conditions.[357]

Health events in response to climate change are also subjects of intense scientific debate. Such as, climate change has the potential to: 1. influence the frequency and transmission of infectious diseases, 2. cold-related and altered heat- mortality and morbidity, and, 3. influencing air and water quality.

In fact, the relationships between weather, climate and human health has really just begun and the health consequences of climate change are difficult to measure and understand. Increases in mean temperatures are expected to result in an increase in the number of warm days and new record high temperatures and warm nights compared to the present. Cold-related stress may decline whereas, heat stress in major urban areas may increase if no adaptation occurs. The *National Assessment* connected the relationships between an increase in adverse air quality to higher temperatures. However, much of the United States is thought to be protected against many different adverse health impacts related to climate change given a very strong public health system, and a high standard of living. Children, the elderly, and the poor are considered to be the most vulnerable to climate change impacts such as these. The costs, benefits, and availability of resources for adaptation are also uncertain.[358]

The Assessment further points out, that coastal areas are more vulnerable to increases in sea level rise and severe weather. Fifty-three percent of the U.S. population lives within the coastal regions. Importantly, changes in storm frequency and intensity are one of the more uncertain impacts of future climate change forecasting. Rises in sea levels increase the potential damage to coastal regions even under current conditions of storm intensities and can endanger coastal ecosystems (if human systems or other barriers) limit the opportunities for migration.[359]

---

357 Except where noted, this section is based on information provided in the U.S. National Assessment, U.S. Global Change Research Program, "Climate Change Impacts on the United States: The Potential Consequences of Climate Variability and Change", 2001, Cambridge, UK, Cambridge University Press.

358 Committee on the Science of Climate Change, National Research Council, *Climate Change Science: An Analysis of Some Key Questions*, *op. cit.*, p. 20.

359 *Ibid.*, p. 20.

Significant climate change will cause disruptions to many U.S. ecosystems, including forests, grasslands, rivers, lakes and wetlands. Contrasting to human systems, the *U.S. National Assessment* argues that ecosystems are the most vulnerable to the projected forecasts and magnitudes of climate change, in part, because these ecosystem adaptation options are limited. At a national level, the direct adaptation economic impacts are projected to be modest. However, the level and extent on a regional basis of harmful impacts will grow. Some economic sectors may be transformed substantially, and there may be significant regional transitions associated with shifts in agriculture and forestry.

Even some of the mid-range scenarios developed by the IPCC point out temperatures that will continue to increase beyond the end of this century, suggesting that assessments that examine only the next 100 years *underestimate* the magnitude of the eventual impacts. For example, if a sustained and progressive drying of the land surface occurred, it would eventually lead to desertification of regions that are now marginally arable, whereby, any substantial melting or breaking up of the Greenland and Antarctic ice caps might cause widespread coastal inundation.[360]

Timeline Events

Scientists have predicted that global average temperatures would increase by 2 to 11 degrees Fahrenheit by 2100 and that sea levels could rise by up to 2 feet. Scientists have also speculated that Glaciers, already receding, will disappear. Epic floods will hit some areas while intense drought will strike others. Humans will face widespread water shortages. Famine and disease will increase. Earth's landscape will transform radically, with a quarter of plants and animals at risk of extinction.

While putting specific dates on these potential contagious events is challenging, this timeline paints the big picture and details Earth's future based on several recent studies and the longer scientific version of the IPCC report, which was made available to *LiveScience*.[361]

360 *Ibid.*, p. 20.

361 Andrea THOMPSON, "Timeline: Earth's Precarious Future," *Live Science*, January 11, 2008. Retrieved from http://www.livescience.com/1433-timeline-earth-precarious-future.html

2011

- More of the world's population now lives in cities rather than in rural areas, with changing patterns of land use occurring. The world population surpassed 7.0 billion. -UN World Population Projections[362]

- Global oil production peaks sometime between 2008 and 2018. Others say this tipping point for oil, known as "Hubbert's Peak", won't occur until after 2020. Once Hubbert's Peak is reached, global oil production will begin an irreversible decline, possibly triggering a global recession, food shortages and conflict between nations over dwindling oil supplies.[363]

2020

- Flash floods will very likely increase across all parts of Europe.[364]

- Less rainfall could reduce agriculture yields by up to 50 percent in some parts of the world.[365]

- World population will reach beyond 8.0 billion people.[366]

2030

- Diarrhea-related diseases will likely increase by up to 5 percent in low-income parts of the world [367]

- Up to 18 percent of the world's coral reefs will likely be

---

362 "U.S. and World Population Clocks," U.S. Census Bureau. Retrieved from http://www.census.gov/main/www/popclock.html

363 Frederik ROBELIUS, Doctoral dissertation, University of Uppsala, Sweden; Robert L. HIRSCH, report, Science Applications International Corporation.

364 James J. MCCARTHY, Osvald F. CANZIANI, Neil A. LEARY, David J. DOKKEN, and Kasey S. WHITE, *Working Group II: Impacts, Adaptation and Vulnerability*, Geneva, Switzerland, Intergovernmental Panel on Climate Change (IPCC), 2001. Retrieved from http://www.ipcc.ch/ipccreports/tar/wg2/index.php?idp=2

365 Ibid.

366 Ibid.

367 Ibid.

lost as a result of climate change and other environmental stresses. In Asian coastal waters, the coral loss could reach 30 percent.[368]

- World population will reach beyond 8.3 billion people.[369]
- Warming temperatures will cause temperate glaciers on equatorial mountains in Africa to disappear.[370] In developing countries, the urban population will more than double to about 4 billion people, packing more people onto a given city's land area. The urban populations of developed countries may also increase by as much as 20 percent.[371]
- By 2040 the Arctic Sea could be ice-free in the summer, and winter ice depth may shrink drastically. Other scientists say the region will still have summer ice up to 2060 and 2105.[372]

2050

- Small alpine glaciers will very likely disappear completely, and large glaciers will shrink by 30 to 70 percent. Austrian scientist Roland Psenner of the University of Innsbruck says this is a conservative estimate, and the small alpine glaciers could be gone as soon as

368 Ibid.

369 U.S. Census Bureau, International Database, June 2011 Update, World Population 1950–2050, 2010.

370 Richard G. TAYLOR, "Recent Glacial Recession in the Rwenzori Mountains of East Africa due to Rising Air Temperature," *Geophysical Research Letters*, 33, 2006.

371 Schlomo ANGEL, Stephen C. SHEPPARD, and Daniel L. CIVCO, "The Dynamics of Global Urban Expansion," World Bank, Transport and Urban Development Department, Washington, D.C., September 2005. Retrieved from http://web.worldbank.org/WBSITE/EXTERNAL/TOPICS/EXTURBANDEVELOPMENT/0,,contentMDK:20970341~menuPK:512046~pagePK:148956~piPK:216618~theSitePK:337178~isCURL:Y,00.html

372 Edward BLANCHARD-WRIGGLESWORTH, Cecilia M. BITZ, and Marika M. HOLLAND, "Influence of Initial Conditions and Climate Forcing on Predicting Arctic Sea Ice," *Geophysical Research Letters*, 38, 2011, L18503.

2037.[373]

- In Australia, there will likely be an additional 3,200 to 5,200 heat-related deaths per year. The hardest hit will be people over the age of 65. An extra 500 to 1,000 people will die of heat-related deaths in New York City per year. In the United Kingdom, the opposite will occur, and cold-related deaths will outpace heat-related ones.[374]
- World population reaches beyond 9.4 billion people.[375]
- Crop yields could increase by up to 20 percent in East and Southeast Asia, while decreasing by up to 30 percent in Central and South Asia. Similar shifts in crop yields could occur on other continents.[376]
- As biodiversity hotspots are more threatened, a quarter of the world's plant and vertebrate animal species could face extinction[377]

2070

- As glaciers disappear and areas affected by drought increase, electricity production for the world's existing hydropower stations will decrease. Hardest hit will be Europe, where hydropower potential is expected to decline on average by 6 percent; around the Mediterra-

---

373 James J. MCCARTHY, Osvald F. CANZIANI, Neil A. LEARY, David J. DOKKEN, and Kasey S. WHITE, *Working Group II: Impacts, Adaptation and Vulnerability, op. cit.*

374 Ibid.

375 US Census Bureau

376 James J. MCCARTHY, Osvald F. CANZIANI, Neil A. LEARY, David J. DOKKEN, and Kasey S. WHITE, *Working Group II: Impacts, Adaptation and Vulnerability, op. cit.*

377 Sandra L. PETERS, Jay R. MALCOLM, and Barbara L. ZIMMERMAN, "Effects of Selective Logging on Bat Communities in the Southeastern Amazon," *Conservation Biology*, 20, 2006, p. 1410-1421.

nean, the decrease could be up to 50 percent. (IPCC)[378]

- Warmer, drier conditions will lead to more frequent and longer droughts, as well as longer fire-seasons, increased fire risks, and more frequent heat waves, especially in Mediterranean regions. (IPCC)

2080

- While some parts of the world dry out, others will be inundated. Scientists predict up to 20 percent of the world's populations live in river basins likely to be affected by increased flood hazards. Up to 100 million people could experience coastal flooding each year. Most at risk are densely populated and low-lying areas that are less able to adapt to rising sea levels and areas that already face other challenges such as tropical storms.[379]
- Coastal population could balloon to 5 billion people, up from 1.2 billion in 1990.[380] Between 1.1 and 3.2 billion people will experience water shortages and up to 600 million will go hungry.[381]
- Sea levels could rise around New York City by more than three feet, potentially flooding the Rockaways, Coney Island, much of southern Brooklyn and Queens, portions of Long Island City, Astoria, Flushing Meadows-Corona Park, Queens, lower Manhattan and eastern Staten Island from Great Kills Harbor north to the Verrazano-Narrows Bridge.[382]

---

378 James J. MCCARTHY, Osvald F. CANZIANI, Neil A. LEARY, David J. DOKKEN, and Kasey S. WHITE, *Working Group II: Impacts, Adaptation and Vulnerability*, *op. cit.*

379 Ibid.

380 Ibid.

381 Ibid.

382 "NASA Looks at Seal Level Rise, Hurricane Risks to New York City," NASA Goddard Institute for Space Studies, October 24, 2006. Retrieved from http://www.giss.nasa.gov/research/news/20061024/

2085

- The risk of dengue fever from climate change is estimated to increase to 3.5 billion people.[383]

2100

- A combination of global warming and other factors will push many ecosystems to the limit, forcing them to exceed their natural ability to adapt to climate change.[384]
- Atmospheric carbon dioxide levels will be much higher than anytime during the past 650,000 years.[385]
- Ocean pH levels will very likely decrease by as much as 0.5 pH units, the lowest it's been in the last 20 million years. The ability of marine organisms such as corals, crabs and oysters to form shells or exoskeletons could be impaired.[386]
- Thawing permafrost and other factors will make Earth's land a net source of carbon emissions, meaning it will emit more carbon dioxide into the atmosphere than it absorbs.[387]
- Roughly 20 to 30 percent of species assessed as of 2007 could be extinct by 2100 if global mean temperatures exceed 2 to 3 degrees of pre-industrial levels.[388]
- New climate zones appear on up to 39 percent of the world's land surface, radically transforming the planet.[389]

---

383 James J. MCCARTHY, Osvald F. CANZIANI, Neil A. LEARY, David J. DOKKEN, and Kasey S. WHITE, *Working Group II: Impacts, Adaptation and Vulnerability*, *op. cit.*

384 Ibid.

385 Ibid.

386 Ibid.

387 Ibid.

388 Ibid.

389 John W. WILLIAMS, Stephen T. JACKSON, and John E. KUTZBACH, "Projected distributions of novel and disappearing climates by 2100 AD," *Proceedings of the National Academy of Sciences*, 104, 2007, p. 5738-5742.

- A quarter of all species of plants and land animals—more than a million total—could be driven to extinction. The IPCC reports warn that current "conservation practices are generally ill-prepared for climate change and effective adaptation responses are likely to be costly to implement."[390]
- Increased droughts could significantly reduce moisture levels in the American Southwest, northern Mexico, and possibly parts of Europe, Africa and the Middle East, effectively recreating the "Dust Bowl" environments of the 1930s in the United States.[391]

2200

- An Earth day will be 0.12 milliseconds shorter, as rising temperatures cause oceans to expand away from the equator and toward the poles, one model predicts. One reason water will be shifted toward the poles is most of the expansion will take place in the North Atlantic Ocean near the North Pole. The poles are closer to the Earth's axis of rotation, so having more mass there should speed up the planet's rotation.[392]

Contemplating some of these events outlined above, draws our attention and focus on some potential solutions that only can be delivered by the characteristics in the next section: the stickiness attributes.

Section 5.2 Stickiness Attributes (S)

It appears from the previous section outlining the timeline of events that the world is headed towards a pivotal *tipping point* sometime around the

390 James J. MCCARTHY, Osvald F. CANZIANI, Neil A. LEARY, David J. DOKKEN, and Kasey S. WHITE, *Working Group II: Impacts, Adaptation and Vulnerability*, *op. cit.*

391 Richard SEAGER, Nicholas GRAHAM, and Celine HERWEIJER, "Blueprints for Medieval Hydroclimate," *Quaternay Science Reviews*, 26, 2007, p. 19-21.

392 Felix W. LANDERER, Johann H. JUNGCLAUS, and Jochem MAROTZKE, "Regional Dynamic and Steric Sea Level Change in Response to the IPCC-A1B Scenario," Journal of Physical Oceanography, 37, 2006, p. 296-312.

year 2100. The research of the *stickiness attribute* of climate change is straightforward: Are the events that are leading us to a potential *tipping point* in 2100 influenced by the media and can we reverse the expert forecasts? In this next section, I look just some of the people, organizations, potential media developments, and events that are characterized by the *stickiness attribute*.

Section 5.2.1 People

Citizens of the Planet: Carbon Dioxide Emissions

Leading climate change researchers have concluded that to protect the planet from potentially catastrophic climate change risk, we must stabilize the atmospheric carbon dioxide concentration at 500 ppm, or even as low as 350 ppm. This would require reducing our total global carbon dioxide emissions to no more than 19.1 billion tons per year, less than half of what's predicted for 2030. In a world now with 7 billion people (August 2011), the question is: how can we shrink carbon emissions to average about 2 1/2 tons per person per year?

To put this objective into perspective, currently a Toyota Corolla, (which happens to be the most popular car in the United States), gets 25 miles to the gallon, and exceeds the 2 ½ ton target for C02 emissions if it is driven just 7500 miles per year. The average driver travels approximately 12,000 miles per year. If driving was our sole source of greenhouse gas emissions, then perhaps it might be a manageable problem. (Another way to consider the issue is, are people ready to cut back that much? If we answer yes, this is by precedent probably false, as the evidence shows that very few individuals have cut back on their carbon producing activities at all). It would appear that most individuals are hoping "*someone else*" will come up with a solution that will fix all of our problems.

The evidence outlined in the previous sections points to major climate changes in the future, but it seems so abstract and so beyond our abilities to try to do anything about it, i.e. a *harder story to tell*, (similar to the International Financial Crisis media reaction). Even though the global climate scientists urge that we should take *action* to reduce global carbon concentrations to as low as 350 ppm - most people don't know *why* and *how* we should do it. Here are several things that are guaranteed about the future: *There will be more people, more money per person, and more pollution.*

The fact is, we have already released too much greenhouse gas, and there appears to be no credible signs that global emissions will decline in the near or medium future, hence, the driving *characteristic* of this *stickiness attribute* with this tipping point, in my opinion, is already well underway.

The carbon mitigation plans that governments are trying to come up with are worthy goals, but the fact is, we are unlikely to invent some kind of new clean technology that will allow us to continue to live without producing greenhouse gases, nor would we be able to come up with some kind of solution to do away with the existing carbon emissions. The fact is, the planet that we live on is going to get hotter. How will we adapt? What is the future for the world's temperature: How hot will it become? And in this study's context, what role will media have?

The 2008 Nobel laureate and columnist in economics, *Paul Krugman*, has argued, "...we are like frogs in a pot slowly heating water, patiently waiting to be cooked when it comes to boil. He says that we know the pot is getting hot, but we are ignorant of the coming doom that climate change will cause. The fact is frogs will actually jump out of the water before it gets too hot, humankind...might just be cooked. Little by little over time, if we continue along the current path, the issue will be one more of adaptation through migration, re-engineering our life support systems, conflict, and world struggle."[393]

Dr. Charles D. Keeling was the first person in the world to develop an reliable and accurate technique for measuring carbon dioxide in the air. He discovered 310 parts per million was the amount back in the 1950's. That is defined as for every million pints of air contained 310 pints of carbon dioxide. By 2005, (the year he died), that number had risen to 380 parts per million. The prediction is that sometime in the next few years it is expected to pass 400 ppm. And, without stronger world response to limit emissions, this number could pass 560 ppm before the end of the century, and alarming doubling what it was before the Industrial Revolution.[394]

393 Matthew E. KAHN, Climatopolis: How our Cities Will Thrive in the Hotter Future, New York, Basic Books, p. 6.

394 Justin GILLIS, "A Scientist, His Work and a Climate Reckoning," *New York Times*, December 21, 2010. Retrieved from http://www.nytimes.com/2010/12/22/science/earth/22carbon.html

"I find it shocking," said Pieter P. Tans, who runs the government monitoring program at the *Mauna Loa Observatory*, Hawaii. "We really are in a predicament here, and it's getting worse every year."[395] "Nature doesn't care how hard we tried," *Jeffrey D. Sachs*, the Columbia University economist said at a recent seminar. "Nature cares how high the parts per million mount. This is running away."[396]

By the late 1960s, nearly a decade after *Dr. Keeling*'s first measurements, the trend of rising carbon dioxide was evident, and scientists began to warn of the potential for a substantial increase in the earths' temperature. In his essay in 1998, *Dr. Keeling* replied to claims that global warming was only a myth, declaring that the only real myth was that: "natural resources and the ability of the earth's habitable regions to absorb the impacts of human activities are limitless."[397]

Even with these statements, Climate Change was not a political issue and largely misunderstood by the media. That changed in 2006, when ex US Vice President *Al Gore's* movie and book, both titled *An Inconvenient Truth,* brought wider public attention to the issues. *The Keeling Curve* was featured in both of these works. Following in 2007, the IPCC, declared that the scientific evidence that the earth was warming had now become unequivocal, and that humans were almost certainly the main cause. *Mr. Gore* and the IPCC jointly won the *Nobel Peace Prize.*

In an interview, *Ralph Keeling* (son of Charles), who had calculated that the carbon dioxide level at Mauna Loa, HI (the observatory where the original samples were taken) was likely to surpass 400 by May 2014, a stickiness moment in mankind's alteration of the atmosphere. "We're going to race through 400 (ppm) like we didn't see it go by," *Dr. Keeling* said.[398]

Researchers

Basic physics of the atmosphere show that carbon dioxide plays a powerful role in maintaining the earth's climate. Even though the amount in the air is relatively small in proportion, the gas is potent at trapping the sun's heat, such that, that it effectively works as a one-way blanket, letting in visible

395 Ibid.
396 Ibid.
397 Ibid.
398 Ibid.

light yet stopping much of the resulting heat from escaping back into space. Without any of this gas, the earth would likely be a frozen wasteland—with its average temperature colder by roughly 60 degrees Fahrenheit.

In recent years, researchers have placed the Keeling measurements in a broader context. Bubbles of ancient air trapped by glaciers have been analyzed, and they demonstrate that over the past 800,000 years, the amount of carbon dioxide in the air varied between roughly 200 and 300 parts per million. What is of interest from these analysis, just before the Industrial Revolution, the level was about 280 parts per million and had remained there for several thousand years. That amount of the gas, was sufficient and produced the equable climate in which human civilization was able to survive.[399]

Other studies also show a close association between carbon dioxide and the temperature of the earth. These geologic records suggest that as the earth began cooling, the amount of carbon dioxide fell, probably because much of it got locked up in the glaciers and polar ice sheets, and that amplified the initial cooling. The gas seemingly also played a major role in increasing the effects of the ice ages, causing by wobbles in the earth's orbit. With this orbital wobble, the earth to begin warming, and a great deal of carbon dioxide then escaped from the ocean, amplifying the warming and providing evidence of carbon dioxides' critical role.

Richard B. Alley, a climate scientist at *Pennsylvania State University*, stated that the wobbles in the earth's orbit were not, by themselves, big enough to cause the large changes of the ice ages, the analysis made sense only when the amplification from carbon dioxide was factored in. "What the ice ages tell us is that our physical understanding of CO2 explains what happened and nothing else does," *Dr. Alley* said. "The ice ages are a very strong test of whether we've got it right."[400] As people on the planet began burning substantial amounts of coal and oil, the carbon dioxide level began to rise. And now, it is about 40 percent higher than before the Industrial Revolution, and this extra gas has been placed into the air since just the late 1970s.

The most reliable scientific estimate is that if the amount of carbon dioxide

399 Ibid.
400 Ibid.

doubles, the temperature of the earth may increase about five or six degrees Fahrenheit, a forecasted number that represents an annual global average, and an immense addition of heat to the planet. This warming would be higher over land, and it would also greatly increase at the poles where a considerable amount of ice would melt, raising sea levels. The deeper parts of the ocean would also absorb a tremendous amount of heat. Moreover, scientists say that an increase of five or six degrees is a actually mildly optimistic outlook. Many project increases as high as 18 degrees Fahrenheit, which would completely transform the planet.[401]

Societies

Most of the world's governments have accepted the science of climate change, however, their efforts to bring emissions under control are far behind. Farms, planes, cement factories, home furnaces, cars, trucks, power plants, steel mills,— typically all emit carbon dioxide or lesser (heat-trapping) gases into the atmosphere. Developed countries, especially the United States, are chiefly responsible for the massive increases that has taken place since the Industrial Revolution. The simple reason: modern civilization is built on burning fossil fuels.

Developed countries have made some advances on reducing the amount energy used to produce a given amount of economic output, attempting to lower their total emissions. However, these efforts are overshadowed by rising energy use in developing countries like China, India, Brazil and parts of Africa. In those areas, economic growth is increasing. A scientific paper referred to China's growth as "the biggest transformation of human well-being the earth has ever seen."[402] China's citizens on average, still use less than a third of the energy per person as Americans. But with 1.3 billion people (four times as many as the United States) China is growing so quickly that it has surpassed the United States and become the world's largest overall user of energy.[403] This rapid growth in developing countries threatens to make the emissions stickiness unstoppable.

Interestingly, emissions actually dropped sharply in Western nations during the International Financial Crisis, particularly in 2009, however this

---

401 Ibid.
402 Ibid.
403 Ibid.

decrease was largely offset by continued growth in the East. And for 2012, global emissions are currently returning to rapid growth, similar to the past decade, rising more than 3 percent a year. Many countries have "in principle" *embraced* the goal of trying to limit global warming to two degrees Celsius, (or 3.6 degrees Fahrenheit), the thinking being that beyond that, the risk would be too great.

Scientists are estimating that about one trillion tons of carbon can effectively be burned and the gases released into the atmosphere (before emissions need to fall to nearly zero). "It took 250 years to burn the first half-trillion tons," *Myles R. Allen*, a leading British climate scientist, stated, "On current trends, we'll burn the next half-trillion in less than 40."[404] Unless there are increased efforts to convert to a new energy system soon, scientists argue, it is impossible to hit the 3.6-degree target, and the risk will increase that global warming will continue its stickiness, out of control towards a *tipping point* by the century's end. "We are quickly running out of time," said *Joseph G. Canadell*, an Australian scientist who tracks emissions.[405]

Section 5.2.2 Organizations

Fuel companies which have lobbied against action on emissions are in fact squandering the world's chance to avoid dangerous climate change. Professor *Bob Watson*, chief scientist at the *US Department for Environment and Rural Affairs*, in an interview with the *Guardian*, *Watson* said,

> "Those that have opposed a deal on climate, which would include elements of the fossil fuel industry, have clearly made making a 2C target much, much harder, if not impossible. They've clearly put the world at risk of far more adverse effects of climate change". Further he pointed out that the decision of former US president George W. Bush to walk away from the Kyoto Protocol, the existing global treaty on carbon emissions, sent a message to other countries not to act. He said, "The last decade was a lost opportunity. Elements within the fossil fuel industry clearly had major implications for the

404 Ibid.

405 Ibid.

Bush administration".[406]

Further, the Copenhagen talks in 2010 failed to deliver a legally binding treaty as originally hoped, only making minor progress on issues such as: financial assistance for the developing world and emissions cuts for rich countries. Scientists say the emissions must fall by 25-40% to have a good chance of staying within the 2C limit.[407] *Watson*, a former head of the Intergovernmental Panel on Climate Change, said,

> "I think we will do well to stabilize between 3 and 4C. Even that is going to take strong political action to decarbonize the energy system and to require us peaking greenhouse gas emissions in the next 10 or more years…We have to make sure we understand what it would mean to see 3-4C. How would we adapt our agriculture, our water resources, coastal protection and human health systems?"[408]

The British government has published a map showing a world warmer by 4C, it details that the rise would be unevenly spread across the globe, coupled with temperature rises larger than 4C in high latitudes, such as the Arctic region. Further, because the sea warms more slowly, land temperatures will increase by an average 5.5C, confirming what scientists say about shrinking yields for all major crops on all regions of production. A 4C rise would impact water availability, with supplies being limited to the forecasted extra billion people by 2080. *Watson* endorses controversial research into geo-engineering techniques, i.e. blocking the sun, as a way to head off dangerous temperature rise – he is one of the most senior figures so far to do so. He says, "We should at least be looking at it."[409] Such solutions at geo-engineering seem beyond comprehension, like the *living story* itself. Imagining the resources and degree of cooperation on an international level seems impossible with today's current means of communication, which are discussed in our next section.

---

406 David ADAM, "Climate Change Sceptics and Lobbyists put World at Risk, says Top Adviser," *Guardian*, November 22, 2009. Retrieved from http://www.guardian.co.uk/environment/2009/nov/22/climate-change-emissions-scientist-watson

407 Ibid.

408 Ibid.

409 Ibid.

Section 5.2.3 Media

The Internet has given rise to the opportunity for other discipline challengers who now question every aspect of the climate change science — physics as an example, whose research dates to 19th century, also shows that carbon dioxide traps heat. However, there are a handful of "experts", adversarial stickiness *salespersons,* who are trying to influence media and Congress from disciplines such as atmospheric physics. They generally accept the same conclusions about the rising carbon dioxide numbers and the increase is caused by human activity, and they further acknowledge that the earth is warming in response. However, they distort the media and seek to place doubt that it will warm nearly as much as (mainstream) scientists say, arguing that the increase is likely to be less than two degrees Fahrenheit, a change they characterize as "manageable."[410]

Among the most notable of these salespersons is *Richard Lindzen*, physicist at the *Massachusetts Institute of Technology,* who argues that as the earth initially warms, cloud patterns will shift in a way that should help to limit the heat buildup. However, climate scientists contend that little evidence to support this view. *Dr. Lindzen* is regularly consulted on Capitol Hill. "I am quite willing to state…unprecedented climate catastrophes are not on the horizon, though in several thousand years we may return to an ice age."[411]

Recent Media Developments

Climategate

In 2011, a trove of e-mail messages and documents which mention scientific discourse pertaining to adjustments in data, has been seized upon by global warming doubters as evidence of a conspiracy to promote the idea of human-driven climate change. Many scientists, however, have said that the contents of the messages and documents do not undercut decades of peer-reviewed science.[412] From the skeptic viewpoint, the prevailing theory about the e-mail messages was that they had been leaked by a whistle-

410 Justin GILLIS, "A Scientist, His Work and a Climate Reckoning," *op. cit.*

411 Ibid.

412 Andrew C. REVKIN and John M. BRODER, "In Face of Skeptics, Experts Affirm Climate Peril," *New York Times*, December 6, 2009. Retrieved from http://www.nytimes.com/2009/12/07/science/earth/07climate.html

blower who should eventually be celebrated. "In my view, not only will he not be prosecuted, but he should not be prosecuted," said *Christopher Monckton*, a policy adviser with the *Science and Public Policy Institute*, a British group concerned chiefly with trying to argue the notion of a climate crisis.[413] *Lord Monckton*, expressed his concern about the economic effects of putting limits on emissions of greenhouse gases, and other such restrictions said, it "...would be devastating to the economies of all countries, particularly poor nations. That's why it's necessary to allow them to burn plenty of fossil fuels because that's the cheapest way to get the electricity that will help to lift them from poverty."[414]

Skeptics contend the messages reveal that researchers attempted to stifle dissent and manipulate findings, and suppress data, with conservative bloggers dubbing it "Climategate". "The e-mails do nothing to undermine the very strong scientific consensus ... that tells us the earth is warming, that warming is largely a result of human activity," said another government scientist *Jane Lubchenco.*[415] A marine biologist and climate researcher, she heads the *National Oceanic and Atmospheric Administration*. In defense of the scientists, Rep. *Jay Inslee*, D-Wash., said, "Somehow the e-mails aren't stopping the Arctic from warming, the oceans from getting more acidic, and glaciers from melting."[416]

Hockey Stick Theory

The *hockey stick theory* of climate change, first described by scientist *Michael E. Mann* in the late 1990s, was also questioned in the above email controversy. The theory suggests that the past 50 years were the hottest in several centuries (if not 1,000 years) and that human activity leading to global warming is to blame. This research was so controversial that *The National Academy of Sciences* studied the theory in depth, and it was included in former Vice President *Al Gore's* documentary on global warming. The *National Academy of Sciences'* conclusions are (essentially) the

413 Tom ZELLER Jr., "And in This Corner, Climate Contrarians," *New York Times*, December 9, 2009. Retrieved from http://www.nytimes.com/2009/12/10/science/earth/10skeptics.html

414 Ibid.

415 Seth BORENSTEIN, "Obama Science Advisers Grilled over Hacked E-mails," *Breitbart*, December 2, 2009. Retrieved from http://www.breitbart.com/article.php?id=D9CBFB901

416 Ibid.

same as the *hockey stick theory* that *Mann* proposed, (and even if *Mann* and others had done no research at all), the world would still be warming and scientists would still be able to show it.[417]

Section 5.2.4 Events

The *IPCC* is currently recognized as one of the leading scientific bodies for the assessment of climate change established by the *United Nations Environment Programme* (UNEP) and the *World Meteorological Organization* (WMO) in 1988, to provide the world with a clear scientific view on the current state of climate change and its potential environmental and socio-economic consequences. It reviews and assesses the most recent scientific, technical, and socio-economic information produced worldwide relevant to the understanding of climate change. It does not conduct any research, nor does it monitor climate related data or parameters. According to the *IPCC*,

> One widely-accepted definition of dangerous climate change is that it begins at a global temperature rise of 2C. The *IPCC* recommends that to have a good chance of avoiding this definition of dangerous climate change, developed countries cut emissions by at least 25 per cent from 1990 levels by 2020, and that global emissions must peak and begin to decline by 2020 at the latest.[418]

According to the I*PCC*, existing research indicates that the earth's surface temperature has risen on average by less than a degree Celsius over the last 140 years, supported by data indicating an unusual rise over this time period when contrasted with the last thousand years. *IPCC* findings also indicated that the 20th century has also been marked by lessened snow and seasonal ice cover and rising sea levels and ocean temperatures. According to the *IPCC Second Assessment Report* released in 1995, "The balance of evidence suggests a discernible human influence on global climate."[419] *The IPCC Third Assessment Report in 2001* reinforced this message: "There

---

417 Ibid.

418 "Copenhagen Climate Accord: Key Issues," *BBC*, December 19, 2009. Retrieved from http://news.bbc.co.uk/2/hi/8422186.stm

419 "IPCC Second Assessment, Climate Change 1995," Intergovernmental Panel on Climate Change, December 1995. Retrieved from http://www.ipcc.ch/pdf/climate-changes-1995/ipcc-2nd-assessment/2nd-assessment-en.pdf

is new and stronger evidence that most of the warming observed over the last 50 years is attributable to human activities...Anthropogenic climate change will persist for many centuries."[420] Indeed, all modeled scenarios reflect temperature increases in the next century.

IPCC Third Assessment Report in 2001 further stated that research indicates the effects of climate change:

> Net losses in biodiversity, increasing frequency on weather-related events e.g. droughts or floods, and even the changing thaw and freeze of ice, are more likely to affect and have a disproportionate impact on vulnerable communities. Examples include the higher risk of coastal settlements to changes in sea-levels, the heightened effect in the tropics and sub-tropics of reduced crop yields, lower water availability in water-stressed regions, and the implications this has for human health in the case of intensified disease transmission and lowered living standards.[421]

The IPCC Third Assessment Report also states, "The effects of climate change are expected to be greatest in developing countries in terms of loss of life and relative effects on investment and the economy."[422] In terms of economic loss, the *Stern Review on the Economics of Climate Change*, published in Oct 2006, concludes that climate change will result in the loss of 5% global GDP every year, possibly rising to 20% GDP if a broader range of impacts is considered. Sociologists have pointed out that when it comes to vulnerable communities, small climate shocks share strong linkages to extreme social instability precipitated by warring for scarce resources made even scarcer.[423] As these stickiness events becomes a global *tipping point*, and the characteristics of this *one dramatic moment* are discussed in the next section.

---

420 "IPCC Third Assessment, Climate Change 1995," Intergovernmental Panel on Climate Change (IPCC), 2001. Retrieved from http://www.ipcc.ch/ipccreports/tar/index.htm

421 Ibid.

422 Ibid.

423 Nicholas STERN, *Stern Review on the Economics of Climate Change*, Her Majesty's Treasury, 2006. Retrieved from http://webarchive.nationalarchives.gov.uk/+/http://www.hm-treasury.gov.uk/stern_review_report.htm

Section 5.3 One Dramatic Moment (TP)

Section 5.3.1 People

Since climate change is recognized as manmade phenomena, small variations in the world population forecasts will have enormous impacts in the long term. As pointed out in earlier sections, as little as one-quarter of a child under the two-child norm, or one-quarter of a child above the norm, would result in world populations ranging from 2.3 billion to 36.4 billion. If fertility levels remain unchanged at today's levels, however, world population would rise to 44 billion in 2100, 244 billion persons in 2150 and 1.34 trillion in 2300. The requirements for air, water, food and shelter for populations of these magnitudes will inevitably create a series of events that will contribute to this global tipping point. As economies and governments attempt to service the demand, breakdowns in supply chains and environmental effects will be catastrophic. The next sections discuss the opportunities and the challenges which lie in the future.

What is essential in the discourse about the *tipping point* for climate change and organizations is the way that information is now presented and transmitted across international borders instantaneously. The societal governing structures that were set up, for example, after WWII, like the United Nations, operated in a media environment whereby there was a certain degree of control in the amount of information and the types of information that was either gathered and/or released. For the future, organizations and governments in the United States, European Union, Arab states, South American continent, Asian region and Africa, will, in effect, have to move in *media sync* as the means addressing the global *tipping point* with climate change. Past approaches of sovereignty, nation states, labels of religious background and ownership of resources may have worked in the past, they will not in a world very different than the one that we are facing with Climate Change. The new realities, equal in magnitude to the events and changes brought on from the Ice Age, or even the beginning of man, are now rapidly being put forth as the questions and agenda of the day and tomorrow regarding who will play important roles in our global future.

Section 5.3.2 Organizations

Based upon this research and how the current and future will media influence an important part in this *real time, living story*, governments and organizations as we know them today, will, in effect, be obsolete in the future when faced with the challenges of climate change. At that time, as we try to hang on to the ancient conventions of who is American, who is European, who is Asian, Russian, Turkish, etc. From the broader perspective as relates to climate change and the tipping point, labels, conventions and national titles will no longer be relevant. The question is, as the worlds populations expand, will we be comfortable with the current system of leaders and decision-makers to govern and steer the course of the world destiny? Ideally, individuals should be chosen because they are representing the greatest perspective on what is good for the global community of people. Unfortunately, as we become keenly aware, in the past 10 years and certainly in the last five, there have been events that clearly have gone beyond our organizational capabilities and reached epidemic proportions. The types of organizations necessary for the future that need to be able to address the magnitude and complexity of these issues and navigate the fundamentals of how the *media story* needs to be responsible and accountable. The charter to support this new organization should be founded on a constitution of *global consciousness*. At this juncture, I have no other way of describing it, other than the understanding that we are not alone anymore. Clearly the reality of dumping tons of CO2 into the environment, unbridled population growth, and using the same energy sources developed during the Industrial Revolution are destroying our future and must change.

The media platforms that we are now seeing and experiencing in 2011 are the beginning of this *global consciousness*. Governments, in the meantime, will (and have already) try to circumvent and establish controls on the media delivery systems. Good examples include Georgia's experience in 2010, China's in the last five years, as well as the Arab spring conflicts where governments have tried to shut down Internet, television, and other media. It is my opinion that in the future, as governments search for means of controlling the populations, will be faced with not humanitarian objectives but military objectives, as the strength and evolution of the military technologies has always been the driving force as a solution to every conflict on our planet.

The contrast now is we have the opportunity and challenge for the global community to really understand the predicament it is faced with, and the leaders will be mandated to listen and find the types of solutions and implement the types of laws and regulations that may effectuate the outcome.

The *Intergovernmental Panel on Climate Change* and other bodies has already issued warnings, and the scientists have backed up their claims with data and research that has been reviewed by their peers in objective forms. The types of governmental agencies that are now known to exist, when faced with such a magnitude of issues associated in the future with *climate change*, requiring the resources and abilities to manage them, will mandate an evolution to some new forms of governmental environmental groups. Without this, the *epidemic* will spread. The *Broken Windows Theory* will manifest in the sense that in the world, media will echo the panic by these ancient organizations and everyone will think that no one is in control and all hope is lost and the Tipping Point will occur.

Section 5.3.3 Media

If there is a need for fundamental and profound shifts in energy production, solutions for how and where people live, sweeping changes in agriculture and forestry and the creation of complex new economies and media systems related to climate change, there is another question: "How are we going to create a *global consciousness* to address these challanges?" The answer is with media influence over the next few decades. It will require a significant effort and establishing funds to execute but a relatively small fraction of the world's activity.

Placed in context with the financial amount necessary to retool the worlds energy approach, *Kevin Parker*, the global head of *Deutsche Bank Asset Management*, who tracks climate policy stated,

> "...the figures people tend to cite don't take into account conservation and efficiency measures that are easily available. And they don't look at the cost of inaction, which is the extinction of the human race. Period. That is not very much compared to the size of the world economy or the financial crisis bailouts".[424]

Álvaro *Umaña Quesada*, the leader of Costa Rica's climate delegation at the Copenhagan Talks, also made the statement,

424 John M. BRODER, "Climate Deal Likely to Bear Big Price Tag," *New York Times*, December 8, 2009. Retrieved from http://www.nytimes.com/2009/12/09/science/earth/09cost.html?pagewanted=all

> "There are great needs for adaptation, where the small island nations are really at risk. Some of them are one severe weather event away from disappearing...The good news is that everybody now is supporting our proposal for financing. The bad news is that it's happening 15 years too late. Without real money on the table, this will be a disaster."[425]

The media, the governments that control them, the corporations and the audiences of the world need to hear the truth from strong leaders and new organizations capable of addressing the magnitude of the media influence to drive the world solutions, as the media continues to represent and play an integral role in this *real time living story*.

If we were to look back a few years from now at the first decade of the 21st century, when the food prices increased, energy prices were out of control, the world population expanded, hurricanes and tornadoes plowed through our cities, floods and droughts set records, entire regions of populations were displaced and governments were toppling, we might ask ourselves: What in the world were we doing? How is it that we didn't panic when the evidence was so obvious that we crossed over some dramatic moment that defines our everyday existence with regard to growth, climate, natural resources and population? "The answer can only be denial," says *Paul Gilding* in his book called *The Great Disruption: Why the Climate Crisis Will Bring an End to the Shopping and the Birth of a New World.* In the book he states,

> When you are surrounded by something so big it requires you to change everything about the way you think and see the world, denial is a natural response. But the longer we wait, the bigger the response required. In order to sustain our current growth rates we are using about 1.5 earths. Having only one planet makes this a rather significant problem[426]

None of this is science fiction, says *Gilding*:

425 Ibid.

426 Paul GILDING, The Great Disruption: Why the Climate Crisis Will Bring On the End of Shopping and the Birth of a New World, New York, NY, Bloomsbury Press, 2011.

> …if you cut down more trees than you grow, you run out of trees, if you put additional nitrogen into the water system, you change the type and quality of the life that water can support. If you thicken the Earth's CO2 blanket, the earth gets warmer. If we do all these things and many more things at once, you change the way the world systems on the planet behave. Along with that comes the social, economic and life-support impacts. This is not speculation; this is high school science."[427]

China's environmental minister, *Zhou Shengxian*, said recently, "In China's thousands of years of civilization, the conflict between humankind and nature has never been as serious as it is today."[428] The Chinese minister is telling us the same thing that *Gilding* is. He says, "The earth is full. We're now using so many resources and putting out so much waste into the earth that we have reached some kind of limit, given current technologies. The economy is going to have to get smaller in terms of physical impact."[429] But none of this will change, without media influencing the *tipping point*.

Section 5.3.4 Events

My research illustrates that we are headed in a *tipping point* direction with media contributing. We are currently caught in two very dramatic moment event pathways: one, where the population growth and more global warming together are, for example, pushing up food prices (which was part of the reason for the 2011 political instability in the Middle East region caused by rising food prices, which led to higher oil prices, which led to higher food prices, which led to more instability). At the same time, all this improved productivity has meant that more people are needed in the factories to make products. As we know, we need more jobs, which means we need more factories. More factories produce more products making more global climate change, and *this* is where the two event pathways meet. This is the same issue that *Gilding* speaks of. As the impact of the eminent *tipping point* arrives, he says optimistically,

---

427 Ibid.

428 Andrew JACOBS, "China Issues Warning on Climate and Growth," *New York Times*, February 28, 2011. Retrieved from http://www.nytimes.com/2011/03/01/world/asia/01beijing.html

429 Thomas L. FRIEDMAN, "The Earth is Full," *New York Times*, June 7, 2011. Retrieved from http://www.nytimes.com/2011/06/08/opinion/08friedman.html

> Our response will be proportionally dramatic, mobilizing as we do in war. We will change a scale and speed we can barely imagine today, completely transforming our economies, including our energy and transport industries, in just a few short decades.[430]

Optimistically, the Climate Change event will be that the *consumer-driven growth model* will no longer be in fashion, and as *Gilding* predicts, we will move more towards a *happiness-driven growth model* based on people working less and owning less, in effect a new global consciousness.

The *tipping point* event will arrive, I would argue, as, "We are headed for a crisis-driven choice," states *Gilding.* "We can allow the collapse to overtake us or develop a new sustainable economic model." *Gilding* feels we would choose the latter. "We may be slow, but we're not stupid."[431]

In lieu of dramatic changes *(global consciousness*) in the world's organizations, economic agendas, media influence and the current direction that this event is evolving, the following sections outline the best case and worst case scenarios identified in the research as to the various events associated with this *tipping point.*

Future Scenarios: US

In more than 3100 US counties, the *Community Climate System Model* (CCSM) predicts that between now and the late 21st century, a typical county's average annual temperature will rise 8°, and its rainfall will decline by 0.3 inches. But these averages conceal huge variations. The model predicts that there are 150 counties whose average temperature will rise by only 3°F, and there are more than 150 counties whose average temperature will rise by more than 12°F. Iowa and North Dakota are examples of states that are expected to grow much warmer. As such, North Dakota is likely to be a more attractive place to live. Historically, the average February temperature in North Dakota has been a frigid 15°F. The CCSM predicts that these will double the 30°F by the end of the century, while August average temperatures will rise from 69° to 83°F.

Some of the more alarming computer predictions focus on the fate of the

430 Ibid.

431 Ibid.

cities along the coasts. In the United States over the last 60 years or more, an enormous number people have chosen to live in US coastal cities from San Diego to Boston. Counties that are located 50 miles from the ocean or a large lake body make up just 13% of the continental US land area. But they accounted for 50% of the US population in the year 2000. The same patterns exist in European countries. One third of the EU population is estimated to live within 50 km of the coast. And in Denmark it is almost 100% as well as 75% in the United Kingdom and the Netherlands. No one is saying that coastal cities aren't beautiful, but if the climate change events that the scientists are predicting occur, the change will take place gradually, and those populations that are living on the coasts and who have invested in structures there are certain to be more impacted. Many of these people have a wait and see attitude as they adapt to the change in the sea levels that could rise as high as 2 feet. This strategy of adaptation makes perfect sense, unless catastrophic events with abrupt climate change unfold. However, should that be the case, coastal cities will disappear in the blink of an eye with the sudden sea level rise.

The question remains: If we subscribe to the sudden nightmare *tipping point* scenario, shouldn't we consider evacuating such cities worldwide? From the research there are no climate models that are making such a prediction. But there are many that are making predictions that the cumulative effects may not be tolerable in a not too distant future.

In contrast to the first two case studies, we might think of it in terms of the size of the event, the magnitude of the *epidemic*, and whether or not we have the solutions available to address the issues. There are two ways to look at this:

One, it becomes obvious with the timeline and events that the amount of media (space) information and the clarity (accuracy) of the content will eventually ring through. The *global consciousness* for how media delivers the content will no longer be cloaked in some kind of profit-making agenda beyond the short-term gains. Both the *Obama Presidential Campaign* and the International Financial Crisis messages were spread as characterized by the tipping point attributes. As this becomes an *epidemic*, there would be no turning back from the eventual outcome due to the complexity of these man-made systems, manipulated in part by the media technologies available. With *climate change*, we have both a man-made problem and a natural process relative to the order of our environment that is playing out in many of the same ways, but also entirely different. Two, as we contrast the three case studies' attributes with each other, the objectives and goals are dramatically different with the first two; the man-made contributions to the attributes leading to the contagiousness and stickiness are very similar to what is occurring with climate change.

From the standpoint of the media involvement and the media manipulation in what may eventually become the government intervention to avoid a global catastrophe, this presents some serious problem-solving for future leaders. Many cities throughout the world are commissioning crystal ball studies to provide a glimpse of what the world might look like by the year 2050. San Diego, for example, has concluded a study that sea level will be 12 to 18 inches higher and the average annual temperature will increase by 4.5°F. This region will require 37% more water being supplied from sources such as the Colorado River, which at that time will be smaller by 20% or more. The fire seasons will start earlier in the annual number of days, as the ideal conditions for big fires will increase by up to 20%. Electricity demands at peak times will increase by more than 70%. And the city is going to be occupied by more and more senior citizens who are typically less able to move in response to impending environmental changes. What is interesting, as even though this information has been provided to San Diego politicians and the populations for some time, the market reaction has been to find solutions to improve the quantities of air conditioning and additional electricity to power it.

Other studies by the *Pacific Institute* along the California coast estimate the sea level rise and the number of people who are going to be experiencing a major flood event. It appears that unless there are significant amounts of population that are affected, as in New Orleans during *Hurricane Katrina*, there really is no way to get the media's attention and the government funds to move these people and their investments to higher ground. The people living in areas at risk will take the gamble and continue to seek to live along the coastal areas.

On the other side of the United States, New York will be greatly affected by climate change. Between 1971 and the year 2000, New York averaged 14 days a year over 90°F. Mean annual temperatures are projected by global climate models to increase roughly 2°F by 2020 and 48°F by 2080. But the climate change could have a different kind of severe effect on New York and many cities like it throughout the world. Climate change raises the likelihood of some very nasty climate-related events taking place, but the risk is ambiguous and is difficult to qualify. Many of the scientists try to sketch out some possible future nasty scenarios, but for cities like New York, we just don't know how much damage will happen and who would suffer the most from such events because the climate scientists are portrayed in the media with statements that couch their positions with no definite statements like "one in 5 million will die" and "more than 100,000 will be injured." And because qualified risk can be difficult to deal with, cities like New York are filled with risk-averse people who will slough off media reports until they are forced to "jump out of the pot," as *Paul Krugman* says.[432]

What kind of risk will New Yorkers face? There is something that climate modelers have predicted called the "triple witching hour" in which climate change raises sea levels and that a major hurricane occurs during high tide. The geographical and environmental implications are clear: Manhattan is surrounded by water--the Atlantic, the Long Island sound, and the Hudson, Harlem, and East Rivers. Ten percent of the city's land mass, including much of the lower Manhattan area and the three airports, are less than 3 meters above sea level. Scenarios that are played out in movies in Hollywood would become a reality in New York. Subway flooding would cripple the city, and already has, not to mention what would happen if the thousands of gallons of sewage line that are part of the rain runoff become flooded and the water treatment plants and sewage plants are swamped.

New York is preparing for the changes in the climate. The subway entrances and exits are least 10 feet above the flood line established by the *Federal Emergency Management Agency*. And new stations will also be more flood-proof, as will many of the major Manhattan projects that are being built. They are being done in such a way as prepare them for the potential disasters. In addition, engineers have gone as far as drawing up preliminary plans for the largest underground complexes in the city, a massive 80 foot deep basement that will extend a block from the banks of the Hudson River. It would be capable of handling a part of the storm surge in the event

432 Paul KRUGMAN, "Boiling the Frog," *New York Times*, July 12, 2009. Retrieved from http://www.nytimes.com/2009/07/13/opinion/13krugman.html

it should come. New York has already had fire drills to this effect during the torrential downpours that were associated with Hurricane Frances in 2004 that inundated the city with more than two inches of rain an hour. Note the recent events in summer 2011 with Hurricane Irene that threaten the eastern seaboard of the US. During these times, hundreds of thousands of commuters were stranded. As rainwater seeped through the tunnel walls and flowed down subway grates and stairwells, some 280 pump rooms next to the subway tracks pulled the water back up to street level. The water then naturally flowed toward the door storm drains, but the storm drains themselves were unable to handle the flow of the water. The result was a catastrophe.

New York City has responded to the challenge of forecasting the climate change impacts by putting together a panel that consists of leading climate change and environmental impact scientists, academics, and private sector practitioners. The city's approach has called for new flood zone maps in the form of a long-term sustainability plan. The idea is to change the building codes and be prepared for the global climate change. The fact is that the people who are the politicians today will no longer be around in 2050 or 2071 when these events will be occurring. Politicians typically have short-term perspective primarily because they are just looking to raise their reelection prospects. New York mayor *Mike Bloomberg* is not typical. As of this writing, he has become a billionaire by creating a company called *Bloomberg Inc.* that collects information and distributes it to Wall Street traders. He's in the media, and one can only imagine the frustration that he has when he hears from leading experts on climate change and they cannot provide him with precise predictions on how and when climate change will strike.

The New York project has yielded some consensus climate predictions concerning how average temperature, rainfall, and sea level rise will be affected by the end of the 21st century. But the question of adaptation to climate change and the average risk is less important than if it's going to be in your backyard and you have the means and the ability to deal with it. Climate modelers are producing topographical maps highlighting geographical areas at risk under certain and various climate scenarios. The *US Army Corps of Engineers* estimates that if a category three hurricane hits New York, nearly 30% of the south side of Manhattan will be flooded. Such estimates raise these questions:

- How will the financial companies in New York survive if employees can't get to work, and the infrastructure that supports their operations is no longer able to function due to the floods of the other servers' shutdowns?
- How will all the middle-class renters who work in all of the financial district jobs get back and forth to keep the economy going?

Who is to come up with the solutions? We put a lot of faith in the engineers and the politicians who are discussing a variety of engineering scenarios to protect coastal cities from rising sea levels. But if one looks today at Europe, for example *Venice*, one can see that the engineers and the politicians have neither the means nor the ability to stop the effects of climate change. In Venice, San Marcos Square is now becoming one of the world's most interesting scuba diving areas. And on most days it is under a half to a meter of water. The politicians and the engineers have developed elaborate plans for constructing a huge foundation system and propping up the city with balloons with structural systems that would cost billions and billions of Euros and raise the foundations relative to rising water levels of all the city's buildings. This race against time, already unfortunately lost, started several years back.

Singapore is another example of a city that is vulnerable to climate change. Much of it is an island less than 15 meters above sea level, generally flat with a population of 4.7 million along its 193 km coastline. Singapore is one of the most densely populated countries in the world. The city has spent millions with land reclamation projects and flood control schemes to alleviate flooding in the low-lying areas of the city.

Some experts are urging to build enormous, retractable storm surge barriers in three locations around New York, including one straddling the Verrazano Narrows and another at Throngs neck, or where Long Island Sound meets the East River. The idea is that such barriers, rising 15 m above sea level, would effectively wall off New York Harbor if a major hurricane should send huge waves toward the city. The optimism behind these technological remedies somehow reassures the public creating a sense of blind faith, - luring them into a false sense of security. The media promotes and reports on the proposals and the audience listens and can't quite comprehend the living story, so they then return to their more manageable daily tasks and issues. Many people have neither the time nor the energy to perform the due-diligence that is necessary to determine what the risk factors are with living in a certain area. People trust the engineers, and the public wants magic bullet solutions. And politicians, at risk of not being reelected, make promises that basically say that there's unlikely to be any problem with climate change. The citizens, in turn, might move to higher ground, if they could, but they can't. The media does little to clarify the issues, the threats, and agendas, as politicians and their engineers say that we can continue to survive and thrive in a hotter world--that we will adapt.

Future Scenarios: World

When asked to *quantify* the impact of *climate change*, scientists come up with a lot of interesting answers, no two of them quite the same. The timeline of events that was included in the previous section (stickiness attribute) is, by most measures, a pretty good estimate of how *climate change* will evolve over time. For the lay person, perhaps the simplest way to understand it is to imagine a distant asteroid somewhere out in space on a collision course with Earth. It's not clear when or where the asteroid will hit, or exactly how severe the consequences will be. But it is clear that when it happens, the consequences will be far worse–and last far longer–than any natural disaster humanity has ever known. That is the threat to the planet that many scientists can agree is posed by climate change. Yet the global response to global warming–with less clarity in the media than real focus — doesn't exactly resemble the mobilizing opening scenes of disaster films like *Armageddon* or *Deep Impact*. Quite the opposite, as fears about other global events, like war, economic collapse, earthquakes, political and technological upheavals, climate change will recede from the public *consciousness*.

A recent 2010 *Gallup Poll* found that a record-high 41% of Americans believe that the threat of global warming is exaggerated in the news media, up from 30% in 2006.[433] Though a majority of Americans are still a "fair amount" or a "great deal" concerned about climate change, that proportion has hardly changed in recent years, even as the preponderance of scientific evidence increasingly supports the danger of global warming and the speed

433 Lydia SAAD, "Increased Number Think Global Warming Is 'Exaggerated'," *Gallup*, March 11, 2009. Retrieved from http://www.gallup.com/poll/116590/increased-number-think-global-warming-exaggerated.aspx

with which it is occurring. The asteroid is out there, and yet we remain reluctant to heed the warnings. Why?

First, most people imagine global warming to be a gradual process, like water slowly coming to boil — so it follows that averting the worst effects of climate change should be as straightforward as turning down the heat. But the climate, immensely complex as it is, doesn't work that way. The real danger could come from tipping points–sharp, sudden changes that could result in, for example, the complete collapse of the ice sheets on Greenland or West Antarctica or the desiccation of the Amazon rainforest.

Second, if we cross these thresholds, the effects could be too swift and terrible for the world to cope–the ice on Greenland alone contains enough water to raise global sea levels by more than 20 feet, which would swallow the coasts. Passing a tipping point would be irreversible, and that is why the possibility keeps climatologists up at night. The key is to comprehend where the *tipping point* is. How much carbon do we have to pump into the atmosphere, and how much warmer does the climate need to be before get there?

A team of researchers led by *Elmar Kriegler* of the *Potsdam Institute for Climate Impact Research in Germany* posed those questions to 43 of world's top climatologists. Their answers, reported in an intriguing study published in the March 16, 20 issue of the *Proceedings of the National Academy of Sciences (PNAS)*, basically concluded that we don't really know. The scientists agreed that there was a significant chance that the tipping points would be crossed this century — or the next — especially if we fail to reduce carbon emissions and if global temperatures rise considerably over the coming decades, which, as we know, is likely to happen without a concerted global effort to cut the CO2 emissions. But the reality is that the climate system remains too complex and the future too difficult to predict as to when exactly when we've passed the point of no return.

This uncertainty has an obvious impact on the media response and reporting on global warming. Scientists can warn us repeatedly that adding billions of tons of CO2 to the atmosphere will eventually cause severe, even irreparable damage to the planet and to us — but they can't tell us exactly when the catastrophe will occur. (Small pieces of it already have — the Arctic ice cap has already shrunk considerably, and dozens of frog species alone have gone extinct thanks to warming.) So climate change inevitably fades from the news headlines, and the public agenda is replaced by more urgent concerns: the recession, wars, terrorism. It's perfectly understandable that many of us would take refuge in the uncertainty and hope that we'll somehow have the climate problem solved before we cross the *tipping point*. That would be a mistake. It may come later — or it may come sooner.

Global Climate: Wars and Population

Although scientists have warned of possible social perils resulting from climate change, the impacts on social unrest and population collapse have been quantitatively investigated. One study used high-resolution *paleoclimatic* models to explore at a macro scale the influence of climate change on the outbreak of war and population which decline during a preindustrial era. It showed that long-term fluctuations of war frequency and population changes followed the cycles of temperature change.

Further analyses demonstrated that cooling impeded agricultural production, which brought about a series of serious social problems, including successive war outbreak, famine, and population decline and price inflation,. The findings suggested that global war–peace events, population, and price cycles in recent centuries have been driven predominantly by long-term climate change. The findings also suggest that social mechanisms that may otherwise mitigate the impact of climate change were not significantly effective during the (study) periods. Climate change it concluded played a more important role and imposed a wider ranging effect on human civilization than has so far been suggested.

This study went further to note that social activities heavily depend on climate as well. Pointing out that temperature probably influences our lives more than any other climatic factor, and human society is especially vulnerable to temperature changes.[434] However, scientific research on social effects tends to focus on the economic costs of current and future climate change and typically neglects the study of how societies have historically reacted to long-term climate change. One possible reason for this might have been the availability and advancement of media forms prevalent historically and identified during the study period (s). In other words, the

434 Panel on Climate Variability on Decade-to-Century Time Scales, National Research Council, "Decade-to-Century-Scale Climate Variability and Change: A Science Strategy," Washington, D.C., National Academy Press, 1998. Retrieved from http://www.nap.edu/catalog.php?record_id=6129

societies effectively did not have the technologies to express their social concerns about how the environment was affecting them and therefore had limited global options to change events. This deficiency is unfortunate, but perhaps helps to better understand how past climate changes may or may not have been influenced human society (and media available). It may help us better understand our future prospects.

David Webster argued that warfare was an adaptive ecological choice in prehistoric societies with limited resources and growing populations, unfortunately, he was not able to use systematic, scientific data to support his conclusion.[435] The concept of environmental conflict has been suggested by several researchers, focusing only on conflicts caused by meteorological events and short-term climate variations.[436] *Patrick Galloway* discovered that long-term climate change controlled population size in middle-latitude regions. However, his findings lacked quantitative precision because of the absence of high-resolution climate records.[437]

A long span study of Chinese history shows that the number of war outbreaks and population collapses in China are significantly correlated with Northern Hemisphere (NH) temperature variations. And that all of the periods of population collapse, dynastic change and nationwide unrest occurred in the cold phases of this period.[438]

---

435 David WEBSTER, "Warfare and the Evolution of the State: A Reconsideration," *American Antiquity*, 40, 1975, p. 464-470.

436 Jonathan COWIE, *Climate and Human Change: Disaster or Opportunity?* New York, Parthenon, 1998; R. Brian FERGUSON, *Warfare, Culture, and Environment*, Orlando, FL, Academic, 1984; Thomas F. HOMER-DIXON, "Environmental Scarcities and Violent Conflict: Evidence from Cases," *International Security*, 19, 1994, p. 5-40; Astri SUHRKE, "Environmental Degradation, Migration, and the Potential for Violent Conflict," in *Conflict and the Environment*, Nils Petter GLEDITSCH (ed.), The Netherlands, Kluwer, Dordrecht, 1997, pp. 255–272.

437 Patrick R. GALLOWAY, "Long-Term Fluctuations in Climate and Population in the Preindustrial Era," *Population and Development Review*, 12, 1986, pp. 1-24.

438 Harry F. LEE, Lincoln FOK, and David D. ZHANG, "Climatic Change and Chinese Population Growth Dynamics over the Last Millennium," *Climatic Change*, 88, 2007, pp. 131-156; David D. ZHANG, C. Y. JIM, George C. S. LIN, Yuan-Qing HE, James J. WANG, and Harry F. LEE, "Climate Change, Wars and Dynastic Cycles in China over the Last Millennium," *Climatic Change*, 76, 2006, pp. 459-477; David D. ZHANG, Jane ZHANG, Harry F. LEE, and Yuan-Qing HE, "Climate Change and War Frequency in Eastern China over the Last Millennium," *Human Ecology*, 35, 2007, pp. 403-414.

The incidence of warfare in the Europe, Asia, Northern Hemisphere and the more arid areas of the NH tends to follow a cyclical pattern, with a turbulent period followed by a relatively tranquil one, then periods of unrest and warfare, following the temperature inversely. This pattern has also appeared at a continental scale, (except for in the late 19th century) when the temperature of the Southern Hemisphere (SH) was its coldest and a great number of wars occurred in the southern part of Africa.[439] Stated another way, periods of (relative) peace and turbulence during the 500 years of the study periods, was a global phenomenon apparently linked to temperature change. The temperature–war connection is significant, and population declines followed every high war peak.[440]

Parallel, the ecological stress triggered by climate change induces population shrinkage of most species, particularly human beings. *Johnson and Gould* demonstrated that the agricultural production of Mesopotamia (present-day Iraq) closely echoed its changing climate, which led to cyclical collapses of its population by famine and wars.[441]

The above points out significant global connections in the timing between temperature change, increased wars, and population growth rates tipping points. These analyses also indicate that cooling may have contributed to widely-separated human tipping points during the cold periods. The paths to those tipping points resulted in a reduction in agricultural production, because the cooling brought about a shortening of the growing season and a lessening of available land for crops. Shortages of food resources (reflected in price rises) instigated wars and conflicts, with population declines.

Social scientists note these phenomena of social order and disorder in his-

439 Peter BRECKE, "Violent Conflicts 1400 A. D. to the Present in Different Regions of the World," Annual Meeting of the Peace Science Society (International), Ann Arbor, MI, October 8–10, 1999.

440 David D. ZHANG, C. Y. JIM, George C. S. LIN, Yuan-Qing HE, James J. WANG, and Harry F. LEE, "Climate Change, Wars and Dynastic Cycles in China over the Last Millennium," *op. cit.* pp. 459–477; David D. ZHANG, Jane ZHANG, Harry F. LEE, and Yuan-Qing HE, "Climate Change and War Frequency in Eastern China over the Last Millennium," *op. cit.* pp. 403–414.

441 Douglas L. JOHNSON and Harvey A. GOULD, "The Effect of Climate Fluctuations on Human Populations: A Case Study of Mesopotamian Society," in *Climate and Development*, Asit K. BISWAS (ed.), Dublin, Tycooly International Limited, 1984, pp. 117-138.

tory during which downturn periods were characterized by a fall in real wages, political crisis, war, inflation, and state. There are many theories and hypotheses that attempt to explain these phenomenon and the dynamics behind the cyclical pattern in history. However, those models cannot explain parallel and spatial occurrence of these phenomenon in widely separated regions that were in different stages of civilization, developed or undeveloped, connected or not cultures, and specific resource, no as means for prediction the timing of such events.

Malthus, as well as *Darwin* and many other ecologists have stated that positive checks and effectively rebalancing the systems occur when population growth exceeds the level of resources based on the assumption that the level of resources needed for basic survival is essentially constant or possibly increasing.[442]

War is an extremely complicated social phenomenon, with many scholars investigating the problem of the causes of war since the days of *Thucydides*. Unfortunately, as we approach the tipping point in this context for Climate Change, scholars have made at best modest progress on the issues related to the phenomenon, even though some members of all of the social sciences have partially addressed it. Some of these theories try to explain certain wars, (and some of the theories may even explain sizable classes of wars), yet none of them approach it broad-scope with todays' information platforms and tools and explain the temporal and spatial patterns of warfare. Although the research is a far stretch to being complete. It still implies that relative food scarcity is a fundamental cause of war outbreaks on various physical and social components and in different geographical regions.

As such, a resource scarcity, due to the increase in Climate Change effects will manifest itself in two ways: 1. A direct cause, in which resource-oriented wars erupted as most of the world's population still struggled to satisfy the lower levels of Maslow's Hierarchy of Needs,[443] and 2. An indirect cause, as food resources become scarce and economic difficulties

442 David D. ZHANG, Peter BRECKE, Harry F. LEE, Yuan-Qing HE, and Jane ZHANG, "Global Climate Change, War, and Population Decline in Recent Human History," *Proceedings of the National Academy of Sciences*, 104, 2007, p. 19214-19219.

443 Abraham Harold MASLOW, *Motivation and Personality*, New York, Harper & Row, 1970.

stemming from that intensified different social contradictions, increasing the incidence of war.

Section 5.4: Summary

Currently, the planet is now in the warmest climatic phase of the past two millennia, (another climatic extreme like the 17th century), which was the coldest period of the past two millennia.[444] Rising of temperatures will, during the short term, increas bio-productivity according to biological principles, recent research suggests that the negative effects of Climate Change on agriculture will be greater than the positive effects.[445]

Significantly, most of the world's population relys on small-scale agriculture, which remains vulnerable to climatic fluctuations. Other direct impacts of Climate Change, such as spread of tropical diseases, increase of extreme weather events, sea level rising, and glacial retreat, would also add costs to current economies that are supported by cheap energy. In severe cases, the increased economic burdens would increase conflict for resources and intensify social conflict and unrest as we have seen in the past and with increased prevalence recently. However, the greater threat from Climate Change comes from the unknown response of the ecosystems because the (current) high global average temperature is continuing to rise at an accelerated speed.

Perhaps we are reaching the *tipping point* at which it will break the balance of a human ecosystem that has been long established at a lower temperature, and a change to key components in the ecosystem will likely cause dramatic moments in human societies dependent on the existing human ecosystem.

However, currently, we now have more robust social and political institutions at both international and national levels to change this path, as well as much more advanced social, media and technological developments.

---

444 Michael E. MANN and Philip D. JONES, "Global Surface Temperatures over the Past Two Millennia," *Geophysical Research Letters*, 30, 2003.

445 Jun FURUYA, Shintaro KOBAYASHI, and Seth D. MEYER, "Economic Impacts of Climate Change on Global Food Supply and Demand," *Japan Agriculture Research*, 39, 2005, p. 121-134; David B. LOBELL and Christopher B. FIELD, "Global Scale Climate–Crop Yield Relationships and the Impacts of Recent Warming," *Environmental Research Letters*, 2, 2007.

Part III
Analysis and Comparisons

INTRODUCTION

The Case Studies presented in the preceding section provide a wide range of data and information that can be analyzed and compared in order to assess whether the Tipping Point Theory provides a model framework and opportunity for addressing the impact of media on global events, and what specific attributes and characteristics of the theory might be involved. While the cases highlight only a very small set of potential examples, they represent specific contemporary events and therefore capture a relatively comprehensive understanding of the application of this theory phenomena.

Despite being limited in number, the case studies reveal certain similarities that they exhibit to be clear and consistent. They also exhibit differences that permit us to highlight the scope of possibilities that occur in the presence of these common ingredients. While the overall limits of possibilities for application and analysis of this theory may not have been exhausted herein, other opportunities might be found to be relevant if additional case studies are identified and studied. It nevertheless allows us to make some conclusions about the relevancy of Tipping Point Theory and media impact on global events in the context examined here. These analysis and comparisons identify the consistent nature of the tipping point attributes and characteristics in each of the case study global events and point out a historical perspective. The Tipping Point Theory applied to the three different case studies; together give us a fundamentally broad base for interpreting the similar elements that might present themselves in future applications.

The global events in these case studies can all be assessed in the context of a specific media impact and information technology advancements that contribute or have contributed to their tipping points. While there are many other issues and effects, the net result allows this to make conclusions about the attributes as they exist. The circumstances are worthy of discussion in the context of international relations as these phenomena continue to unfold and provide opportunities for world leaders and world populations in the future. With this process of first identifying the characteristics in the case studies, and now proceeding in this part to analyze and compare them, we begin to understand and develop a sense of how relevant the connection is between media and global events.

In this context, the analysis and comparisons also highlight the way the Tipping Point Theory, as applied in the context of media impact and global events, provides an excellent mechanism for anticipating, observing and perhaps influencing global event outcomes.

Media Impacts and Global Events Website:

For further information please visit the: Media impact and Global Events Website: http://mdgparis.typepad.com/global_media_and_world_ev/

This website tracks, highlights, categorizes and provides a articles and commentary related to Tipping Point Attributes and Characteristics, as well as information and recent updates related specifically to the three case studies included in this version and other Media and Global Event issues.

CHAPTER SIX ANALYSIS

Putting the Tipping Point attributes and characteristics into an analytical context provides challenges for exhibiting the influences of media over short and long period of times. Even with the evidence of the particular characteristic, some of these influences may be difficult to identify. However, for the attribute and characteristics identified in each of the case studies, I propose a bracketed timescale on the order of years as a finite duration for the analysis, and this timescale will then enable me to qualitatively measure and exhibit, on a relative scale, the media impact in terms of the tipping point attributes and characteristics as researched and identified for each global event. The three case studies highlight that there are people, organizations, media, and events inherently critical to development and potential for a tipping point to occur, and with basis for influence from the media sectors. Progressively, each case study expands the duration timescale window of the attribute and characteristics analysis, from the relatively short timeframe of the Obama Presidential Campaign of one year (2008 plus), to the four-year (plus) duration of the International Financial Crisis of 2007-2011, and the evolving thirty plus years duration focus on Climate Change (2000-2030 and beyond). The purpose is three-fold: (1) contrasting and comparing the attributes and characteristics from a very finite timescale to a broader scope to identify similarities and differences (2) identifying fundamental philosophies, trends, and media delivery systems and technology that may be prevalent, and (3) providing for the three case studies to be measured qualitatively relative to the identified characteristic importance and influence on the tipping point attribute (one dramatic moment).

The following should be noted regarding the limits to quantity of characteristics identified for the purposes of sizing the research scope and magnitude accordingly for this version. First, while I strove to provide a complete survey of the detail of the many potential characteristics that might have been included for each of the case studies, the research continues to evolve and grow and, perhaps inadvertently, the content on relevant issues was unjustly included given recent discoveries that have come to bear on the potential application of the theory. For this, I merely am reinforced by the dynamics of how media is in many ways captured by the changing flux of these phenomena as well. And second, the research and data is limited given the breadth of information that exists and the fundamental complexity of this application. This has indeed confirmed my admiration for the scientists, scholars, media sources, authors and world leaders whose work and fine efforts proceeded mine and was deemed salient to the discussion. In as much as was practical and applicable in the scope of this work, I have attempted to assimilate these perspectives and findings herein and duly note and credit their origins and context with the resources, fact-checking and formatting approaches and graphic and text tools available. If ever there was a shortcoming in my approach, was my focus on the theory analysis, with a genuine objective develop and answer questions as they arose and ultimately exhibit my findings and conclusions for future events. I fully admit in this context (and current research formatting protocol), invariably, some rules were adjusted regarding the research to move the project forward and support the arguments and not constrained by these issues. In the following sections I discuss the methodology and illustrate its application to each of the case studies.

Methodology

What I have developed is a qualitative ratio analysis framework for graphically exhibiting the relative scalable media impact with each timescale and for each attribute and characteristic identified. Each case study chapter that proceeded identified a broad range of characteristics that correlated to a media influence on the evolution of the tipping point. As a principal domain of this application I show how one might approach and provide a coherent representation of the tipping point attributes, characteristics, and relationships to global events as presented over several different durations of time, subject to some qualitative interpretations but nevertheless accurate enough to permit qualitative analysis.

The qualitative ratio analysis framework provides the opportunity to analyze the different attributes and characteristics and compare their performance measured by the qualitative scale. In the same way that financial experts analyze annual reports, I looked at the attributes in succession, i.e. time duration and use this tool to identify patterns relative to the tipping point attributes and characteristics. Similarly, this framework allows each case study to be interpreted, analyzed, and compared.

Case studies used in this manner are sometimes used to describe phenomena. For example, findings about mental health in the longitudinal case studies conducted by Vailant.[1] The adaptation of this framework as a viable research tool has emerged, in part, as a convenient and meaningful technique to capture a time-framed picture of an aggregate of values that can be construed as a unit or collective-characteristics and performance. While methodological disagreements among practitioners of this approach might continue, nevertheless as of this writing, I have an obligation to reveal how the research was conducted and how collected evidence was handled and interpreted.

In order to be convinced that this approach has merit, I strove to develop a relationship between argument and evidence applying a best practice approach to make this determination; in short, to increase the believability of my findings whereby I identify early in the analysis a clear statement of the conceptual relationship of the attributes and characteristics and readily determine how this qualitative ratio analysis framework translated the researchable questions or issue, or series of questions or issues. In addition, I specifically relate to the nature of the case study undertaken. The longer the time frame over which the case study is conducted, the more difficult it was to ensure accurate representation, hence the need for an applicable framework adaptable to all three case studies for analysis and comparison purposes.

1 George E. VAILLANT, *Adaptations to Life*, Boston, MA, Little Brown, 1977.

There are four (4) major issues relating to the ability to convince and generalize the application of the qualitative ratio analysis framework:

- First, context(s) to be represented in a conceptually clear manner so that the reader will find them convincing.
- Second, findings to be provided from collected information that has been verified.
- Third, evidence to be provided that the case has been conducted in a manner that is consistent with the principles of trustworthiness - in particular the type and extent of triangulation and the presence of an audit trail should have been documented- as described by Lincoln and Guba (1985)[2] or, stated differently, that the criteria for internal and external validity as explicated by Yin (1994).[3]
- Fourth, analysis and comparisons to be believable. Due to the considerable variation of each of the case studies and general nature of the qualitative research, I felt I had an obligation to exhibit how evidence is interpreted as well as identifying my own viewpoints as opposed to just researcher's footnotes.

Researchers have a number of choices they can make when interpreting evidence to help the reader follow their perspective, such as using computer-based interpretations like Atlas/ti (Muhr, 1997),[4] using constant comparison (Strauss & Corbin, 1990),[5] or a procedure that emphasizes contextual

---

2 Yvonne S. LINCOLN and Egon G. GUBA, *Naturalistic Inquiry*, Beverly Hills, CA, Sage, 1985.

3 Robert K. YIN, *Case Study Research: Design and Methods* (2nd ed.) Newbury Park, CA, Sage, 1994.

4 Thomas MUHR, *Atlas/ti: The Knowledge Workbench, Version 4.1*, Berlin, Scientific SoftwareDevelopment, 1997.

5 Anselm L. STRAUSS and Juliet M. CORBIN, *Basics of Qualitative Research: Grounded Theory Procedures and Techniques*, Newbury Park, CA, Sage, 1990.

quotations and head-notes (Kvale, 1996; Strauss, 1987).[6] The selected procedure will, of course, vary as a function of perspective and is not limited to the illustrations given.

My illustrative, graphical, and visual approach provides important information gathered and analyzed during the research in the context of the case studies. And through a qualitative (numerical) ratio framework to judge the evidential basis of each case study (Bachor, 2000; Davis & Bachor, 1999),[7] I have suggested that a ratio can be computed. This ratio is the value and element point raised within a characteristic typically by the three attributes identified within each case study. I researched for a similar set of characteristics that was persistent in all three of the case studies. In particular, the Obama Presidential Campaign study. I observed that the media lag time was particularly short in relation to influence and impact, particularly with the Internet. This reinforced the fact that it had a more *real time* definition, similar patterns of influential characteristics that were transferred quickly via the media.

Moreover, it is the direct influence between media and global events that creates the successive tipping point attributes that evolve and compete in context with other events and media contributions that propagate and are diffused through media. Of note is that very few media events evolve and compete for attention within a relatively large set of broader topics that are evident in the media environment. Identification of these case study characteristics has proved difficult, and some characteristics presented themselves continuously, crossing over attribute timeframes, appearing to grow and then diminish, while another characteristic during the same attribute timeframe may have presented itself without significant shifts in the media attention or impact. As a result, the dynamics of this analysis could be the subject of intense interest to researchers in media, the political process, and related global issues, with the focus here being mainly qualitative, it may

6 Steiner KVALE, *Interviews. An Introduction to Qualitative Research Interviewing*, Thousand Oaks, CA, Sage, 1996; Anselm L. STRAUSS, *Qualitative Analysis for Social Scientists*, Cambridge, UK, Cambridge University Press, 1987.

7 Daniel G. BACHOR, "Rethinking Case Study Research Methodology," paper presented at the Special Education National Research Forum, Helsinki, May 2000; T M. DAVIS and Daniel G. BACHOR, "Case Studies as a Research Tool in Evaluating Student Achievement," paper presented at the Canadian Society for Studies in Education Conference, Sherbrooke, Canada, June 1999.

indeed overlook some scientific techniques for undertaking the quantitative analysis of the question as a whole.

Utilizing these tipping point attributes and characteristics and constructing the qualitative ratio analysis framework as defined above, I can now effectively exhibit these ratios by these characteristics for each of the tipping point attributes and see their relative context. Again, an important point to note at the outset is that the total number of characteristics of each attribute is by no means inclusive and would require additional study and analysis. Rather, the intention here has been to highlight those characteristics that are salient to the discussion and analysis of each attribute. The approach was to identify a minimum set of characteristics for each tipping point attribute that can be analyzed and exhibited for the three case studies that exhibit a relationship to our question of media impact on global events.

Another question that has grown out of this research is *when* does the media impact occur, before or after the global event? One common assertion is the event occurs, and then the media propagates information about it after. However, that may have been case with old media types, but certainly this notion has lost its credibility given the real-time influences of current and future media technology. Another important characteristic definition that needs to be discussed is whether the people, organizations, media and global events can be truly labeled in such a manner? Are these the only characteristics to consider? To address this question and provide a filter that works well in practice, I only used characteristics that were readily identified, via Google or related search engines, books and journals assembled during this project, libraries and archives visited, and my own firsthand personal observations and accounts, in order to include as characteristics to analyze. Otherwise there would be such a multitude of characteristics to identify and analyze that the dataset would be overwhelming.

I've developed this qualitative ratio analysis framework for analyzing the distinctive characteristics for the tipping point attribute timeframes for each of the case studies, with the intention of presenting *scalable* (numerical) values for identifying and comparing them. These efforts are some of the first qualitative ratio analysis of how the Tipping Point theory can be applied to media impact on global events and the dynamics of how information is propagated between media and the public. It also points out, in particular, the existence, or lack thereof, of a perception of the lag time between the peak of attention in the media and the respective influence on the global event. Using this tipping point methodology in these case studies certainly provides one interpretation and potentially one solution for our third and most pressing case study: Climate Change. Media may hold some very real options for how we as a civilization go about the business of the future of the planet. My approach opens up the opportunity to pursue additional questions that before had been effectively impossible to conceptualize. For example,

- *How can we characterize the dynamics of media impact on key global events?*
- *How does information change and influence the evolution of the tipping point baseline as it propagates?*
- *Might it be possible to use this tipping point model over longer periods of time, in a way that is essential to discovering the core solution to climate change?*

One could combine the approaches here into several multidiscipline approaches towards addressing scientific, political, cultural and financial issues associated with this phenomenon. And more generally, it appears useful to further understand the media impact on the different tipping point attributes and characteristics as exhibited during global events.

Extracting from the research in the proceeding chapters, I began to analyze the case studies with the goal of understanding the attributes, characteristics and relationships between them as they unfold. Looking at the purposes of the case studies and the research questions that were posed earlier, one can see how the attributes took place in relative groupings of people, organizations, media, and events, and the net results. I attempt to identify and/or quantify the relative impact among them. This study of the relationships evolves and becomes more important as I analyze their impact on the outcome. In any case, with the third case study, Climate Change, the overall research question is trying to point out that by analyzing these attributes it might influence and predict and/or help avoid a potential global tipping point from occurring.

An explanation of the notation for analyzing the relationships and attributes is in order, as qualitative ratio analysis framework identifies people, organizations, media impact, and events that occurred during the case study and influenced the ultimate outcome. One way to measure and determine the one dramatic moment of each is to quantify the relative impact of the various issues and in context with others of scalable importance. My aim is to provide a sense of qualitative influence and pneumatic control as to how these various attributes led to the ultimate outcome.

With this tipping point analysis three attributes are identified in the *Qualitative Ratio Analysis Framework*: Contagiousness (C), Stickiness (S), and, One Dramatic Point (TP). The notations indicate either a positive attribute relationship, i.e., +C, prevalent with the originating issue, or a –C, indicating a negative relationship and so on. The tables and graphics that follow summarize the qualitative research on the various attributes recalling these relative values and attempt to identify important relationships in relation to the events and media influence. The important point is that the relative relationships between the attributes are chosen based upon the research of the subject matter, evaluation, and in some cases, researched opinion.

For the purposes of this tipping point analysis, the values for the relationships between the attributes and the characteristics range between values summarized between 1 to 10, or a *raw score*, with 1 being a very weak indicator and 10 being a very strong indicator. And as a way of understanding the approach and conveying our information effectively, what is also shown are graphs illustrating a *smooth score*, which is helpful when depicting our analysis using line graphs, especially over time. With the large number of characteristics in each of the case studies such as ours, whereby values that zigzag up and down a lot, the key is to try to separate out the meaningless or temporary fluctuations from the underlying, long-run changes, transitions and trends that occur central to the characteristics. Essentially, the *smooth score* substitutes for the *raw score* a new number, which is the average of the characteristic immediately before and after it. The intent is to present the data by reducing the chart information to the essentials.

The logic of our tipping point analysis qualitative ratio analysis framework is that these rules govern the identification of key areas of the case study research and provide a means of control over what characteristics and issues were included as part of each case study. For example, the influence of the media and the messages delivered by and with the current media technology that existed in 2008, providing the tipping point for presidential hopeful Barack Obama over his rival John McCain during the presidential election is fundamental to that analysis.

Easily, one can interpret these attributes and characteristics from many perspectives; however, the intent of our tipping point analysis is to define where and when the one dramatic moment occurred during each case study and compare this to the other two case studies for a similar analysis. This qualitative ratio analysis framework for analyzing these attributes is simply a look at the sequence of events in a chronological manner to observe the way they each developed and how, over the duration of the case study life, media influenced the global event.

Section 6.1 Analysis: Obama Presidential Campaign Case Study

Introduction: Qualitative Ratios

The approach for this case study was to analyze the media delivery systems and technology available that were being used during the campaign and influenced the tipping point attributes. Important to the analysis, in terms of contagiousness and stickiness attributes resulting in voter influence for the candidate, does the analysis indicate a direct relationship between the *real time* characteristic referenced and Obama's victory? Extracting from the research in Chapter 3, I analyzed the attributes with the goal of identifying the characteristics and understanding the relationships between them as the campaign unfolded. With the research question above and the analysis methodology, what follows are the tipping point qualitative ratios and graphic summary of how the attributes and characteristics were influential relative to people, organizations, media and events. It identifies and quantifies the relative impact and relationships among them. This study of the attribute relationships evolves and become more important in context of the impact on the outcome. The same series of rules governed the research and provided a means of control over what characteristics/issues were included as part of this case study. The influence of the media and the messages delivered by and with the technology that led to the tipping point for the Obama Presidential Campaign is presented. The influence of the media and the messages delivered by and with the technology provided for the tipping point. Clearly, one can interpret these characteristics/issues and attributes from many perspectives; however, the intent of our tipping point analysis is to define where and when the one dramatic event occurred during the Obama Presidential Campaign and then compare these in Chapter 7 to the other two case studies. This method for analyzing the attributes is simply to look at the sequence of events in a chronological manner and observe the way the campaign developed and how the various media sectors played their role. The relationships between the characteristics and various media delivery systems led to a historical tipping point in the 2008 presidential campaign. The following qualitative ratios reveal an actual correlation between media and the outcome of the campaign.

Section 6.1.1 Contagiousness Attribute (C)

Date: 5-Sep-11 Start Time Frame: October 1, 2007 *
Revised: End Time Frame: February 1, 2008 *

Section: 6.1.1 Obama Presidential Campaign: Contagiousness Attribute

			McCain			Obama	
Qualitative ratio scale			**Raw score**	**Smooth score**		**Raw score**	**Smooth score**
	Neutral 0	0			0		
Characteristic							
People		0			0		
George Bush			-2	-1		2	2
Economy			-3	-2		3	3
Iraq war			-3	-1		3	3
Public opinion			0	0		4	3
John McCain		0		0	0		2
Veteran/proven			3	1		-2	0
Temper/out of touch/too old			-2	0		2	-1
Barack Obama		0		0	0		-1
Risky/not ready to lead			3	1		-2	-2
Rev. Wright			3	2		-3	-3
Racial issue			2	2		-4	-3
Underworld connections			2	1		-5	-2
Organizations		0		0	0		0
American voter/frustration			-5	-3		5	3
Opinions/war/economy			-6	-5		5	4
Previous elections			-6	-3		4	4
Republican/conservative			2	-2		-2	3
Democrats/liberals			-2	-1		2	2
Bush			-3	-2		3	3
Iraq			-5	-4		5	4
Taxes			-5	-3		5	5
Economy/who could solve?		0		-2	0		4
McCain			-2	-2		4	4
Obama			-3	-2		4	4
"Chicago machine"			0	-1		3	3
Media		0		0	0		0
"Real Time"			-5	0		5	3
Radio			3	2		3	2
Internet news			2	2		3	2
Google stories			0	1		2	2
TV news			1	1		3	2
Economy			-2	0		3	3
Ad campaigns			1	1		4	3
Age			-1	0		2	2
Two young			1	0		0	1
Trustworthy			2	1		-1	0
Internet "viral"			-1	0		1	0
US Citizen			1	0		0	0
Events	notes: do not add*	0		0	0		0
	space *						
	space *						
	space *						
Economy	note position on chart		-3	-2		3	2
	space *						
	space *						
DOW	note postion on chart		-4	-3		4 *	3
	space *						
	space *						
Wall Street	note position on chart		-5	-3		5	3
	space *						
	space *	0		0	0		0
–	space *						

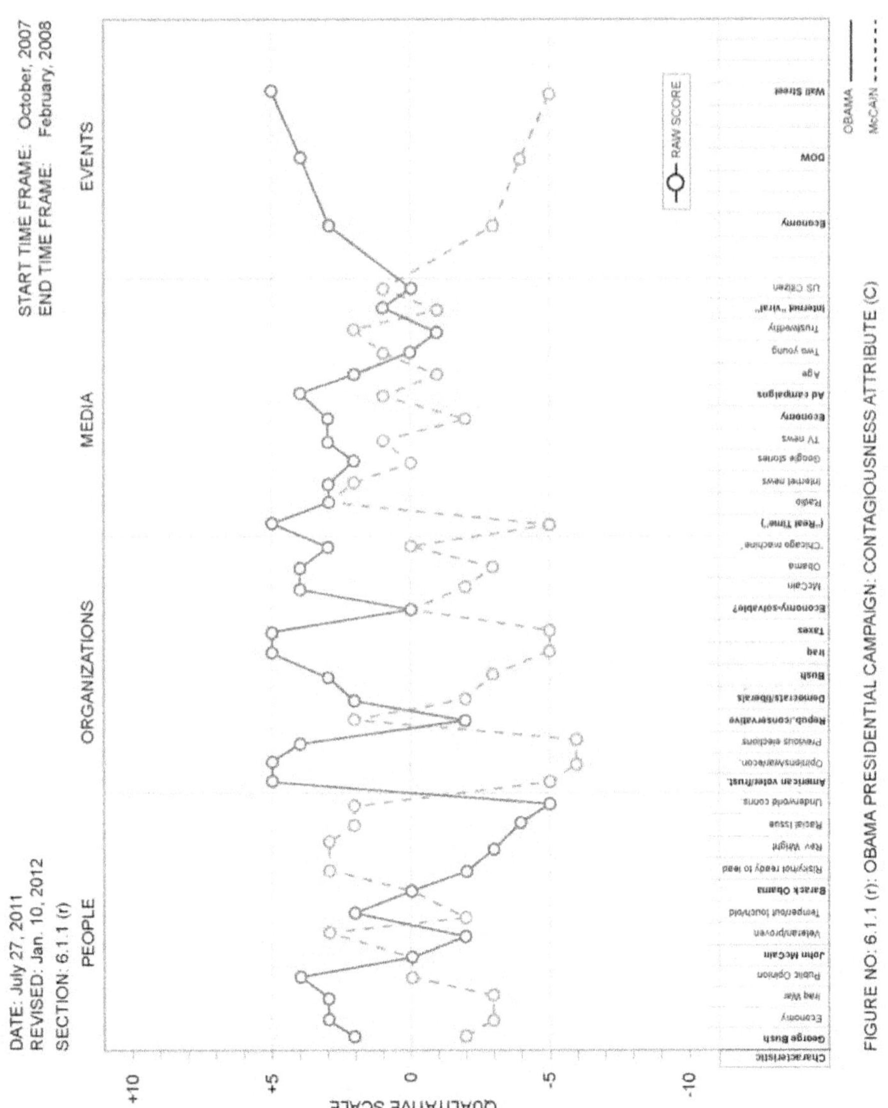

FIGURE NO: 6.1.1 (r): OBAMA PRESIDENTIAL CAMPAIGN: CONTAGIOUSNESS ATTRIBUTE (C)

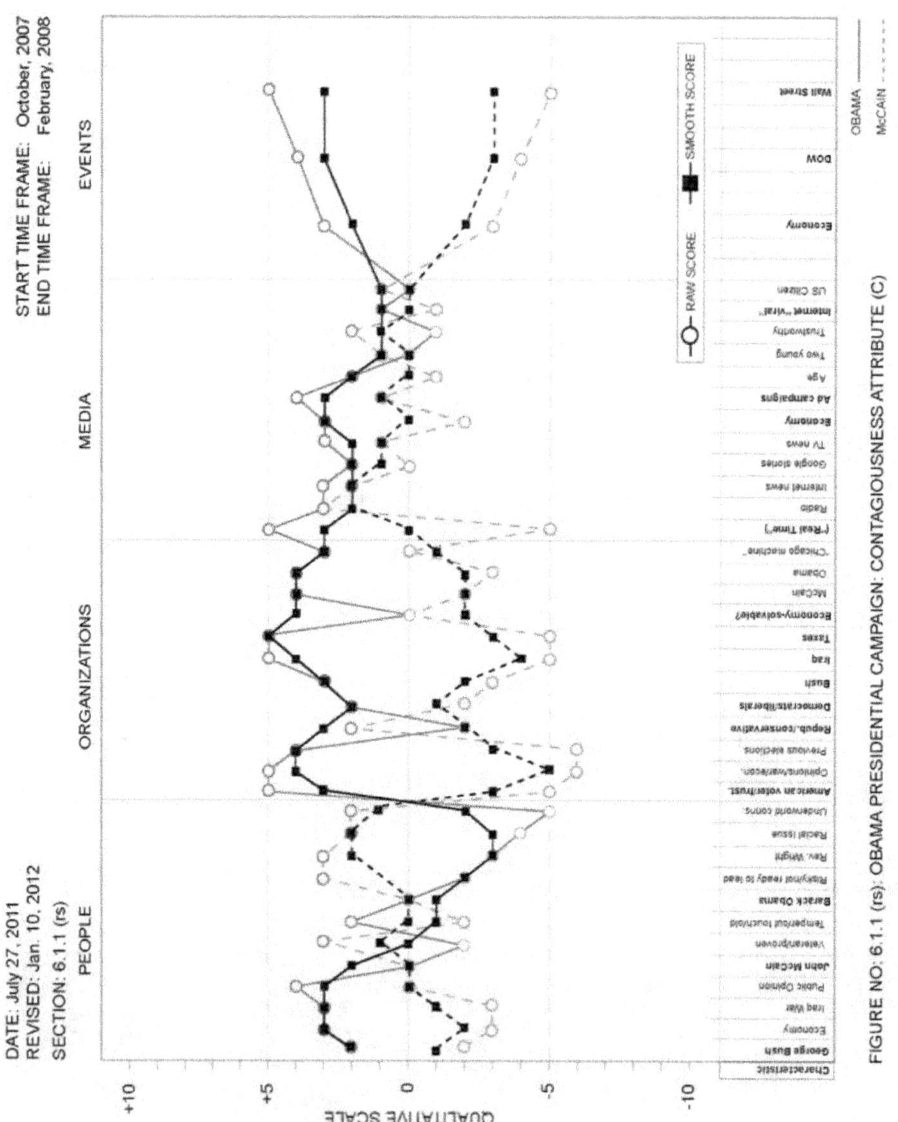

FIGURE NO: 6.1.1 (rs): OBAMA PRESIDENTIAL CAMPAIGN: CONTAGIOUSNESS ATTRIBUTE (C)

Section 6.1.2 Stickiness Attribute (S)

Date: 5-Sep-11
Revised:

Start Time Frame: February 1, 2008
End Time Frame: June 1, 2008

Section: 6.1.2 Obama Presidential Campaign: Stickiness Attribute

Qualitative ratio scale		McCain Raw score	McCain Smooth score		Obama Raw score	Obama Smooth score
Characteristic						
People	0		0	0		0
Joe Biden		-4	-2		6	3
Voting record		-2	-2		2	2
Sarah Palen		-3	-3		1	1
Experience		-5	-3		2	2
Gender		-3	-3		1	1
"Trooper gate" *		-5	-3		3	2
McCain	0		-3	0		1
"Heartbeat away"/age		-5	-3		4	2
Competence		3	0		0	1
Obama	0		0	0		0
Budget experience		4	1		0	2
Media exposure		-3	0		4	3
Organizations	0			0		0
Democratic	0			0		
Convention		-4	-2		5	3
"Change versus same"		-5	-3		6	4
Biden speech		-6	-3		6	5
Obama speech		-6	-2		6	3
Republican	0		0	0		1
Convention		2	1		0	0
Palen speech		3	2		0	0
"Maverick appeal"		5	3		-1	0
Distance Bush		-1	1		0	0
Media	0		0	0		0
"Real Time"		-5	-3		5	3
Economy capability		-6	-4		3	3
Wall Street/perception fault		-7	-5		6	5
Bush link		-8	-4		7	6
TV debates		-2	-3		7	6
Tax increases		3	-2		3	5
VP candidates/speeches		4	-1		5	5
Speeches/ad campaigns		1	-1		7	6
Shared values		-2	-2		5	5
Technology		-5	-3		7	6
Frequency		-2	-2		8	7
Agenda		2	-1		6	5
Events	0		0	0		0
Energy/gas		3	1		5	3
Tax issues		3	1		4	4
DOW drop		-3	0		6	5
Wall Street		-4	-1		7	6
Offshore drilling		3	0		-3	4
Obama lead?		-5	-2		5	4
National security		3	0		0	3
Economy		-7	-3		5	4
Hurricane		0	-2		2	3
Iraq war		-4	-3		3	3
Afghanistan		-5	-4		4 *	4
Public anxiety		-7	-5		7	5

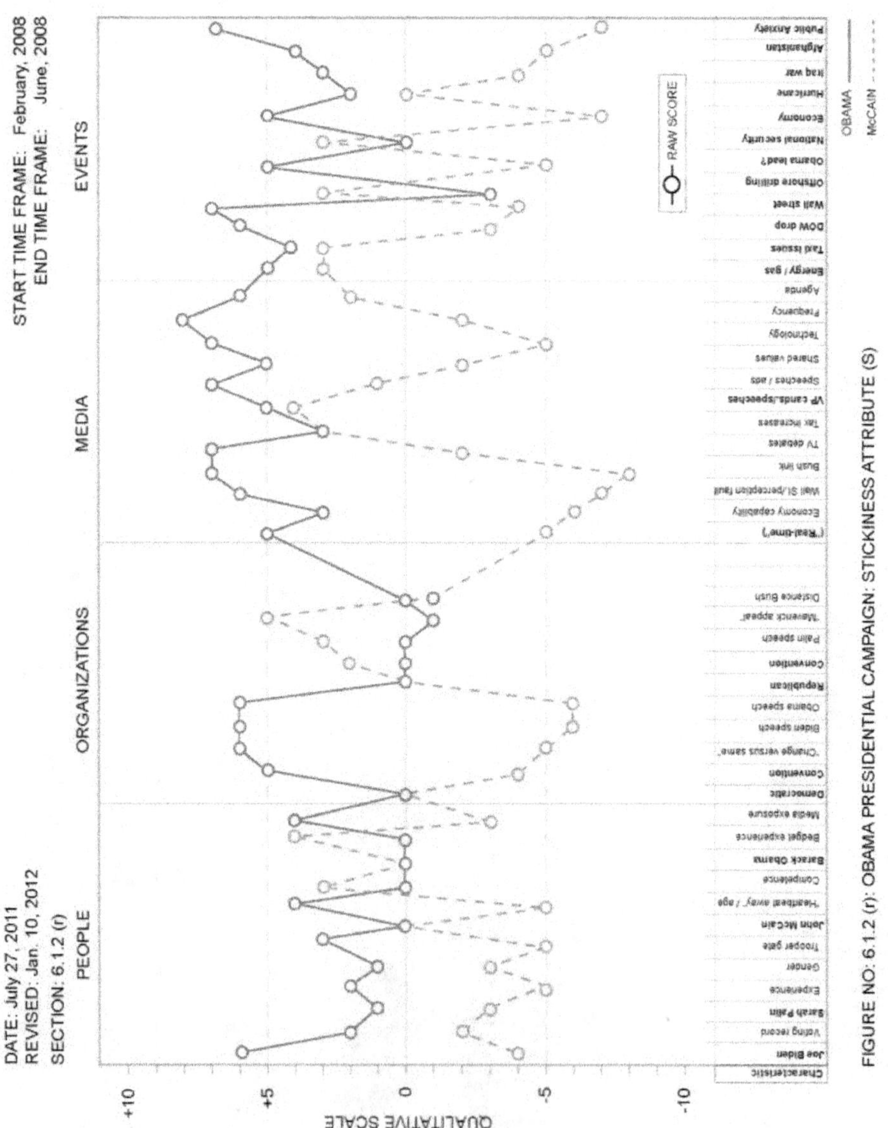

FIGURE NO: 6.1.2 (r): OBAMA PRESIDENTIAL CAMPAIGN: STICKINESS ATTRIBUTE (S)

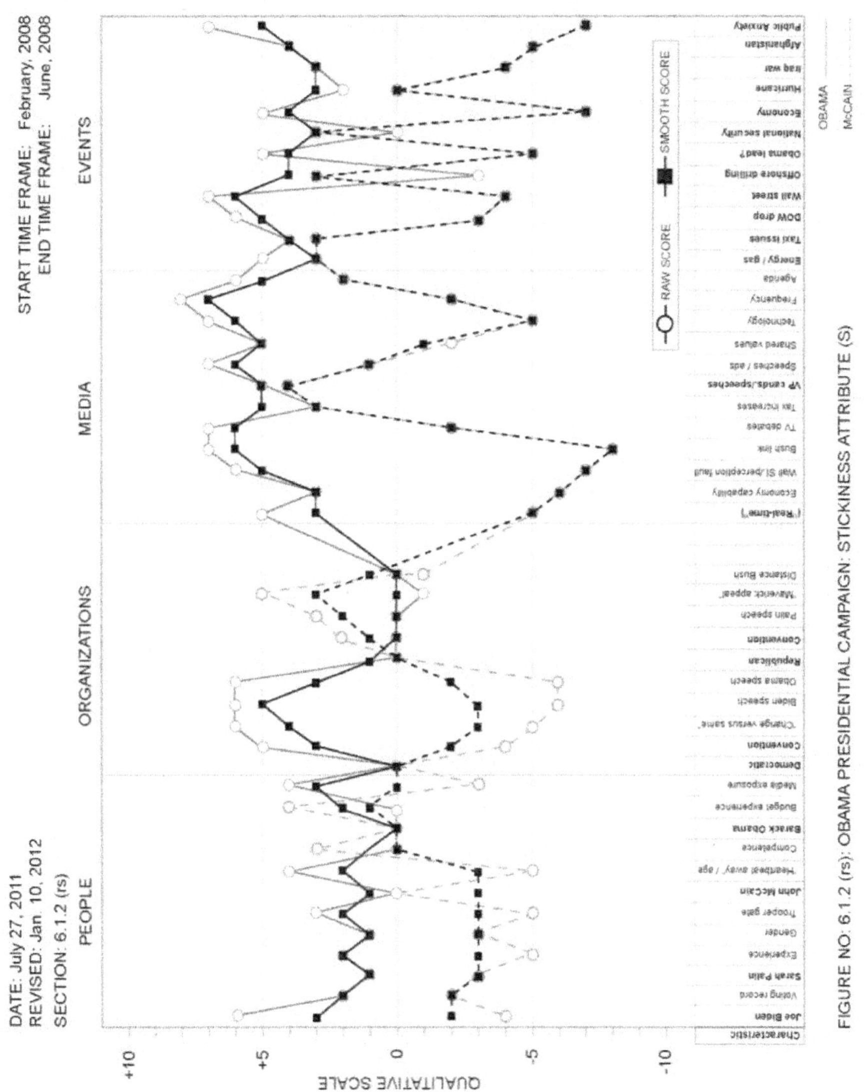

FIGURE NO: 6.1.2 (rs): OBAMA PRESIDENTIAL CAMPAIGN: STICKINESS ATTRIBUTE (S)

Section 6.1.3 One Dramatic Moment: The Tipping

Date: 5-Sep-11 Start Time Frame: June 1, 2008
Revised: DEC 31 2011 End Time Frame: November 6, 2008

Section: 6.1.3 Obama Presidential Campaign: One Dramatic Moment Attribute

		Obama			McCain	
Qualitative ratio scale		**Raw score**	**Smooth score**		**Raw score**	**Smooth score**
Characteristic						
People	0		0	0		0
Public opinion polls		-5	-3		5	3
John McCain		-6	-4		6	4
Barack Obama		-5	-5		7	6
Unemployment: September 5, 2008		-6	-6		8	7
"Fundamentals of the economy" September 15, 2008		-9	-7		10	9
Debates: October 15, 2008		-6	-6		7	8
Election day: November 5, 2008		0	0		9	9
Organizations						
Republicans	0			0		0
"Economic freefall"		-7	-3		8	4
"Out of touch"		-6	-5		6	6
"Fundamentals of the economy are strong"		-9	-6		10	8
Democrats	0		-3	0		7
Link Bush		-5	-5		5	8
"Fundamentals"		-9	-3		10	9
Strength of campaign		0	0		7	7
"Spread the wealth"		3	1		-3	3
"Joe the plumber" October 12, 2008		5	3		-4	2
Debates 15-Oct-08		-1	1		6	3
Banking situation		-3	-1		3	0
Media	0		0	0		0
"Real-time"		-5	-1		7	4
Radio		2	0		5	5
Internet news		2	1		6	6
TV news		3	2		6	6
Ad campaigns		3	2		8	7
Internet "viral"		-3	0		7	7
E-mails		-7	-5		7	7
Text messaging		-6	-6		7	7
Videos		-6	-6		5	6
Cell phones		-3	-5		5	7
Digital technology/innovation		-5	-5		9	8
Micro-targeting		-7	-5		8	7
Events	0		0	0		0
Economy		-5	-3		5	3
DOW October 15, 2008 735 points		-5	-5		5	4
Wall Street		-7	-7		5	5
"Fundamentals": September 15, 2008		-9	-9		10	7
Lehman Brothers		-6	-7		9	8
Bailouts: October 3, 2008		-6	-6		9	9
AIG		-6	-6		6	8
Other banks		-6	-3		9	9
Tax issues		2	0		7	8
Healthcare/ so security		2	1		7	7
Congressional debates		1	0		5	7
Public anxiety		-6	-3		9	8
	0		0	0		0

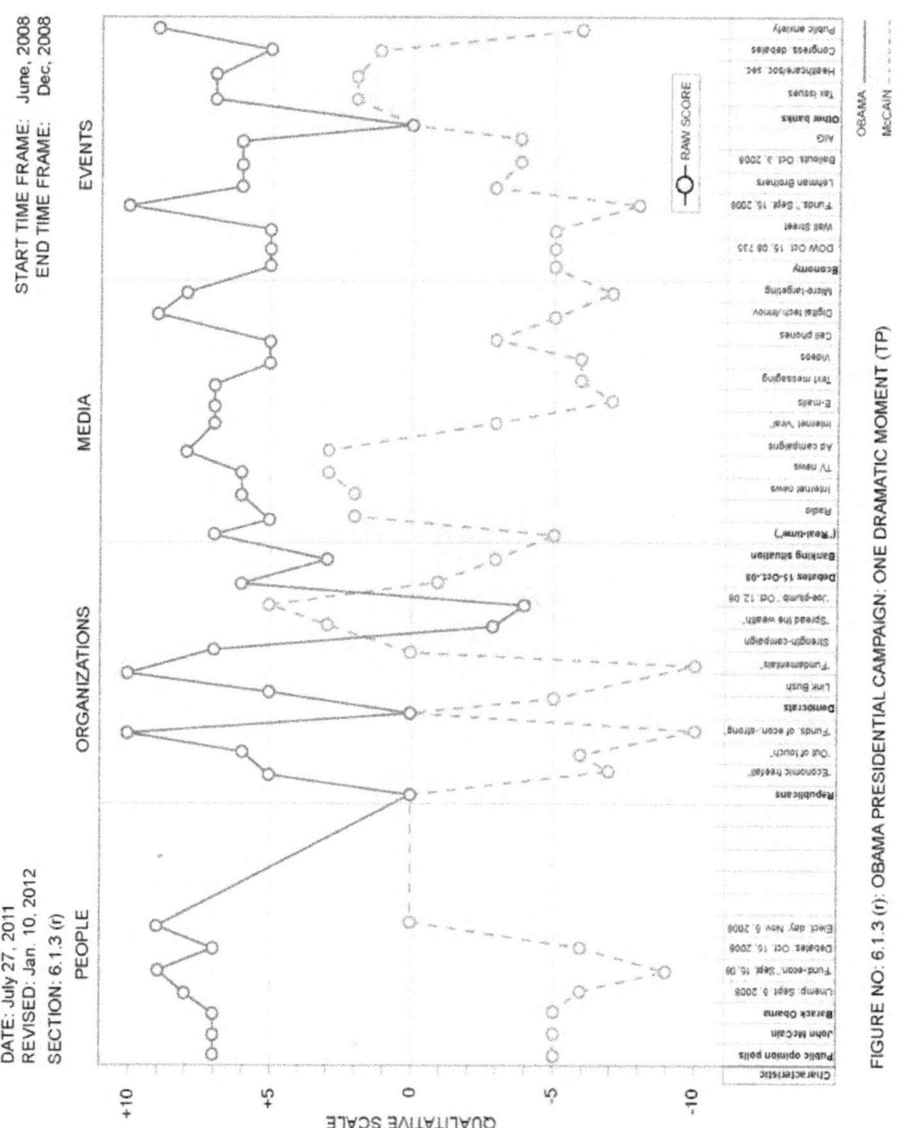

FIGURE NO: 6.1.3 (r): OBAMA PRESIDENTIAL CAMPAIGN: ONE DRAMATIC MOMENT (TP)

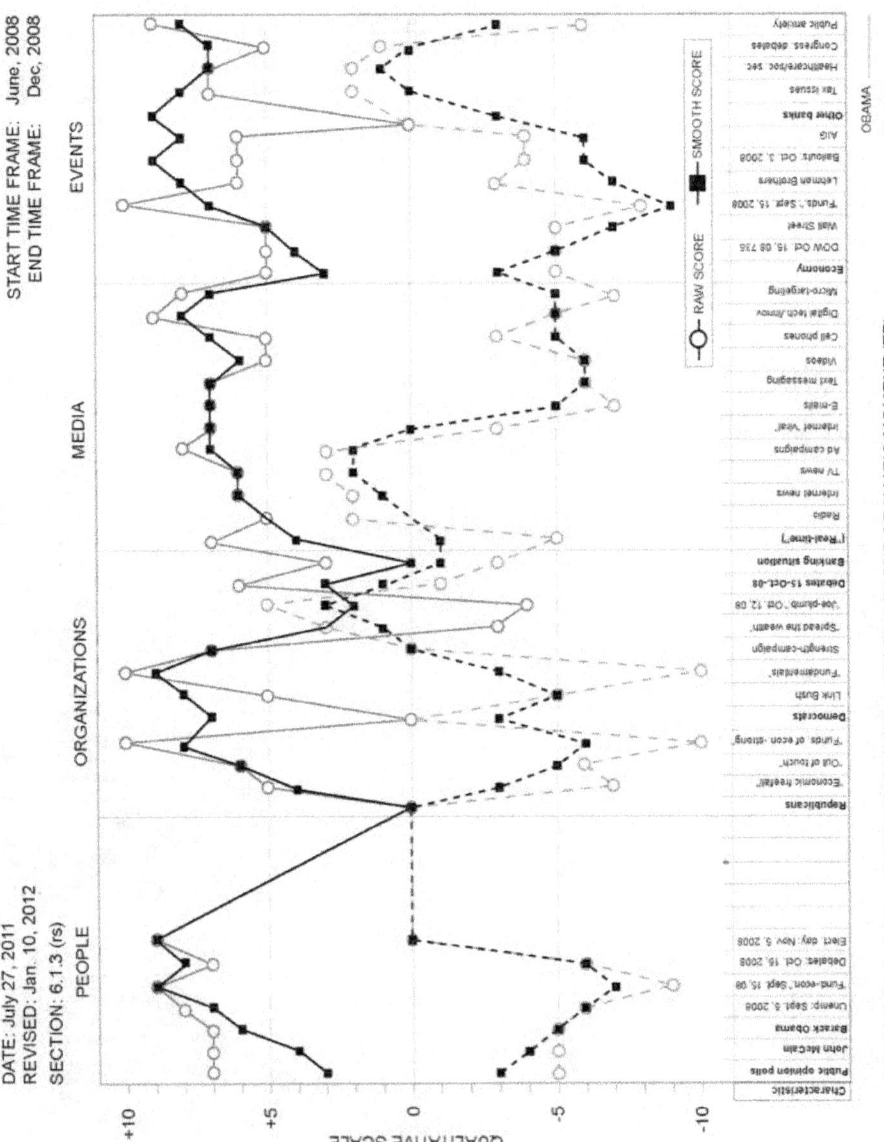

FIGURE NO: 6.1.3 (rs): OBAMA PRESIDENTIAL CAMPAIGN: ONE DRAMATIC MOMENT (TP)

Section 6.1.4 Obama Presidential Campaign

Compilations

On November 4, 2008, Barack Obama became the first African-American to be elected president of the United States. He gained almost 53% of the popular vote and 365 electoral votes. The popular vote percentage was the best showing for any presidential candidate since George H. W. Bush in 1988 and not since Bill Clinton, whose 379 votes in 1996. He won Colorado, Nevada, Virginia, Indiana, Florida, Ohio, and North Carolina, all states that were won by President George W. Bush in 2004. A bylaw received more total votes than any presidential candidate in history, totaling well over 69 million votes.

In response to the first research question, did the media influences have a direct impact on the presidential hopeful Barack Obama victory? From these overwhelming results one can see that the media coverage of the economy issue provided the necessary momentum and stickiness to propel Obama to his tipping point on or about the middle of September 2008. In addition, Joe Biden also made history by being the first Roman Catholic to be elected vice president, and after serving in the Senate for 36 years prior, was the longest serving senator to become vice president.

With regard to the another important question, was there a direct correlation between the media frequency and content of the messages during the campaign? The Obama campaign raised enormous amounts of money that was spent throughout the media sectors on delivering messages to the voters and contributed to the outcome. Future campaigns will copy the Obama approach by offering similar forms of messages that can be proliferated on the Internet almost immediately creating a communication vehicle capitalizing on the interactive character and potential of future media delivery systems.

Candidates who are willing to subscribe to the new media platforms and to spend (and find investors to spend for them to raise more cash) to increase and expand their stickiness momentum largely will have the advantage against candidates who are unwilling to please prospective patrons and utilize these advantages in the same way. For example, big oil companies which had an influence on previous campaigns' strategies, may actually hurt future candidates rather than help sway voter opinion due to the associated negative impacts and links to the environment related to fossil fuels and climate change. In contrast, another possibility is the better-financed candidate might micro-target (saturate) his audience and reach voters without the benefit of rebuttal from the other candidate, which as the social platforms currently illustrate, is risky, as in a truly democratic societies the opportunity to defend one's position and one's agenda is paramount and would be canceled out. Rather than electing a better person with the better policies and better agenda, the American voters might be influenced by only one candidate who has the ability to use (flood) the media with enough micro-messages that distort the candidates' positions and the real potential for democratic solutions. With the media developing in real-time, such strategies may prove detrimental. Nevertheless, these point some interesting complexities as to how media forms in this context are influential.

As I turn to the second case study, the International Financial Crisis 2008-2010, similar patterns in the contagiousness and stickiness attributes are prevalent, and ultimately, the one dramatic moment tipping point is impacted by many of the same types of media communication delivery systems that delivered the messages and contributed to the Obama Presidential Campaign *epidemic*.

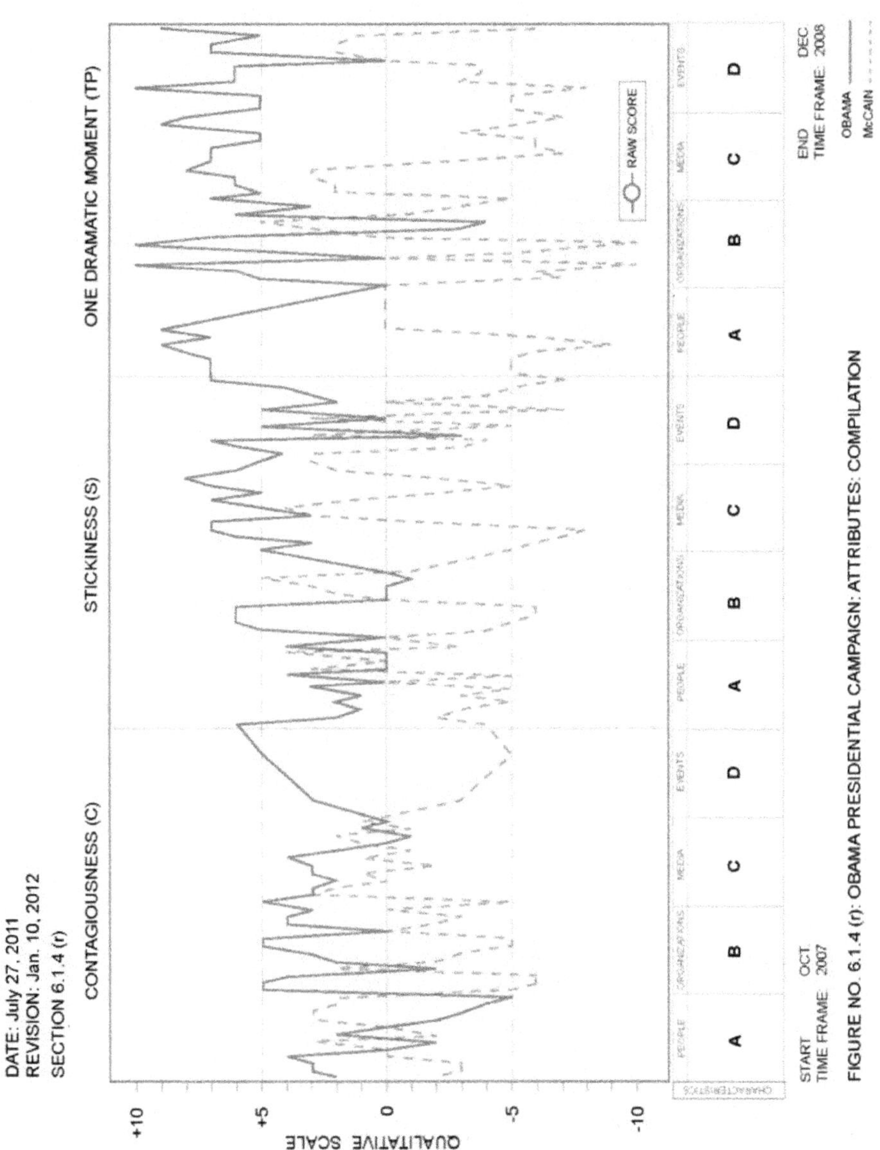

FIGURE NO. 6.1.4 (r): OBAMA PRESIDENTIAL CAMPAIGN: ATTRIBUTES: COMPILATION

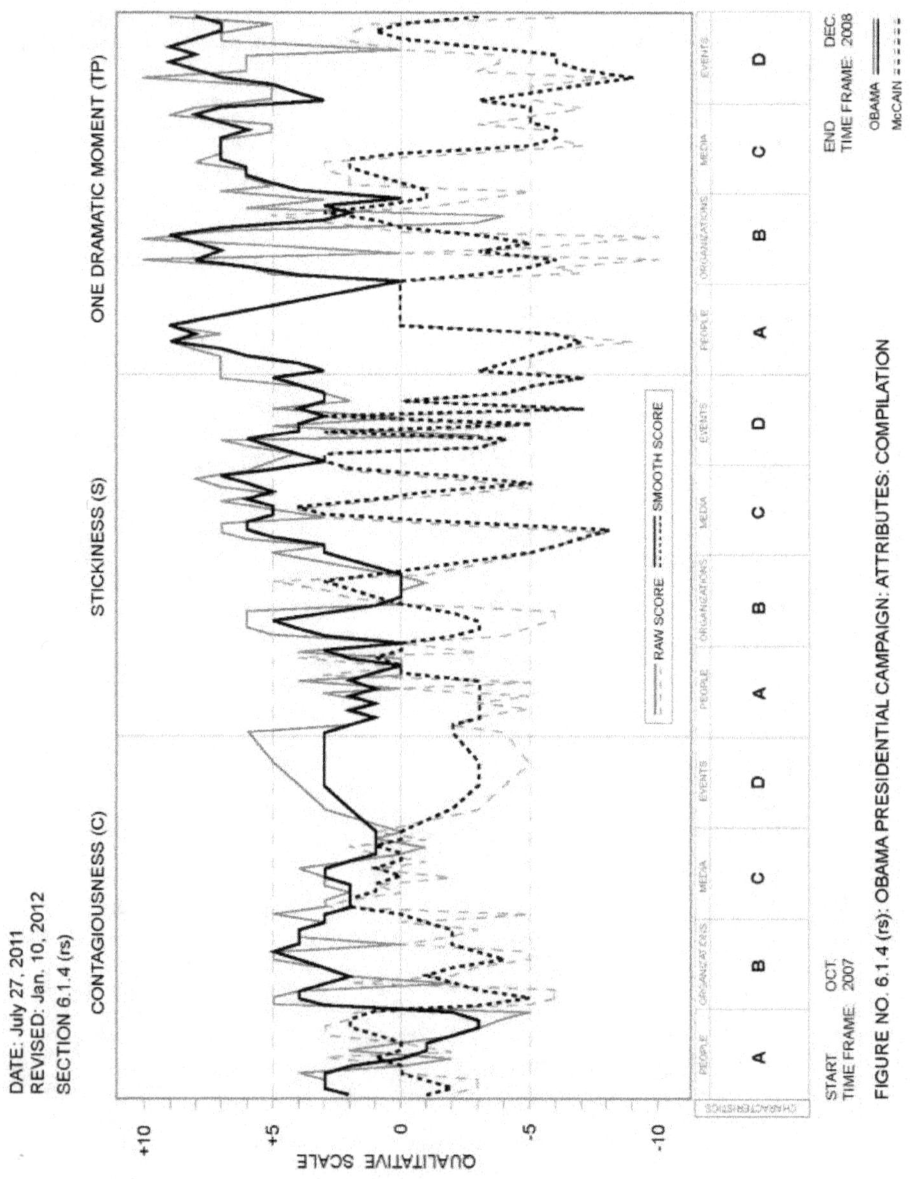

FIGURE NO. 6.1.4 (rs): OBAMA PRESIDENTIAL CAMPAIGN: ATTRIBUTES: COMPILATION

Section 6.2 Analysis: International Financial Crisis 2007-2011 Case Study

Introduction: Qualitative Ratios

The approach for this case study is to analyze the media influence during the International Financial Crisis 2007- 2010 in two key areas: The first, with regard to the contagiousness and stickiness attributes, was there a *living story* in the media that contributed to the systemic international financial crisis? Second, which relationships between the attributes and characteristics and various media delivery systems led to the historic international financial crisis tipping point? Extracting from the research in Chapter 4, I analyzed the attributes with the goal of identifying the characteristics and understanding the relationships between them as the 2007-2010 international financial crisis unfolded. With the research questions above and the analysis methodology, what follows are the tipping point qualitative ratios and graphic summary of how the attributes and characteristics were influential relative to people, organizations, media and events. It identifies and quantifies the relative impact and relationships among them. This study of the attribute relationships evolves and become more important in context of the impact on the outcome. The same series of rules governed the research and provided a means of control over what characteristics/issues were included as part of this case study. The influence of the media and the messages delivered by and with the technology that led to the tipping point for the International Financial Crisis of 2007-2010 is presented. The influence of the media and the messages delivered by and with the technology that provided for the tipping point for the International Financial Crisis of 2007-2010. Clearly, one can interpret these characteristics/issues and attributes from many perspectives; however, the intent of our tipping point analysis is to define where and when the one dramatic event occurred during the International Financial Crisis and its origins and then compare these in Chapter 7 to the other two case studies. This method for analyzing the attributes is simply to look at the sequence of events in a chronological manner and observe the way the international financial crisis developed and how the various media sectors played their role, ultimately contributing to the worst global financial meltdown since the 1930s.

Section 6.2.1 Contagiousness Attribute (C)

Point (TP)

Date:	5-Sep-11	Start Time Frame:	January 2007
Revised:		End Time Frame:	January 2008

Section: 6.2.1 International Financial Crisis: Contagiousness Attribute

Qualitative ratio scale		Raw score	Smooth score
Characteristic			
People	0		
Baby boomers		5	3
Manufacturing loss		2	2
Untrained workers		2	1
Politics	0		0
Culture wars		-2	-1
Nixon		-3	-2
Carter		-2	-1
Reagan		2	1
Clinton		4	3
Bush		6	4
World leaders		3	3
Bank directors		2	2
Organizations	0		0
Banks		3	3
Auction rate/security system		4	4
Bank runs		5	5
Wall Street		5	5
LBOs		6	5
Deregulation		4	4
PIKS/derivatives		3	4
Technological instruments		6	5
Trading tools		6	5
Internet revolution		7	6
Gov. organizations		3	5
Private sector		4	4
Media	0		0
"Living story"		5	3
Conservatives		1	4
Liberals		7	5
Bank risk		5	5
Subprime mortgages		6	5
Housing		5	5
Bush		6	5
Obama		1	4
Big business failure		7	5
Bank sector		7	6
Stimulus package/tarp		1	5
US auto industry		7	3
Events	0		0
Bank failures		6	3
Stock indexes		7	5
Equity value		5	5
Credit defaults		6	5
Liquidity		6	6
Trade deficits		6	6
Banking shakeout/subprime lending		8	7
US financials/GDP		5	6
European financials		5	5
US reserves		3	4
"Warnings ignored"		8	6
CDOs		5	3

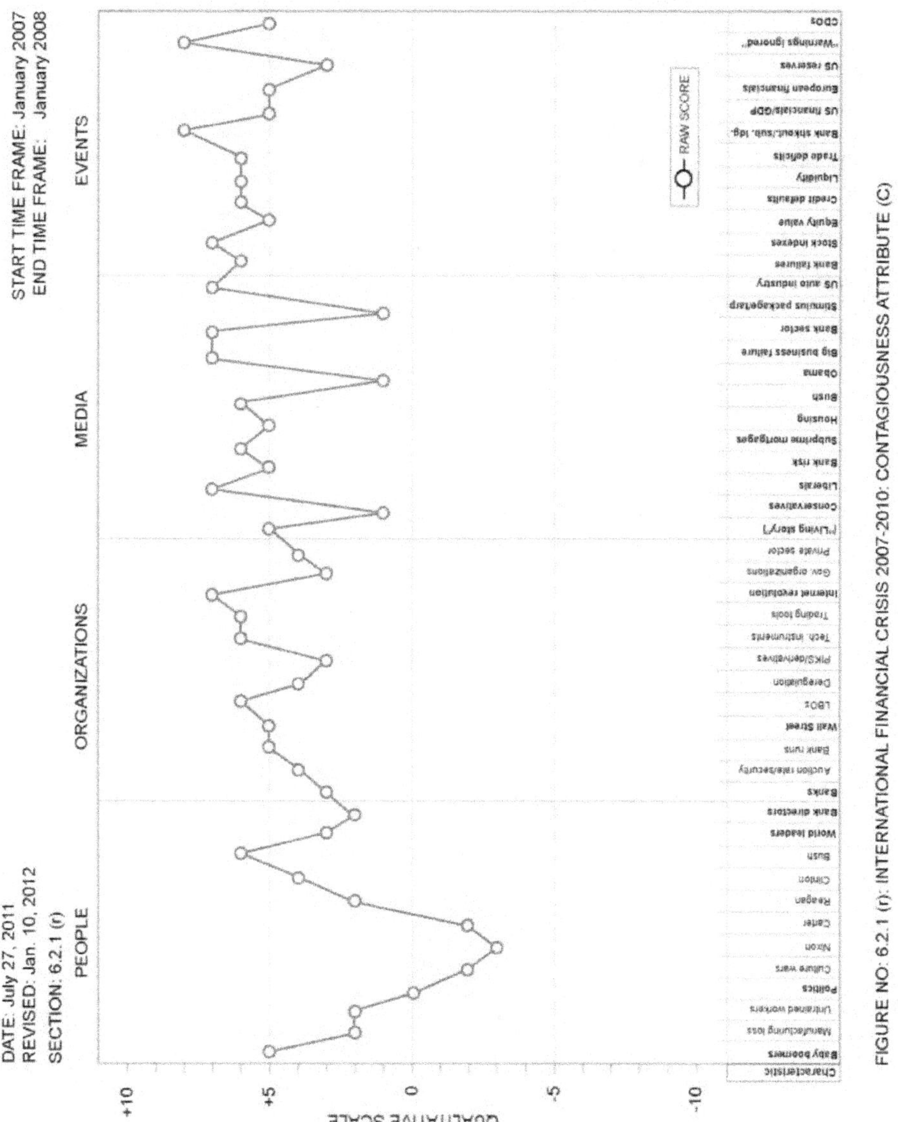

FIGURE NO: 6.2.1 (r): INTERNATIONAL FINANCIAL CRISIS 2007-2010: CONTAGIOUSNESS ATTRIBUTE (C)

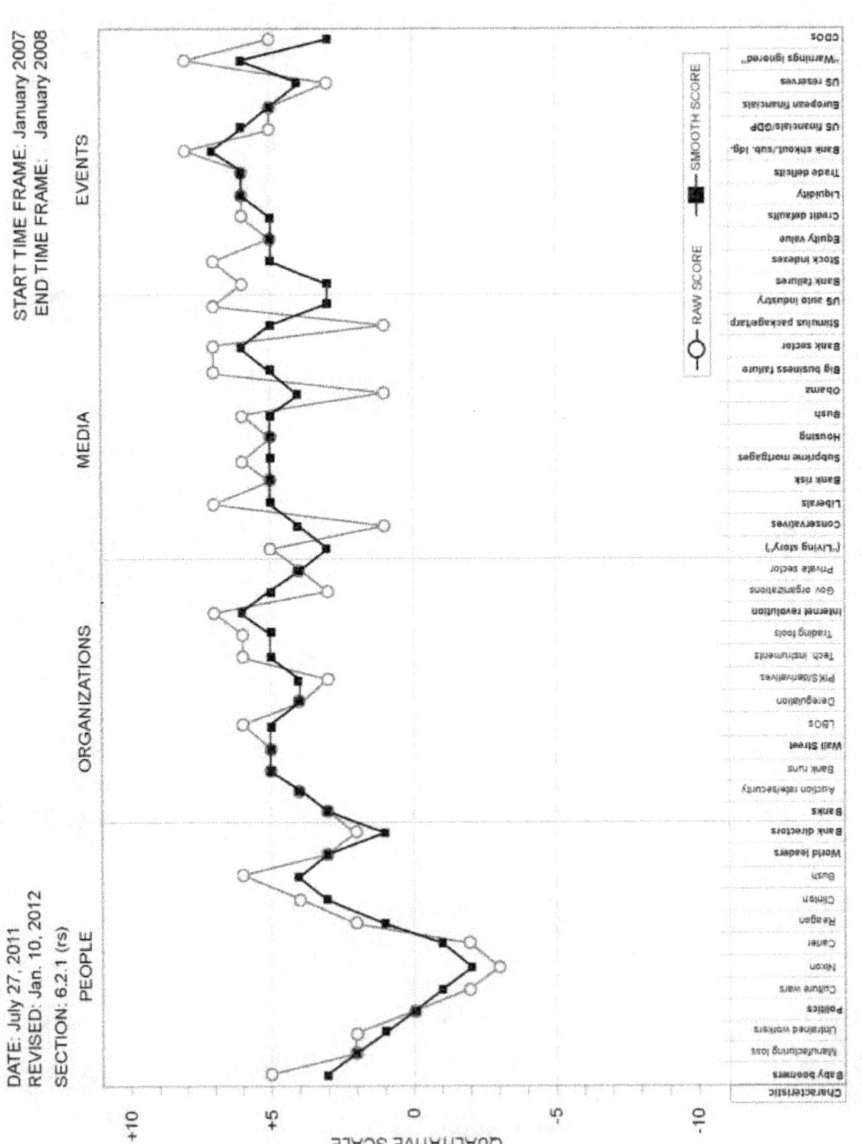

FIGURE NO: 6.2.1 (rs): INTERNATIONAL FINANCIAL CRISIS 2007-2010: CONTAGIOUSNESS ATTRIBUTE (C)

Section 6.2.2 Stickiness Attribute (S)Point (TP)

Date: 5-Sep-11 Start Time Frame: January 2008
Revised: End Time Frame: January 2009

Section: 6.2.2 International Financial Crisis: Stickiness Attribute

Qualitative ratio scale		Raw score	Smooth score
Characteristic			
People	0		0
Alan Greenspan		3	2
Federal Reserve/FMOC		1	4
American property owners		5	4
American borrowers		5	3
Others	0		2
Henry Paulson		4	3
Benard madoff		3	3
Timothy Geithner		2	2
Robert Gibbs		1	2
Ben Bernanke		2	1
Organizations	0		0
Banks			
Citibank		7	3
Merrill Lynch		7	5
Other World Bank failures		8	7
Subprime lending		9	8
Application process		6	6
Credit scoring		6	6
Financial instruments		8	7
Mortgage-backed securities		8	4
Media	0		0
"Livingstory"		9	5
Banking/subprime/defaults		8	7
Commercial paper/loans		7	7
Mental recession?		9	8
Public reaction		9	6
Competition with other events		2	4
Presidential campaign		3	3
Iraq war		2	2
Hurricanes, wildfires		1	1
Time delay/"easier story to tell"		-5	0
Gas prices		5	3
Public attention/New York/Washington DC		4	2
Events	0		0
Recession		6	3
Housing defaults		7	5
Gas prices		6	6
Crisis in banking		9	7
Bailouts		9	8
Stimulus package		3	7
US auto industry		8	7
Subprime lending/Fannie Mae and Freddie Mac		7	6
Government actions		5	6
Media themselves		9	8
Financial innovation/risk-taking/"gaussian copula"		9	7
Elections		5	4

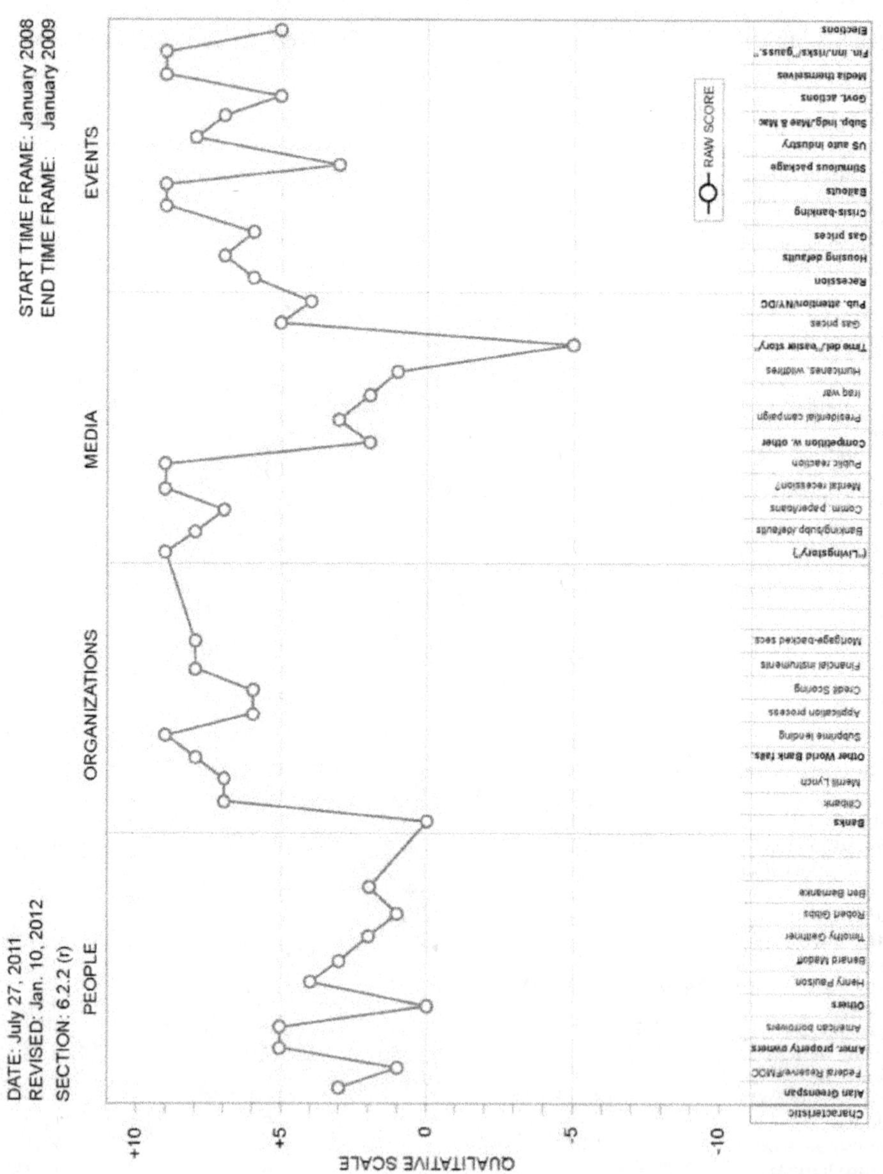

FIGURE NO: 6.2.2 (r): INTERNATIONAL FINANCIAL CRISIS 2007-2010: STICKINESS ATTRIBUTE (S)

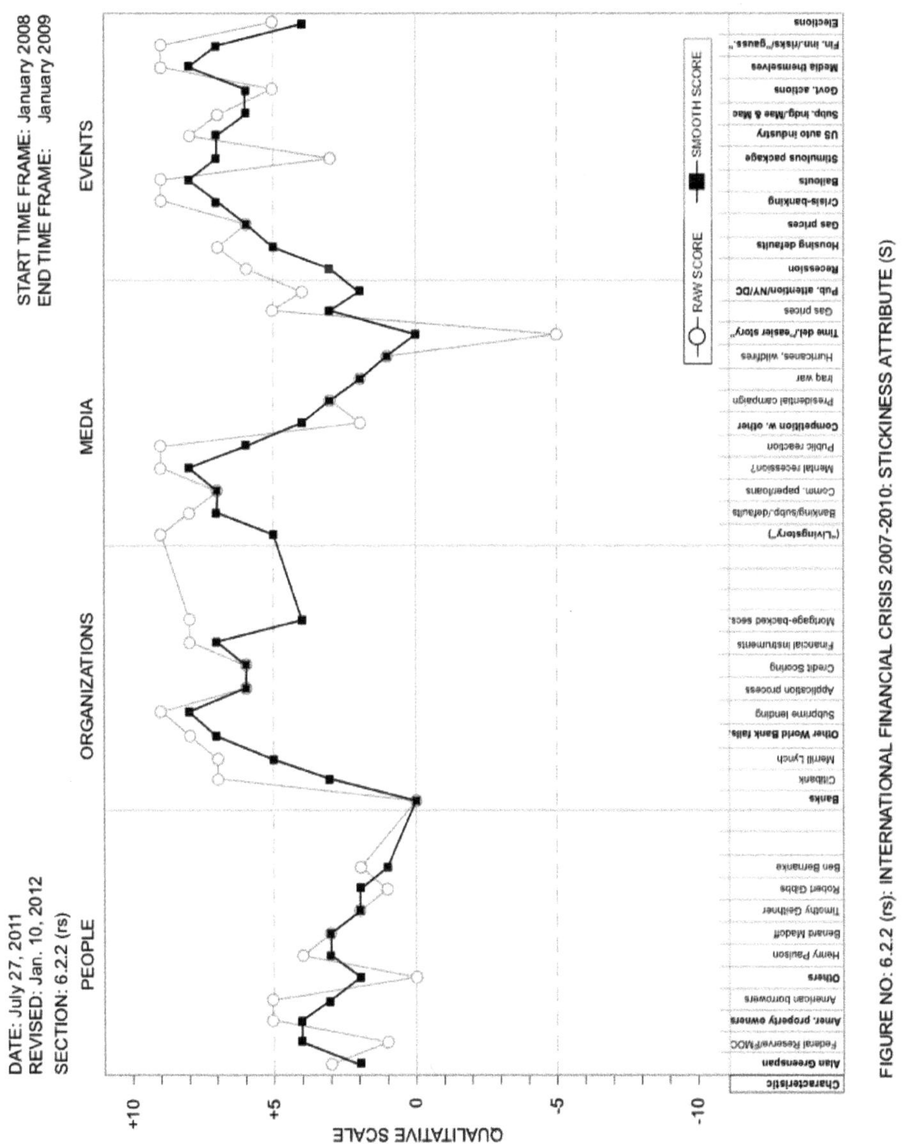

FIGURE NO: 6.2.2 (rs): INTERNATIONAL FINANCIAL CRISIS 2007-2010: STICKINESS ATTRIBUTE (S)

Section 6.2.3 One Dramatic Moment: The Tipping Point (TP)

Date: 5-Sep-11 Start Time Frame: January 2009
Revised: End Time Frame: January 2010

Section: 6.2.3 International Financial Crisis: One Dramatic Moment Attribute

Qualitative ratio scale		**Raw score**	**Smooth score**
Characteristic			
People	0		0
Alan Greenspan		3	2
Timothy Geithner		1	3
Bank directors		6	4
Regulators		-1	4
Government officials		4	4
Bush		7	5
Obama		1	3
Others	0		1
Donald Trump		1	1
Warren Buffett		2	1
Organizations	0		0
Shadow banking		9	5
Derivatives		9	7
Off sheet balances		9	8
Credit default swaps CDS		9	9
Over-the-counter OTC		9	9
Deregulation		8	8
Securities and exchange		7	8
Stock markets		9	9
DOW		10	7
Congressional debates		4	6
Bailouts		-2	3
Stimulus package		-3	2
Media	0		0
"Living story"		10	5
"Bad news versus good news"		10	7
"Warnings ignored"		9	8
Market rebound		5	5
Competing stories -healthcare, terrorism		4	4
Bailouts/stimulus package		3	5
Media influence		9	7
Newspapers		4	6
Radio		5	7
TV		9	8
Websites		7	8
Viral Internet/blogs		9	8
Cell phones/video		7	4
Events	0		0
"Denial thinking"		7	3
"Social virus"		8	6
"Rippling effect"		9	7
"Information cascade"		9	8
Subprime disaster		10	9
Financial institutions		9	9
Housing "myth"		8	9
Stock markets		9	8
Debates/stimulus package		4	6
Government reports		5	7
Banking crisis		10	8
Global market reaction/impacts		9	4

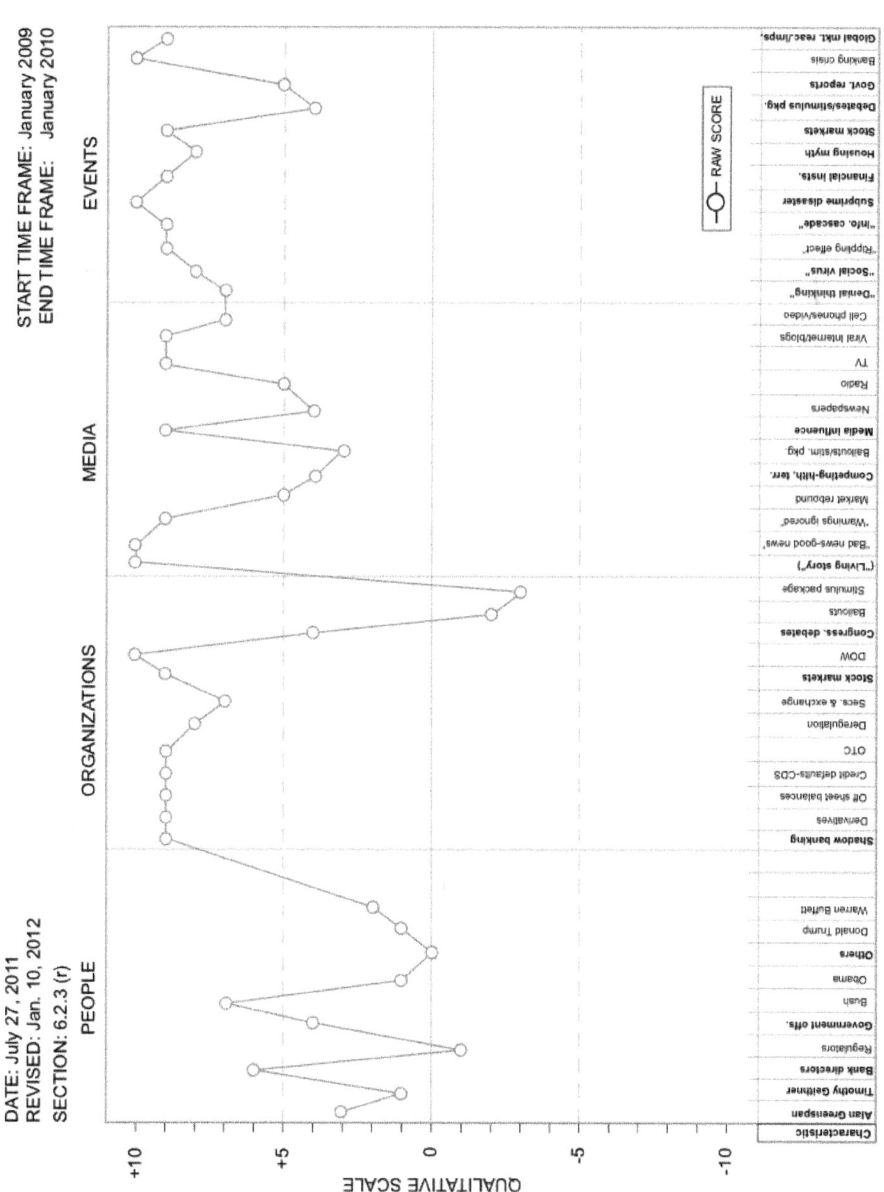

FIGURE NO: 6.2.3 (r): INTERNATIONAL FINANCIAL CRISIS 2007-2010: ONE DRAMATIC MOMENT (TP)

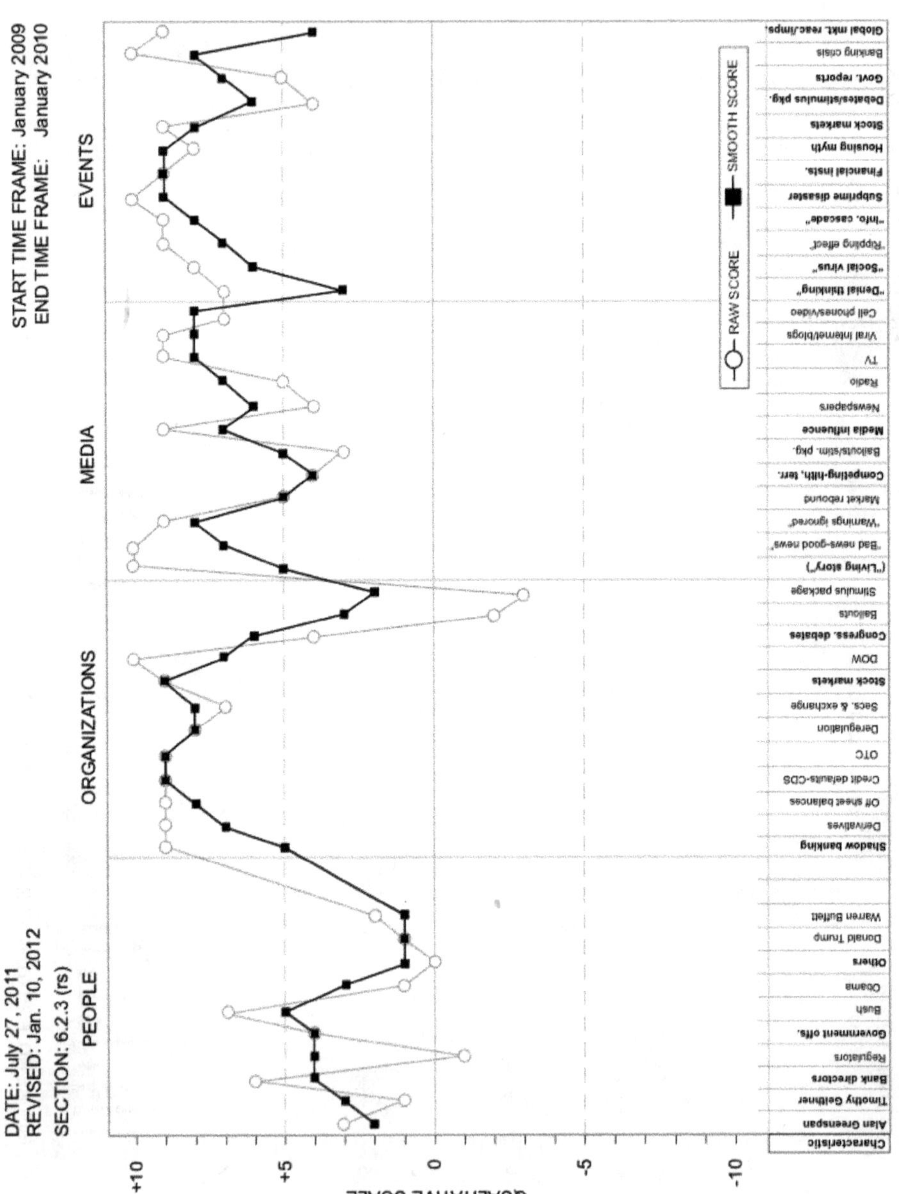

FIGURE NO: 6.2.3 (rs): INTERNATIONAL FINANCIAL CRISIS 2007-2010: ONE DRAMATIC MOMENT (TP)

Section 6.2.4 International Financial Crisis 2007-2010:

Compilations

The 2007 - 2010 International Financial Crisis has been called by leading economists the worst financial since the Great Depression of 1930s with declines in consumer wealth estimated in the trillions of US dollars contributing to the failure of key businesses, requiring substantial financial support by governments, and leading to a significant decline in overall economic activity. In response to our first research question, the contagiousness and the stickiness ***living story*** was being delivered by worldwide media that influenced the credit freeze that brought the global financial systems to the brink of collapse during the last quarter of 2008. The central banks introduced $2.5 trillion of government funds, the largest injection of liquidity into the credit markets and banking systems in world history.

Another research question uniquely links the media delivery systems to the crisis as it profiled the global housing bubble, which peaked in the United States during 2006 and chronicled and spread the epidemic as the value of complex securities tied to housing prices to plummeted and damaged financial institutions globally. It impacted the global stock market, which suffered large losses during 2008. Economies worldwide slowed in late 2008 and early 2009 as credit was tight and international trade declined.

As we turn to our final case study, Climate Change, similar patterns are prevalent in the contagiousness and stickiness attributes, and ultimately, what could be the world's one dramatic moment, or tipping point, which is characterized by many of the same types of media communication delivery systems that delivered the messages and that contributed and influenced the outcome in the first two case studies.

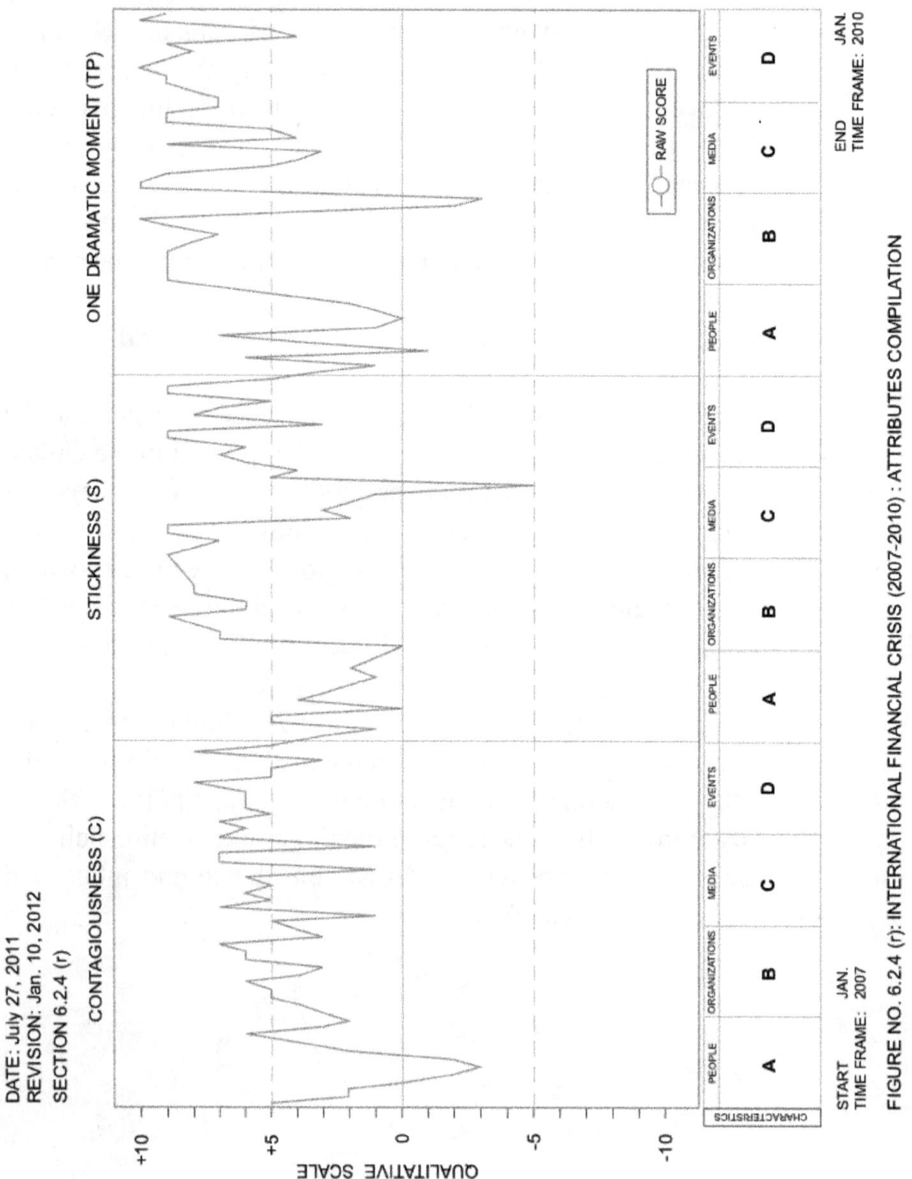

FIGURE NO. 6.2.4 (r): INTERNATIONAL FINANCIAL CRISIS (2007-2010) : ATTRIBUTES COMPILATION

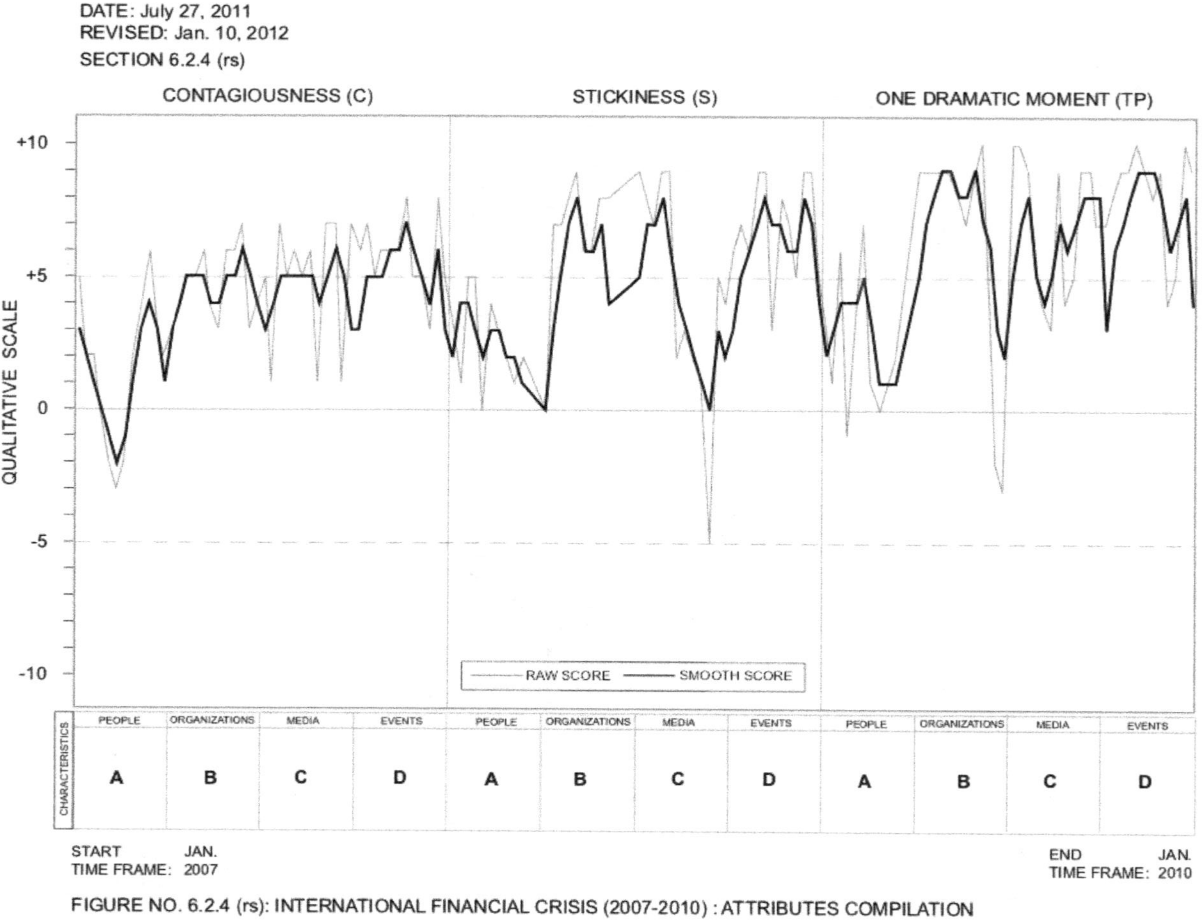

FIGURE NO. 6.2.4 (rs): INTERNATIONAL FINANCIAL CRISIS (2007-2010) : ATTRIBUTES COMPILATION

Section 6.3 Analysis: Climate Change Case Study

Introduction: Qualitative Ratios

With the third case study, Climate Change, I fundamentally focused overall on analyzing each of the tipping point attributes and characteristics similar to the first two case studies in order to identify those that can be understood for the future, and be predicted. It became evident that complex global media systems which are engaged and manipulated, ultimately, could influence this case study outcome. The approach for this case study was to analyze the media environments and technology available and their relationships to climate change and then to answer these research questions:

- Does media contagiousness and stickiness attributes influence the world's behavior as it relates to potential climate change?
- What are the relationships between these attributes and characteristics and various media environments that may lead to a tipping point in climate change?
- Can media influence and predict and/or avoid a potential world tipping point from occurring with climate change, rather, can complex global media systems be engaged and executed with a global consciousness to influence the outcome?

Extracting from the research in Chapter 5, I analyzed the attributes with the goal of identifying the characteristics and understanding the relationships between them as they occur. With the research questions above and the analysis methodology, what follows are the tipping point qualitative ratios and graphic summary of how the attributes and characteristics were/ and are influential relative to people, organizations, media and events. It identifies and quantifies the relative impact and relationships among them. This study of the attribute relationships evolves and become more important in context of the impact on the outcome. The same series of rules governed the research and provided a means of control over what characteristics/issues were included as part of this case study. The influence of the media and the messages delivered by and with the technology are included that may lead to the tipping point for the Climate Change is presented. The influence of the media and the messages delivered by and with the technology that provide an opportunity for the tipping point application. Clearly, one can interpret these characteristics and attributes from many perspectives; however, the intent of our tipping point analysis is to define where and when the one dramatic event may occur and then compare these in Chapter 7 to the other two case studies. The goal is to identify the actions and reactions of the various media sectors along the climate change journey and identify the potential relationships of these attributes.

Section 6.3.1 Contagiousness Attribute (C)

Date:	5-Sep-11	Start Time Frame:	January 2010
Revised:		End Time Frame:	January 2030

Section: 6.3.1 Climate Change: Contagiousness Attribute

Qualitative ratio scale		Raw score	Smooth score
Characteristic			
People	0		0
7 billion people		5	5
Human activity		7	4
Scientists		1	3
Industry Agendas		6	3
Government leaders		1	1
Corporate lobbyists		-2	0
University "think tanks"		1	1
Al Gore		2	0
Pres. Bush		-3	-3
Organizations	0		0
IPCC		2	1
Wikileaks		0	3
Energy industries		8	6
oil		7	5
Coal		8	6
Nuclear		5	5
Politics		1	2
US		3	3
Religion		4	3
Special-interest groups		-2	0
Environmental groups		2	2
Scientific organizations		3	1
Media	0		0
"Harder story to tell"		-5	-1
"age of mis-information"		-4	-2
Oral culture		2	0
Internet distortion		-3	-1
TV and cable TV		1	0
Radio		1	1
Print and newspapers		0	0
Viral blogs textos e-mails		2	0
Standard of accuracy		-4	-2
Government campaigns		-1	-1
Political pressure on scientists		-3	-3
Media cover-up?		-5	-3
Events	0		0
Greenhouse effect		5	
1990 to 2100 : 1.4° to 5.8°		7	
Climate models		5	
Adaptation		-1	
Health effects/disease		1	
Sea levels		2	
Ability to change		0	
risk aversion/ denial		-2	
Migration		1	
Resources		2	
Conflict		5	
Valuation of ecosystem		4	

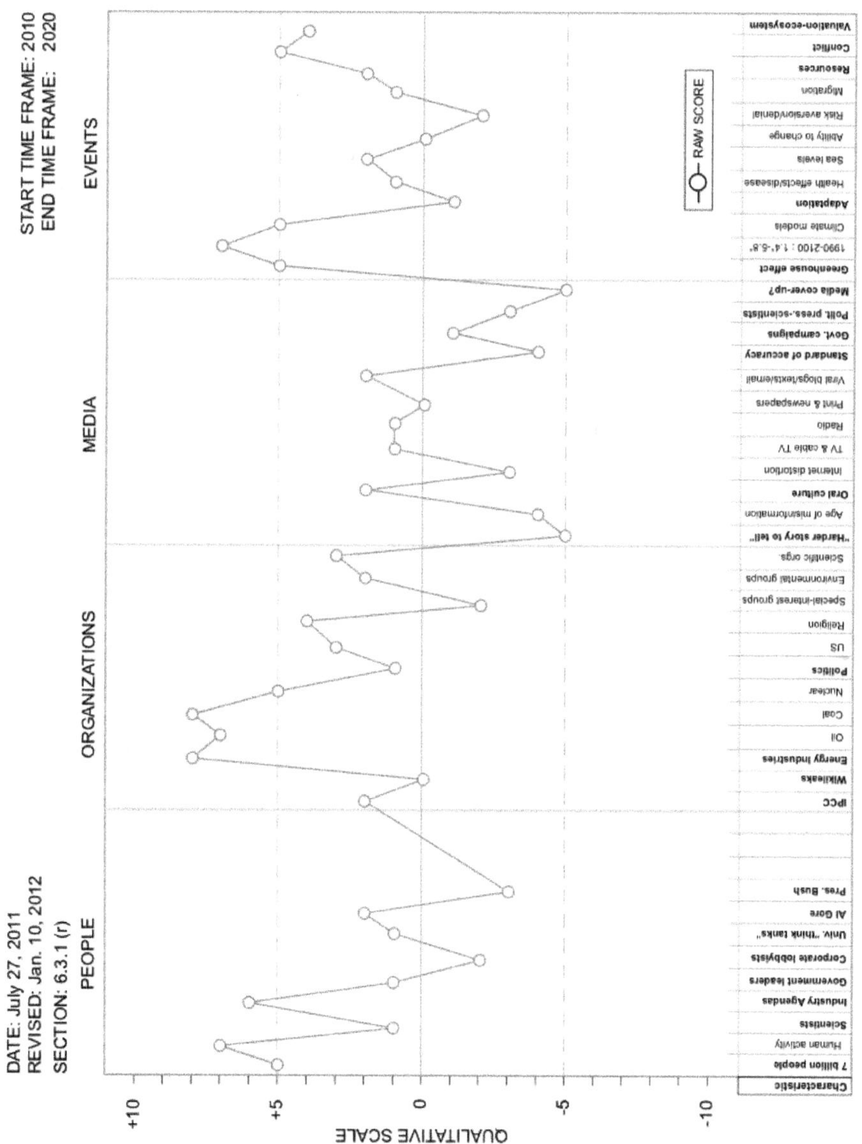

FIGURE NO: 6.3.1 (r): CLIMATE CHANGE: CONTAGIOUSNESS ATTRIBUTE (C)

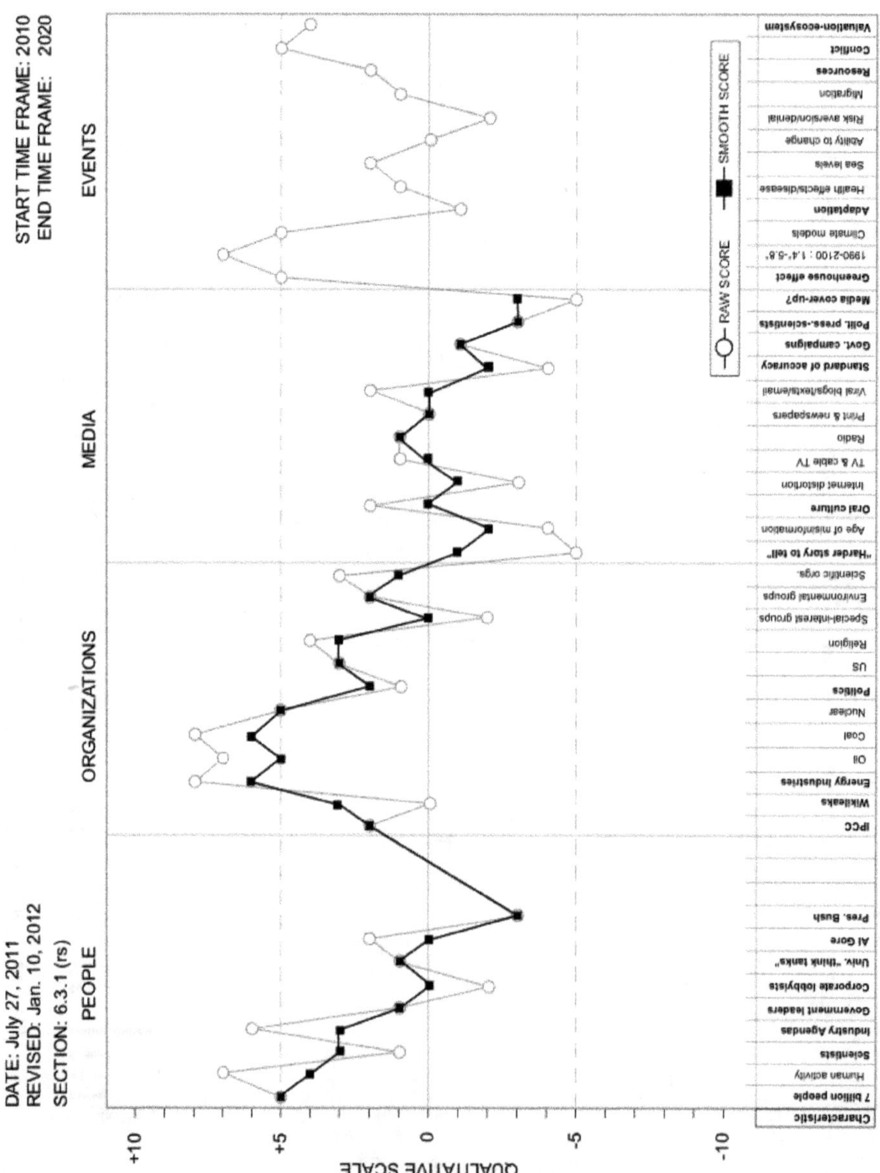

FIGURE NO: 6.3.1 (rs): CLIMATE CHANGE: CONTAGIOUSNESS ATTRIBUTE (C)

Section 6.3.2 Stickiness Attribute (S)

Date: 5-Sep-11 | Start Time Frame: January 2030
Revised: | End Time Frame: January 2100

Section: 6.3.2 Climate Change: Stickiness Attribute

Qualitative ratio scale			Raw score	Smooth score
Characteristic				
People		0		0
Citizens of the planet			6	3
CO2 levels			8	4
Scientists			0	4
Keeling	Keeling curve		2	2
Miles R. Allen			1	1
Joseph cannadel			1	1
George Bu!	1992		-2	0
Al Gore	2006		2	1
Populations			6	4
Developed countries			7	5
undeveloped countries			6	4
Organizations		0		0
US Department of energy			1	1
Bob Watson			1	1
IPCC			3	0
Bush administration	Congress 1998		-3	-1
Obama administration			0	0
Kyoto			1	1
Copenhagen			1	1
United Nations			2	2
World meteorological organizations			2	2
National Academy of Sciences			2	2
Al Gore			3	2
Other scientists			2	1
Media		0		0
"Real-time"			5	4
"living story"			6	5
"Harder story to tel"l			9	7
Distorted media space			8	7
Doubts			7	6
"Climategate"			2	3
Internet			3	3
Blogs textos e-mails			3	3
Television and cable TV			1	2
Newspapers			1	1
Radio			1	1
Geo technical solutions			0	0
Events		0		
Temperature change: 5- 6°F or 18° F versus 3.6° F			8	6
CO2 up 25% by the year 2020			9	7
Adaptation			3	4
Droughts			5	5
Floods			5	5
Food scarcity			5	5
Capital Investments			1	3
Economies			2	5
Quality of life			9	7
Conflict			8	4

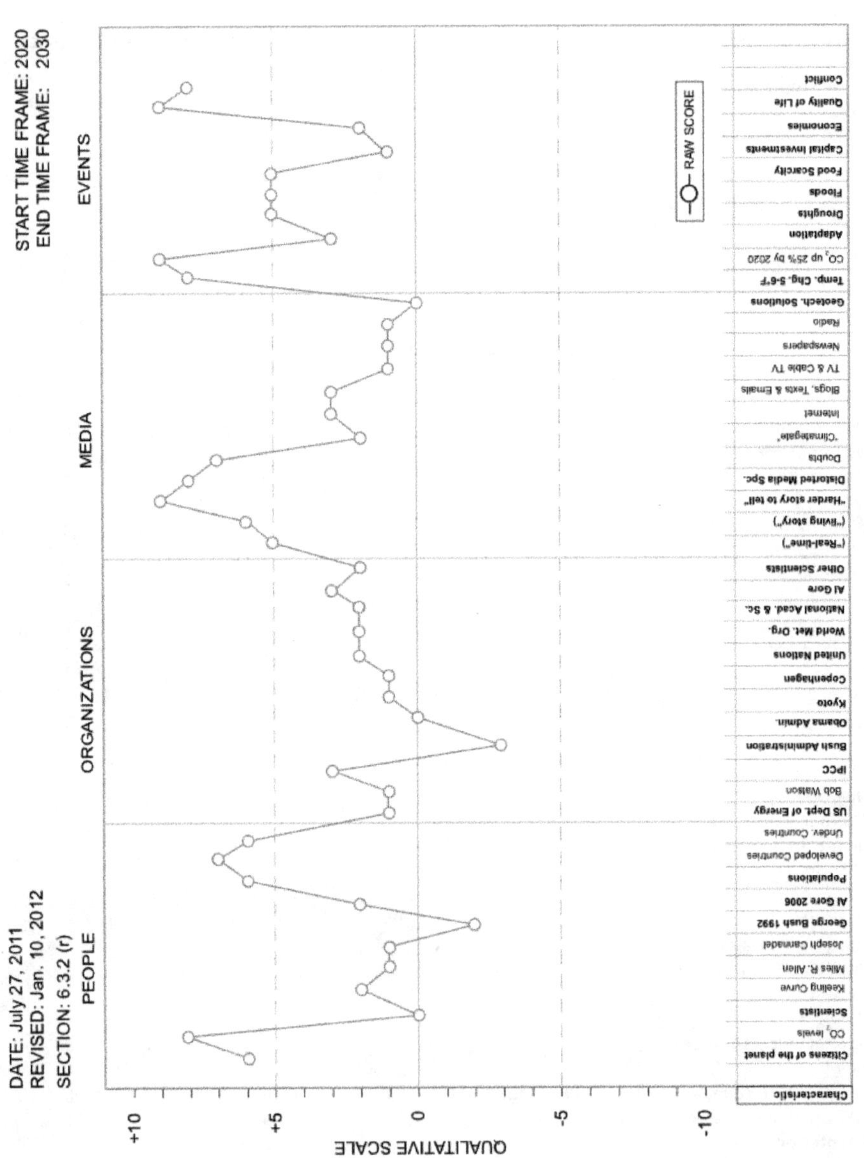

FIGURE NO: 6.3.2 (r): CLIMATE CHANGE: STICKINESS ATTRIBUTE (C)

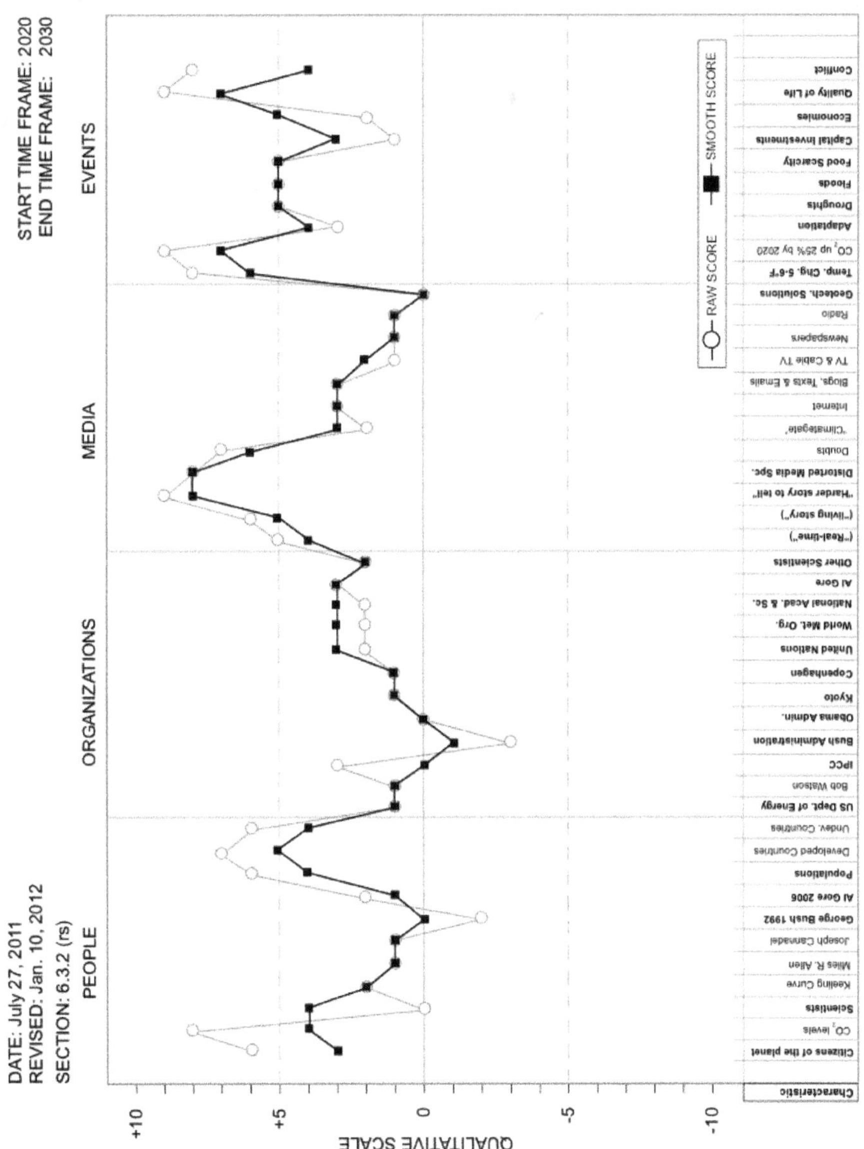

FIGURE NO: 6.3.2 (rs): CLIMATE CHANGE: STICKINESS ATTRIBUTE (C)

Section 6.3.3 One Dramatic Moment: The Tipping Point (TP)

Date: 5-Sep-11 Start Time Frame: January 2100
Revised: End Time Frame: January 2140

Section: 6.3.3 Climate Change: One Dramatic Moment Attribute

Qualitative ratio scale		Raw score	Smooth score
Characteristic			
People	0		0
World Impacts		6	5
Population		7	6
Resources		5	5
Air		6	6
Water		6	6
Food		7	6
Shelter		5	5
Other		6	6
War/ conflict		8	5
Organizations	0		0
Generations of leaders	0		
Forefathers		-1	0
Present		-4	-1
Future		0	0
International borders		2	1
USA		2	2
European Union		3	2
Arab states		2	1
South America		0	0
Asia		-5	-2
African Union		-6	-3
New World environmental groups		0	-1
Media	0		0
"Global consciousness"		7	3
Social media platforms		8	6
Other	0		5
Government intervention		4	5
Media events		8	7
Food/ energy prices		7	7
Population		8	7
Hurricanes/tornadoes/floods/ droughts		7	7
Displaced regions		7	7
Topple governments		9	8
"Denial thinking"		6	7
Media management		2	3
Events	0		0
Climate change revolution		9	5
"Global consciousness"		10	7
Other			
"Crisis driven change"		10	8
Scenarios			
Best case			
Year 2100			
Events:New York, Venice, Singapore, etc.		10	9
Worst-case			
Year 2140			
Social unrest, war, chaos, 36.4 billion people		10	5

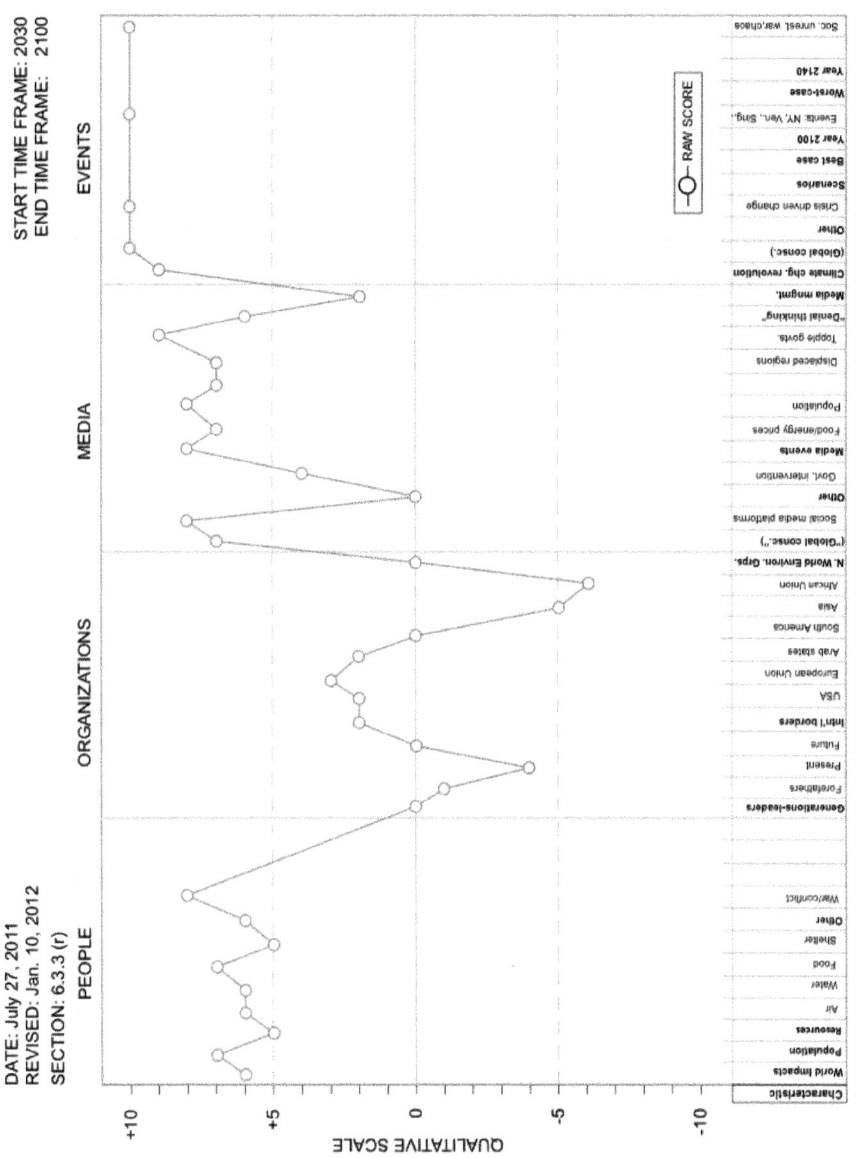

FIGURE NO: 6.3.3 (r): CLIMATE CHANGE: ONE DRAMATIC MOMENT (TP)

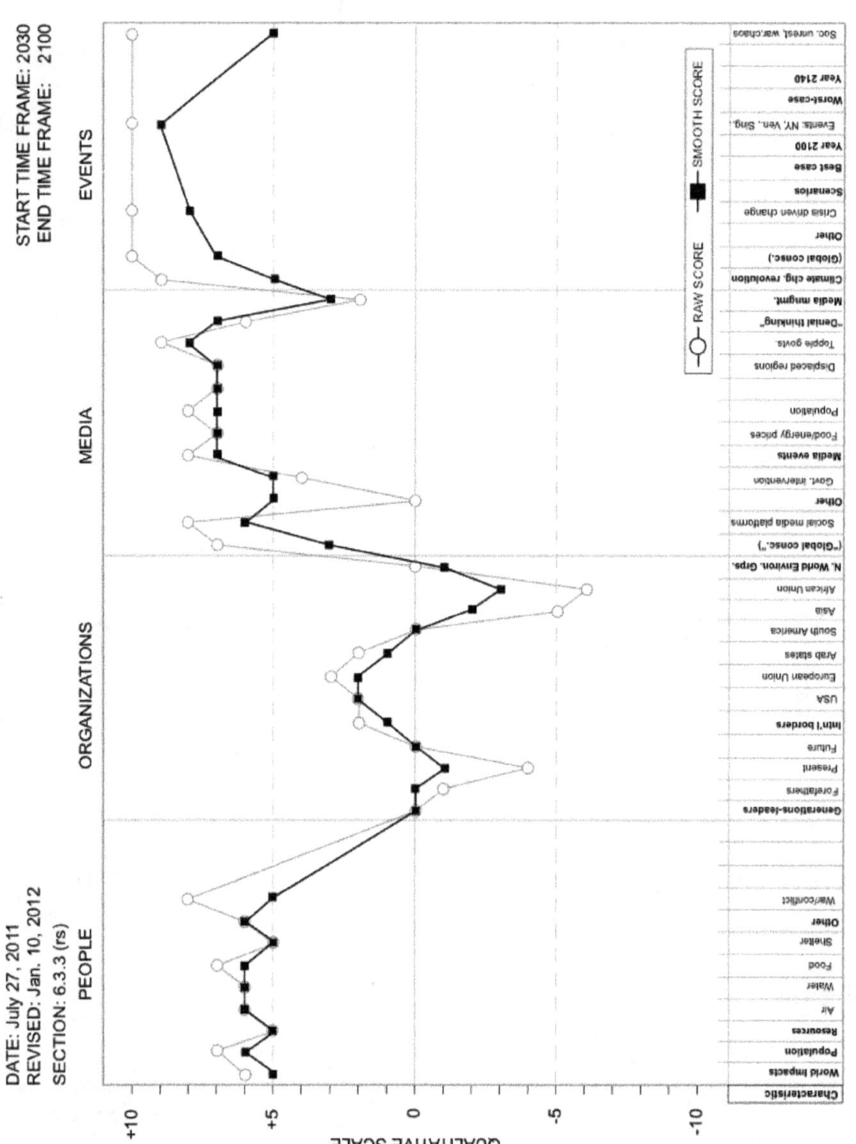

FIGURE NO: 6.3.3 (rs): CLIMATE CHANGE: ONE DRAMATIC MOMENT (TP)

Section 6.3.4 Climate Change:

Compilations

Parameters in this case study were outlined for the various climate change tipping point attributes and characteristics. The goal was to identify the actions and reactions involved in the climate change *living story* and identify the potential *global consciousness* inter-relationships of these attributes and characteristics. The intent here was to address the research questions. From the research, characteristics and their relationships were identified and used in construction of our tipping point qualitative ratio analysis framework. These represent the key people, organizations, media, and events that impact this global event.

The influence of the media and the messages delivered by and with the media technology is a complicated issue to identify a future tipping point. One can easily interpret these attributes and characteristics from many perspectives. However, the intent of our qualitative ratio analysis framework is to define where and when the one dramatic event might occur and compare this to the other two case studies for similar analysis. This method for analyzing these attributes was simply look at the sequence of events in chronological manner and observe the way they develop and how the various media sectors play their role.

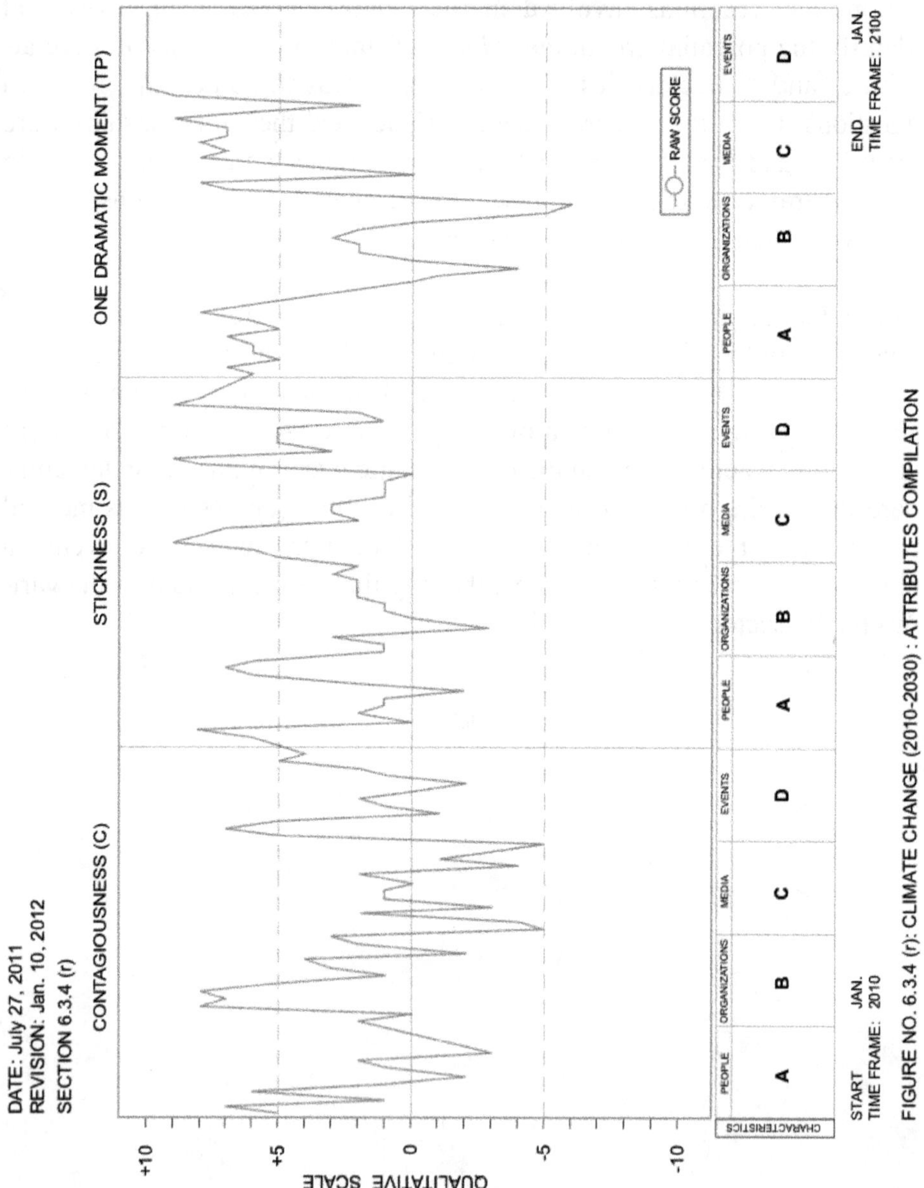

FIGURE NO. 6.3.4 (r): CLIMATE CHANGE (2010-2030) : ATTRIBUTES COMPILATION

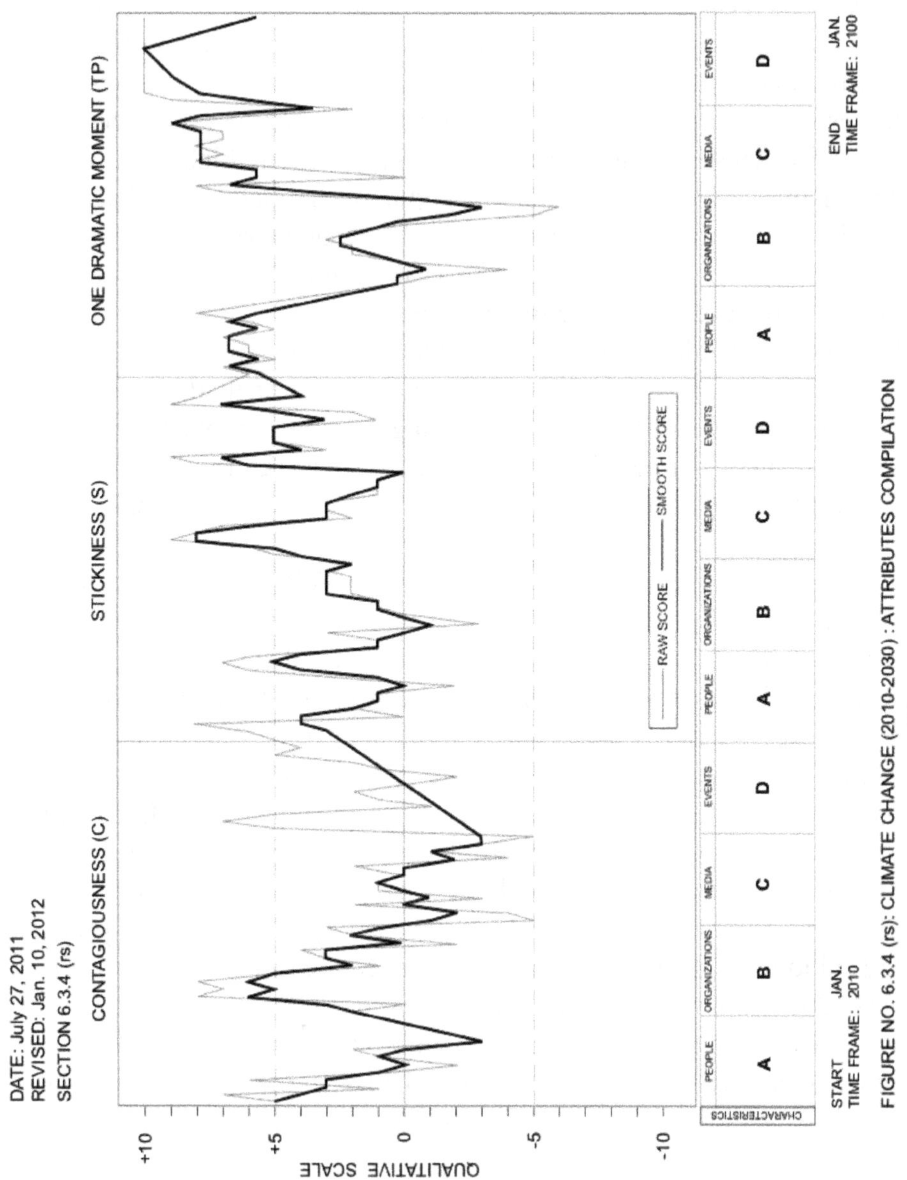

FIGURE NO. 6.3.4 (rs): CLIMATE CHANGE (2010-2030) : ATTRIBUTES COMPILATION

Section 6.4 Summary

For each of the three case studies, one clearly could review the media content and make some broad-stroke generalizations about the occurrence of these tipping point phenomena. However, the spreading contagion during the Obama Presidential Campaign piggybacked with the plummeting stock market during the International Financial Crisis and the current dazed and confused policymakers facing the issue of Climate Change, merely reinforces the basic premises and evolutions of the tipping point phenomena. As each of these tipping points approach(ed), with unthinkable and finally irreversible end results, it prompted populations to take radical action and required governments and leaders to make changes whether they liked the outcome or not, sometimes to the frustration of many, however drastic the moves may have been. One might assume that there was some carryover from the Bush administration to the Obama campaign that reinforced his agenda and pledges to the American people that propelled him into office. However, the media frenzy created a huge source of momentum and ultimately a huge source of campaign donations. Certainly there was broad support for McCain during this time and a lot of unhappy voters.

During the International Financial Crisis 2007-2010, there was the consistent failure by the media and the public to understand conceptually the broad spectrum and complexity of the crisis that was unfolding. How widespread and serious the crisis was, for example. At the time (and maybe even now), we don't know. Many months have passed since this *living story* was carried. Headlines show the nation states throughout the world are still suffering from severe financial and budget troubles. Governments lack the resources for a full investigation and a means for correcting the magnitude of the problems. With the International Financial Crisis 2007-2010, the banking industry had little incentive to correct their processes to lead to their insolvency that deconstructed the markets in late 2008 and early 2009. But those markets have long since returned to normal, in part because everyone knows that banks will be bailed out if they get in trouble, as is the case throughout the European Union in mid 2011-2, with the issues surrounding the Greek, Italian, and Portuguese economies.

The fact is with many of these stories you can't believe what is being told in the media and who is accountable. As US officials are grappling with increasing the national debt levels reaching to gargantuan proportions, one wonders where it all is leading, as the average American taxpayer each (in

August 2011), owed 125,000 USD as part of the national debt. Who can you believe? And recently (early July 2011), a global world event within the media sector exhibited similar tipping point phenomena. The News Corp. phone hacking scandal that involved the Murdoch publishing Empire, the British government and Scotland Yard played out in macro fashion (in billions of dollars in value, lost revenue, and loss of life) with the same attributes and characteristics of the prototypical tipping point case study.

Within a period of weeks the world media audience was riveted on the contagiousness, stickiness, and what lead to a dramatic tipping point for the Murdoch empire relative to the scandal that unfolded crossing economic, cultural, and political lines within British society and media environments. The characteristics can be easily identified with a tipping point context of people--the editors, the police commissioner, reporters, the politicians, and the presidents of companies; the organizations--news organizations, political parties, parliament, and the Metropolitan Police Department; media--both as a participant–News Corp. and the watchdog journalists that covered the story for the various other media sectors; and events–illegal hacking of telephones, e-mails and voicemails, payments and settlements to avoid scrutiny, the evidence that was ignored, the players that were arrested, hearings that were held in broadcast live, the percentage of news coverage by media in covering a story of one of their own, the government and corporate apologies that could be analyzed much in the same way as we have done with our case studies with the qualitative ratio analysis framework which would show when the tipping point occurred in this recent and somewhat ironic global event. This event did nothing more than compete for the media space in a world that has now lost objective perspective on the information that is being presented to them. Remembering, in comparison to scientific phenomena that is analyzed and reviewed by peers, the real-time unfolding of this event had no fact checking or means to qualify the information that was being presented. Most individuals did not have the filters, or the energy, or the expertise to evaluate and analyze the substance in the reporting and the relevance of the topic.

This is an easier media story to tell. All the while, the world's most pressing issue of climate change was moved to the back pages of the *global consciousness*. Our analysis here for each of the case studies underscores the reality that the clock is ticking.

Proceeding to chapter 7, I attempt to place the people, organization, media, and events of the three tipping point case studies into comparative context for the purposes of contrasting their similarities and differences. I also look at each case study historically in context with similar events of their type and historical tipping points and influenced by the media systems available at that time.

Media Impacts and Global Events Website

For further information please visit the
Media impact and Global Events Website:

http://mdgparis.typepad.com/global_media_and_world_ev/

This website tracks, highlights, categorizes and provides a articles and commentary related to Tipping Point Attributes and Characteristics, as well as information and recent updates related specifically to the three case studies included in this version and other Media and Global Event issues.

CHAPTER 7
COMPARISONS

Introduction

When comparing the media impact on global events, part of the criteria for the starting point was developing a representation for the appropriate qualitative measurement of the attributes and their characteristics. This was done in the preceding Chapter 6 with the qualitative ratio analysis framework system that summarized and identified when the tipping points had occurred. The other issue that I feel that I only touched on briefly in the research is that media information remains territorially bound in many respects, i.e. whereby it is limited by where I was able to find and analyze data. For example, much of the data and resources regarding climate change were found relative to the United States. In that regard, it underscores my view on what the global media culture might miss presenting key issues during an era in which media flows consistently over national borders and differing climate and cultural regions when it is presented different languages and different formats. Based on these considerations, my preference was leaning towards the transcultural approach to the research and inevitably in the comparisons of the case studies. This approach assumes beginning with one state as a natural center of a comparison, in this case the US, but in effect it points to more complex issues arising for carrying out the comparisons between different media sectors and the three case study attributes and characteristics that cross over territorial borders. To make these comparisons understandable, we must first agree that my research has a bit of container thinking to its structure and how the research was presented.

Overall, I have attempted a comparison approach that provoked me to think about when and why tipping points occur and their applications to global events in such a way that territoriality and associated politics, while important, were not wholly part of the legitimate perspective when considering the outcomes. Traditional or old media is indeed a complicated communication process that sometimes can be focused around relatively centralized power structures, in contrast to new mass media, which is marked by a more multi-centered power structure, for example, the Internet. In this context, I approached the comparisons of the case studies from a highly generalized perspective with the neither the intent to either validate or invalidate the phenomenon about tipping points, which were analyzed in chapter six and the media environments presented in chapter two. What is problematic for the comparisons, particularly when considering the third case study, is that they can be criticized for the generalities that were made given the complexity of the size and magnitude and diversity and sheer quantity it encompasses, and, it has not ended in duration.

Assumptions from the beginning as to how to interpret agendas for national cultures and the application of the tipping points approach may be more harmful than helpful. As such, in this context specific cultural interrelationships are difficult at best to compare and outline herein. This permits me to focus on the defined framework of attributes and characteristics as a vehicle to describe, and compare and contrast the relationships with tipping point phenomena, which may have more substance. Having said that, the Internet is an effective medium for assembling and analyzing research. At this juncture in time, media has become a formidable power on the global stage with the rise of multimedia conglomerates, deregulated and private communications systems, and advanced technological innovations. With the globalization of media and communication, media technologies and industries have created a global culture in which people from all over the world can watch and share experiences, from war and humanitarian disasters, to sports and entertainment, to the free-market capitalism and advertisements, which make us all the world's media consumers. Extracting from the analysis and research in the preceding chapters, I describe and compare the attributes sequentially for each of the three case studies with the goal of identifying the *relationships* between them. This comparison is organized by the relative groupings of people, organizations, media, and the events.

These groupings identify and describe the *relative* influence. My study of the relationships evolves and become more important as I compare these in context with the media systems in place using the attributes themselves and as a benchmark for understanding some of the media developments and technological advances. In any case, the third case study, Climate Change, poses the overall research question as to how to predict the *one dramatic moment* for the world and to understand (and anticipate) to the extent that these attributes evolve within complex global media systems, which can be engaged, manipulated and executed to influence the outcome. Additionally, all of the attributes and characteristics that were described in the case studies, ranging from a shorter timeframe of approximately one year for the Obama Presidential Campaign, to the duration of three years for the International Financial Crisis, and the on-going current and future events related to Climate Change, are similarly characterized by specific people, organizations, media, and events that have an influence.

The following sections offer the detailed descriptions of the comparisons of these various factors, highlighting their similarities and differences and providing observations that can derived from them. Obviously, media types are the focus for this exercise - their historical context, development, and influence on populations and the structures of economies. That focus then turns to the development of these media types with historical context for each of the case studies. An interesting aspect that emerges from the application of this exercise is that significant global events that occurred in the past followed similar tipping points evolutions (or sequence), which in effect led to their one dramatic moment, yet perhaps the means for analyzing and predicting them with current state-of-the-art methods is not available. In this context, and with the varied historical narratives that were generated with the attributes and characteristics, a comparison of the case studies yields some striking similarities. However the respective attribute descriptions reveal significant differences in these case studies, reflecting perhaps the technological sophistication and limitation of media types at the time for influencing tipping points.

The media issues that were examined in the case studies cover a range of examples that are sometimes extremely small, not only in absolute qualitative terms, but also relative to the size of audience of the media environments at the time. Despite their varying scale and magnitude, the case studies exhibit considerable comparison value when searching for similarities and differences that might be extrapolated towards even larger applications.

It ultimately rests with the world's nation states where specific questions pertaining to the effect and impact of these phenomena need to be addressed and where specific resources might be employed for implementing methods as a means of predicting and managing global tipping points, particularly Climate Change. The case studies vary widely, but when combined and compared, one can perceive certain common traits, most notably for Climate Change with regard to the influence between media on populations and response.

From a cross-section of descriptions with each attribute and the characteristics that occurred within the case studies, it is interesting to note the interdependence of the factors as they are influenced by the media on these global events. This is not to say that all global events are capable of being analyzed and compared in this fashion, which is due to the complexities and size, and arguably, some experts will claim, as they have throughout much of history, that the very development and existence of such phenomena are associated with external factors outside human control. Rather, the descriptive comparisons show results of modern media forces acting out in the environments that affect smaller nation states as they are not independent enough on their own to avoid being part of the larger phenomena.

One can conclude from these factors that the comparison value of the case studies is relatively high, albeit some questions remain relative to the strategic implementation and adoption to address such large content of issues, which will mandate all present and future nations and state involvement for finding solutions, particularly with Climate Change.

The following comparisons highlight the media influence during the sequential attributes for each of the case studies for the purposes of defining where the similarities and differences are relevant, how these affected the outcome and are depicted in the graphic summary for all three. The intent is to illustrate the attribute and characteristic similarities and differences over the evolving media lifecycle of each event in order to draw some conclusions further to their existence and relationships. The patterns and trends that emerge via this synbook of this application provide further discoveries about the nature of global events and the media impact.

Section 7.1 Obama Presidential Campaign

Section 7.1.1 Contagiousness Impacting this Global Event

The economy and the unpopular incumbent (the disapproval of the presidency of George W. Bush) alone might have been enough for Obama to win as the McCain campaign was nonresponsive to the economic issues. The Obama campaign spent more than 14 million USD to broadcast ads to familiarize the public with McCain's loyalty to the Bush agenda. McCain was 72 years old, and his age as a potential liability was being reinforced loudly and clearly in the media. Coverage about the perception of youth was rampant in the media, as was Obama's' age at 47 vigorous, energetic, and brimming with fresh ideas. The erratic nature and temperament of McCain was covered extensively in the media arena. This contagiousness feeling of frustration continued into 2008 election and media reinforced the effect during the campaign. The on-going economic collapse was reinforced as the media treated this as a major story.

While most of the developments in the media contagiousness occurred in nationally televised broadcasts and ads, the Obama campaign also opened a media assault on McCain's reputation on radio with repackaged biographies. The Obama campaign also increased the contagiousness in the media culture, such as with news reports, opinion columns, and comedy on TV that already existed. By the time the American voters entered the voting booth, a contagious majority had concluded, with media reinforcement, that McCain's age was more worrisome than Obama's background.

The US voter was anxious, and three quarters of the US population believed that the nation was on the wrong track, and when the Dow lost more than 4000 points to a close on October 7, 2008 at 9477 points, a majority of the voters, 53%, felt that the Democrats were better able to handle the economy, which then became the leading campaign and media contagiousness issue.

Section 7.1.2 Stickiness Impacted this Global Event

The Obama campaign sidestepped the media by notifying its supporters electronically that Delaware Senator Joseph Biden had been given the nod for the Democratic vice presidential position. Obama was constantly using new media to push and promote his campaign ahead of traditional old media. There was a consistent focus in the media on the politics, and those who watched Senator Obama during the convention were more impressed by him than those who viewed the republican candidates. Also television contributed to his media stickiness. The information that was disseminated by each of the campaign teams was done so in such a way via the new media that the influence and impact could be correlated to the number of the dollars spent to reach the voters.

However, the economy's presence as a central issue, *real time* story of the campaign meant that the media influence was indeed linked to the delivery systems and the way the messages were timed. Media consumers, i.e. voters, were more likely during the campaign to see the economy as a central national issue. TV, journals, and Internet sources were reporting the same conclusion. And the perception and belief that electing McCain meant a continuation of the same Bush policies was a media theme that was propelled widely. The country was on the wrong track as it related to economic concerns, and that was the conclusion that most global media was putting forth. The Obama campaign's messages on broadcast, cable, and radio media delivery systems:

- Obama shared voter values.
- Obama could handle the economy better than McCain.
- McCain equaled Bush.

In essence, these were the critical stickiness characteristics of the Obama campaign, which continued to drive home media perceptions that were all too important to the Obama candidacy. With their substantial bankroll, the Obama campaign had time to test and analyze the media message delivery and how they would be deployed with the new technology mediums.

Focusing on the energy issues, the media made the oil and energy security as the national purpose. During the campaign, gas prices were at four dollars and five dollars a gallon, with no end in sight. With the drilling issue a popular stickiness characteristic, media exposure focused the energy prices and framed them as a cause for the United States' failing economy. The stickiness of the energy issue and the economy led to a two-pronged media momentum shift away from the Republicans during the campaign.

Section 7.1.3 One Dramatic Moment impacting this Global Event

The media couldn't contain themselves as the economic collapse dominated the media, and media had all the one dramatic moment momentum needed when on September 15, 2008 John McClain stated: "The fundamentals of the economy are strong." The economy was becoming unhinged, and media would overwhelm the voter decisions. Democrats bridged from stickiness to the one dramatic moment capitalizing in the media on McCain's comment. The media was overwhelmed reporting on the Lehman Brothers' collapse, the Dow Jones averages plunging, and story after story about economic disaster occurring in the US markets. The fundamental statement was screaming capital letters on the search engines, and was being linked to "job losses at 605,000 for the year, September foreclosures at 9800 a day, etc…"[8] Also central to the media momentum towards the tipping point was the Democrats' branding McCain as "erratic," as McCain moved from one position on the crisis to another. This feeling of *herky-jerkiness* translated into a media public perception of how he would handle the presidency if elected. For McCain's strategy team, the economy really took the campaign away. Obama's strategy during this time was to use "a nation in trouble" with home foreclosures, lost jobs, high gas prices, record deficits, national debt that had never been higher, and the fact that the country in just few months had begun to historic economic meltdown.

The economy was the central event to the agenda for the public and the media. From mid-January 2008 through Election Day, economy was the front, middle, and foremost on the media agenda. During the post-convention run-up, media activity about the economy, the foreclosure rates, the Dow dropping, and the slide of personal wealth became the momentum of enormous proportions for the American voter. As media technology opened up

---

8 Linked Search Engine Associations, "Covering the Great Recession: Why Did Coverage of the Economy Decrease?" Pew Research Center's Project for Excellence in Journalism, October 5, 2009, Retrieved from http://www.journalism.org/analysis_report/why_did_coverage_economy_decrease

new ways to inform, engage, and mobilize during the campaign, it also provided opportunities to insulate and send deceptive messages. The heavily financed Obama campaign's regular barrage of e-mails blanketed voters with reinforcing information that reframed all the events from their campaign's point of view and continued to offer a strategy rebuttal arguments to go after the Republicans in media. McCain's statement "The fundamentals of the economy are in good shape," coupled with Obama's deep pockets, created a media convulsion during the campaign. In retrospect, Obama had little to do but to ride the epidemic of voter concern and momentum to the campaign's one dramatic moment, the *tipping point*.

Section 7.2 International Financial Crisis 2007 - 2010

Section 7.2.1 Contagiousness Impacting this Global Event

Baby boomers and politicians fostered the birth and rearing of the organizations that were developed and contributed to the contagiousness attribute of the International Financial Crisis 2007-2010. Baby boomers, the generation from the 1950s, and 40 years of government investment behind implementing the Internet including most of its core technologies built it into a working worldwide system, essentially, shifting the strategy and *organizational model from government* to a *private sector control model* in 1995. Timothy Geithner, when president of the New York Federal Reserve Bank, attributed the financial problems to merely a housing bubble; however, it was in fact, a whole range of badly designed financial contagious arrangements. On Wall Street investors and institutions, fearful of unregulated instruments, started to pull out their funds, and it became the epicenter of the financial crisis. The media was consumed with these events. The 2007- 2010 International Financial Crisis was as a *living story* in the media; a story which was always evolving to keep their audiences focused and tuned in. Three top *living stories* dominated:

- Efforts to help revive the failing banking sector
- The battle over the stimulus package
- The struggles of the U.S. auto industry

When it came to the biggest economic storylines, the media was very influential, and there was one key metric for identifying who was controlling coverage—the lead source in each story.[9] There was a dominance of Obama Administration players in the news narrative on the economy. The visibility of the president and his administration far exceeded that of any other source as Obama was the lead in 14% of the economy stories. Meanwhile, the Labor Department was releasing figures showing the greatest job loss records in 42 years. In his response to these figures, Obama stated a phrase that added to the contagiousness during this time: "In the midst of our greatest economic crisis since the Great Depression…"[10] The media reacted almost proportionally, conversely when media deployed: "They [investors] see the first signs of an economic spring, if you would—a few blooming flowers," UBS Financial Services analyst *Art Cashin* told ABC's World News Tonight.[11] With these later statements the media coverage dropped off dramatically, hence, the correlation with bad news as a contagiousness characteristic.

The crisis of the media *living story* contagiousness rapidly developed and continued to spread. The financial crisis would yield the biggest banking shakeout since the 1980s savings-and-loan meltdown. The U.S. unemployment rate increased to 10.2% by October 2009, the highest rate since 1983 and roughly twice the pre-crisis rate. And finally, another key contagiousness characteristic of the financial crisis was the bursting of the United States housing bubble, which peaked in approximately 2005–2006.

Section 7.2.2 Stickiness Impacting this Global Event

From 2000 until mid-2005, the United States of America experienced a housing boom, which was part of a global real estate bubble that was pronounced the greatest in history. American property owners and borrowers had learned how to ride down the interest rate curve with abandon and were *stuck* to it in such a way that they kept going back to the well

---

9 A lead media salesperson, per Gladwell, is someone who is featured in at least 50% of a story.

10 "Remarks of President Barack Obama, Weekly Address," The White House, Washington, D. C., February 7, 2009. Retrieved from http://www.whitehouse.gov/blog_post/compromise1

11 "Covering the Great Recession: Why Did Coverage of the Economy Decrease?" Pew Research Center's Project for Excellence in Journalism, October 5, 2009, p. 2. Retrieved from http://www.journalism.org/analysis_report/why_did_coverage_economy_decrease

again and again. The proliferation of new affordable products and devices to make houses available to more marginal credit clients contributed to the crisis as predatory behavior in the subprime banking industry epidemic in the banking sector, and then big banks and investment banks reported some 20 billion in losses, primarily in their prime subprime-based CDOs portfolios. What makes this important as a stickiness characteristic and so devastating is not the absolute size of the subprime and risky mortgages, but how during this time these were packaged and resold and entered their way into the entire global financial system.

The media's *living story* of the financial crisis shifted repeatedly from a narrative about mortgages to one about recession, then a banking crisis, and then largely about gas prices—with a changing storyline and one that differed from medium to medium. The connection between media *living story* and stickiness was uneven. Sometimes coverage lagged months behind economic activity when the information was dependent on government data. Other times, the *living story* tracked events erratically, trying to "leapfrog" perceptions in front of events, as with housing and inflation.

As events of the financial crisis were easier to tell, (as in the case of gas prices), coverage was closely tied to what was actually (*real time*) occurring in the marketplace. The financial crisis was a bigger media *living story* in older forms--print, the three network evening newscasts, and traditional news radio—and a noticeably smaller one in the newer—the more opinion-oriented platforms of cable TV and talk radio. Parts were a bigger story in one medium than another with some media generally less concerned overall. Gas prices, for instance, was a bigger TV story. Banking and housing were bigger in print. And unless there was a clear political issue to argue about, the economy did not tend to be much of story. The economy was one of those *living stories* in which public attitudes play a central role. During the financial crisis, the public was focused on the living story in some ways before the media. But to some degree Wall Street was significantly influenced by consumer psychology. And the media information the public is operating by is a major determinant of that psychology.

With the nervousness came the panic selloffs. The *living story* events during the International Financial Crisis were perhaps too large and too complicated and presented such a psychological block to both the media, the general public, as well as government officials. It was simply too difficult to follow, interpret, report and understand. In fact, there was no way of avoiding the stickiness. George Soros commented, "The super-boom got out of hand when the new products became so complicated that the authorities could no longer calculate the risks and started relying on the risk management methods of the banks themselves."[12] Similarly, the rating agencies relied on the information provided by the originators of synthetic products. "It was a shocking abdication of responsibility."[13] The value of U.S. subprime mortgages was estimated at $1.3 trillion as of March 2007, with over 7.5 million first-lien subprime mortgages outstanding.[14] Wall Street banks were eager to make fast profits. And the media was reporting on the growing evidence that such mortgage frauds may be the cause of the crisis for these reasons: 1. Media echoed the reality that U.S. households and financial institutions became increasingly indebted or overleveraged during the years preceding the crisis. 2. This increased their vulnerability to the collapse of the housing bubble and worsened the ensuing economic downturn, while market participants did not accurately measure the risk inherent with financial innovation (such as MBS and CDOs) or understand its impact on the overall stability of the financial system. 3. These losses and events were widely reported in all media sectors. 4. Finally, in 2008, the stickiness became a tipping point when the financial system's foundation swallowed up trillions of dollars and put the survival of the global banking system in serious peril.

Section 7.2.3 One Dramatic Moment Impacting this Global Event

Timothy Geithner stated in June of 2008 that the financial system had reached its tipping point: "The combined effect of these factors was a finan-

12 George SOROS, "The Worst Market Crisis in 60 Years," *Financial Times*, January 22, 2008, Retrieved from http://www.ft.com/cms/s/0/24f73610-c91e-11dc-9807-000077b07658.html#axzz1jtkkWJ7H

13 Ibid.

14 "Will Subprime Mess Ripple through the Economy?" MSNBC, March 13, 2007. Retrieved from http://www.msnbc.msn.com/id/17584725#.Txf6qmOonus; Ben S. BERNANKE, "The Subprime Mortgage Market," Remarks by Governor Ben S. Bernanke at the Federal Reserve Bank of Chicago's 43rd Annual Conference on Bank Structure and Competition, Chicago, Illinois, May 17, 2007. Retrieved from http://www.federalreserve.gov/boarddocs/speeches/2005/20050414/default.htm

cial system vulnerable to self-reinforcing asset price and credit cycles."[15] Economists, such as *Paul Krugman* and others, expounded in the media, "Politicians and government officials should have realized that they were re-creating the kind of financial vulnerability that made the Great Depression possible."[16] When Fed Chairman *Alan Greenspan* lobbied to keep the derivatives market unregulated. The U.S. Congress allowed the self-regulation of the derivatives market enacting the Commodity Futures Modernization Act of 2000. Derivatives, including credit default swaps (CDS) were used to hedge or speculate against credit risks. The CDS outstanding volume increased 100-fold from 1998 to 2008, with debt covered from during November 2008 ranging from US$33 to $47 trillion.

The largest economic crisis since the Great Depression was covered in the media essentially from the top down. The perspective has been slanted overwhelmingly from the direction of the political administration and corporate business interests, as the typical citizen turned out to be a victim of the financial crisis, and not the primary actor in the media depiction of it.

Interestingly, the influence and impact of the media subsided when the level of coverage and worrying began to ease, whereby: 1. following the *living story*, the media was like a doctor monitoring the blood pressure of the patient. When there was good news economically, the media coverage trailed off. Media coverage began to move in an inverse relationship with the markets during this time; as stocks began their steady climb, press coverage of the economy generally began falling off. As the Dow moved over 8000, coverage of the economy plunged. The changes in coverage was affecting the ordinary citizen, and as Americans were getting mixed signals through the press and the media, and there was less bad news about the economy as time went on. Signs of the good news began to coincide with the decrease in economic media coverage. 2. Media saturation levels, with economic stories competing for media space, were another key reason the coverage of the economy in the media declined over time. An example was

15 Timothy GEITHNER, "Reducing Systemic Risk in a Dynamic Financial System," Speech, *Federal Reserve Bank of New York*, June 9, 2008. Retrieved from http://www.newyorkfed.org/newsevents/speeches/2008/tfg080609.html

16 Paul KRUGMAN, *The Return of Depression Economics and the Crisis of 2008*, *op. cit.*; Paul KRUGMAN, "Financial Reform 101," *New York Times*, April 1, 2010. Retrieved from http://www.nytimes.com/2010/04/02/opinion/02krugman.html?adxnnl=1&adxnnlx=1326978494-WOo7/m5tevHSi/qRiQCY5A

that the Washington-based congressional battles over the major issues of the stimulus package had subsided and along with them much of the media coverage. The stimulus battle took place in February and March and was eventually signed into law on February 17. The stimulus coverage in the media was almost a third of all the news, however, with the rise of other non economic stories, in fact impeded it for the attention of the media market as the year continued to move forward.

The International Financial Crisis was covered by the media in all sectors, with newspapers, network and cable television, radio news, and news websites all devoted more than a quarter of their storylines to economy-related subjects. There were major differences in the way that the media have focused on the economic news, particularly,

- The newspaper media sector consistently devoted the most attention to the economic financial crisis, yet newspapers had their own political agenda, in effect, creating their own momentum.
- Three major commercial broadcast networks stood out for their emphasis on the impact of the economic crisis on the ordinary American citizen.
- Commercial news reporting websites derived most of their revenue from covering financial news for business clients.
- Radio depended in large part on the type of the program.

The International Financial Crisis tipping point was a combination of factors that led to an epidemic of "denial thinking", as it was spread in a viral manner by the media and leadership institutions. Indeed, we would like to conclude that the world is led by intelligent minds that act independently of the media events surrounding them; however, the magnitude of the contagiousness and stickiness attributes influencing the systems and thought patterns played a role in our "collective reality." In a sense, media oversight and arrogance exerted a growing influence over the meltdown of the world economy. Perhaps we could also argue, with the kind of thinking and media influence that persists, the *tipping point* has yet to end.

Section 7.3 Climate Change

Section 7.3.1 Contagiousness Impacting this Global Event

First, all of the world's leading scientists and academics seemed to all be speaking with the same voice. They all are making essentially the same statement: "... the world's climate is changing dangerously, and humans are to blame." The scientists have been telling us the truth when they say the world is at risk. And second, if we listen to those who are manipulating the media, we are in trouble. The *Intergovernmental Panel on Climate Change (IPCC)* concludes that the global surface temperature will probably rise a further 1.1 to 6.4°C (2.0 to 11.5°F) during the twenty-first century.[17] Scientists understand that even a small increase in the average temperature of the globe could throw off the equilibrium that existed on the earth since a long time before the beginning of mankind, and scientists warn about global melting of the glaciers in the collapsing ice caps. They also warn about the floods and droughts and rising tides. Not a single scientist was found to have taken exception to the consensus position.[18]

Misleading counter arguments exist as some of the biggest deterrents of action on climate change originating in the fossil fuels energy industry, and, particularly the oil industry. Global leaders continued to not be in agreement. The *Bush* administration implemented an industry-formulated disinformation campaign designed to mislead the American public on global warming and to forestall limits on "climate polluters."[19] *Pope Benedict*

17 Gerald A. MEEHL, Thomas F. STOCKER, William D. COLLINS, Pierre FRIEDLINGSTEIN, Amadou T. GAYE, Jonathan M. GREGORY, Akio KITOH, Reto KNUTTI, James M. MURPHY, Akira NODA, Sarah C.B. RAPER, Ian G. WATTERSON, Andrew J. WEAVER, and Zong-Ci ZHAO, "Global Climate Projections," in *Climate Change 2007: The Physical Science Basis. Contribution of Working Group I to the Fourth Assessment Report of the Intergovernmental Panel on Climate Change*, S. Solomon, D. Qin, M. Manning, Z. Chen, M. Marquis, K.B. Averyt, M. Tignor and H.L. Miller (eds.), 2007, Cambridge, UK and New York, NY, Cambridge University Press.

18 James HOGGAN and Richard D. LITTLEMORE, *Climate Cover-up: The Crusade to Deny Global Warming*, Vancouver, Canada, Greystone Books, 2009, p. 20.

19 Tim DICKINSON, "The Secret Campaign of President Bush's Administration To Deny Global Warming," *Rolling Stone*, June 20, 2007. Retrieved from http://www.desmogblog.com/sites/beta.desmogblog.com/files/The%20Secret%20Campaign%20of%20President%20Bush%20rolling%20stone.pdf

XVI stood before a half a million people on a hillside near the Adriatic city of Loreto on the annual Save Creation Day, and said that world leaders must make courageous decisions to save the planet "before it is too late."[20] The UK government-commissioned *Stern Review* on the economic effects of Climate Change, stated *Tony Blair's* assessment showed that scientific evidence of global warming was "overwhelming" and its consequences "disastrous."[21]

In our current information age, the media finds it almost impossible to stay up to speed on every issue, especially, when it has to do with science. Media contagiousness influence on the general public contributes to the confusion through conflicting stories that attempt to minimize the problem and exaggerate the solutions making it more difficult for the public to understand the *living story*. There is not a peer-review system set up for the media and the journalists and the reporters, as they pick up information as it is available on the Internet, cable, and newspapers around them and regurgitate the storylines back into their own reporting. The problem is that it is past the time for those responsible in global media to check their facts and start to share them, ethically and responsibly, as the public deserves the truth.

The *Hadley Model* of the United Kingdom, and the *Canadian Climate Model* predict very different averaged temperature increases for the globe (2.7 and 4.4°C) and (4.9 and 7.9°F)[22] respectively by the year 2100. But with each, the potential increases are significant. The earth's environmental landscape will transform radically. Putting specific dates on (traumatic) potential global events is challenging and exhibits a daunting effort to solve our future reality, yet is a paramount rallying point for media interests and global leaders. Having said that, given the contagiousness of this event will

20 Philip PULLELLA, "Pope Urges, Save the Planet Before it's too Late," *Reuters*, September 2, 2007. Retrieved from http://www.enn.com/top_stories/commentary/22598/print

21 "Climate Change Fight 'Can't Wait'," *BBC*, October 31, 2006. Retrieved from http://news.bbc.co.uk/2/hi/business/6096084.stm

22 *Climate Change 2001: The Scientific Basis*, Contribution of Working Group I to the Third Assessment Report of the Intergovernmental Panel on Climate Change (IPCC), H.T. Houghton, Y. Ding, D.J. Griggs, M. Noguer, P.J. van der Linden, X. Dai, K. Maskell, and C.A. Johnson (eds.), Cambridge and New York, Cambridge University Press, 2001.

continue, the U.S. society is likely to able to *adapt* to most of the climate change impacts on human systems, however these adaptations a coupled with substantial cost for agriculture and forestry, water, human health, and coastal regions.

Section 7.3.2 Stickiness Impacting this Global Event

Leading climate change researchers have concluded that to protect the planet from potentially catastrophic climate change risk, we must stabilize the atmospheric carbon dioxide concentration at 500 ppm, or even as low as 350 ppm. This would require reducing our total global carbon dioxide emissions to no more than 19.1 billion tons per year, less than half of what is predicted for 2030.

The stickiness impact of this event is already moving forward. The United Nations has declared the scientific evidence that the earth was warming is substantiated. They say "…fossil fuel industry, have clearly made achieving the 2°C target much, much harder, if not impossible. They've clearly put the world at risk of far more adverse effects of climate change."[23]

As societies began using substantial amounts of coal and oil in the 19th century, the carbon dioxide rose, and it is now about 40 percent higher than before the Industrial Revolution, and people have put half the extra gas into the air since the late 1970s.

Scientists agree that an increase of five or six degrees is an optimistic outlook. They point out an increase as high as 18 degrees Fahrenheit is possible, which would transform the planet. Growth in developing countries threatens to take the emissions problem to the tipping point, and scientists argue on the improbability to hit the 3.6-degree target (reduced emissions), and the risk will increase that climate change could be an epidemic and towards a tipping point by century's end.

The Hockey Stick theory of climate change has suggested that the past 50 years had been the hottest in several centuries, (if not 1,000 years), and

---

23 David ADAM, "Climate Change Sceptics and Lobbyists put World at Risk, says Top Adviser," *Guardian*, November 22, 2009. Retrieved from http://www.guardian.co.uk/environment/2009/nov/22/climate-change-emissions-scientist-watson

that man-made activities are to blame. Yet, the stickiness reinforces the influence on US Congress to generally accept the rising carbon dioxide numbers, recognizing that the increase is caused by human activity, and acknowledging that the earth is warming.. But they distort the media space based on short term political agendas..

Developments in media politics of climate change provide evidence of a conspiracy to debate the idea of human-driven climate change. Climate change skeptics contend researchers manipulated and suppressed data. Conclusions are essentially the same, theory or no theories, the world is still warming and scientists would still demonstrate it.

In order to avoid the tipping point event associated with dangerous climate change, developed countries must cut emissions by at least 25 per cent from 1990 levels by 2020, and global emissions must peak and begin to decline by 2020 at the latest. If not, significant global changes are likely to occur: losses in biodiversity and increasing frequency on weather-related events e.g. droughts or floods, with a disproportionate impact on vulnerable communities. The effects of climate change are expected to be greatest in developing countries in terms of loss of life and relative effects on investment and the economy. Finally, as this stickiness continues, sociologists have pointed out that when it comes to vulnerable communities, small climate shocks share strong linkages to extreme social instability, precipitated by warring for scarce resources made even scarcer.

Section 7.3.3 One Dramatic Moment Impacting this Global Event

The requirements for air, water, food, and shelter for populations of these magnitudes will inevitably create a series of *global tipping points*. As economies and governments attempt to service the demand, breakdowns in supply chains and environmental effects will be catastrophic.

While issues of sovereignty and nation states and labels of religious background and ownership of resources may have worked in a world very different than the one that we are facing, the new realities, similar to the changes like the Ice Age, or even the beginning of man, are now rapidly being put forth as the questions of the day. The cost of media inaction could be the extinction of the human race.

Perhaps, first question which should be proactively included in the media *global consciousness* discussions: "So how much is this going to cost to save the planet?" The short answer is trillions of dollars over a few decades. It is a significant sum but a relatively small fraction of the world's total economic output.[24] "The good news is that everybody now is supporting our proposal for financing," said *Dr. Umaña*, the Costa Rican delegate. "The bad news is that it's happening 15 years too late. Without real money on the table, this will be a disaster."[25]

The *amount* of media (space) information and the *clarity* (accuracy) of the content will eventually ring through. The *global consciousness* for how media delivers the content will no longer be cloaked in some kind of profit-making agenda beyond the short-term gains.

In summary, the planet is currently caught in two very detrimental pathways: one, where population growth and global warming together are driving the demand for resources, and two, at the same time, improved productivity means more factories that produce more products, making more global warming, and the two pathways meet.

The series of tipping points for Climate change will take place gradually, as some populations will be affected in the short term, while whole regions and continents will later be impacted. Unfortunately, many of the media and those in leadership positions have a wait and see attitude as they *adapt* to the change. While true, Climate Change is both a man-made problem and a natural process relative to the order of our environment, the media role and contributions to the characteristics leading to the contagiousness and stickiness are very similar to what is occurring with the first two case studies. A new media *global consciousness* will be necessary to avoid a global catastrophe, *tipping point* and, this will require very serious problem-solving for future leaders.

---

24 John M. BRODER, "Climate Deal Likely to Bear Big Price Tag," *New York Times*, December 8, 2009. Retrieved from http://www.nytimes.com/2009/12/09/science/earth/09cost.html?pagewanted=all

25 Ibid.

Section 7.4 Comparisons

With regard to the description of what is considered an global event that is in fact impacted by media, the case studies here have much in common in as much as these events coexisted both in physical reality and real-time in the media. And as defined by their duration and their characteristics, each reached across broad platforms of differing media technology to reach their respective audiences.

Case Study Similarities and Differences

The specific case study attributes and characteristics, although different from each other, occurred in different sectors of the global agendas and completely dominated the respective sector. The Obama Presidential Campaign - political, the International Financial Crisis - economic, and Climate Change, perhaps involving these sectors and more, and in this context - cultural, crossing over nation-state borders. Nevertheless, each case study was largely impacted by the media environments by their very definition of being global events.

The Obama Presidential Campaign introduced several interlocking dynamics that led to his election that were influenced by the technological media tools available and deployed, as well as the crisis financially on Wall Street. In contrast, the International Financial Crisis 2007-2010 followed similar patterns of earlier financial crisis. Not only were they amplified and to a degree, manipulated by the media, short-term gains by both the banking sectors and investment houses and the governmental institutions benefited and profited from its occurrence.

The Climate Change study is altogether different. A closer examination shows that even though the other two case studies had similar patterns with regard to their attributes and characteristics that were played out in the media environments, they were largely a function of the agendas--they were driving the objectives economically and politically. The Climate Change history shows that in the case of global environmental changes, there exist economic and political benefits. For example, some countries may have more control and viable access to fossil fuels or more abundant sea and foodstuffs. However these strategies are merely tactics that are doomed by the convergence of climate change event. These are linked in part to man-made activities and reports by the media environments.

Stated another way, comparing the first two case studies in the same context as the third, is difficult at best. However, as stated early on, the objective is to demonstrate how the media similarities might effectuate the outcome in a positive way for Climate Change, rising above political and economic nation-state agendas. There are many factors that create a natural resistance among nation states to relinquish control of their media resources, and the viability of cooperation at such a large scale diminishes the comfort level of boundaries that states are normally accustomed to imposing. However, the Climate Change issue mandates that we address the solutions from a different vantage point and that we may have at our disposal current and future media technology to achieve this.

There now appears to be the seeds of a *global consciousness*, grown from the media similarities in the first two case study evidence, in *real time* as *living stories*, with social media and database sharing that allows for immediate dissemination of content information for action.

Section 7.5 Future Technologies: Opportunities and Constraints

Although media impact on global events points out a fundamental phenomenon of dynamic relationships between how the attributes and characteristics lead to their ultimate tipping points, when coupled with the diplomatic missions of nation states, the idea of casting this theory across territorial lines becomes indeed a complex undertaking. Despite the relatively sparse amount of published research about tipping points relative to media impacts on global events, the topic presented in the context of Climate Change, provides a springboard for diplomats, scholars, and other analysts a potential for addressing future projects.

With new theories and analysis it is difficult to create methodologies of analyzing complex phenomena to progress past the point where detailed methods and implementation measures can be employed and deployed at such scale. This may in fact be a reflection of a variety of conditions, and ultimately it suggests that world community generally does not understand the impact of media in this context on their own nationalistic events and/or the global events occurring around them.

The reasons for this are unclear since the case studies examined in this context, by defining and analyzing their attributes and characteristics, can all be considered relevant in applying this theory. One possibility is that these suggestions are so conceptual, in a very general sense, and give little consideration to the subtleties that can change media influence on a specific global event. Another possibility is the assumption that the scale and magnitude of these events are so extreme that application theoretically is impossible given the changing dynamics within the case studies themselves.

Why this Might Work

Gauging by the potential of future media technology to disseminate and deploy, in real time, information, data and research about the world around us, it provides clear opportunities as to what will be required by nation states and world leaders to take into account their responsibilities and roles for addressing Climate Change. In a general sense, the Tipping Point Theory applied to the Climate Change issue offers some solutions if such nation states can determine their relationships towards the overall event. At this time there are such organizations (such as the Intergovernmental Panel on Climate Change) and other nonpartisan media entities that are only beginning to propagate the problems and the solutions. The convergence of characteristics that will lead and could favor the success of the global momentum (*global consciousness*) towards addressing Climate Change needs to occur with fundamental systems that are driven by global political, economic, and cultural objectives.

Why this May not Work

First, a cautionary note, along with future forms of media technological developments, there rests the possibility of certain nation states putting in motion a chain of events that are ultimately dictated by their own view of survival. This may or may not amount to intervention of normal media processes as well as information systems that carry content.

Understanding the application of the Tipping Point theory may sometimes preclude its being acknowledged as a viable concept in such cases. The sizable dimensions and the impacts of the media and populations that might be involved in some of the applications may preclude its being a success. Yet, with the magnitude of media scale and potential impact on global events, the approach that is outlined here is sometimes not adequate. The analysis of the factors conducive to the success or failure of the Tipping point theory could make it doubtful that the application could be resolved with differing nation-state agendas, which are substantial impediments to success of the theory. And ultimately, the intensity of the potential conflicts of interest, politically, economically, and culturally provide major impediments for addressing the relationships between nation states and the key media players impacting the events at such global scale.

Comparisons: Summary

These case studies show that media impact can have an effect on global events, and they also demonstrate a satisfactory framework for addressing the attributes and characteristics that can evolve into tipping points. In addition, the comparisons of these case studies provide a body of information that allows us to deduce general circumstances that might make the relationships between media and global events more viable. By reviewing the attributes and characteristics in each of these case studies, the set of conditions that may have contributed to the tipping points was arrived at, and from this we can make judgments about conditions that may lead to the outcome.

The case studies bring into light the potential determinants for success or failure of our Tipping Point theory. By considering these overall attributes and the magnitude qualitatively of the characteristics specific to the individual case studies, one can identify situations in which future media and global event phenomena might be a downside and highlight an appropriate option for nation states to consider in their efforts to address future events. And, we might also determine when such an application may have little chance of succeeding, for example: The comparisons of the case studies showed that all of them succeeded in following the specific attribute progression from *contagiousness*, to *stickiness* and the *one dramatic moment*, however, the issues of the media influence and control over these events is a complex analysis.

In addition, the case studies all showed that new media developments led to new solutions and new challenges. During the Obama Presidential Campaign, the micro-targeting of Internet messages could easily have been a tactic that the McCain organization could have employed or couching of his "fundamentals of the economy of strong statement" -contagiousness could have been presented from an opposing perspective in the media, thereby capturing the benefits of the media tools available. During International Financial Crisis, the pure saturation crossed all media forms, lead to irreversible stickiness with the net effect of snowballing the viral effect of the economic downturn and the financial and governmental reactions worldwide. Such drawbacks must be assessed in their own right in order to determine the future net effect on the issue of Climate Change with media technology that may be positive or negative, and whether it will be desirable for nation states to tolerate and/or manage the issues that may exist as we move forward in time.

These types of questions give rise to more fundamental ones, such as: Whether these issues of media impact on global events are inherent to our concepts of who we are as mankind and how we interact, and/or whether the problems that arise in the context of the predictions for global change can be addressed in the same context as those studied here and can be anticipated and avoided? To examine the possible answers to such questions, one has to consider that the case studies point out that there is an immediate net relationship between media and global events, and this has been evolving through time. The opportunities to reach larger audiences of populations across territorial boundaries are a tangible objective and certainly can be weighed against the impacts that may be detrimental to us all. More importantly, the long-term problems weigh against the benefits of such global media consciousness makes no broader impact worldwide when it relates to Climate Change.

When we examine more closely the relationships in media, we can see that it is being betrayed for Climate Change and chosen number of factors contributing to the opposition and global agendas. The research about this question always mentions the fact that there are agendas being manipulated for short-term monetary and political gains, which allows us to conclude that the role for media in the future is one of being a major influence, effectuating a positive outcome.

Recent events throughout the Arab region during the summer of 2011 point out territorial boundaries create obstacles that are clearly only referenced on maps and printed matter. The demonstrations and social unrest poured out of this region via cell phones, social media, and a *real-time* coverage whereby existing regimes were unable to contain the phenomena, and it led to individual *tipping points* that changed the history of these countries. The same impact on an international scale will be evident when we reach our critical *one dramatic moment* as relates to Climate Change. The limitations of map-drawn boundaries and printed matter regulations devised for strategy and security of nation states will fall by the wayside when facing the scale of the Climate Change imperatives as relates to population migration in search of food and water, resources for survival, and ultimately the air we breathe.

Having compared these case studies, some judgments about the attributes and the characteristics contribute in a general sense to their *one dramatic moment*. While each case study contains some unique elements to accommodate the specific situation at hand, it is logical to assume that the results of the analysis and comparisons of them reflect some of the common characteristics that can be identified to link media impact with these global events, for example:

People

It appears that individuals create conditions that are conducive to the evolving nature of the attributes in each of the case studies. In each of the case study there are individuals who represent an opportunity for populations to follow their lead, whether political, economic, or cultural. It provides an opportunity for opposing entities to challenge, presenting the essential ingredients for moving through evolution of the attributes towards a tipping point.

Organizations

The organizations in each of the case studies provide a potential source of conflicting agendas, and I point out a presence of resources that can be manipulated via the media deployment. This kind of media activity and the likelihood that organizations influence the amount and types of information that is distributed, in essence, maximizes the media impact on events from a tipping point standpoint, and again the understanding of the role of the attributes influence which strategic decisions are implemented and deployed via the media sectors. In the past there were fewer nation states that would have such agendas; however, given the state-of-the-art media, in the future it becomes more and more likely that they will move towards a *global consciousness*.

Media

The case studies demonstrate with a range of media audiences that the people and organizations involved work towards the *phenomena* of the *tipping point*. In short, the phenomena of *one dramatic moment* can keep a story line on the path towards its own self determinism that can only be concluded in this manner. Each of the case studies here generated some opposition released at the time and considered in the media with broader public awareness that allowed contrary opinions to become more wide spread.

Events

The ability of an event as a *living story* to be told to a population in such a way as it is understood and followed clearly was demonstrated in each of our case studies as being both a contributing characteristic and detrimental if the incident is too complex in the case of Climate Change. Throughout history, when an event involved a longer duration and affected larger populations, the media was involved in defining positions and influencing outcomes. With the evolving *global consciousness*, one hopes this will improve.

Section 7.6 Tipping Point Attribute Compilations: Historical Comparisons

Putting the *Tipping Point* attributes and characteristics into a historical context provides challenges for exhibiting the influences of media over short and long period of times. Even with the evidence of the particular characteristic, some of these influences may be difficult to identify. However, for the attribute and characteristics identified in each of the case studies, I propose to also visit the measures of similar events and exhibit, on a relative scale, the media impact in terms of their tipping point attributes and characteristics as researched and identified for each global event. The historical comparison of the three case studies highlight that there are people, organizations, media, and events inherently critical to development and potential for a tipping point to occur, and with basis for influence from the media sectors

The purpose is three- fold: (1) contrasting and comparing the attributes and characteristics from a very historical context and broadly identify similarities and differences (2) identifying fundamental trends, media delivery systems and technology that may be prevalent, and (3) providing for the three case studies to be measured qualitatively relative to other world events with similar characteristic importance and influence on the tipping point attribute. It should be noted that there are limits to the number of similar events and quantity of characteristics identified for historical comparisons and the sizing the research scope and magnitude accordingly for this version.

Using the tipping point methodology as applied in the case studies certainly provides a basis for historical comparisons. Media may hold some very real options for how we as a civilization go about the business of the future world events. My approach strives to open up the opportunity to pursue additional questions that before had been effectively impossible to conceptualize. For example,

- Can we characterize the dynamics of media impact on key global events?
- Does information change and influence the evolution of the tipping point baseline as it evolves and propagates?
- Is it be possible to use this tipping point model over long periods of time, in a way that is essential to discovering the core solution to other world event and ultimately, climate change?

Granted, one could combine the approaches here into several multidiscipline approaches towards addressing scientific, political, cultural and financial issues associated with this phenomenon. And more generally, it appears useful to further understand the media impact on the different tipping point attributes and characteristics as exhibited during global events.

Extracting from the research in the proceeding chapters, I present the case studies with the goal of understanding the attributes, characteristics and relationships in a historical perspective. Looking at the purposes of the case studies and the research questions that were posed earlier, one can see how the attributes took place in relative groupings of people, organizations, media, and events, and the net results. I attempt to identify and/or qualify the relative impact among them. This study of the relationships evolves and becomes more important relative to the overall research question of trying to point out that by analyzing these attributes it might influence and predict and/or help avoid a potential global tipping point from occurring.

Obama Presidential Campaign (2007-2008)

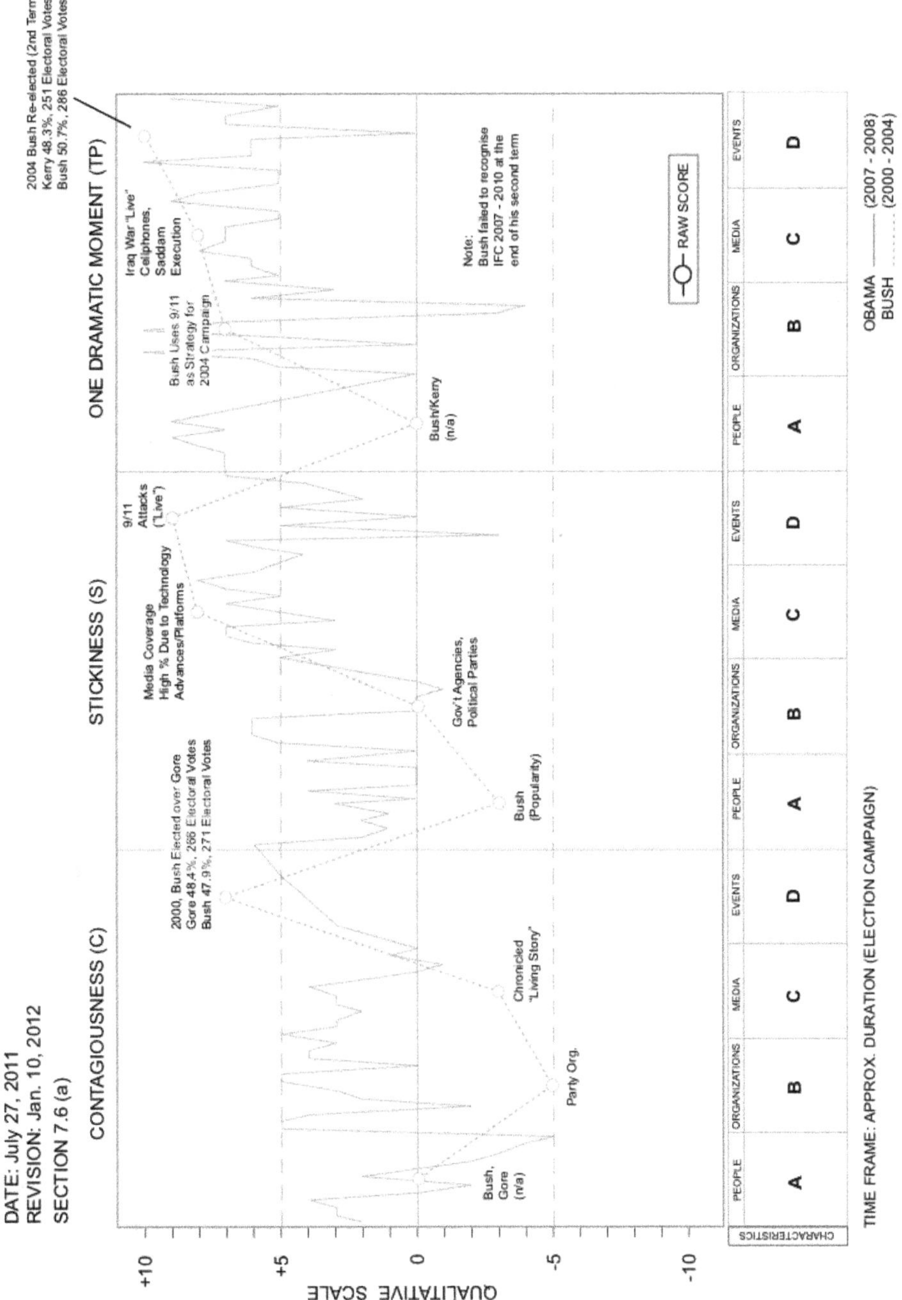

FIGURE NO. 7.6 (a): PRESIDENTIAL CAMPAIGNS: ATTRIBUTES: COMPARISONS: HISTORICAL

International Financial Crisis (2007-2011)

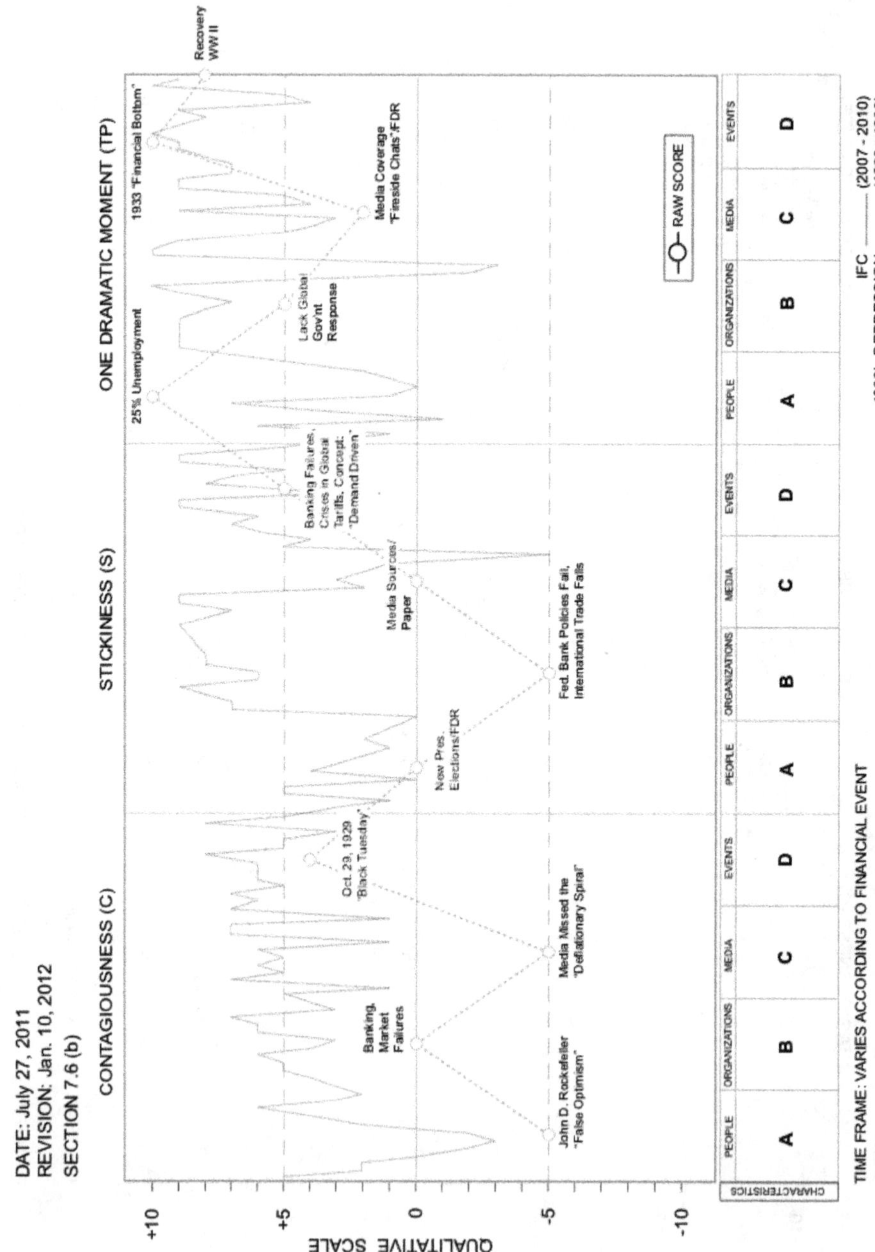

FIGURE NO. 7.6 (b): FINANCIAL CRISIS: ATTRIBUTES: COMPARISONS: HISTORICAL

Climate Change (2000-2030)

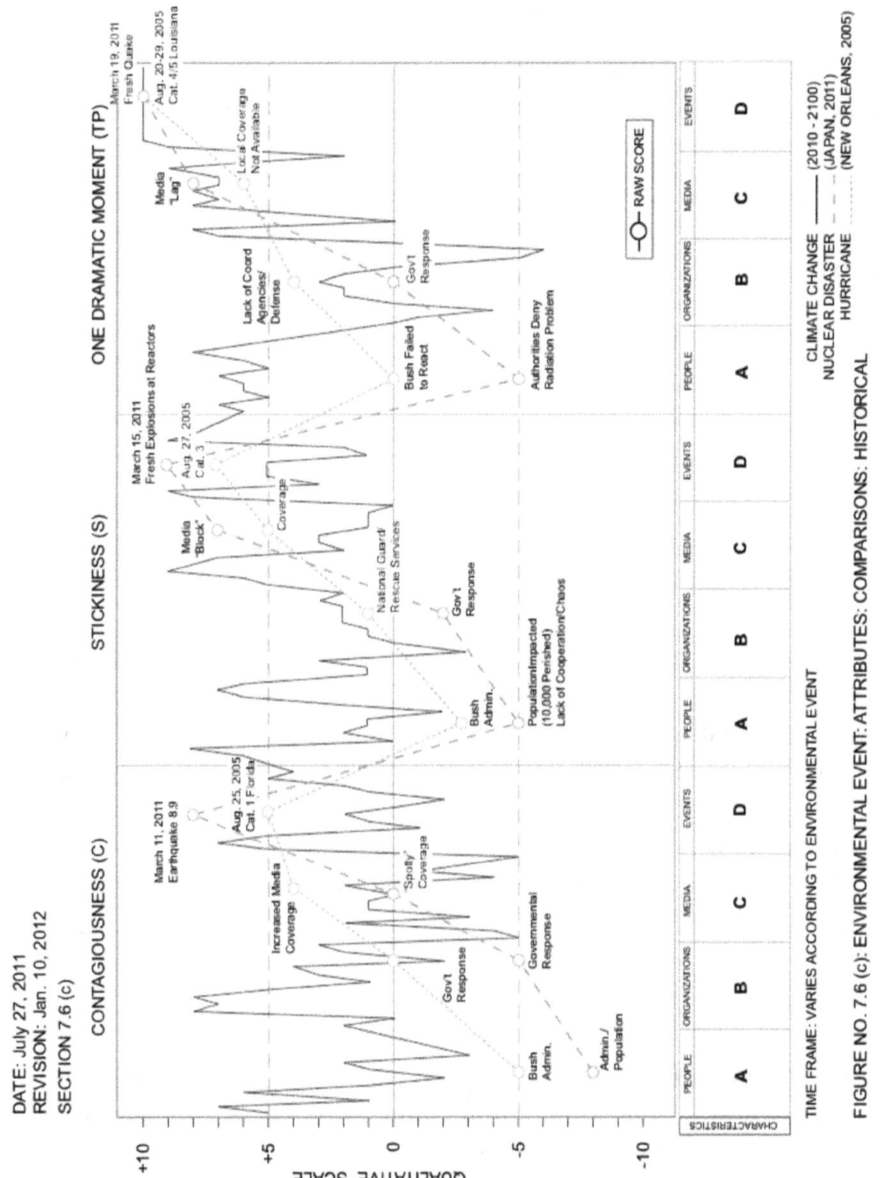

FIGURE NO. 7.6 (c): ENVIRONMENTAL EVENT: ATTRIBUTES: COMPARISONS: HISTORICAL

Section 7.7 Media Development: Global Events: Historical Dateline

A few decades ago media reporting was through newspapers, radio, and television. Things are different now as we are witnessing a revolution of people-oriented reporting of global events. This element of intimate knowledge of the event being reported has dramatically changed. This revolution has intrinsically altered the way events become more personal and more accurate – however more subjective.

As highlighted in the case studies and analysis and comparisons, there are three (3) key milestones when comparing historical media development relative to a dateline context that can now be best described as:

Real Time

Cyber culture is a phenomena associated with the Internet and network communications

Media are the cultural objects that use technology for distribution and exhibition.

Media today is a mix between older cultural conventions for data representation, access, (and manipulation), and recent *real time* technological conventions. In order for this approach to be of maximum benefit, development of a much more comprehensive comparative analysis would be required, which would correlate the history of technology with social, political, and economical histories with the significant milestones. Technology offers some unique insights into what were previously only identified with manual techniques.

Living Story

The avant-garde is about new ways of accessing and analyzing information, whereby, algorithms, this essential part of the *living stories*, do not depend on technology, but can be executed by humans. Media has increased quality of the content and frequency of communication between people all over the world and the Internet.

Global Consciousness

> Changes in the new media environment create a series of milestones in the concept of *global consciousness* of influence. A trend of the *global consciousness* is not only as a geographical expansion from a nation to worldwide, particularly as the population of the world increases and barriers to entry and access are removed. Virtual communities are being established online and transcend geographical boundaries, thereby eliminating social limitations. The new media connects like-minded others worldwide as a foundation for a *global consciousness*. Society doesn't follow a script based on the course of technological change, since many factors, including individual inventiveness and entrepreneurialism, intervene in the process of science, technical innovation and social interactions.

What I propose to highlight in the dateline of historical Tipping Point milestones applied to a time context, population growth and media development context. Questioning whether, in fact, this theory presents the leading edge equations for understanding current and future context for world events. Ultimately these milestones show what drives world societies closer together or further apart. And if similar tipping point attributes and characteristics were evident if one were to expand the scope and complexity of this version? Supporting the notion, whether or not the great shift taking place in the world now, proves to be less about the domain of individual cultures and more about *global consciousness*.

Media Impacts and Global Events Website

For further information please visit the
Media impact and Global Events Website:

http://mdgparis.typepad.com/global_media_and_world_ev/

This website tracks, highlights, categorizes and provides a articles and commentary related to Tipping Point Attributes and Characteristics, as well as information and recent updates related specifically to the three case studies included in this version and other Media and Global Event issues.

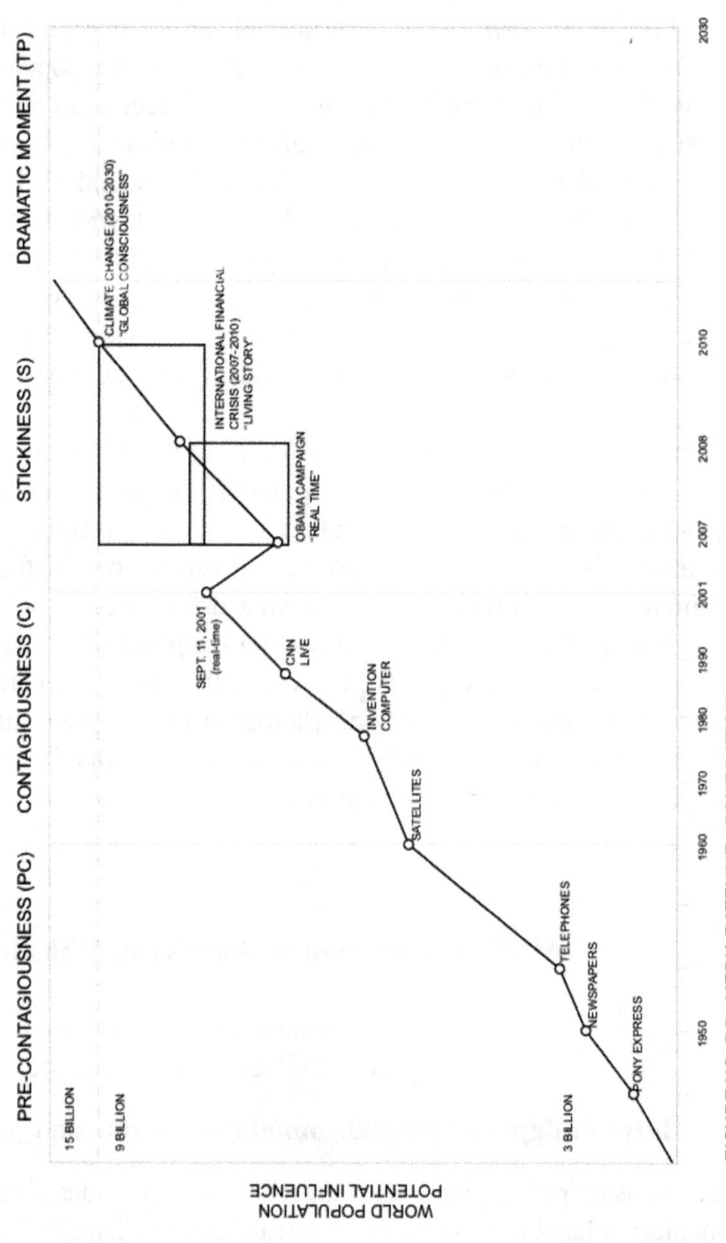

FIGURE NO: 7.7 : MEDIA DATELINE : COMPILATION

CHAPTER 8
CONCLUSIONS

The application of the Tipping Point theory in the context of global events and media impact provides a conceptual framework for understanding the role of media and international events and provides for understanding of how society can respond and develop around it. Through this process, the tipping points attributes and characteristics are recognized as a means by which international events may be analyzed in the context of media influence. Underlining these phenomena is the notion that events on a worldwide scale can be analyzed and predicted. A simple application of this phenomenon suggests that if a window is broken and left unrepaired, i.e. the international financial system, whereby, if it appears that the system is unregulated, unmanaged, or that no one cares about it and no one is in charge, soon more windows will be broken, and the condition will spread. In countries or regions with lack of financial oversights and monitoring regulation are all the equivalent of broken windows.[26] Perhaps, in keeping with the example, such broken windows promote invitations to further financial tipping points - as is evident in events in Ireland and Greece that affected the entire European Union in 2011-2. This is the epidemic of finance. The effects are contagious - just as a trend is contagious. It can start

26 Wilson and Kelling argue that impacts and events are the evitable result of disorder.

with just one broken window (or country financial failure) and spread like a virus, sometimes instantaneously, particularly if the message is delivered via television or internet, to an entire region or population in the world. The impetus to engage in a certain type of behavior is not necessarily coming from a certain kind of person or culture, but from a feature of the environment, i.e. the financial sector–banking.

Further, the Broken Window Theory postulates that if a particular behavior in a community (or world) goes unaddressed, it signals that nobody cares about the community (or world) resulting in additional behavior of the same type. Given that current information technology has evolved with the Internet, text messaging, Twitter, and a 24-hour media cycle, this creates a combustible mix indeed. This also provides an opportunity for the application of conceptual framework for understanding tipping points to evolve together with the idea of embracing international momentum or the global media consciousness to create legal instruments and policies with these developments that might influence the world's most pressing issue: Climate Change.

In addition, as a potential mechanism for international relations, media tipping points and global events has a wide variety of applications; among them is a process of dissemination of unbiased, factual information and resolution of disputes between countries and regions. Since some countries and regions are driven by different growth and economic objectives, particularly between developed and undeveloped nations, understanding the context of their potential tipping point contributions, actions or reactions and how this is being portrayed by the media and disseminated on a worldwide scale.

"What if the pollution coming from our island nations was threatening the very existence of the major emitters?" stated President *Marcus Stephens* of the tiny island state of *Nauru*, speaking on behalf of some 14 island states vulnerable to disappearing. "What would be the nature of today's (climate change) debate under those circumstances?"…"Climate change is a threat to international peace and security," *Mr. Stephens* said to the *UN Security Council* in June of 2011, comparing it to nuclear proliferation or terrorism given its potential to destabilize governments and create conflict.[27]

I would argue the application of the Tipping Point theory has the potential to change the very nature of our approach to these phenomena as countries start to understand the interdependent relationships and responsibilities. The Tipping Point's conceptual framework can offer an alternative path towards analyzing and adjusting future impacts. The cases examined in this current version demonstrate that tipping points analyzed in the context of media and its impact on global events shows, indeed, that there can be success in viewing the trends and sequential development of world events in this manner. It could be also argued that for this reason Tipping Point theory could be used to address the media role with regard to the climate change issue.

I recognize the conceptual framework that has been put forth is an option which may not fully explain all the results beyond my initial premises. While there may be several possible explanations for this, one, is the particularly difficult task of trying to analyze and assemble all of the data, opinions, and research relative to the size of each specific case study. As evidenced by the data and documentation employed in presenting this framework, there are virtually limitless opportunities to refine and focus the strengths of this argument.

Having said that, the fact that climate change is such a large-scale global event, the application of Tipping Points in this context may yet to give birth to a known practice and a further refined systematic process for recognition, analysis, or consideration as a potential model for addressing the media impact on global events, even though this potential was recognized in the isolated comments and sources that were found and cited throughout the three case studies.

Stated another way, tipping points can become incorporated into the structure of the international system of media relationships and could become almost routine for countries to incorporate the same global consciousness objectives - such as establishing a secure climate change agenda with deployment of resources and technological means coupled with diplomatic

27 "The Environment in the News," United Nations Environment Programme, July 22, 2011. Retrieved from www.unep.org/cpi/briefs/2011July22.doc, p. 9.

missions and infrastructure as a way of meeting the goals associated with such a formidable task.

Despite my argument that tipping points are connected to global events, which unfold and are influenced during the attributes and characteristics in the analysis here, it is likely that a parallel future objective to addressing the tipping point for climate change should recognize and focus on the lack of knowledge and the understanding of the impacts by the world's growing population on our environment and how media holds the key to our very existence.

The degree of certainty that it is necessary for our world leaders to develop solutions merely serves the dispute, that this, as with any large-scale human endeavor, requires the deployment and execution of new concepts and approaches mandated by survival on the world stage. A committee panel of scientists, former government officials, and national security experts in October of 2011 were already urging the US government to begin researching a radical and drastic fix to avoid climate change disaster by directly manipulating the Earth's climate to lower temperatures. This committee proposed extreme engineering techniques, which included scattering particles in the air to mimic the cooling effect of volcanoes and stationing orbiting mirrors in space to reflect sunlight. The panel stated that it was time to begin researching and testing such ideas, "…just in case the climate system reaches a tipping point and the swift remedial action was required."[28]

Everyone has to understand what is at stake. Basically the current body of climate change proposals fall into two broad groups, one, which is widely known as *climate remediation*, which concerns carbon dioxide *removal* from the atmosphere. What is good about these is they are "generally uncontroversial and don't introduce new global risks," according to *Ken Caldeira*, a climate expert at *Stanford University* and a panel member.[29] The controversy arises more with the second group of techniques, termed *solar radiation management* approaches, which involve physically manipulating the amount of solar energy that bounces back into space before it can be absorbed by the year. The problem with these techniques is that they

28 Cornelia DEAN, "Group Urges Research Into Aggressive Efforts to Fight Climate Change," *New York Times*, October 4. 2011. Retrieved from http://www.nytimes.com/2011/10/04/science/earth/04climate.html.

29 Ibid.

pose a risk of upsetting the Earth's natural rhythms. With them, *Dr. Caldeira* states, "The real question is what are the unknowns: Are you creating more risk than you are alleviating?"[30] *Joe Romm*, a fellow at the Center of American Progress, has made a similar point, comparing geo-engineering to a dangerous course of chemotherapy and radiation to treat a condition that otherwise is curable through diet and exercise or, in this case, emissions reduction.

The bottom line is that many countries fault developed nations and the United States in particular, for government inaction on climate change, especially given its longtime role as the chief contributor to the problem. *Frank Loy*, a former Under Secretary of State who is now the nation's chief climate negotiator, suggests that people around the world would see past these issues if the United States embraced geo-engineering studies, provided that it was "very clear about what kind of research is undertaken and what the safeguards are."[31] Clearly media could deliver these messages.

The case studies in this version showed that there is nothing inherent in the phenomena of the tipping point attributes and characteristics that would prevent such an application from being used in resolving the issue of climate change. A broad range of factors involved with climate change, the history and future development of media, and global impact suggests that we stand a better chance of yielding positive results in some circumstances than others.

The tipping points analyzed in the Obama Presidential Campaign and the International Financial Crisis 2007-2010, viewed by measureable impact, point out the difference required for the issue as large as Climate Change. Whereby, there were many attributes and characteristics shared by first two case studies that can be applied to Climate Change, and in a sense, the conceptual framework produced a positive result vis-à-vis a methodology for categorizing and exhibiting the specific attributes of contagiousness, stickiness, and the one dramatic point in their evolution and the media's role and importance.

From another perspective, the analysis utilizing Tipping Points Theory

30 Ibid.

31 Ibid.

would appear to at least offer a chance of success in addressing the media impact on Climate Change issue, given the scope, magnitude and impact of the event in terms of population effects, country resources, and/or economic activity involved, which if not resolved, could become the subject of a very high intensity conflict worldwide between nations. Meanwhile, attributes that are unique to the Climate Change issue must be taken into account when weighing the viability of using tipping points and evolving media technology to address them. Thus, tipping points as applied in this context to media impact and global events may be a means of addressing certain world issues such as climate change.

This also raises the question as to whether or not applying Tipping Point theory universally to media impacts on all global events is legitimate. This remains a subject for further research. Nonetheless, the case studies presented here fall within the limits of what can be analyzed, and what can be used conceptually for addressing the further developments of the Climate Change issue and other global events with similar characteristics. Further applications of this concept in the context of media impact and global events may bring to light more clearly where the opportunities are and allow a more refined approach to be developed.

The case studies presented here provide evidence that the phenomenon of tipping points as a means of analyzing media impact and global events is certainly practical on an international scale, and with greater visibility of this approach and practice, would bring it in more fully into focus with acceptance as a recognized conceptual framework.

Media Impacts and Global Events Website

For further information please visit the
Media impact and Global Events Website:

http://mdgparis.typepad.com/global_media_and_world_ev/

This website tracks, highlights, categorizes and provides a articles and commentary related to Tipping Point Attributes and Characteristics, as well as information and recent updates related specifically to the three case studies included in this version and other Media and Global Event issues.

Discussion Questions:

1. Does the solution lie (for influencing world event tipping points) in the technological revolution and the conscience of man's morality to survive?

2. What is the relation between global communications and national/international events? Are they a cause of or an effect of change? Can they be explained or verified by either of these?

3. Do media cause these attributes to occur and/or does it promote or reflect tipping points or misrepresent international events?

4. What is global about global media?

5. How much does government's control influence international global communications?

6. Are national cultures threatened by developments in international communications?

7. Does the Internet threaten old media?

8. Do new communication technologies lead to a more or less democratic world?

9. Is the world divided into communication-rich and communication-poor regions? What are the consequences of such divides as it relates to events?

10. Will global super intergovernmental powers, with resources and capacity far beyond the UN and European Union, China and US systems be created? And will they be able to craft a solution?

11. Will the demand and need for resources and economics force an agenda of mass media imperialism? Consider China, Africa, the US, Russia, and other nation states with nuclear and technological advancements and media tools.

12. What are the socio and psychological effects on populations in relation to their level of technological advancements and maturity about the world stage, and how will these actors play the game?

13. What is the relationship between the worldwide development of state-of-the-art technological "tools" of communication and scope and impact of particular events?

14. Can the frequency and magnitude be correlated in a timeline historically through the development of these tools and delivering systems?

15. Can the frequency spikes be correlated between the dates of media innovation and introduction/intervention?

16. Where and how were populations and systems impacted and events influenced/changed?

17. With this statistical data, what trends can be identified?

18. Is there a relationship between first world and third world perceptions and technology, and how and at what rate is this changing as technology continues to develop?

19. What are the possible outcomes, if the trends are quantified and verified?

20. How and what can be done to reverse/influence/control the trends?

21. Can we fix climate change?

BIBLIOGRAPHY

PART ONE REFERENCES
CHAPTER 1: TIPPING POINT THEORY

CONDON, William, "Cultural Microrhythms," in *Interaction Rhythms*, 1974, New York, Human Sciences.

FRIEDMAN, Thomas, *The World is Flat: A Brief History of the Twenty-first Century*, New York, Farrar, Straus and Giroux, 2005.

GLADWELL, Malcolm, *The Tipping Point: How Little Things can Make a Big Difference*. New York, Back Bay Books, 2002.

GRANOVETTER, Mark, "Threshold Model of Collective Behavior," *The American Journal of Sociology*, 83, 1978, pp. 1420–1443.

GRODZINS, Morton, *The Metropolitan Area as a Racial Problem*. Pittsburgh, University of Pittsburgh Press, 1958.

LINKOLA, Pentti, "The Doctrine of Survival and Doctor Ethics," 1992.

National Security Agency (NSA), *Information Operations Roadmap* (National Security Archive Electronic Briefing Book No. 177), October 30, 2003.

SCHELLING, Thomas, “Dynamic Models of Segregation,” *Journal of Mathematical Sociology*, 1, 1972, pp. 143–186.

United Nations Department of Economic and Social Affairs/Population Division (UNDES), “World Population in 2300 to be around Nine Billion Persons,” December 9, 2003. Retrieved from http://www.un.org/apps/news/story.asp?NewsID=12439

U.S. Census Bureau, *International Database, June 2011 Update, World Population 1950–2050*, 2010. Retrieved from http://www.census.gov/population/international/data/idb/worldpopgraph.php

WELLS, Gary and PETTY, Richard, “The Effects of Head Movement on Persuasion: Compatibility and Incompatibility of Responses,” *Basic and Applied Social Psychology*, 1, 1989, pp. 219–230.

WILSON, James and KELLING, George, “Broken Windows. The Police and Neighbourhood Safety,” *Atlantic Magazine*, 3, 1982, 29–38. Retrieved from http://www.theatlantic.com/magazine/archive/1982/03/broken-windows/4465/

CHAPTER 2: MEDIA

ATTON, Chris, “Reshaping Social Movement Media for a New Millennium,” *Social Movement Studies*, 2, 2003, pp. 3–15.

BOYD, Clark, “BBC News – North Korea creates Twitter and YouTube presence,” *BBC*, August 18, 2010. Retrieved from http://www.bbc.co.uk/news/world-us-canada-11007825

BRODZINSKY, Sibylla, “Facebook Used to Target Colombia’s FARC with Global Rally,” *The Christian Science Monitor (Boston)*, February 4, 2008. Retrieved from http://www.csmonitor.com/World/Americas/2008/0204/p04s02-woam.html

CARVIN, Andy, “Welcome to the Twitterverse,” *National Public Radio*, February 28, 2009. Retrieved from http://www.npr.org/templates/story/story.php?storyId=101265831

CASTELLS, Manuel, *The Rise of the Network Society (The Information Age: Economy, Society and Culture, Volume 1)*, Hoboken, Wiley-Blackwell, 1996.

CLEE, Nicholas, "The Bookseller," *Guardian Unlimited*, March 1, 2003, Retrieved from http://www.guardian.co.uk/books/2003/mar/01/featuresreviews.guardianreview30

CROSBIE, Vin, "What is New Media?" 1998, *Sociology Central*. Retrieved from http://www.sociology.org.uk/as4mm3a.doc

CROTEAU, David and HOYNES, William, (2003). *Media Society: Industries, Images and Audiences* (3rd edition). Thousand Oaks, Pine Forge Press, 2003.

DOUGLAS, Nick, "Twitter Blows Up at SXSW Conference," *Gawker*, March 12, 2007. Retrieved from http://gawker.com/243634/twitter-blows-up-at-sxsw-conference

DURHAM, Meenakshi, and KELLNER, Douglas, *Media and Cultural Studies: Keyworks (KeyWorks in Cultural Studies)*, Malden, MA and Oxford, UK, Blackwell Publishing, 2001.

Edelman, *Edelman Trust Barometer 2008*, 2008. Retrieved from http://www.edelman.com/trust/2008/TrustBarometer08_FINAL.pdf

Edelman, *Edelman Trust Barometer 2010*. 2010. Retrieved from http://www.edelman.com/trust/2010/

FELDMAN, Tony, *An Introduction to Digital Media*, London, UK, Routledge, 1997.

FLEW, Terry and HUMPHREY, Sal, "Games: Technology, Industry, Culture," in *New Media: An Introduction* (second edition), 2005, South Melbourne, Australia, Oxford University Press, pp. 101–114.

GOLDMAN, Russell (January 5, 2007). "Facebook Gives Snapshot of Voter Sentiment". ABC News. Retrieved March 23, 2010.

GRIER, Thom, *et al.*, "The 100 Greatest Movies, TV Shows, Albums, Books, Characters, Scenes, Episodes, Songs, Dresses, Music Videos, and Trends that Entertained Us Over the 10 Years," *Enter-*

tainment Weekly, 1079/1080, December 11, 2009, 74–84.

JACOBS, Andrew, "Chinese Woman Imprisoned for Twitter Message," *New York Times*, November 18, 2010. Retrieved from http://www.nytimes.com/2010/11/19/world/asia/19beijing.html

JOSHI, Rajmohan, *Encyclopaedia of Journalism and Mass Communication: Media and Mass Communication*, New Delhi, India, Gyan Publishing House, 2006, p. 95.

KAPLAN, Andreas and HAENLEIN, Michael, "Users of the World, Unite! The Challenges and Opportunities of Social Media," *Business Horizons*, 53, 2010, pp. 59–68.

KAZENIAC, Andy, "Social Networks: Facebook Takes Over Top Spot, Twitter Climbs," *Compete Pulse blog,* February 9, 2009. Retrieved from http://blog.compete.com/2009/02/09/facebook-myspace-twitter-social-network/

KELLNER, Douglas, "New Technologies, Technocities, and the Prospects for Democratization," in *Technocities*, 1999, London, UK, Sage, pp. 186–204.

KELLNER, Douglas, "Globalization and Technopolitics," in *The Future of Revolutions: Rethinking Radical Change in the Age of Globalization*, 2003, New York, Zed Books, pp. 180–194.

LEARY, Brent, "Overemphasis on Brand Building Leads to Mistrust, *Inc.*, March 24, 2010. Retrieved from http://technology.inc.com/2010/03/22/overemphasis-on-brand-building-leads-to-mistrust/

LERNER, David, *The Passing of Traditional Society: Modernizing the Middle East*, New York, The Free Press, 1958.

LEVY, Steven, "Twitter: Is Brevity the Next Big Thing?" *Newsweek*, April 30, 2007. Retrieved from http://www.msnbc.msn.com/id/17888481/site/newsweek/

LINNELL, Nathan, "Social Media Influence on Consumer Behavior," *Search Engine Watch*, May 3, 2010. Retrieved from http://searchenginewatch.com/article/2049190/Social-Media-Influence-on-Consumer-Behavior

LISTER, Martin, DOVEY, Jon, GIDDINGS, Seth, GRANT, Ian, and KELLY, Kieran, *New Media: A Critical Introduction*, London, UK, Routledge, 2003.

MARMURA, Stephen, "A Net Advantage? The Internet, Grassroots Activism and American Middle-Eastern policy," *New Media & Society*, 10, 2008, pp. 247–271.

MANOVICH, Lev, "New Media from Borges to HTML," in *The New Media Reader*, 2003, Cambridge, The MIT Press, pp. 16–23.

MCCOMBS, Maxwell and SHAW, Donald, "The Agenda-Setting Function of Mass Media," *Public Opinion Quarterly*, 36, 1972, pp. 176–187.

MCLUHAN, Marshall, *The Gutenberg Galaxy: The Making of Typographic Man*, London, UK, Routledge and Kegan Paul, 1962; Marshall MCLUHAN, *Understanding Media: The Extensions of Man*, Toronto, Canada, McGraw-Hill, 1964.

MCLUHAN, Marshall and QUENTIN, Fiore, *The Medium is the Message*, Hardwired, San Francisco, 1967, pp. 8–9, 26–41.

Press release, "Media Advisory M10-012 – NASA Extends the World Wide Web Out into Space," NASA, January 22, 2010. Retrieved from http://www.nasa.gov/home/hqnews/2010/jan/HQ_M10-012_ISS_Web.html

MOROZOV, Eugenie, "The Net Delusion: The Dark Side of Internet Freedom," *PublicAffairs*, 2011.

PRESTON, Paschal, *Reshaping Communications: Technology, Information and Social Change*, London, UK, Sage, 2001.

Quantcast, "Facebook.com," October 31, 2011. Retrieved from http://www.quantcast.com/facebook.com

REED, Thomas Vernon, "Will the Revolution be Cybercast?: New Media, the Battle of Seattle, and Global Justice," in *The Art of Protest: Culture and Activism from the Civil Rights Movement to the Streets of Seattle*, 2005, Minneapolis, University of Minnesota Press, pp. 240–285.

RHEINGOLD, Howard, *The Virtual Community: Homesteading on the Electronic Frontier*, Cambridge, The MIT Press, 2000.

ROBERTS, Laura, "North Korea Joins Facebook," *The Daily Telegraph (London)*, August 21, 2010. Retrieved from http://www.telegraph.co.uk/technology/facebook/7957222/North-Korea-joins-Facebook.html

SCHORR, Angela, SCHENK, Michael, and CAMPBELL, William, *Communication Research and Media Science in Europe*, Berlin, Germany, Mouton de Gruyter, 2003.

Second Life, http://secondlife.com/whatis/#Be_Creative

SHANE, Scott, *Dismantling Utopia: How Information Ended the Soviet Union*, Chicago, Ivan R. Dee, 1994.

SHANE, Scott, "Spotlight Again Falls on Web Tools and Change," *New York Times*, January 29, 2011, para. 12.

SNIDERMAN, Zachary, "North Korea's Newly Launched Twitter Account Banned by South Korea," *Mashable.com*, August 19, 2010. Retrieved from http://mashable.com/2010/08/19/north-korea-twitter-banned/

SULLIVAN, Michelle, "'Facebook Effect' Mobilizes Youth Vote," *CBS News*, November 3, 2008. Retrieved from http://www.cbsnews.com/stories/2008/11/04/politics/uwire/main4568563.shtml

Staff writer, "13th Annual Webby Special Achievement Award Winners," *The Webby Awards*, n.d. Retrieved from http://www.webbyawards.com/webbys/specialachievement13.php/; Ian PAUL, "Jimmy Fallon Wins Top Webby: And the Winners Are…," *PC World*, May 5, 2009. Retrieved from http://www.pcworld.com/article/164374/jimmy_fallon_wins_top_webby_and_the_winners_are_.html

TURKLE, Sherry, "Who am We?" *Wired*, 4.01, January 1996.

VOLKMER, Ingrid, *News in the Global Sphere. A Study of CNN* and its Impact on *Global Communication*. Luton, UK, University of Luton Press, 1999.

WARDRIP-FRUIN, Noah and MONTFORT, Nick (eds.), *The New Media Reader*. Cambridge, The MIT Press, 2003.

WASSERMAN, Herman, "Is a New Worldwide Web Possible? An Explorative Comparison of the Use of ICTs by Two South African Social Movements," *African Studies Review*, 50, 2007, pp. 109–131.

WELLS, Roy, "41.6% of the U.S. Population has a Facebook account," *Social Media Today*, August 8, 2010. Retrieved from http://socialmediatoday.com/index.php?q=roywells1/158020/416-us-population-has-facebook-account

WESSEL, Rhea, "Activist Investors Turn to Social Media to Enlist Support," *The New York Times DealBook*, March 24, 2011.

WILLIAMS, Raymond, *Television: Technology and Cultural Form*, London, UK, Routledge, 1974.

"Your World, More Connected," Twitter, August 1, 2011. Retrieved http://blog.twitter.com/2011/08/your-world-more-connected.html; Twitter Search Team, "The Engineering Behind Twitter's New Search Experience," *Twitter Engineering Blog (blog of Twitter Engineering Division)*, May 31, 2011. Retrieved from http://engineering.twitter.com/2011/05/engineering-behind-twitters-new-search.html

PART TWO REFERENCES
CHAPTER 3: OBAMA PRESIDENTIAL CAMPAIGN 2007-2010

ANDREWS, Wyatt, "Reality Check: The Cost Of Obama's Pledges," CBS News, October 29, 2008. Retrieved http://m.cbsnews.com/relatedfullstory.rbml?feed_id=0&catid=4557520&videofeed=36

BENJAMIN, Mark, "It's 3 a.m. Who do You Want Answering the Phone?" Salon, March 6, 2008. Retrieved from http://www.salon.com/2008/03/06/commander_in_chief_2/

BENTLEY, John, "McCain Says "Fundamentals" Of U.S. Economy Are Strong," CBS News Politics, September 15, 2008. Retrieved from http://www.cbsnews.com/8301-502443_162-4450366-502443.html

BROWN, Peter A., "Bush not an Albatross," Boston Herald, January 15,

2012. Retrieved from http://www.bostonherald.com/news/opinion/op_ed/view.bg?articleid=1084447&srvc=next_article

DE MORAES, Lisa, "Obama Enters the League of Must-See TV," Washington Post, October 31, 2008. Retrieved from http://www.washingtonpost.com/wp-dyn/content/article/2008/10/30/AR2008103002536.html

GLADWELL, Malcolm, The Tipping Point: How Little Things can Make a Big Difference. New York, Back Bay Books, 2002.

GOODMAN, Peter, "Market Suffers as Investors Weigh Relentless Trouble," New York Times, October 15, 2008.

"Growing Doubts About McCain's Judgment, Age and Campaign Conduct," Pew Research Center for the People and the Press, October 21, 2008.

HARRIS, Sam, "When Average isn't Good Enough," Los Angeles Times, September 3, 2008. Retrieved from http://articles.latimes.com/2008/sep/03/news/OE-HARRIS3

HOMAN, Timothy R., "U.S. Economy: Consumers, Government Propel Growth (Update2)," Bloomberg, October 29, 2009. Retrieved from http://www.bloomberg.com/apps/news?pid=newsarchive&sid=aCi2EYr.5RhY

KENSKI, Kate, HARDY, Bruce W. and JAMIESON, Kathleen Hall, The Obama Victory: How Media, Money, and Message Shaped the 2008 Election, New York, Oxford University Press, 2010, p. 71.

KOLBERT, Elizabeth, "The 1992 Campaign: The Media; Perot's 30-Minute TV Ads Defy the Experts, Again," New York Times (Late Edition), Oct 27, 1992, p. A.19

MCCAIN, John, "2008 third presidential debate against Barack Obama," October 15, 2008, Hofstra University, Hempstead, New York.

"McCain, Obama Blast Regulators, Managers for Wall Street Woes,"

CNN Politics, September 15, 2008. Retrieved from http://articles.cnn.com/2008-09-15/politics/wall.street.candidates_1_wall-street-financial-markets-financial-crisis?_s=PM:POLITICS

NEWPORT, Frank, "Bush Job Approval at 25%, His Lowest Yet," Gallup Poll, October 6, 2008, Retrieved from http://www.gallup.com/poll/110980/bush-job-approval-25-lowest-yet.aspx

"Obama Launches Historic Campaign," BBC, August 29, 2008. Retrieved from http://news.bbc.co.uk/2/hi/americas/7586375.stm

OSTROM, Mary Anne, "Google CEO Eric Schmidt to Stump for Obama," Denver Post, October 10, 2008. Retrieved from http://www.denverpost.com/entertainment/ci_10769458?source=rss

PASEK, Josh, ROMER, Daniel and JAMIESON, Kathleen Hall, "America's Youth and Community Engagement: How Use of Mass Media Is Related to Civic Activity and Political Awareness in 14-to-22-Year-Olds," Communication Research, 33, 2006, p. 115–35.

PETERS, Jeremy W., "Political Blogs Are Ready to Flood Campaign Trail," New York Times, January 29, 2011. Retrieved from http://www.nytimes.com/2011/01/30/business/media/30blogs.html?pagewanted=all

RUTENBERG, Jim, "Taking to the Airwaves," New York Times, July 29, 2008. Retrieved from http://thecaucus.blogs.nytimes.com/2008/07/29/taking-to-the-airwaves/

RUTENBERG, Jim, "Candidates Clash over Character and Policy," New York Times, October 15, 2008. Retrieved from http://www.nytimes.com/2008/10/16/us/politics/16debate.html?pagewanted=all

STIRLAND, Sara Lai, "Obama's Secret Weapons: Internet, Databases and Psychology," Wired, October 29, 2008. Retrieved from http://www.wired.com/threatlevel/2008/10/obamas-secret-w/

TEO, Dawn, "Obama Campaign Buys Channel 73 on Dish Network," Huffington Post, October 2, 2008. Retrieved from http://www.huffingtonpost.com/dawn-teo/obama-campaign-buys-chann_b_131105.html

XENOS, Michael and BENNETT, W. Lance, "The Disconnection in Online Politics: The Youth Political Sphere and US Election Sites, 2002-2004," Information, Communication, and Society, 10, 2007, p. 443–64.

CHAPTER 4: INTERNATIONAL FINANCIAL CRISIS 2007-2010

ALTMAN, Robert C., "The Great Crash, 2008, A Geopolitical Setback for the West," *Foreign Affairs*, January/February 2009. Retrieved from http://www.foreignaffairs.com/articles/63714/roger-c-altman/the-great-crash-2008

AMIN, Samir, "Financial Collapse, Systemic Crisis?" World Forum for Alternatives, Caracas, October 2008. Retrieved from http://www.globalresearch.ca/index.php?context=va&aid=11099

BAHMANI, Sahar, "Understanding the Current Recession and Its Global Impact," *Gulf Coast Economics Association, 2009 Conference Proceedings*, Savannah Georgia, November 5, 2009, p. 11. Retrieved from http://gulfcoastecon.org/63312/62060.html

"Bailout is Law," *CNN Money*, October 4, 2008. Retrieved from http://money.cnn.com/2008/10/03/news/economy/house_friday_bailout/index.htm

BAILY, Martin Neil and ELLIOT, Douglas J., "The U.S. Financial and Economic Crisis: Where Does It Stand and Where Do We Go From Here?," Initiative on Business and Public Policy at Brookings, June 2009. Retrieved from http://www.brookings.edu/papers/2009/0615_economic_crisis_baily_elliott.aspx

BAJAJ, Vikas, "Home Prices fall for 10th Straight Month," *New York Times*, December 26, 2007. Retrieved from http://www.nytimes.com/2007/12/26/business/27home-web.html

BARR, Colin, "The $4 Trillion Housing Headache," *CNN Money*, May 27, 2009. Retrieved from http://money.cnn.com/2009/05/27/news/mortgage.overhang.fortune/index.htm

BERNANKE, Ben S., "The Global Savings Glut and the U.S. Current Account Deficit," Remarks by Governor Ben S. Bernanke at the Homer Jones Lecture, St. Louis, Missouri, March 10, 2005. Retrieved from http://www.federalreserve.gov/boarddocs/speeches/2005/20050414/default.htm

BERNANKE, Ben, "The Economic Outlook," Testimony before the Joint Economic Committee, October 20, 2005. Retrieved from http://www.house.gov/jec/hearings/testimony/109/10-20-05bernanke.pdf

BERNANKE, Ben S. "The Subprime Mortgage Market," Remarks by Governor Ben S. Bernanke at the Federal Reserve Bank of Chicago's 43rd Annual Conference on Bank Structure and Competition, Chicago, Illinois, May 17, 2007. Retrieved from http://www.federalreserve.gov/boarddocs/speeches/2005/20050414/default.htm

BOGLE, John C., *The Battle for the Soul of Capitalism*, Yale University Press, New Haven, CT.

BROCKES, Emma, "He Told Us So," *Guardian*, January 24, 2009. Retrieved from http://www.guardian.co.uk/business/2009/jan/24/nouriel-roubini-credit-crunch

"Buffett Warns on Investment 'Time Bomb'," *BBC News*, March 4, 2003. Retrieved from http://news.bbc.co.uk/2/hi/2817995.stm

BUSH, George W., "President's Weekly Radio Address," August 6, 2005. In Robert J. Schiller, *The Subprime Solution: How Today's Global Financial Crisis Happened, and What to Do about It*, Princeton University Press, Princeton, NJ, p. 40.

"The Changing Narrative: How the News Media have Covered the Slowing Economy," *Analysis Report, Pew Research Center's Project for Excellence in Journalism*, August 8, 2001, p. 2. Retrieved from http://www.journalism.org/files/Economy%20report.pdf

"Covering the Great Recession: How the Media Have Depicted the Economic Crisis," *Pew Research Center, Project for Excellence in Journalism*, October 5, 2009. Retrieved from http://pewresearch.org/pubs/1365/great-recession-media-coverage-driven-by-government-officials-and-business

"Covering the Great Recession: Why Did Coverage of the Economy Decrease?" *Pew Research Center's Project for Excellence in Journalism*, October 5, 2009, p. 2. Retrieved from http://www.journalism.org/analysis_report/why_did_coverage_economy_decrease

COY, Peter, MILLER, Rich, YOUNG, Lauren, and PALMERI, Christopher, "Is a Housing Bubble About to Burst?" *Bloomberg Businessweek*, July 19, 2004. Retrieved from http://www.businessweek.com/magazine/content/04_29/b3892064_mz011.htm

COY, Peter, "What Good are Economists Anyway"? *Bloomberg Businessweek*, April 16, 2009. Retrieved from http://www.businessweek.com/magazine/content/09_17/b4128026997269.htm

"Criminal Fraud: Mortgage Fraud Scandal Brewing," *Real News*, May 13, 2009. Retrieved from http://therealnews.com/t2/index.php?option=com_content&task=view&id=31&Itemid=74&jumival=3708

"CSI: credit crunch," *Economist*, October 18, 2007. Retrieved from http://www.economist.com/specialreports/displaystory.cfm?story_id=9972489

"The Disappearing Dollar," *Economist*, December 2, 2004. Retrieved from http://www.economist.com/node/3446249

"Executive Summary," International Monetary Fund, January 2009. Retrieved from http://www.imf.org/external/pubs/ft/weo/2009/01/pdf/exesum.pdf

"Existing-Home Sales Fall in 41 States," *Associated Press*, August 15, 2007. Retrieved from http://www.msnbc.msn.com/id/20279235/

DAUBLE, Jennifer, "Billionaire Investor Warren Buffett Today on CNBC's 'Squawk Box'," *CNBC Squawk Box*, March 9, 2009. Retrieved from http://www.cnbc.com/id/29598302/CNBC_TRANSCRIPT_CNBC_S_BECKY_QUICK_SITS_DOWN_WITH_BILLIONAIRE_INVESTOR_WARREN_BUFFETT_TODAY_ON_CNBC_S_SQUAWK_BOX

"Declaration of the Summit on Financial Markets and the World Economy," Office of the Press Secretary, The White House, November 15, 2008. Retrieved from http://georgewbush-whitehouse.archives.gov/news/releases/2008/11/20081115-1.html

"Delinquencies and Foreclosures Increase in Latest MBA National Delinquency Survey," Mortgage Bankers Association, September 5, 2008. Retrieved from http://www.mbaa.org/NewsandMedia/PressCenter/64769.htm

"Delinquencies Continue to Climb in Latest MBA National Delinquency Survey," Mortgage Bankers Association, November 19, 2009. Retrieved from http://www.mbaa.org/NewsandMedia/PressCenter/71112.htm

FACKLER, Martin, "Trouble Without Borders," *New York Times*, October 23, 2008. Retrieved from http://query.nytimes.com/gst/fullpage.html?res=9B00E2DC103FF937A15753C1A96E9C8B63&ref=martinfackler

FIGLEWSKI, Stephen, SMITH, Roy C., and WALTER, Ingo, "Geithner's Plan for Derivatives," *Forbes*, May 18, 2009. Retrieved from http://www.forbes.com/2009/05/18/geithner-derivatives-plan-opinions-contributors-figlewski.html

GASSMAN, James K., "What to Learn from the Fall of Enron, a Firm that Fooled So Many," *International Herald Tribune*, December 10, 2001, p. 10.

GEITHNER, Timothy, “Reducing Systemic Risk in a Dynamic Financial System,” Speech, Federal Reserve Bank of New York, June 9, 2008. Retrieved from http://www.newyorkfed.org/newsevents/speeches/2008/tfg080609.html

“Giant Pool of Money Wins Peabody,” National Public Radio, This American Life, April 5, 2009. Retrieved from http://www.pri.org/stories/business/giant-pool-of-money.html

GLADWELL, Malcolm, The Tipping Point: How Little Things can Make a Big Difference, New York: Back Bay Books, 2002, p. 7.

GOEL, Suresh, Crisis Management: Master the Skills to Prevent Disasters, Global India Publications, New Delhi, India, p. 183.

GORDON, Robert, “Did Liberals Cause the Sub Prime Crisis?” *American Prospect*, April 7, 2008. Retrieved from http://prospect.org/article/did-liberals-cause-sub-prime-crisis

“Government Support for Financial Assets and Liabilities Announced in 2008 and Soon Thereafter ($ in billions),” FDIC Supervisory Insights Summer 2009, Federal Deposit Insurance Corporation, Retrieved from http://www.fdic.gov/regulations/examinations/supervisory/insights/sisum09/si_sum09.pdf

GREENSPAN, Alan, The Age of Turbulence: Adventures in a New World, Penguin Press HC, New York.

GREENSPAN, Alan and KENNEDY, James, “Sources and Uses of Equity Extracted from Homes,” Divisions of Research & Statistics and Monetary Affairs, Federal Reserve Board, Washington, D.C., March 2007. Retrieved from http://www.federalreserve.gov/pubs/feds/2007/200720/200720pap.pdf

GULLAPALLI, Diya and ANAND, Shefalli, “Bailout of Money Funds Seems to Stanch Outflow,” *Wall Street Journal*, September 20, 2008. Retrieved from http://online.wsj.com/article/SB122186683086958875.html?mod=article-outset-box

"A Helping Hand to Homeowners," *Economist*, October 23, 2008. Retrieved from http://www.economist.com/node/12470547?story_id=12470547

HOLMES, Steven A., "Fannie Mae Eases Credit to Aid Mortgage Lending," *New York Times*, September 30, 1999. Retrieved from http://www.nytimes.com/1999/09/30/business/fannie-mae-eases-credit-to-aid-mortgage-lending.html

"Home Equity Extraction: The Real Cost of 'Free Cash'," *Seeking Alpha*, April 25, 2007. Retrieved from http://seekingalpha.com/article/33336-home-equity-extraction-the-real-cost-of-free-cash

KEDROSKY, Paul, "How Enron Ran Out of Gas," *Wall Street Journal*, October 29, 2001, p. A22.

KRUGMAN, Paul, The Return of Depression Economics and the Crisis of 2008, New York, WW Norton, 2009, pp. 168–169.

KRUGMAN, Paul, "Revenge of the Glut," *New York Times*, March 1, 2009. Retrieved from http://www.nytimes.com/2009/03/02/opinion/02krugman.html?_r=1

KRUGMAN, Paul, "Reagan Did It," *New York Times*, May 31, 2009. Retrieved from http://www.nytimes.com/2009/06/01/opinion/01krugman.html

KRUGMAN, Paul, "Financial Reform 101," *New York Times*, April 1, 2010. Retrieved from http://www.nytimes.com/2010/04/02/opinion/02krugman.html?adxnnl=1&adxnnlx=1326978494-WOo7/m5tevHSi/qRiQCY5A

LABATON, Stephen, "Agency's '04 Rule Let Banks Pile Up New Debt," *New York Times*, October 3, 2008. Retrieved from http://www.nytimes.com/2008/10/03/business/03sec.html

LAMBERT, Richard, "Crashes, Bangs & Wallops," *Financial Times*, July 19, 2008. Retrieved from http://www.ft.com/cms/s/0/7173bb6a-552a-11dd-ae9c-000077b07658.html#axzz1jmaY8v3M

LANDER, Mark, "West is in Talks on Credit to Aid Poorer Nations," *New York Times*, October 24, 2008. Retrieved from http://www.nytimes.com/2008/10/24/business/worldbusiness/24iht-24emerge.17215442.html?pagewanted=all

LEE, Susan, "The Dismal Science: Enron's Success Story," *Wall Street Journal*, December 26, 2011, p. A11.

LEWIS, Michael, "The End of Wall Street's Boom," *Portfolio.com*, November 11, 2008. Retrieved from http://www.portfolio.com/news-markets/national-news/portfolio/2008/11/11/The-End-of-Wall-Streets-Boom

MANKIW, Gregory, "How to Avoid Recession? Let the Fed Work," *New York Times*, December 23, 2007. Retrieved from http://www.nytimes.com/2007/12/23/business/23view.html?ex=1356066000&en=3337604c8708710a&ei=5090&partner=rssuserland&emc=rss

MAX, Sara, "The Bubble Question, How Will Rising Interest Rates Affect Housing Prices?" *CNN Money*, July 27, 2004. Retrieved from http://money.cnn.com/2004/07/13/real_estate/buying_selling/risingrates/

MIHM, Stephen, "Dr. Doom," *New York Times*, August 15, 2008. Retrieved from http://www.nytimes.com/2008/08/17/magazine/17pessimist-t.html?pagewanted=all

"Minutes of the Federal Open Market Committee," Board of Governors of the Federal Reserve System, June 23-24, 2009, Washington D.C. Retrieved from http://www.federalreserve.gov/monetarypolicy/fomcminutes20090624.htm

MORGENSON, Gretchen, "A Bank Crisis Whodunit, With Laughs and Tears," *New York Times*, January 29, 2011. Retrieved from http://www.nytimes.com/2011/01/30/business/30gret.html

MORRIS, Charles, R., The Two Trillion Dollar Meltdown: Easy Money, High Rollers, and the Great Crash, New York, PublicAffairs, 2008.

"Multinational Arrangements," *World Academy Online*, June 2009. Retrieved from http://worldacademyonline.com/article/33/460/multinational_arrangements.html

NASTASE, Marian, CRETU, Alina Stefania, and STANEF, Roberta, "Effects of Global Financial Crisis," *Review of International Comparative Management*, 10, 2009, p. 695. Retrieved from www.rmci.ase.ro/no10vol4/Vol10_No4_Article9.pdf

NOCERA, Joe, "As Credit Crisis Spiraled, Alarm Led to Action," *New York Times,* October 1, 2008. Retrieved from http://www.nytimes.com/2008/10/02/business/02crisis.html

NORRIS, Floyd, "Another Crisis, Another Guarantee," *New York Times*, November 24, 2008. Retrieved from http://www.nytimes.com/2008/11/25/business/25assess.html?hp

"Open Market Operations," Board of Governors of the Federal Reserve System, January 26, 2010. Retrieved from http://www.federalreserve.gov/monetarypolicy/openmarket.htm

PHILIPPON, Thomas, "The Future of the Financial Industry," Finance Department of the New York University Stern School of Business at New York University, Stern on Finance blog. Retrieved from http://sternfinance.blogspot.com/2008/10/future-of-financial-industry-thomas.html

POWELL, Michael, "Crises in Japan Ripple Across the Global Economy," New York Times, March 20, 2011. Retrieved from http://www.nytimes.com/2011/03/21/business/global/21econ.html?pagewanted=all

RealtyTrac Staff, "U.S. Foreclosure Activity Increases 75 Percent in 2007," RealtyTrac, January 30, 2008. Retrieved from http://www.realtytrac.com/content/press-releases/us-foreclosure-activity-increases-75-percent-in-2007-3604?accnt=64847

REILLY, David, "Banks' Hidden Junk Menaces $1 Trillion Purge," *Bloomberg*, March 25, 2009. Retrieved from http://www.

bloomberg.com/apps/news?pid=newsarchive&sid=akv_p6LBNIdw&refer=home

SAKOLSKI, Aaron M., *The Great American Land Bubble: The Amazing Story of Land Grabbing, Speculations, and Booms from Colonial Days to the Present Time*, Johnson Reprint Corp., New York, NY.

SALMON, Felix, "Recipe for Disaster: The Formula That Killed Wall Street," *Wired Magazine*, February 23, 2009. Retrieved from http://www.wired.com/techbiz/it/magazine/17-03/wp_quant?currentPage=all

SCHILLER, Robert J., The Subprime Solution: How Today's Global Financial Crisis Happened, and What to Do about It, Princeton University Press, Princeton, NJ, p. 47.

SOROS, George, "The Worst Market Crisis in 60 Years," *Financial Times*, January 22, 2008, Retrieved from http://www.ft.com/cms/s/0/24f73610-c91e-11dc-9807-000077b07658.html#axzz1jtkkWJ7H

"Spending Boosted by Home Equity Loans: Greenspan," *Reuters*, April 23, 2007. Retrieved from http://www.reuters.com/article/2007/04/23/us-usa-greenspan-equity-idUSN2330071920070423

STEVERMAN, Ben and BOGOSLAW, David, "The Financial Crisis Blame Game," *Bloomberg Businessweek*, October 18, 2008. Retrieved from http://www.businessweek.com/investor/content/oct2008/pi20081017_950382.htm?chan=top+news_top+news+index+-+temp_top+story

"Ted Spread," *Bloomberg*. Retrieved from http://www.bloomberg.com/quote/!TEDSP:IND

TIMRAOS, Nick and BRAY, Chad, "SEC Brings Crisis-Era Suits," *Wall Street Journal*, December 17, 2011. Retrieved from http://online.wsj.com/article/SB10001424052970203733304577102310955780788.html

TRUMP, Donald, CBS Early Show, March 6, 2009.

"United States GDP Growth Rate," *Trading Economics*. Retrieved from http://www.tradingeconomics.com/united-states/gdp-growth

"U.S., European Bank Writedowns, Credit Losses," *Reuters*, November 5, 2009. Retrieved from http://www.reuters.com/article/2009/11/05/banks-writedowns-losses-idCNL554155620091105?rpc=44

WALLISON, Peter J., "The True Origins of This Financial Crisis," *American Spectator*, February 6, 2009. Retrieved from http://spectator.org/archives/2009/02/06/the-true-origins-of-this-finan

"Will Subprime Mess Ripple through the Economy?" *MSNBC*, March 13, 2007. Retrieved from http://www.msnbc.msn.com/id/17584725#.Txf6qmOonus

WILSON, James and KELLING, George, "Broken Windows. The Police and Neighbourhood Safety," *Atlantic Magazine*, 3, 1982.

WOLF, Martin, "Japan's Lessons for a World of Balance-Sheet Deflation," *Financial Times*, February 17, 2009. Retrieved from http://www.ft.com/intl/cms/s/0/774c0920-fd1d-11dd-a103-000077b07658.html#axzz1jtkkWJ7H

WOLF, Martin, "Reform of Regulation has to Start by Altering Incentives," *Financial Times*, June 23, 2009. Retrieved from http://www.ft.com/intl/cms/s/0/095722f6-6028-11de-a09b-00144feabdc0.html#axzz1jtkkWJ7H

ZUCKERMAN, Mortimer, "The Economy Is Even Worse Than You Think," *Wall Street Journal Opinion section*, July 14, 2009. Retrieved from http://online.wsj.com/article/SB124753066246235811.html

CHAPTER 5: CLIMATE CHANGE

ADAM, David, "Climate Change Sceptics and Lobbyists put World at Risk, says Top Adviser," *Guardian*, November 22, 2009. Retrieved from http://www.guardian.co.uk/environment/2009/nov/22/climate-change-emissions-scientist-watson

"Administration To Deny Global Warming," *Rolling Stone*, June 20, 2007. Retrieved from http://www.desmogblog.com/sites/beta.desmogblog.com/files/The%20Secret%20Campaign%20of%20President%20Bush%20rolling%20stone.pdf

"An Increase in GOP Doubt About Global Warming Deepens Partisan Divide," *Pew Research Center for the People and the Press*, May 8, 2008. Retrieved from http://pewresearch.org/pubs/828/global-warming

BELL, Larry, "Hot Sensations vs. Cold Facts," Forbes, January 28, 2011. Retrieved from http://www.forbes.com/sites/larrybell/2011/01/28/hot-sensations-vs-cold-facts-3/

BELL, Larry, *Climate of Corruption: Politics and Power Behind the Global Warming Hoax*, Austin, TX, Greenleaf Book Group, 2011, p. 84.

BODEN, Thomas A., MARLAND, Gregg, and ANDRES, Robert J., "Global, Regional, and National Fossil-Fuel CO2 Emissions," Carbon Dioxide Information Analysis Center, Oak Ridge, TN, 2006. Retrieved from http://cdiac.ornl.gov/trends/emis/overview_2006.html

BORENSTEIN, Seth, "Obama Science Advisers Grilled over Hacked E-mails," *Breitbart*, December 2, 2009. Retrieved from http://www.breitbart.com/article.php?id=D9CBFB901

BOWEN, Alex and RANGER, Nicole, *Mitigating Climate Change Through Reductions in Greenhouse Gas Emissions: the Science and Economics of Future Paths for Global Annual Emissions*, policy paper, London, UK, Grantham Research Institute for Climate Change and the Environment, 2009.

BOYCOFF, Maxwell T. and BOYCOFF, Jules M., "Balance as Bias: Global Warming and the US Prestige Press," *Global Environmental Change*, 14, 2004, p. 125-136.

BRECKE, Peter, "Violent Conflicts 1400 A. D. to the Present in Different Regions of the World," Annual Meeting of the Peace Science Society (International), Ann Arbor, MI, October 8–10, 1999.

BRODER, John M., "Climate Deal Likely to Bear Big Price Tag," *New York Times*, December 8, 2009. Retrieved from http://www.nytimes.com/2009/12/09/science/earth/09cost.html?pagewanted=all

BROHAN, P., KENNEDY, J J., HARRIS, I., TETT, S. F. B., and JONES, P. D., "Uncertainty Estimates in Regional and Global Observed Temperature Changes: A New Data Set from 1850," *Journal of Geophysical Research Atmospheres*, 111, 2006, D12106.

BUHAUG, Halvard, *Second IMO GHG Study 2009*, London, UK, International Maritime Organization (IMO), 2009. Retrieved from http://www.imo.org/blast/blastDataHelper.asp?data_id=27795&filename=GHGStudyFINAL.pdf

CAMPBELL, Duncan, "White House Cuts Global Warming from Report," *Guardian*, June 20, 2003. Retrieved from http://www.guardian.co.uk/environment/2003/jun/20/climatechange.climatechangeenvironment

CHARNEY, Jule G., "Carbon Dioxide and Climate: A Scientific Assessment," National Academy of Sciences Summer Studies Center, Washington, D.C., National Academy of Sciences, 1979. Retrieved from www.atmos.ucla.edu/~brianpm/download/charney_report.pdf

CLARKE, Leon E., EDMONDS, James A., JACOBY, Henry D., PITCHER, Hugh M., REILLY, John M., and RICHELS, Richard G., "Scenarios of the Greenhouse Gas Emission and Atmospheric Concentrations," U.S. Climate Change Science Program and the Subcommittee on Global Change Research, Washington, D.C., Department of Energy, Office of Biological and Environmental Research, 2007. Retrieved from http://www.climatescience.gov/Library/sap/sap2-1/finalreport/

Climate Change 2001: The Scientific Basis, Contribution of Working Group I to the Third Assessment Report of the Intergovernmental Panel on Climate Change (IPCC), H.T. Houghton, Y. Ding, D.J.

Griggs, M. Noguer, P.J. van der Linden, X. Dai, K. Maskell, and C.A. Johnson (eds.), Cambridge and New York, Cambridge University Press, 2001.

"Climate Change Fight 'Can't Wait'," *BBC*, October 31, 2006. Retrieved from http://news.bbc.co.uk/2/hi/business/6096084.stm

"Climate Chaos: Bush's Climate of Fear," *BBC*, June 1, 2006. Retrieved from http://news.bbc.co.uk/2/hi/programmes/panorama/5005994.stm

COILE, Zachary, "How the White House worked to scuttle California's climate law", San Francisco Chronicle, September 25, 2007. Retrieved from http://articles.sfgate.com/2007-09-25/news/17261302_1_auto-emissions-greenhouse-gases-e-mails

Committee on the Science of Climate Change, National Research Council, *Climate Change Science: An Analysis of Some Key Questions*, Washington, D.C., National Academies Press, 2001.

"Copenhagen Climate Accord: Key Issues," *BBC*, December 19, 2009. Retrieved from http://news.bbc.co.uk/2/hi/8422186.stm

COWIE, Jonathan, *Climate and Human Change: Disaster or Opportunity?* New York, Parthenon, 1998.

DEN ELZEN, Michel and HOHNE, Niklas, "Reductions of Greenhouse Gas Emissions in Annex I and non-Annex I Countries for Meeting Concentration Stabilisation Targets," *Climatic Change*, 91, 2008, p. 247-274.

DEN ELZEN, Michel G. J., VAN VUUREN, Detlef P., and VAN VLIET, Jasper, "Postponing Emission Reductions from 2020 to 2030 Increases Climate Risks and Long-Term Costs," Climatic Change, 99, 2010, p. 313-320.

DICKINSON, Tim, "The Secret Campaign of President Bush's

DONEY, Scott C., FABRY, Victoria J., FEELY, Richard A., and KLEYPAS, Joan A., "Ocean Acidification: The Other CO2 Problem," *Annual Reviews*, 1, 2009, pp. 169-192.

EILPERIN, Juliet, "Climate Researchers Feeling Heat From White House," *Washington Post*, April 6, 2006. Retrieved from http://www.washingtonpost.com/wp-dyn/content/article/2006/04/05/AR2006040502150_pf.html

Emissions Scenarios, Intergovernmental Panel on Climate Change (IPCC), Nebojsa Nakicenovic and Rob Swart (eds.), Cambridge and New York, Cambridge University Press, 2000.

European Commission Joint Research Centre (JRC)/Netherlands Environmental Assessment Agency (PBL), Emission Database for Global Atmospheric Research (EDGAR), 2009, release version 4.0. Retrieved from http://edgar.jrc.ec.europa.eu/overview.php?v=40

FARKAS, Tamás, *The Investor's Guide to the Energy Revolution*, Raleigh, NC., Lulu.com, 2008, p. 234.

FERGUSON, R. Brian, *Warfare, Culture, and Environment*, Orlando, FL, Academic, 1984.

FREUDENBURG, William, "The Effects of Journalistic Imbalance on Scientific Imbalance: Special Interests, Scientific Consensus and Global Climate Disruption," *Climate Change: Global Risks, Challenges and Decisions, IOP Conf. Series: Earth and Environmental Science* 6, 2009 532011.

FRIEDMAN, Thomas L., "The Earth is Full," *New York Times*, June 7, 2011. Retrieved from http://www.nytimes.com/2011/06/08/opinion/08friedman.html

FURUYA, Jun, KOBAYASHI, Shintaro, and MEYER, Seth D., "Economic Impacts of Climate Change on Global Food Supply and Demand," *Japan Agriculture Research*, 39, 2005, p. 121-134.

GALLOWAY, Patrick R., "Long-Term Fluctuations in Climate and Population in the Preindustrial Era," *Population and Development Review*, 12, 1986, pp. 1-24.

GILDING, Paul, *The Great Disruption: Why the Climate Crisis Will Bring On the End of Shopping and the Birth of a New World*, New York, NY, Bloomsbury Press, 2011.

GILLIS, Justin, "A Scientist, His Work and a Climate Reckoning," *New York Times*, December 21, 2010. Retrieved from http://www.nytimes.com/2010/12/22/science/earth/22carbon.html

GOLDSTEIN, Natalie and COOK, Kerry Harrison, *Global Warming*, New York, Checkmark Books, 2010, p. 164.

"Groups Say Scientists Pressured On Warming," *CBS News*, February 11, 2009. Retrieved from http://www.cbsnews.com/stories/2007/01/30/politics/main2413400.shtml

HAMILTON, Tyler, "Fresh Alarm over Global Warming," *Toronto Star*, January 1, 2007. Retrieved from http://www.thestar.com/article/166819

HIRSCH, Robert L., report, Science Applications International Corporation.

HOEGH-GULDBERG, Ove and BRUNO, John F., "The Impact of Climate Change on the World's Marine Ecosystems," *Science*, 18, 2010, pp. 1523-1528.

HOGGAN, James and LITTLEMORE, Richard D., *Climate Cover-up: The Crusade to Deny Global Warming*, Vancouver, Canada, Greystone Books, 2009, p. 19.

HOHNE, Niklas, BLUM, Helcio, FUGLESTVEDT, Jan, SKEIE, Ragnhild, KUROSAWA, Atsushi, HU, Guoquan, LOWE, Jason, GOHAR, Laila, MATTHEWS, Ben, NIOAC DE SALLES, Ana, and ELLERMANN, Christian, "Contributions of Individual Countries Emissions to Climate Change and Their Uncertainty," *Climate Change*, 106, 2011, pp. 359-391.

HOMER-DIXON, Thomas F., "Environmental Scarcities and Violent

Conflict: Evidence from Cases," *International Security*, 19, 1994, p. 5-40.

"IPCC Second Assessment, Climate Change 1995," Intergovernmental Panel on Climate Change, December 1995. Retrieved from http://www.ipcc.ch/pdf/climate-changes-1995/ipcc-2nd-assessment/2nd-assessment-en.pdf

"IPCC Third Assessment, Climate Change 1995," Intergovernmental Panel on Climate Change (IPCC), 2001. Retrieved from http://www.ipcc.ch/ipccreports/tar/index.htm

JACOBS, Andrew, "China Issues Warning on Climate and Growth," *New York Times*, February 28, 2011. Retrieved from http://www.nytimes.com/2011/03/01/world/asia/01beijing.html

JOHNSON, Douglas L. and GOULD, Harvey A., "The Effect of Climate Fluctuations on Human Populations: A Case Study of Mesopotamian Society," in *Climate and Development*, Asit K. BISWAS (ed.), Dublin, Tycooly International Limited, 1984, pp. 117-138.

KAHN, Matthew E., *Climatopolis: How our Cities Will Thrive in the Hotter Future*, New York, Basic Books, p. 6.

KLUGER, Jeffrey, "A Climate of Despair," Time, April 1, 2001. Retrieved from http://www.time.com/time/magazine/article/0,9171,104596,00.html

KRUGMAN, Paul, "Boiling the Frog," *New York Times*, July 12, 2009. Retrieved from http://www.nytimes.com/2009/07/13/opinion/13krugman.html

LANDERER, Felix W., JUNGCLAUS, Johann H., and MAROTZKE, Jochem, "Regional Dynamic and Steric Sea Level Change in Response to the IPCC-A1B Scenario," Journal of Physical Oceanography, 37, 2006, p. 296-312.

LEE, Harry F., FOK, Lincoln, and ZHANG, David D., "Climatic Change and Chinese Population Growth Dynamics over the Last Millennium," *Climatic Change*, 88, 2007, pp. 131-156.

LOBELL David B., and FIELD, Christopher B., "Global Scale Climate–Crop Yield Relationships and the Impacts of Recent Warming," *Environmental Research Letters*, 2, 2007.

MANN, Michael E. and JONES, Philip D., "Global Surface Temperatures over the Past Two Millennia," *Geophysical Research Letters*, 30, 2003.

MASLOW, Abraham Harold, *Motivation and Personality*, New York, Harper & Row, 1970.

MCCARTHY, James J., CANZIANI, Osvald F., LEARY, Neil A., DOKKEN, David J., and WHITE, Kasey S., *Working Group II: Impacts, Adaptation and Vulnerability*, Geneva, Switzerland, Intergovernmental Panel on Climate Change (IPCC), 2001. Retrieved from http://www.ipcc.ch/ipccreports/tar/wg2/index.php?idp=2

MCNEIL, Ben I. and MATEAR, Richard J., "Southern Ocean Acidification: A Tipping Point at 450-ppm Atmospheric CO2," *Proceedings of the National Academy of Sciences*, 105, 2008, pp. 18860-18864.

MEEHL, Gerald A., STOCKER, Thomas F., COLLINS, William D., FRIEDLINGSTEIN, Pierre, GAYE, Amadou T., GREGORY, Jonathan M., KITOH, Akio, KNUTTI, Reto, MURPHY, James M., NODA, Akira, RAPER, Sarah C.B., WATTERSON, Ian G., WEAVER, Andrew J., and ZHAO, Zong-Ci, "Global Climate Projections," in *Climate Change 2007: The Physical Science Basis. Contribution of Working Group I to the Fourth Assessment Report of the Intergovernmental Panel on Climate Change*, S. Solomon, D. Qin, M. Manning, Z. Chen, M. Marquis, K.B. Averyt, M. Tignor and H.L. Miller (eds.), 2007, Cambridge, UK and New York, NY, Cambridge University Press.

MEINSHAUSEN, Malte, HARE, Bill, VAN VUUREN, Detlef P., DEN

ELZEN, Michel, and SWART, Rob, "Multi-Gas Emission Pathways to Meet Climate Targets," *Climate Change*, 75, 2006, pp. 151–194.

MEINSHAUSEN, Malte, RAPER, Sarah, and WIGLEY, Tom, "Emulating IPCC AR4 Atmosphere-Ocean and Carbon Cycle Models for Projecting Global-Mean, Hemispheric and Land/Ocean Temperatures: MAGICC 6.0," *Atmospheric Chemistry and Physics*, 8, 2008, pp. 6153-6272.

MEINSHAUSEN, Malke and RAPER, Sarah, *The Rising Effect of Aviation on Climate; Project Report OMEGA—Aviation in a Sustainable World*, Manchester, UK, Manchester Metropolitan University, 2009.

MEINSHAUSEN, Malte, MEINSHAUSEN, Nicolai, HARE, William, RAPER, Sarah C. B., FRIELER, Katja, KNUTTI, Reto, FRAME, David J., and ALLEN, Myles R., "Greenhouse-Gas Emission Targets for Limiting Global Warming to 2 °C," *Nature*, 458, 2009, pp. 1158-1162.

METZ, Bert, DAVIDSON, Ogunlade, BOSCH, Peter R., DAVE, Rutu, and MEYERS, L. A. (eds.), *Climate Change 2007: Mitigation. Contribution of Working Group III to the Fourth Assessment Report of the Intergovernmental Panel on Climate Change*, Cambridge, UK and New York, NY, Cambridge University Press, 2007. Retrieved from http://www.ipcc.ch/publications_and_data/ar4/wg3/en/contents.html

MOONEY, Chris, *The Republican War on Science*, New York, Basic Books, 2005.

NABEL, Jane, MACEY, Kirsten, and CHEN, Claudine, "PRIMAP Reference Data for LULUCF Accounting," Potsdam Real-time Integrated Model for probabilistic Assessment of emissions Paths (PRIMAP). Retrieved from www.primap.org

NABEL, Julia, ROGELJ, Joeri, CHEN, Claudine M., MARKMANN,

Kathleen, GUTZMANN, David J., and MEINSHAUSEN, Malte, "Decision Support for International Climate Policy—the PRIMAP Emission Module," *Environmental Modelling and Software*, 26, 2011, pp. 1419-1433.

"NASA Looks at Seal Level Rise, Hurricane Risks to New York City," NASA Goddard Institute for Space Studies, October 24, 2006. Retrieved from http://www.giss.nasa.gov/research/news/20061024/

Panel on Climate Variability on Decade-to-Century Time Scales, National Research Council, "Decade-to-Century-Scale Climate Variability and Change: A Science Strategy," Washington, D.C., National Academy Press, 1998. Retrieved from http://www.nap.edu/catalog.php?record_id=6129

PETERS, Sandra L., MALCOLM, Jay R., and ZIMMERMAN, Barbara L., "Effects of Selective Logging on Bat Communities in the Southeastern Amazon," *Conservation Biology*, 20, 2006, p. 1410-1421.

PORTER, Henry, "Fiddling as the Planet Burns," The Observer, June 19, 2005. Retrieved from http://www.guardian.co.uk/politics/2005/jun/19/greenpolitics.climatechange

"President Bush Discusses Global Climate Change," Office of the Press Secretary, The White House, June 11, 2001. Retrieved from http://georgewbush-whitehouse.archives.gov/news/releases/2001/06/20010611-2.html

PULLELLA, Philip, "Pope Urges, Save the Planet Before it's too Late," *Reuters*, September 2, 2007. Retrieved from http://www.enn.com/top_stories/commentary/22598/print

PURVIS, Andrew, "Heroes of the Environment: Angela Merkel," *Time*, October 17, 2007. Retrieved from http://www.time.com/time/specials/2007/article/0,28804,1663317_1663319_1669897,00.html

REVELLE, Roger and SEUSS, Hans, "Carbon Dioxide Exchange between Atmosphere and Ocean and the Question of an Increase of

Atmospheric CO2 during the Past Decades," *Tellus*, 9, 1957, p. 18-27.

REVKIN, Andrew C. and BRODER, John M., "In Face of Skeptics, Experts Affirm Climate Peril," *New York Times*, December 6, 2009. Retrieved from http://www.nytimes.com/2009/12/07/science/earth/07climate.html

REVKIN, Andrew C. and BRODER, John M., "Facing Skeptics, Climate Experts Sure of Peril," *New York Times*, December 7, 2009, p. A1, A8.

RIAHI, Keywan, GRUBLER, Amulf, and NAKICENOVIC, Nebojsa, "Scenarios of Long-Term Socio-Economic and Environmental Development under Climate Stabilization," *Technological Forecasting and Social Change*, 74, 2007, pp. 887-935.

ROBELIUS, Frederik, Doctoral dissertation, University of Uppsala, Sweden.

ROGELJ, Joeri, CHEN, Claudine, NABEL, Julia, MACEY, Kirsten, HARE, William, SCHAEFFER, Michiel, MARKMANN, Kathleen, HOHNE, Niklas, ANDERSEN, Katrine Krogh, and MEINSHAUSEN, Malte, "Analysis of the Copenhagen Accord Pledges and its Global Climatic Impacts—A Snapshot of Dissonant Ambitions," *Environmental Research Letters*, 5, 2010, 034013.

ROGELJ, Joeri, NABEL, Julia, CHEN, Claudine, HARE, William, MARKMANN, Kathleen, MEINSHAUSEN, Malte, SCHAEFFER, Michiel, MACEY, Kirsten, and HOHNE, Niklas, "Copenhagen Accord pledges are paltry," *Nature*, 464, 2010, pp. 1126-1128.

"Rudd Ratifies Kyoto," *The Age*, December 3, 2007. Retrieved from http://www.theage.com.au/news/national/rudd-ratifies-kyoto/2007/12/03/1196530553722.html

SAAD, Lydia, "Increased Number Think Global Warming Is 'Exaggerated'," *Gallup*, March 11, 2009. Retrieved from http://www.gallup.com/poll/116590/increased-number-think-global-warming-exaggerated.aspx

SEAGER, Richard, GRAHAM, Nicholas, and HERWEIJER, Celine, "Blueprints for Medieval Hydroclimate," *Quaternay Science Reviews*, 26, 2007, p. 19-21.

SILVERMAN, Jacob, LAZAR, Boaz, CAO, Long, CALDERA, Ken, and EREZ, Jonathan, "Coral Reefs May Start Dissolving When Atmospheric CO2 Doubles," *Geophysical Research Letters*, 36, 2009, L05606.

SMITH, Steven J. and WIGLEY, T.M.L., "Multi-Gas Forcing Stabilisation with the MiniCAM," *Energy Journal* (special issue 3), 2006, pp. 373–391.

"Smoke, Mirrors & Hot Air: How ExxonMobil uses Big Tobacco's Tactics to Manufacture Uncertainty on Climate Science," Cambridge, MA, Union of Concerned Scientists, 2007. Retrieved from http://www.ucsusa.org/assets/documents/global_warming/exxon_report.pdf

STEINACHER, Marco, JOOS, Fortunat, FROLICHER, Thomas L., PLATTNER, Gian Kasper, and DONEY, Scott, "Imminent Ocean Acidification in the Arctic Projected with the NCAR Global Coupled Carbon Cycle-Climate Model," *Biogeosciences*, 6, 2009, pp. 515-533.

STERN, Nicholas, *Stern Review on the Economics of Climate Change*, Her Majesty's Treasury, 2006. Retrieved from http://webarchive.nationalarchives.gov.uk/+/http://www.hm-treasury.gov.uk/stern_review_report.htm

STERN, Nicholas, *Deciding Our Future in Copenhagen: Will the World Rise to the Challenge of Climate Change?* public lecture, London, UK, Grantham Research Institute for Climate Change and the Environment, 2009.

SUHRKE, Astri, "Environmental Degradation, Migration, and the Potential for Violent Conflict," in *Conflict and the Environment*, Nils Petter GLEDITSCH (ed.), The Netherlands, Kluwer, Dordrecht, 1997, pp. 255–272.

THOMPSON, Andrea, "Timeline: Earth's Precarious Future," *Live Science*, January 11, 2008. Retrieved from http://www.livescience.com/1433-timeline-earth-precarious-future.html

U.S. National Assessment, U.S. Global Change Research Program, "Climate Change Impacts on the United States: The Potential Consequences of Climate Variability and Change", 2001, Cambridge, UK, Cambridge University Press.

United Nations Department of Economic and Social Affairs/Population Division (UNDES), "World Population Prospects, The 2008 Revision," 2008. Retrieved from http://www.un.org/esa/population/publications/wpp2008/wpp2008_highlights.pdf

United Nations Environment Program (UNEP) Chief Scientists Office, "How Close Are We to the Two Degree Limit?" UNEP Governing Council Meeting & Global Ministerial Environment Forum, February 24-26, 2010, Bali, Indonesia.

United Nations Framework Convention on Climate Change (UNFCCC), June 28, 2002, FCCC/INFORMAL/84. Retrieved from http://unfccc.int/resource/docs/convkp/conveng.pdf

United Nations Framework Convention on Climate Change (UNFCCC) Secretariat, "Negotiating Text. Note by the Secretariat," Bonn, Switzerland, United Nations Office, August 13, 2010, FCCC/AWGLCA/2010/14.

United Nations Framework Convention on Climate Change (UNFCCC) Secretariat, "Compilation of Pledges for Emission Reductions and Related Assumptions Provided by Parties to Date and the Associated Emission Reductions," Bonn, Switzerland, United Nations Office, May 20, 2010, FCCC/KP/AWG/2010/INF.1. Retrieved from http://unfccc.int/resource/docs/2010/awg12/eng/inf01.pdf

United States. "Restoring the Quality of Our Environment," Environmental Pollution Panel, President's Science Advisory Committee, Washington, D.C., White House,1965.

"U.S. and World Population Clocks," U.S. Census Bureau. Retrieved from http://www.census.gov/main/www/popclock.html

VAN VUUREN, Detlef P., LUCAS, Paul L., and HILDERINK, Henk, "Downscaling Drivers of Global Environmental Change: Enabling Use of Global SRES Scenarios at the National and Grid Levels," *Global Environmental Change*, 17, 2007, pp. 114-130.

VERON, John E. N., HOEGH-GULDBERG, Ove, M. LENTON, Tim, LOUGH, Janice M., OBURA, David O., PEARCE-KELLY, Paul, SHEPPARD, Charles R.C., SPALDING, Mark, STAFFORD-SMITH, M.G., and D. ROGERS, Alex, "The Coral Reef Crisis: The Critical Importance of <350 ppm CO2," *Marine Pollution Bulletin*, 58, 2009, pp. 1428-1436.

VICTOR, David G., *Climate Change: Debating America's Policy Options*, New York, Council on Foreign Relations Press, 2004, p. 143-144.

WEBSTER, David, "Warfare and the Evolution of the State: A Reconsideration," *American Antiquity*, 40, 1975, p. 464-470.

"White House 'Eviscerated' CDC Testimony Regarding Climate Change and Health," *Associated Press*, October 24, 2007. Retrieved from http://www.commondreams.org/archive/2007/10/24/4772

WILLIAMS, John W., JACKSON, Stephen T., and KUTZBACH, John E., "Projected distributions of novel and disappearing climates by 2100 AD," *Proceedings of the National Academy of Sciences*, 104, 2007, p. 5738-5742.

WISE, Marshall, CALVIN, Katherine, THOMSON, Allison, CLARKE, Leon, BOND-LAMBERTY, Benjamin, SANDS, Ronald, SMITH, Steven J., JANETOS, Anthony, and EDMONDS, James, "Implications of Limiting CO2 Concentrations for Land Use and Energy," *Science*, 324, 2009, pp. 1183-1186.

"World Energy Outlook 2009," International Energy Agency, Paris, France, 2009. Retrieved from http://www.worldenergyoutlook.org/docs/weo2009/WEO2009_es_english.pdf

"World Population in 2300 could Stabilize at 9 Billion, UN Estimates," United Nations News Centre, November 4, 2004. Retrieved from http://www.un.org/apps/news/story.asp?NewsID=12439

ZABARENKO, Deborah, "US Climate Scientists Allege White House Pressure," Reuters, January 30, 2007. Retrieved from http://www.commondreams.org/headlines07/0130-10

ZANCHI, Giuliana, "The Article 3.3 and 3.4 Activities of the Kyoto Protocol: Requirements and Choices," in *Stima del carbonio in foresta: metodologie ed aspetti normative*, Roberto Pilli, Tommaso Anfodillo, and Elena Dalla Valle (eds.), Pubblicazione del Corso di Cultura in Ecologia Atti del 42° Corso, Università di Padova, 2006, pp. 161-183. Retrieved from http://www.carbonpro.org/docs/public/Kyoto_protocol/Zanchi.pdf

ZELLER Jr., Tom, "And in This Corner, Climate Contrarians," *New York Times*, December 9, 2009. Retrieved from http://www.nytimes.com/2009/12/10/science/earth/10skeptics.html

ZHANG, David D., JIM, C. Y., LIN, George C. S., HE, Yuan-Qing, WANG, James J., and LEE, Harry F., "Climate Change, Wars and Dynastic Cycles in China over the Last Millennium," *Climatic Change*, 76, 2006, pp. 459-477.

ZHANG, David D., BRECKE, Peter, LEE, Harry F., HE, Yuan-Qing, and ZHANG, Jane, "Global Climate Change, War, and Population Decline in Recent Human History," *Proceedings of the National Academy of Sciences*, 104, 2007, p. 19214-19219.

ZHANG, David D., ZHANG, Jane, LEE, Harry F., and HE, Yuan-Qing, "Climate Change and War Frequency in Eastern China over the Last Millennium," *Human Ecology*, 35, 2007, pp. 403-414.

PART THREE REFERENCES
CHAPTER 6 ANALYSIS

ADAM, David, "Climate Change Sceptics and Lobbyists put World at Risk, says Top Adviser," *Guardian*, November 22, 2009. Retrieved from http://www.guardian.co.uk/environment/2009/

nov/22/climate-change-emissions-scientist-watson

BACHOR, Daniel G., "Rethinking Case Study Research Methodology," paper presented at the Special Education National Research Forum, Helsinki, May 2000.

BRODER, John M., "Climate Deal Likely to Bear Big Price Tag," *New York Times*, December 8, 2009. Retrieved from http://www.nytimes.com/2009/12/09/science/earth/09cost.html?pagewanted=all

Climate Change 2001: The Scientific Basis, Contribution of Working Group I to the Third Assessment Report of the Intergovernmental Panel on Climate Change (IPCC), H.T. Houghton, Y. Ding, D.J. Griggs, M. Noguer, P.J. van der Linden, X. Dai, K. Maskell, and C.A. Johnson (eds.), Cambridge and New York, Cambridge University Press, 2001.

"Climate Change Fight 'Can't Wait'," *BBC*, October 31, 2006. Retrieved from http://news.bbc.co.uk/2/hi/business/6096084.stm

"Covering the Great Recession: Why Did Coverage of the Economy Decrease?" Pew Research Center's Project for Excellence in Journalism, October 5, 2009, p. 2. Retrieved from http://www.journalism.org/analysis_report/why_did_coverage_economy_decrease

DAVIS, T. M. and BACHOR, Daniel G., "Case Studies as a Research Tool in Evaluating Student Achievement," paper presented at the Canadian Society for Studies in Education Conference, Sherbrooke, Canada, June 1999.

Dean, Cornelia, "Group Urges Research Into Aggressive Efforts to Fight Climate Change," *New York Times*, October 4. 2011. Retrieved from http://www.nytimes.com/2011/10/04/science/earth/04climate.html.

DICKINSON, Tim, "The Secret Campaign of President Bush's Administration to Deny Global Warming," *Rolling Stone*, June 20, 2007. Retrieved from http://www.desmogblog.com/sites/beta.desmogblog.com/files/The%20Secret%20Campaign%20of%20President%20Bush%20rolling%20stone.pdf

GEITHNER, Timothy, "Reducing Systemic Risk in a Dynamic Financial System," Speech, *Federal Reserve Bank of New York*, June 9, 2008. Retrieved from http://www.newyorkfed.org/newsevents/speeches/2008/tfg080609.html

GILLIS, Justin, "A Scientist, His Work and a Climate Reckoning," *New York Times*, December 21, 2010. Retrieved from http://www.nytimes.com/2010/12/22/science/earth/22carbon.html

HOGGAN, James and LITTLEMORE, Richard D., *Climate Cover-up: The Crusade to Deny Global Warming*, Vancouver, Canada, Greystone Books, 2009, p. 20.

KRUGMAN, Paul, *The Return of Depression Economics and the Crisis of 2008*, *op. cit.*; Paul KRUGMAN, "Financial Reform 101," *New York Times*, April 1, 2010. Retrieved from http://www.nytimes.com/2010/04/02/opinion/02krugman.html?adxnnl=1&adxnnlx=1326978494-WOo7/m5tevHSi/qRiQ-CY5A

KVALE, Steiner, *Interviews. An Introduction to Qualitative Research Interviewing*, Thousand Oaks, CA, Sage, 1996.

LINCOLN, Yvonne S. and GUBA, Egon G., *Naturalistic Inquiry*, Beverly Hills, CA, Sage, 1985.

MEEHL, Gerald A., STOCKER, Thomas F., COLLINS, William D., FRIEDLINGSTEIN, Pierre, GAYE, Amadou T., GREGORY, Jonathan M., KITOH, Akio, KNUTTI, Reto, MURPHY, James M., NODA, Akira, RAPER, Sarah C.B., WATTERSON, Ian G., WEAVER, Andrew J., and ZHAO, Zong-Ci, "Global Climate Projections," in *Climate Change 2007: The Physical Science Basis. Contribution of Working Group I to the Fourth Assessment Report of the Intergovernmental Panel on Climate Change*, S. Solomon, D. Qin, M. Manning, Z. Chen, M. Marquis, K.B. Averyt, M. Tignor and H.L. Miller (eds.), 2007, Cambridge, UK and New York, NY, Cambridge University Press.

MORGENSON, Gretchen, "A Bank Crisis Whodunit, With Laughs and Tears," New York Times, January 29, 2011. Retrieved from http://www.nytimes.com/2011/01/30/business/30gret.html

MUHR, Thomas, *Atlas/ti: The Knowledge Workbench, Version 4.1*, Berlin, Scientific SoftwareDevelopment, 1997.

PULLELLA, Philip, "Pope Urges, Save the Planet Before it's too Late," *Reuters*, September 2, 2007. Retrieved from http://www.enn.com/top_stories/commentary/22598/print

"Remarks of President Barack Obama, Weekly Address," The White House, Washington, D. C., February 7, 2009. Retrieved from http://www.whitehouse.gov/blog_post/compromise1

SOROS, George, "The Worst Market Crisis in 60 Years," *Financial Times*, January 22, 2008, Retrieved from http://www.ft.com/cms/s/0/24f73610-c91e-11dc-9807-000077b07658.html#axzz1jtkkWJ7H

STRAUSS, Anselm L. and CORBIN, Juliet M., *Basics of Qualitative Research: Grounded Theory Procedures and Techniques*, Newbury Park, CA, Sage, 1990.

STRAUSS, Anselm L., *Qualitative Analysis for Social Scientists*, Cambridge, UK, Cambridge University Press, 1987.

"The Environment in the News," United Nations Environment Programme, July 22, 2011. Retrieved from www.unep.org/cpi/briefs/2011July22.doc, p. 9.

VAILLANT, George E., *Adaptations to Life*, Boston, MA, Little Brown, 1977.

"Will Subprime Mess Ripple through the Economy?" MSNBC, March 13, 2007. Retrieved from http://www.msnbc.msn.com/id/17584725#.Txf6qmOonus; Ben S. BERNANKE, "The Subprime Mortgage Market," Remarks by Governor Ben S. Bernanke at the Federal Reserve Bank of Chicago's 43rd Annual Conference on Bank Structure and Competition, Chicago, Illinois, May 17, 2007. Retrieved from http://www.federalreserve.gov/boarddocs/speeches/2005/20050414/default.htm

YIN, Robert K., *Case Study Research: Design and Methods* (2nd ed.) Newbury Park, CA, Sage, 1994.

CHAPTER 7 COMPARISONS

MEEHL, Gerald A., STOCKER, Thomas F., COLLINS, William D., FRIEDLINGSTEIN, Pierre, GAYE, Amadou T., GREGORY, Jonathan M., KITOH, Akio, KNUTTI, Reto, MURPHY, James M., NODA, Akira, RAPER, Sarah C.B., WATTERSON, Ian G., WEAVER, Andrew J., and ZHAO, Zong-Ci, "Global Climate Projections," in *Climate Change 2007: The Physical Science Basis. Contribution of Working Group I to the Fourth Assessment Report of the Intergovernmental Panel on Climate Change*, S. Solomon, D. Qin, M. Manning, Z. Chen, M. Marquis, K.B. Averyt, M. Tignor and H.L. Miller (eds.), 2007, Cambridge, UK and New York, NY, Cambridge University Press.

"Climate Change Fight 'Can't Wait'," *BBC*, October 31, 2006. Retrieved from http://news.bbc.co.uk/2/hi/business/6096084.stm

"Covering the Great Recession: Why Did Coverage of the Economy Decrease?" Pew Research Center's Project for Excellence in Journalism, October 5, 2009, p. 2. Retrieved from http://www.journalism.org/analysis_report/why_did_coverage_economy_decrease

"Remarks of President Barack Obama, Weekly Address," The White House, Washington, D. C., February 7, 2009. Retrieved from http://www.whitehouse.gov/blog_post/compromise1

"Will Subprime Mess Ripple through the Economy?" MSNBC, March 13, 2007. Retrieved from http://www.msnbc.msn.com/id/17584725#.Txf6qmOonus; Ben S. BERNANKE, "The Subprime Mortgage Market," Remarks by Governor Ben S. Bernanke at the Federal Reserve Bank of Chicago's 43rd Annual Conference on Bank Structure and Competition, Chicago, Illinois, May

17, 2007. Retrieved from http://www.federalreserve.gov/boarddocs/speeches/2005/20050414/default.htm

ADAM, David, "Climate Change Sceptics and Lobbyists put World at Risk, says Top Adviser," *Guardian*, November 22, 2009. Retrieved from http://www.guardian.co.uk/environment/2009/nov/22/climate-change-emissions-scientist-watson

BRODER, John M., "Climate Deal Likely to Bear Big Price Tag," *New York Times*, December 8, 2009. Retrieved from http://www.nytimes.com/2009/12/09/science/earth/09cost.html?pagewanted=all

Climate Change 2001: The Scientific Basis, Contribution of Working Group I to the Third Assessment Report of the Intergovernmental Panel on Climate Change (IPCC), H.T. Houghton, Y. Ding, D.J. Griggs, M. Noguer, P.J. van der Linden, X. Dai, K. Maskell, and C.A. Johnson (eds.), Cambridge and New York, Cambridge University Press, 2001.

DICKINSON, Tim, "The Secret Campaign of President Bush's Administration to Deny Global Warming," *Rolling Stone*, June 20, 2007. Retrieved from http://www.desmogblog.com/sites/beta.desmogblog.com/files/The%20Secret%20Campaign%20of%20President%20Bush%20rolling%20stone.pdf

GEITHNER, Timothy, "Reducing Systemic Risk in a Dynamic Financial System," Speech, *Federal Reserve Bank of New York*, June 9, 2008. Retrieved from http://www.newyorkfed.org/newsevents/speeches/2008/tfg080609.html

GILLIS, Justin, "A Scientist, His Work and a Climate Reckoning," *New York Times*, December 21, 2010. Retrieved from http://www.nytimes.com/2010/12/22/science/earth/22carbon.html

HOGGAN, James and LITTLEMORE, Richard D., *Climate Cover-up: The Crusade to Deny Global Warming*, Vancouver, Canada, Greystone Books, 2009, p. 20.

KRUGMAN, Paul, *The Return of Depression Economics and the*

Crisis of 2008, *op. cit.*; Paul KRUGMAN, "Financial Reform 101," *New York Times*, April 1, 2010. Retrieved from http://www.nytimes.com/2010/04/02/opinion/02krugman.html?adxnnl=1&adxnnlx=1326978494-WOo7/m5tevHSi/qRiQ-CY5A

MORGENSON, Gretchen, "A Bank Crisis Whodunit, With Laughs and Tears," New York Times, January 29, 2011. Retrieved from http://www.nytimes.com/2011/01/30/business/30gret.html

PULLELLA, Philip, "Pope Urges, Save the Planet Before it's too Late," *Reuters*, September 2, 2007. Retrieved from http://www.enn.com/top_stories/commentary/22598/print

SOROS, George, "The Worst Market Crisis in 60 Years," *Financial Times*, January 22, 2008, Retrieved from http://www.ft.com/cms/s/0/24f73610-c91e-11dc-9807-000077b07658.html#axzz1jtkkWJ7H

CHAPTER 8: CONCLUSIONS

Dean, Cornelia, "Group Urges Research Into Aggressive Efforts to Fight Climate Change," *New York Times*, October 4. 2011. Retrieved from http://www.nytimes.com/2011/10/04/science/earth/04climate.html.

"The Environment in the News," United Nations Environment Programme, July 22, 2011. Retrieved from www.unep.org/cpi/briefs/2011July22.doc, p.

INDEX

www.ingramcontent.com/pod-product-compliance
Lightning Source LLC
Chambersburg PA
CBHW080453110426
42742CB00017B/2881

* 9 7 8 0 9 8 4 7 6 3 8 3 2 *